Professional Joomla

Professional
Joomla!

Dan Rahmel

Wiley Publishing, Inc.

Professional Joomla!

Published by
Wiley Publishing, Inc.
10475 Crosspoint Boulevard
Indianapolis, IN 46256
www.wiley.com

Copyright © 2007 by Wiley Publishing, Inc., Indianapolis, Indiana

Published simultaneously in Canada

ISBN: 978-0-470-13394-1

Manufactured in the United States of America

10 9 8 7 6 5 4 3 2

Library of Congress Cataloging-in-Publication Data is available from Publisher.

I'd like to dedicate this book to the noble spirit of contributors to the Joomla! project.
They make the Web a better place for us all.

Credits

Acquisitions Editor
Jenny Watson

Development Editor
Kevin Shafer

Technical Editor
Chris Davenport

Production Editor
Angela Smith

Copy Editor
Foxxe Editorial Services

Editorial Manager
Mary Beth Wakefield

Production Manager
Tim Tate

Vice President and Executive Group Publisher
Richard Swadley

Vice President and Executive Publisher
Joseph B. Wikert

Project Coordinator, Cover
Adrienne Martinez

Compositor
Laurie Stewart, Happenstance Type-O-Rama

Proofreader
Sossity Smith

Indexer
Jack Lewis

Anniversary Logo Design
Richard Pacifico

About the Author

Dan Rahmel is an author best known for his work with database systems, PHP, and Visual Basic. He has more than a dozen years of experience designing and implementing information systems and client-server solutions using MySQL, Microsoft SQL Server, Microsoft Access, and Visual FoxPro. He began work as a writer for various magazines, including *DBMS*, *American Programmer*, and *Internet Advisor*. He is the author of more than a dozen books, and his writing has been translated into numerous languages, including Chinese, Japanese, Spanish, French, and Portuguese. In 2006, Focal Press issued a special edition of *Nuts and Bolts Filmmaking: Practical Techniques for the Guerilla Filmmaker* (Focal Press, 2004) for release in India.

Acknowledgments

Long before I typed the first letter of this book, the Joomla development team spent untold hours creating an application that has been adopted all around the world. Needless to say, this book would not exist without their tireless efforts to make Joomla the world-class application it is today. As with most people who use Joomla regularly, I cannot thank them enough for their astonishing creation.

I want to thank the people at Wrox — especially given their patience while we tried to build this book atop the ever-changing landscape of a beta product. My thanks to Kit Kemper who help me refine what at the time was only a vague idea for a book. To Jenny Watson, who had to suffer through my many refinements to the text and the delays imposed by such tinkering. My gratitude to Chris Davenport, the technical editor whose insightful suggestions and wise recommendations made the book dramatically better. Thank you Kevin Shafer for coming through at the worst of crunch times and doing a phenomenal job pulling everything into line. I'd also like to thank Ami Frank Sullivan, Kirk Bateman, and everyone else at Wiley who worked tirelessly to produce this book.

I must thank the twin stars of my life — my wife Elizabeth and daughter Alexandra — for giving my world significance. With seldom a complaint, Elizabeth put up with the strain of late nights and lost weekends, and I thank you from the bottom of my heart. Meeting you was the best thing that ever happened to me.

I'd like to thank my siblings (David and Darlene) and friends (Joel Harris, Juan Leonffu, Greg Mickey, John Taylor, Ed Gildred, Don Murphy, and Weld O'Connor) for their unconditional support. I'm very grateful to Sandra Villagran for doing such a wonderful job keeping the munchkin happy.

Most of all, I'd like to thank you, the reader. By buying this book, you make it possible for all of us in the publishing industry to labor to produce good work. I hope the information in this book will play a part in helping you achieve your dreams. Thanks.

Contents

Contents

Contents

Contents

Contents

Introduction

At the heart of every Web site project is the need to organize and present content. For the last 10 years, static sites have dominated the Internet landscape, and site maintenance has been a laborious and often frustrating process. Web masters had to cope with thousands of line of HTML code across a mass of Web page files. However, employing a dynamic site required a large amount of custom coding and potential unforeseen security loopholes.

The release of the Joomla content management system (CMS) in 2005 opened a new age of affordable, advanced Web site deployment. Content management was now possible without any programming required, yet the flexibility of the Joomla system allowed the creation of robust add-ons to augment the CMS. As tens of thousands of developers flocked to Joomla and the availability of add-ons reached critical mass (almost 1700 at last count), Joomla became the most important noncommercial CMS in the world. It has become a major force in allowing Web masters to perform site deployment and management without the grueling effort.

This widespread adoption has opened numerous opportunities for professional Joomla developers. With the number of downloads of the Joomla system having surpassed 2.5 million by mid-2007, developers can find a ready audience for their work. Whether you're creating an XHTML-compliant template to sell to a subscription site, providing expert Joomla consulting services, or releasing a Joomla extension into the open source community for widespread adoption, there is a place for you in the wide world of Joomla.

With the diverse needs of professional readers in mind, I wrote this book with the intention that you would turn the last page with an understanding of Joomla second only to full-time developers or the Joomla development team members. Between these covers, I have tried to provide examples of the two main areas of the professional Joomla field: development and deployment.

For *development*, there are chapters focusing on implementing custom templates, creating all three types of Joomla extensions (modules, components, and plug-ins), utilizing cutting-edge Ajax technology in Joomla add-ons, using a professional development environment with source code control, adopting design patterns for best programming methods, and much more.

You will even be delving into the internal structure of the Joomla framework itself to give you a complete behind-the-scenes education. Learning the fundamentals of the Joomla structure will allow you to better develop add-ons that better take advantage of the riches that Joomla offers.

For *deployment*, you'll examine the underlying technologies (PHP, Apache, and so on) that can be tuned to offer the best system performance. General administration, search engine optimization (SEO), interfacing with outside content, security configuration, Lightweight Directory Access Protocol (LDAP) authentication setup — all of the topics are covered.

I hope you come away from this book with many ideas for modifying and extending Joomla to meet the needs of yourself and/or your customers. I've spent dozens of hours digging into the underlying code of the Joomla framework and have come away with a vast appreciation of the brilliant work done by the Joomla team. I suspect that the more you work with Joomla, the more you'll share my admiration for this open source wonder.

Who This Book Is For

Professional Joomla! will be appeal to Web developers, hobbyists, Web designers, small and medium-sized businesses, e-commerce merchants, and nonprofit organizations. The broad interest in acquiring professional Joomla skills goes beyond the normal development community, since companies that have adopted Joomla technology host every type of Web site and range from real estate firms to fitness companies to funeral homes.

This book is of particular interest to bloggers, corporate content creators, and support specialists. However, anyone with access to a Web-hosting site that allows PHP/MySQL content deployment (which includes popular sites such as `GoDaddy.com`, `Rochen.com`, and `SiteGround.com`) will be able to deploy a Joomla! site with all of the features shown in this book.

To use this book effectively, you should already have completed at least a basic installation experience with Joomla. If you are already familiar with earlier versions of Joomla, you will have no trouble with any of the techniques or features. Joomla updates retain enough continuity that, aside from menu reorganization, the core aspects of handling a Joomla system have remained unchanged. Programming Joomla has been altered dramatically, however, so be sure to pay close attention to the examples and note boxes that make explicit the new way of doing things.

Additionally, there is a great deal of PHP programming involved, so basic skills in this area are also necessary to harness the power of the instructions of this book. Knowledge of Web server configuration is recommended but not required if you are running your site on a remote host.

With each chapter, I have tried to build on the chapters that precede it. Therefore, although the book can be read nonsequentially, I recommend that you read at least the first six chapters in order. After that, there is a lot more flexibility to skip to areas of particular interest without becoming confused regarding some Joomla-specific topic that was skipped.

What This Book Covers

Joomla! is a free, open source, and cross-platform (Windows, Linux, and MacOS) CMS. This book focuses on the new Joomla version 1.5 and all of the features (not just new ones) that it provides. Wherever possible, I have noted the differences between the previous version 1.0.x and the new version to aid users in making the transition to a new deployment.

The programming and editing tools required to complete the book examples are, like Joomla, free and freely available (aside from the specific implementation demonstrations with programs such as Adobe Dreamweaver and Microsoft Frontpage). For all programs and extensions that are used, I've included the Web address of the individual home pages where they may be downloaded.

How This Book Is Structured

This book is organized in the likely stages of interest that an intermediate Joomla user would want to follow to progress to becoming a professional user. It begins with installation configuration and progresses to extending the Joomla system through the creation of custom templates, modules, components, and plug-ins. What follows are professional deployment issues that are described, from building virtual communities to interfacing with outside content to SEO.

This book includes the following chapters:

❑ *Chapter 1: "Introducing Joomla"* — This chapter describes the various aspects of Joomla that will be embraced by Web masters, Web designers, and Web developers.

❑ *Chapter 2: "The Finer Points of Installation and Configuration"* — This chapter introduces the four servers of a Joomla system (Joomla!, PHP, MySQL, and Apache/IIS), and shows how each may be installed and configured for maximum performance. Additionally, the recommended differences in settings between staging and deployment servers are elaborated.

❑ *Chapter 3: "Developing Custom Templates"* — This chapter steps through the process of creating a custom template from scratch. Template structure is first examined with a primitive Hello World template. This template is then expanded into a comprehensive three-column Joomla template that uses CSS for column layout. Finally, advanced template creation techniques are described, including how to create a template family, generating a custom *favicon* for the page, and incorporating a cell-phone-centric template.

❑ *Chapter 4: "Adding and Modifying Available Extensions"* — This chapter surveys many available extensions and details their basic configuration and use. The Joomla Extensions Directory (JED) is reviewed, and examples of the various extension categories (Site Features and Management, Organizations and eCommerce, Site Content, and Site Interactivity) are provided.

❑ *Chapter 5: "Developing Simple Extensions: Modules"* — This chapter follows the complete process of creating a module from scratch. Starting with a simple Hello World program, the structure and use of the module extension type is revealed. Two progressively more complex development projects follow with the Holiday Greetings module using a custom table to display definable holiday greetings and the Contact Us module demonstrating access to the native Joomla tables from an extension.

❑ *Chapter 6: "Advanced Extensions: Components"* — This chapter covers the development of a form-based guestbook component. The entire professional development process is covered here from the setup of the Eclipse integrated development environment (IDE) to the use of SVN for source code control to the adoption of phpDocumentor to automatically generate project documentation.

❑ *Chapter 7: "Joomla and Ajax"* — This chapter demonstrates how to create two Ajax components that can be used to add dynamic data retrieval to Joomla. After the structure of Ajax interaction is outlined, a Joomla-Ajax component is created that can be accessed by any Web page. Moving to a more real-world example, an Ajax module and component package is introduced with the component supplying the back-end connectivity and the Joomla front-end module providing the interactive display.

❑ *Chapter 8: "Design Patterns and Joomla"* — This chapter examines the technique of using conceptual models known as *design patterns* to solve common programming problems. A number of design patterns are summarized, and their uses in the design of part of the Joomla framework are highlighted. Then, a step-by-step tour of creating a component using the MVC pattern provides an example for adopting design patterns within Joomla development.

❑ *Chapter 9: "Hooking into the Joomla Foundation: Plug-ins"* — This chapter begins by describing the Joomla plug-in system and events that may be registered to activate routines in the plug-in. A Hello World plug-in shows the basic event activation that can add a greeting to an article. Next, you are provided with a guided tour of the creation of a text abbreviation replacement plug-in that can dynamically replace abbreviated text with the expanded text on the fly. This text alteration is performed only on the article display, thereby leaving the content in the database intact. Finally, a general outline of the Joomla framework itself is presented.

❏ *Chapter 10: "Building Joomla Communities"* — This chapter focuses on the process of creating and retaining a virtual community. Beginning with the plan and design phase, the method provides an outline for defining the target audience for a virtual community site. Once the community is determined, various Joomla extensions are examined that can give a Joomla site community features. Further instruction is provided on the best practices for deploying and maintaining the community.

❏ *Chapter 11: "Managing a Professional Deployment* — This chapter describes the measures that you can take to have a successful deployment. In addition to procedures given to setting debugging settings, configuring automated testing, and transferring a Joomla site from a staging/test server to deployment server, tuning information is provided for MySQL and LDAP authentication.

❏ *Chapter 12: "Interfacing with Outside Content"* — This chapter examines extra-site interaction in the form of external content, managing affiliate programs, business interaction via Electronic Data Interchange (EDI), and custom extranet interaction. This chapter demonstrates how to program custom Joomla extensions to address extranet services, and includes a Joomla component that dynamically performs screen scraping, a component to interface to the Google Map service, and an extension to use the USPS.com ZIP code finder service.

❏ *Chapter 13: "Search Engine Optimization (SEO) and Search Engine Marketing (SEM)"* — This chapter covers the techniques and procedures that can be used to tune a Joomla site for both SEO and SEM. In addition to demonstrating the Joomla! SEO configuration parameters, the advantages of using other Joomla features such as metadata, breadcrumbs, and sitemaps are identified, and their importance to SEO is highlighted. A general procedure for optimizing your site is provided, as well as an examination of the effects of technology such as Flash and JavaScript on page ranking.

❏ *Chapter 14: "Joomla Security"* — This chapter introduces many of the best configuration settings to ensure Joomla site security. A summary of the primary types of attacks that may be expected against a Joomla system (as well as remedies for such attacks) is provided. Information regarding security settings for each individual server (Apache/IIS, PHP, MySQL, and Joomla!) is provided.

❏ *Chapter 15: "What Joomla Can't Do"* — This chapter evaluates the major shortcoming of the system when compared with industrial-grade CMS systems. Limited capabilities in the areas of version control, file conversion, security, load balancing, replication, groupware functionality, and portal capabilities are all examined.

❏ *Chapter 16: "Spotlight on Successful Joomla Sites"* — This chapter surveys a variety of popular sites that use Joomla for their Web deployment. Each site summary includes details about the site (such as template used, default screen size, and so on), as well as the third-party extensions the site uses to add functionality.

What You Need to Use This Book

Aside from Joomla (which is available for free download), there are no essential software requirements to use the examples in this book. Perhaps the largest downloadable application demonstrated is the Eclipse IDE, which runs about 230MB and reasonably requires a high-speed connection to retrieve the installer. Other downloads generally fall into the 10MB to 20MB range.

This book was written to be as platform-independent as possible. Because a large majority of interaction with the Joomla system occurs through the Web-based Administrator interface, the instructions will apply, regardless of the operating system or browser used. When configuration details are specific to a particular operating system, I have tried to include the necessary individual instructions for Linux, MacOS, and Windows.

Conventions

To help you get the most from the text and keep track of what's happening, a number of conventions have been used throughout the book.

> **Boxes like this one hold important, not-to-be forgotten information that is directly relevant to the surrounding text.**

Tips, hints, tricks, and asides to the current discussion are offset and placed in italics like this.

As for styles in the text:

❑ Important new terms and important words are *highlighted* when we introduce them.

❑ Keyboard strokes are shown like this: Ctrl+A.

❑ Filenames, URLs, and code within the text are shown like this: `persistence.properties`.

❑ When paths are specified in the body text, the backslash (\) character is used as a directory separator for standardization, although UNIX-based platforms use the forward slash (/) instead.

❑ Code is presented in the following two ways:

```
In code examples we highlight new and important code with a gray background.
The gray highlighting is not used for code that's less important in the present
context, or has been shown before.
```

Source Code

As you work through the examples in this book, you may choose either to type in all the code manually, or use the source code files that accompany the book. All of the source code used in this book is available for download at www.wrox.com. Once at the site, simply locate the book's title (either by using the Search box or by using one of the title lists), and click the Download Code link on the book's detail page to obtain all the source code for the book.

Because many books have similar titles, you may find it easiest to search by ISBN; for this book the ISBN is 978-0-470-13394-1.

Once you download the code, just decompress it with your favorite compression tool. Alternately, you can go to the main Wrox code download page at www.wrox.com/dynamic/books/download.aspx to see the code available for this book and all other Wrox books.

Errata

We make every effort to ensure that there are no errors in the text or in the code. However, no one is perfect, and mistakes do occur. If you find an error in one of our books (such as a spelling mistake or faulty piece of code), we would be very grateful for your feedback. By sending in errata you may save another reader hours of frustration and, at the same, time you will be helping us provide even higher-quality information.

To find the errata page for this book, go to www.wrox.com and locate the title using the Search box or one of the title lists. Then, on the book details page, click the Book Errata link. On this page, you can view all errata that has been submitted for this book and posted by Wrox editors. A complete book list including links to each's book's errata is also available at www.wrox.com/misc-pages/booklist.shtml.

If you don't spot "your" error on the Book Errata page, go to www.wrox.com/contact/techsupport .shtml and complete the form there to send us the error you have found. We'll check the information and, if appropriate, post a message to the book's errata page and fix the problem in subsequent editions of the book.

p2p.wrox.com

For author and peer discussion, join the P2P forums at p2p.wrox.com. The forums are a Web-based system for you to post messages relating to Wrox books and related technologies, and to interact with other readers and technology users. The forums offer a subscription feature to email you topics of interest of your choosing when new posts are made to the forums. Wrox authors, editors, other industry experts, and your fellow readers are present on these forums.

At http://p2p.wrox.com, you will find a number of different forums that will help you not only as you read this book but also as you develop your own applications. To join the forums, just follow these steps:

1. Go to p2p.wrox.com, and click the Register link.
2. Read the terms of use, and click Agree.
3. Complete the required information to join, as well as any optional information you wish to provide, and click Submit.
4. You will receive an email with information describing how to verify your account and complete the joining process.

You can read messages in the forums without joining P2P, but to post your own messages, you must join.

Once you join, you can post new messages and respond to messages other users post. You can read messages at any time on the Web. If you would like to have new messages from a particular forum emailed to you, click the Subscribe to this Forum icon by the forum name in the forum listing.

For more information about how to use the Wrox P2P, be sure to read the P2P FAQs for answers to questions about how the forum software works, as well as many common questions specific to P2P and Wrox books. To read the FAQs, click the FAQ link on any P2P page.

1

Introducing Joomla!

If you're reading this book, you likely already know that Joomla is becoming one of the most widely adopted new Web technologies. The Joomla Content Management System (CMS) provides an easy-to-use graphical user interface for Web site construction and maintenance. A novice Web user can quickly master the rudiments of Joomla and create a beautiful full-featured site, as shown in Figure 1-1, without knowing any Hypertext Markup Language (HTML). This book assumes that you are beyond the basics of site setup and want to master the Joomla system to make your Web site (or sites) world class — and you'll learn all that between these covers.

Figure 1-1: The default installation demonstrates design sophistication with a pill menu, a search box, some rounded display menus, an online poll, and the automatic page layout.

The method you use to master Joomla will depend on your needs and your role in the deployment of a Joomla Web site. This chapter explains how various Joomla users (Web masters, Web designers, and Web developers) will use this book to focus on learning the skills and technology that suits their needs and desires.

In all of the examples that will be presented in this book, I've tried to present the information as clearly and unambiguously as possible. I know you are here to master Joomla — not necessarily the other technologies (such as MySQL, CSS, PHP, and so on) that Joomla rests atop. There are other excellent books from Wiley that will help you do just that. The goal of this book is to help you complete any Joomla projects that you intend to create and deploy.

Therefore, I've tried to present a solid basic explanation of everything that is being done so that, even if you're not a master of Cascading Style Sheets (CSS), for example, you'll be able to follow the examples easily enough to reach your goal.

Getting to Know Joomla

Joomla is one of the key applications initiating the rebirth of the World Wide Web into what pundits are calling Web 2.0. Unlike Web 1.0, where most Web sites were manually administered and interaction was minimal, 2.0 is defined by automated administration, intrasite and intersite communication, virtual communities, and dynamic interaction. Joomla embraces all of these new advances and provides a CMS that allows an advanced Web site to be created and managed by a small group of people (perhaps as small as one person). A Joomla Web site can rival the capabilities and presentation of a multi-million-dollar Web site. And best of all — Joomla is completely, *100 percent free.*

Joomla burst onto the scene in 2005. Since then, it has seen exponential growth both among Web masters and Web developers. Literally tens of thousands of Joomla Web sites have sprung up around the globe. To match that expansion, the developer community has grown to more than 45,000 registered developers as of this writing. Hundreds are active every day on the Joomla forums, sharing information, tips, and new code.

New plug-ins and templates are constantly appearing to extend the robust capabilities already included with the default Joomla installation. With all this activity around Joomla, it's hard not to become dazzled with the possibilities that it affords.

This book will help you join the revolution by taking you through the deployment, development, and design of an advanced Joomla site. You'll learn how to modify and extend Joomla. You'll learn how to tune Joomla so that, as your Web presence soars and the number of simultaneous visitors would threaten to bring a normal site to its knees, your Joomla installation will handle the load without breaking a sweat. This book will help you if you want to use Joomla to do the following:

- ❏ Develop a commercial plug-in to provide some functionality that is useful to some of the 2.5 million Joomla users.
- ❏ Create an e-commerce store where you can not only sell your wares but also create an online community that makes repeat business the rule, rather than the exception.
- ❏ Design a template or open a template store where users can subscribe to use your template to make their site a work of art.

❏ Publish a political opinion blog site with reference to every kind of supporting documentation for your point of view — at the same time polling your readers to find out the topics they think are important.

❏ Get in on the lucrative field of setting up other people's CMS deployments. The information in this book will give you the competitive edge.

❏ Start a personal Web site with picture galleries (of your kids, special events, and so on) and forums where your relatives can stay in touch.

This book will give you the knowledge to pursue all of these diverse paths, and more. In this exciting new world where many grandmothers know HTML, the limits of mastering Joomla are set mostly by your ambition. Joomla makes even difficult development, if not a joy, at least rewarding. It also opens the gateway to CMS development in the same way that CMS applications are beginning to bring order to the chaos of Web site maintenance.

Flexibility Makes Joomla the CMS of Choice

Before CMS applications became widespread, the Web was beginning to buckle under the weight of the vast amount of content that needed to be managed. Creating a site of individual pages was severely limiting and made maintenance of even a medium-sized Web site incredibly expensive in time and resources. Custom-designed sites with dynamic coded execution using PHP or Active Server Pages (ASP) were not only expensive to implement, but the potential for severe bug problems and security breaches made them a precarious solution.

CMSs such as Joomla dramatically reduce the maintenance costs for large and small Web sites alike. By organizing all of the content in a database and separating it as much as possible from the presentation aspects and the program code, much greater administrative flexibility is available through a CMS than most other methods of Web site deployment.

The Joomla CMS leverages technology to create a system that is not *one-size-fits-all*, but instead *one-size-modifiable-to-fit-anyone*. Joomla is robust enough that it can be modified, extended, and expanded to handle a majority of all needed Web solutions.

> Just because Joomla can fill nearly every Web need doesn't mean that it *should* be used in this fashion. There's an old saying that when you're a hammer, everything looks like a nail. There are applications where using Joomla would not be the best choice. For that reason, I've included Chapter 15, "What Joomla Can't Do." It is important to understand the shortcomings of any program, especially before you begin a large project.
>
> Many of Joomla's limitations (such as fine granular security) can be overcome with a combination of custom coding and available extensions. It is up to you to determine if surmounting these boundaries is even wise to attempt, or whether it might not be a better idea to choose another application with out-of-the-box features more appropriate to your project.

With the release of version 1.5, Joomla has really pulled ahead of the rest of the CMS pack. Gone is the somewhat convoluted application structure of previous revisions. The new foundation boasts a clear and powerful application framework that makes creating everything from new templates to plug-ins a breeze.

Version 1.5 implements a much better model of separating code from presentation design. The new structure helps Web designers and graphic artists, who won't have to struggle with the programming instructions in order to create a new template. It also lets developers craft the logic of the system autonomously from many of the display considerations.

Who Needs This Book

If you have been using Joomla for any length of time, you probably understand the basics pretty well. You know how to add content, register users, add sections and categories, upload a new template, and how to install an extension (plug-in, component, or module). That's just the tip of the iceberg of Joomla's power. The areas you'll want to focus on will vary with the role you play in Joomla deployment.

Web masters can focus on the implementation, deployment, and administration of the Joomla site. Web designers can fashion the artwork and presentation that produce a visually outstanding site interface. Web developers can embrace the flexibility of extension programming to master the art of add-on creation.

Web Masters

Web masters probably have the broadest responsibility in terms of polishing a Joomla Web site. The Web master always has final responsibility for the site functioning properly. That makes understanding the underlying technology critical. Regardless of whether you're a Web master who runs a single hobbyist Web site or an organizational administrator overseeing a large multi-server Joomla deployment, most of the information in this book will prove useful for you.

Joomla is a complicated system. Although the barrier to entry is extremely low given the ease of system installation, mastering Joomla will open up a cornucopia of extra functionality that is simply unavailable to beginners. Not only will your Joomla implementation be optimized for the best performance, but it will also be important that you ensure that the site is secure from hackers.

You may have Joomla designers and/or developers working for you, in which case this book will provide an excellent roadmap of what is possible within the Joomla application framework. If you're the entire design and development team rolled into one, nearly all of the content will be relevant. Your administrative tasks will almost certainly include direct or indirect administration of the site itself.

For Web master administrators, the book includes the tools and techniques to let you do the following:

❑ Build online virtual communities through Joomla interaction technology to harness the Web trend embodied by sites such as MySpace and YouTube.

❑ Maintain the Web server, the Joomla site, and the SQL database back end so that they work together like a well-oiled machine.

❑ Back up your Joomla data, as well as the site and all of the configuration settings.

❑ Plan your site using Search Engine Optimization (SEO) techniques, and optimize Joomla for search engine spidering.

❑ Maintain security on your system by securing your site and defending against attacks from hackers.

❑ Discover the techniques used by professional Joomla sites to establish a Web presence and maintain a proactive site.

❑ Tune the Joomla system for maximum performance. Everything from optimal design to server tuning will be covered.

❑ Load-balancing and load-testing your Joomla site and performing multi-site management.

❑ Determine if Joomla fits your needs, or whether you need to invest in a high-end CMS.

There are many other aspects of administration that will be covered in the book under the specific technology area where they apply (such as using LDAP for authentication). At a minimum, be sure to skim the material that may not seem to directly apply to your role or capabilities.

Web Designers

Web designers have a more specific role than Web masters. The Web master will often choose the direction and functionality that the site will have to offer. A Web designer is then selected by an individual, company, or organization to render the site as a Web presence that meets specified needs. In Joomla, designers have found an excellent platform for client work, as well as the prospect of independent income in the Joomla template market. The number of commercial template vendors is large, and the field seems to be quite lucrative.

Most of the commercial template sites use a subscription model, whereby customers pay a monthly or yearly fee to have unlimited access to all of the templates on the site. This model is a boon for Web designers because each site needs to continually update its stock with new templates. To keep existing customers, there is regular work for numerous Web designers. If you're a Web designer, you'll find plenty of useful information in this book to keep you on the bleeding edge of your profession.

New designers should find a robust introduction to template planning and construction. Because effective template design requires a combination of PHP code, images, and CSS, it takes a fair amount of forethought and guidance to properly design a template. You will find descriptions of all parts of the process.

Even if you've never written any code in your life, the coding guide included in this book will help you to construct a template with a plug-and-play style. As long as you read and understand the general function of the code presented, you'll be able to plug it into the right place.

Advanced designers will be able to hone their skills by following the real-world advice, as well as adding advanced functionality such as Ajax capabilities to Joomla pages. Further, the search engine optimization techniques and the internationalization sections will put you at the top of your field.

On the design side, you'll learn the following:

❑ How to modify the code and style sheets of existing templates.

❑ The process of creating a new template from scratch so that you can see precisely the minimum that is needed and how more advanced templates avoid limitations.

❑ A procedure for authoring new modules that can be plugged into any template.

❑ How to leverage the new Ajax client-side technology to give your Joomla site a responsive, cutting-edge interface.

❑ The planning methods that ensure your site can be internationalized and support multi-language content.

❑ How to fit current extensions (such as polls, classified ads, and picture galleries) into your over-all site design for a more substantial Web presence.

❑ The ins and outs of customizing CSS to give the site a unified look-and-feel.

❑ Guidelines for ensuring your design complies with the Web Content Accessibility Guidelines (WCAG) for people with disabilities.

Web designers are generally hired very early in the site-creation process, and the more they know about Joomla before beginning, the greater the technology that Joomla offers can be leveraged. Particularly in the arena of template construction, taking advantage of the Joomla features can produce a site that not only excels now but is also maintainable and can be reasonably updated in the future. Web designers can also take greatest advantage of the extensions that are developed to supplement the system.

Web Developers

Those performing Web development will find the Joomla platform to be the most flexible and yet the most straightforward development framework of any CMS. Since the upgrade to version 1.5, the entire structure of Joomla has been rewritten to provide a framework that is much more than just a CMS. The Joomla CMS itself is actually an application that executes within the broader Joomla framework. That means that you can do nearly any size of development project on top of the Joomla framework — including developing a completely new CMS (if there were any reason to do so).

You don't have to start at the bottom, though. Examining and modifying existing Joomla extensions (plug-ins, components, and modules) is perhaps the best way to hone your Joomla skills. Once you have a grasp of how existing extensions work within the system, the Joomla world is your oyster. As you progress through this book, you will learn how to create advanced extensions and even deliver a slick client-side Ajax interface implementation. You'll learn how the design patterns that Joomla embraces can be used to structure your own development.

After you've mastered the extensions interface, you can move on to modifying the Joomla system itself, or to participating in group development and deployment. There is plenty of opportunity for collaboration with the more than 45,000 registered Joomla developers. By the time you turn the last page of this book, you'll be at the very top of that skill pyramid. The growth of Joomla has been paralleled by the increase in job opportunities, with an online job market filled with Joomla postings. The economic incentive to maximize your skills is certainly there.

On the development side, *Professional Joomla* will teach you how to do the following:

❑ Develop a plug-in with examples from the simplest Hello World plug-in to advanced reporting e-commerce solutions.

❑ Apply the professional development techniques of design patterns to your Joomla project.

❑ Use scripting with the Ajax technology for snappy client-side interaction without having to requery the server.

❑ Navigate the structure of the Joomla framework so that modifications to the system are possible.

❑ Use and modify existing extensions to add any functionality to your Joomla site that is missing in the default installation.

❑ Adapt a PHP development environment to Joomla code development for proper coding and documentation capabilities.

❑ Implement source code control through Subversion (SVN) to allow team development of a Joomla template, plug-in, component, or module.

❑ Manage a professional deployment from staging server to deployment server.

Developers will find Joomla a fertile platform for both personal and professional satisfaction. Many have already taken the plunge yet have had to sort through sometimes arcane instruction to master even the fundamentals. This book will give you a clear roadmap to attaining the skills you need, with a minimum of confusion or extra work.

Joomla Version 1.0 and Mambo Users

For readers new to the CMS world, Joomla was born in 2005 when the development team left the Mambo community en masse and took the Mambo foundation source code with them. The initial release of Joomla showed little difference from Mambo version 4.5.2.3 under the hood. Even the extensions were interoperable between the Mambo and Joomla.

It was with Joomla 1.5 that the great departure from previous versions began. The entire architecture had been rebuilt as an object-oriented PHP framework. The changes were fundamental enough that neither 1.0 extensions nor templates operate in the newer versions (except in legacy mode). This upgrade provides many opportunities for increased capabilities and the refining of previous template/plug-in/components/modules. It can also produce a great deal of distress because items that worked perfectly in the old system will no longer function in the new.

As a Web master, developer, or designer, it is important for you to understand the implications of this fork from the Mambo system. To meet your own needs or those of your clients, you may be forced to run the new Joomla server in legacy mode if the items that you need have yet to be upgraded to the new system. However, if you run the Joomla server in legacy mode, you will be sacrificing the capabilities and performance gains provided by the new system (and they are substantial).

> With past Joomla versions, deploying a high-traffic site was problematic because Joomla had a tendency to slow down significantly during peak access. The original Joomla application processed one monolithic PHP code block for each page access — whether the page used all of the features it contained or not.
>
> In Version 1.5, the Joomla team addressed this problem and practically eliminated it. The code was refactored so that only those features and modules used by the requested Web page are actually loaded and executed. This new method provides tremendous performance increases on high-volume sites.

I have tried to include pointers and tips wherever possible to allow you to reconcile older development with that of the new. One of the greatest things about the open source community is the fact that it is an open source — you have the source code. If you encounter a component that you need, but it is unavailable for the new Joomla system, given the proper motivation and time, you are not out of luck. You can potentially upgrade it yourself. I'll provide some tips and guidelines in the appropriate areas to help Joomla 1.0 users or those moving from Mambo to ease the transition.

Summary

The Joomla system is a platform that can be mastered by many people with different needs, including Web masters, Web designers, and Web developers. Whatever the reason for your adoption of Joomla, this chapter has provided an overview how this book will help you do the following:

❑ Understand and communicate the value of using a CMS system like Joomla. The new Web 2.0 is a world of automated content management, dynamic interaction, and virtual communities. Joomla is the CMS that makes the opportunities of the new technology available to everyone from individuals to large organizations with an exceptional price tag — free.

❑ Improve your skills as a *Joomla Web master* for deploying and administering a Joomla site. Whether you are an individual Web master with a hobbyist site or a person overseeing a multi-server Joomla installation, the book will show you how to build a Web community, maintain the server, provide security for the content and users, and perform SEO on the site.

❑ Refine the site look-and-feel if you are a *Joomla Web designer*. You will not only learn to create and modify Joomla templates (for fun, for contract employment, or for one of the many commercial template sites), but you will come to understand how to ensure that the site complies with internationalization and accessibility guidelines.

❑ Create plug-ins, components, and modules if you are a *Joomla Web developer*. You will understand the underlying framework structure so that you will even be able to modify Joomla itself. Since almost every aspect of the system is controlled through either CSS or PHP files, almost any desired alteration will be possible.

❑ Upgrade source code, templates, and other technology from earlier Joomla versions or current Mambo installations.

Chapter 2 examines the finer points of installation and configuration of a Joomla site. While basic deployment of Joomla is pretty much a turnkey solution, refining the settings that allow for optimal performance is both an art and a science. By studying the operational choices of the various servers, you can make your Joomla site run like a well-oiled machine.

2

The Finer Points of Installation and Configuration

Four different server technologies must work in concert for Joomla to function properly. If Apache can't execute PHP, or PHP can't connect to MySQL, or Joomla can't write into the MySQL database, the system fails. This chapter will help you configure each interlocking server system to work properly in unison. Each server is controlled by a list of directives or configuration settings, and making sure those settings are optimal will ensure that the system functions properly.

Additionally, various techniques describing the fine-tuning of each aspect of the system will help your server respond to Web requests most efficiently to create the best user experience. By customizing these settings to suit the needs of your Joomla system, you will be able to squeeze a great deal more performance out of the same hardware.

Four Servers in the Joomla System

In the Joomla server constellation (see Figure 2-1), there are four servers that dynamically interact: the Web server, the PHP execution engine, MySQL database server, and the Joomla server itself. I'm using the term *server* loosely in this definition because PHP and Joomla don't execute as independent servers. However, my broader definition will help you understand how to approach operation and configuration, since both PHP and Joomla effectively serve Web pages and require independent configuration.

The foundation of the system is the Web server that supplies the HTTP hosting capabilities. Joomla can run successfully on either Apache Web server or Microsoft Internet Information Server (IIS). While Apache can execute on dozens of operating systems (Windows, MacOS, and dozens of UNIX variants), IIS only runs on the Windows platform. Aside from providing the HTTP serving foundation, the Web server also plays host to the PHP engine and the Joomla server.

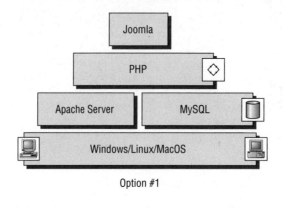

Option #1

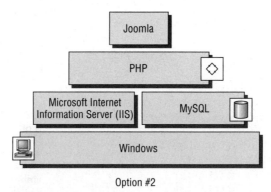

Option #2

Figure 2-1: The four servers that make up the Joomla system

Within the Joomla system, the PHP engine executes the Joomla application. Joomla uses the PHP plug-in to address the MySQL server where all of the Joomla data is stored. While Joomla configuration settings are stored in the `configuration.php` file, almost all other data (including content, sections, categories, extension installation information, and so on) is stored in the MySQL database.

The minimum requirements for the servers that Joomla requires are:

- ❑ PHP 4.3.x or above with the MySQL, XML, and Zlib modules activated
- ❑ MySQL 3.23.x or above
- ❑ Apache 1.13.19 or above

Your choices regarding how these servers will be deployed will have far-reaching implications for the success of your Joomla site.

Installation Choices

You have probably already had some experience with Joomla installation, but I'll provide a short overview so that you may consider the different installation possibilities. When you are making choices about the configuration, you must decide between local or remote deployment, select the platform Joomla will use, determine the method of performing the installation, and pick which Web server to use.

Although most of the options will hinge more on the target deployment conditions than personal preferences, you should evaluate the positives and negatives so that you can understand the ramifications of each selection. You should pay attention to the differences in deployment when performing your evaluation, since it is not unusual to use a different platform for development and testing than will be used for the final deployment. It is common to use Windows or Mac OS for the staging server, while the final site will be launched on a Linux Web server. By noting the variations at the start, you will have an easier time making the deployment transfer.

Local Installation or Remote Deployment

The first installation decision is whether Joomla will be installed locally or remotely. You may have a Web service provider such as `GoDaddy.com` or `SiteGround.com` that will be serving your Web site. In these cases, all of the primary server software, including PHP and MySQL, are already installed and available for use. Activating Joomla is simply a matter of uploading the Joomla installation image and completing the process. If you're installing locally, you have much more to do.

Following are some of the advantages of a local installation:

❑ *Configuration freedom* — You can set up each Joomla server to exactly match your needs. The Web host providers for a remote installation will only rarely allow access to root configuration settings because of the potential danger to their system and other users.

❑ *Thorough system knowledge* — You will almost certainly have more knowledge of the system if you perform the setup and maintenance. That knowledge can translate not only to better system performance but also to a greater understanding of the possibilities and limits of the system when it comes to the development of extensions, components, and plug-ins.

❑ *Potential server performance* — Running your own system gives you complete control to dedicate the maximum amount of resources to the Joomla site. When you use a remote installation, it is likely you'll be sharing database execution and Internet connectivity with a great number of fellow subscribers. That can lead to servers bogging down, and your performance will suffer in peak usage times.

❑ *Backup flexibility* — With a local installation, you have the option of implementing backup procedures that can include everything from a simple manual backup to a mirrored server drive. On a remote installation, creating a backup of the current site installation and content can be tedious and require separate manual procedures for the files (through FTP) and the database (through some type of administration interface).

Following are some of the disadvantages of local installation:

❑ *More work* — With a local installation, you are also responsible for the setup and maintenance of the server. That includes configuration to most effectively divide the server resources among the various servers executing on the machine.

❑ *Potential server performance* — Although having your own dedicated server is likely to give you better performance than a remote installation, this is not always the case. Web host providers spend a great deal of energy ensuring that their servers are optimized for peak performance. They also tend to use more expensive equipment because of the load being placed on it.

❑ *Failover safety* — Most host providers implement some type of redundancy in the system to ensure that their client's Web sites don't go down. This may include backup Domain Name System (DNS) servers, automatic failover hard drive mirrors, clustering, battery backups, and a number of other technologies that ensure that a client site continues to function properly in the event of a system failure. It is difficult and expensive to implement this type of safety net for an individual local server.

If you would like to have a local installation but don't have a business-grade Internet connection, look into co-location options provided by your local Internet service providers (ISPs). Many ISPs have excellent pricing that allows you to locate your server on their premises and hook into their Internet backbone for a fee.

Choice of Platform: Windows, Linux, or MacOS

The choice of a platform can be a difficult one, and there are too many variables involved in the decision that will be particular to your situation to list here. It may boil down to your comfort level with a given operating system, or the consideration of licensing fees (Linux is free, while Windows and MacOS both require licensing fees). While the platform choice may affect performance, it shouldn't have a significant effect on the Joomla installation process. Most Joomla administration occurs through the Web interface, so the platform is immaterial to the interaction with the system.

Further, Joomla uses the PHP and MySQL technologies, which are very nearly identical on all of the platforms. Therefore, you are going to be interacting with the system in much the same manner regardless of the platform.

Installation of Individual Servers or Combined Installation

You can choose to individually install each piece of server software or use a combined installer such as XAMPP (pronounced as either "x-amp" or "zamp"). When describing an installation setup, administrators often use acronyms such as WAMP, LAMP, or MAMP. These acronyms indicate the target platform providing the first letter (W = Windows, L = Linux, and M = MacOS) of the operating systems, and the other three letters representing the servers to be installed (Apache, MySQL, and PHP). The most popular combined installer is called XAMPP, where the X represents a variable, since the installers are available for all three operating systems. The two "PPs" in "XAMPP" indicate PHP and Perl software, both of which are included with the installation. Although Joomla doesn't use Perl, it won't affect server performance.

XAMPP installers overcome one of the major obstacles to open source deployment: packaging. Open source developers are notorious for releasing software that, while stable when executing alone, breaks integration with existing versions of other necessary software. (For example, a new Apache version will no longer work with the stable version of PHP.) An XAMPP installer avoids these problems by shipping only fully compatible versions together. That means that you can download a single installer, execute it, and have an integrated server system up and running in very little time.

While the XAMPP installer provides easy and quick installation for staging or testing, it has some serious disadvantages. Central among those is the problem of security. The default installations of the servers in the XAMPP package leave all avenues of security penetration wide open. Further, there are many unneeded applications (such as Perl), extensions, and modules included in the install that can bog down your system. In fact, the amount of space used on your local drive will be more than three times greater than if you installed the servers needed for Joomla separately.

If you are a beginner, an XAMPP installer is fantastic to get you up and running in a short time. If you're slightly more advanced, even though you're sure to run into a problem or two, individual installations may be the way to go.

Keep in mind that the platform may also help determine how you want to perform the installation. For example, on the MacOS, Apache server is already natively installed — it needs only to be activated. Likewise, if you're going to use IIS as your Web server on the Windows platform, it is likely already installed. The servers included would create redundancy for the existing technology, and at worst they may conflict with servers already in place.

Choice of Web Server: Apache or Microsoft Internet Information Server (IIS)

If you are running on the Windows platform, you have a choice to make for the Joomla Web server: You can run either Apache or Microsoft Internet Information Server (IIS). The choice is a difficult one for several reasons. The primary reason to use Apache on Windows is that compatibility between Joomla and Apache is well tested and understood. However, there are several reasons why you might want to choose IIS instead:

❑   *Native SSL support* — SSL security is natively supported in IIS on Windows. As of this writing, an Apache user would have to do a custom compilation of the Apache server to obtain Secure Sockets Layer (SSL) capabilities. The distribution binaries do not include this security.

❑   *Tuned performance* — Microsoft spends a great deal of time and money making sure that IIS is optimized for maximum performance on Windows. While Apache runs well, it is truly optimized for the Linux platform or another UNIX variant.

❑   *Integrated directory security* — IIS understands the directory security native to Windows and even works with Microsoft's Active Directory infrastructure. Using Apache requires a partial integration of Windows security permissions with the Apache system.

❑   *Bundled FTP server* — The default installation of IIS includes a File Transfer Protocol (FTP) server that can be useful for administration of both the central Joomla system as well as provided extra capabilities to a variety of Joomla extensions (such as upload/download capabilities to an image gallery component).

❑   *Most IIS components already installed* — On the Windows platform, most of the components needed for executing IIS are integrated into the operation system. This means that the install footprint of IIS is very small, since only a few extra pieces of technology need to be placed on the system.

To install Joomla on the Windows platform, first ensure that IIS is running properly. You can test for IIS by going to the Control Panel ➪ Add or Remove Software. Click on the Windows Components button, find the Internet Information Server list item, and determine if it is checked. If not, check the installation box and perform the installation. When IIS is running properly, you should be able to type the following URL into your browser and see the default Web page:

```
http://localhost
```

Before you can run Joomla, you must install PHP and MySQL so that the execution and database technology is available. You can obtain PHP from the following URL:

```
http://www.php.net
```

Follow the PHP installer as you normally would. At the Web Server page of the Installation Wizard, choose your version of IIS, as shown in Figure 2-2. The PHP installer will automatically configure IIS to work with PHP.

That's about it! Even though PHP doesn't notify you that a reboot is required, it is. You must reboot your machine for the `Path` variable to be set to address the new PHP directory. If you have any problem getting PHP working, check the `Path` variable by opening the Control Panel ⇨ System and clicking on the Environment Variables on the Advanced tab. Edit the `Path` variable (see Figure 2-3) to include a reference to your PHP directory. This directory will likely be located at the root of your local drive (for example, `c:\`) or in your programs directory (for example, `c:\Program Files\`).

If the PHP engine still isn't running properly (see the next section for a way to test it), try checking if there is a `PHP.ini` in your `Windows` directory. If so, ensure that it is configured to point to the proper directory. If not, try copying the `PHP.ini` there. You should stop and restart the server to make sure the PHP extension is reset after any change.

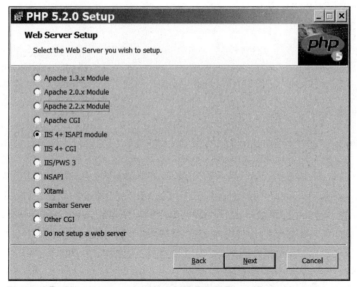

Figure 2-2: Choose your version of IIS for PHP configuration.

Steps in the Joomla Installation Process

Joomla installation is relatively easy for an experienced computer user. This section summarizes the installation steps, so if you haven't gone through the process, this will familiarize you with the basic features.

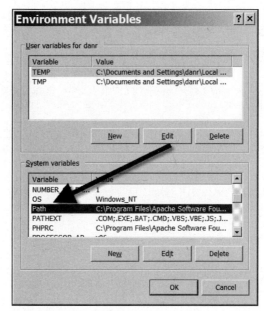

Figure 2-3: Edit the Path variable to ensure that it includes the PHP directory.

Start the installation by downloading the current Joomla image (from `www.joomla.org`) to a local drive. Expand the archive (either a `.zip`, `.tar.gz` and `.tar.bz2` file), and place the Joomla files in your Web server directory. In a remote installation, you can use an FTP program such as the free FileZilla to upload the files in the root directory on the Web server.

> *Before you begin installing on a remote server, you should check to ensure that PHP is functioning properly. You can easily perform this test by creating a file with your text editor (such as Notepad) named* `test.php` *and putting in a single line that reads* `<?php phpinfo(); ?>`. *Save the file and upload it to the remote server. When you access the file (with a URL such as* `http://www.example.com/test.php`*), you will be presented with a multipage screen of PHP configuration parameters. If PHP isn't executing properly, contact your ISP. Be sure to delete this file after it has executed properly because it can reveal a great deal about your Web server to a potential hacker. Additionally, a* `phpinfo()` *page is securely included in the Joomla Administrator interface, so you can obtain the information there.*

Once the files have been copied on the Web site directory, access the `index.php` file through your Web browser. You should see the first Joomla installation screen shown in Figure 2-4. The first screen holds a list box that shows all the languages available for installation. You can select the desired language and click the Next button to proceed with the installation.

The next screen (see Figure 2-5) enables you to do a pre-installation check to ensure that all of the necessary parts of the system work. If any of the parameters are not set as required by Joomla, you can skip to the "Configuring PHP" section for an explanation of the configuration options to make the necessary changes.

Figure 2-4: The first Joomla installation page allows configuration of the destination language.

The next screen requires you to confirm compliance with the GNU General Public License. Clicking the Next button will take you to the Database configuration screen (see Figure 2-6). This screen will allow you to configure the URL of the MySQL server (often just `localhost` on a local installation), enter the database login, set the database where the Joomla data will be stored, and select the collation sequence to be used by Joomla. Note that some remote Web providers will not allow a program to create a new database. If this is the case with your ISP, simply create the database yourself and enter the database name on this screen. The Joomla installer will create the necessary tables within it. In the Advanced Settings tab at the bottom of the screen, there are also parameters that let you select whether to back up or drop any existing data.

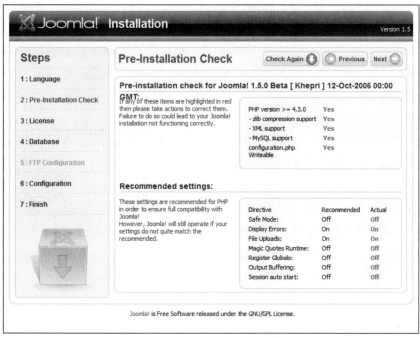

Figure 2-5: The Pre-Installation Check screen will confirm all of the necessary server functionality is working.

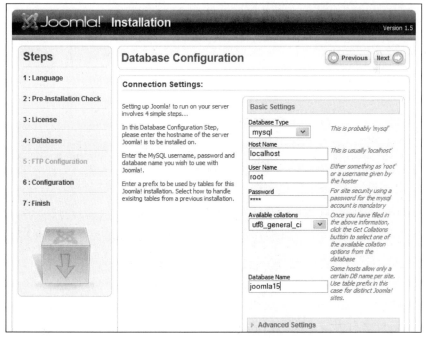

Figure 2-6: The Database Configuration screen lets you set the database account and database name parameters.

The Main Configuration screen (see Figure 2-7) enables you to define parameters for your site. Here you can set the site name, the administrator password, and choose to install sample data if you wish. Clicking on the Install Sample Data button will write the data into the MySQL database, which provides a good test to ensure that connectivity is working properly with the database server.

The Finish screen tells you that the configuration is complete and provides buttons either to move to the opening page of the Joomla site, or execute the Administrator interface.

If there is an error along the way where the installer just fails, be sure to turn on the error reporting in PHP (see the section "Modifying PHP Error Reporting" later in this chapter). Sometimes errors will be generated that the Joomla system doesn't catch, and only by viewing the PHP errors generated (which are invisible without the proper directive) can you diagnose the problem.

Figure 2-7: The Main Configuration screen allows you to set the site name, administrator password, and install sample data.

Configuring Apache Web Server

To obtain the best performance on your Joomla server, you need to start at the bottom: the Apache server. Apache server is one of the most tried and tested Web servers in the world. It's used to run some of the biggest Internet Web sites and some of the tiniest. More than 70 percent of the world's sites use Apache for Web serving. Because of the worldwide deployment and testing, Apache stable releases tend to be rock solid. If a problem is encountered, usually the trouble can be traced back to a faulty configuration, rather than a fault in the server itself.

While initial installation of Apache is easy, there can be difficulties in configuring the system to exactly meet your server needs. In the main configuration file (httpd.conf), there are more than three dozen different directives. Many of the directives overlap and affect not only the operation of the server but also security and performance as well.

Configuration Files

When optimizing Apache to run Joomla most effectively, you will have to check all the configuration directives that the Web server uses. The recommended settings are not one-size-fits-all. How you configure the Web server is governed largely by how you see your audience. Do you have thousands of users who will be visiting your Joomla site for a few minutes and leaving? Or, are you trying to make your site a portal where users will spend a majority of their Web time logged in to your site?

Setting the correct values for some parameters such as those relating to timeouts will take some experience, but you can adjust some settings immediately to make your life as a Joomla administrator easier. The most important directives for Joomla include DirectoryIndex, LogLevel, and ServerRoot.

DirectoryIndex Directive

This directive defines what index file will be accessed by the Web server. By default, the directive is set to DirectoryIndex index.html, which means that only index.html will be returned to a visitor if a directory without a file is requested. Since Joomla uses index.php to execute, you must add a PHP attribution to ensure that your server functions correctly.

If you look in the httpd.conf file, you should find the following directive:

```
# DirectoryIndex: sets the file that Apache will serve if a directory is requested
<IfModule dir_module>
    DirectoryIndex index.html
</IfModule>
```

For Joomla to execute properly, you need to add the PHP file as a default index page. To accomplish this, you only need an index.php reference before the HTML reference, like this:

```
DirectoryIndex index.php index.html
```

The next time a user enters a URL without a file reference (such as http://localhost/), the directory will first be searched for index.php and the index.html file will only be used if the PHP file can't be found.

LogLevel Directive

The LogLevel sets how verbose the system will make the error log entries. When initially learning Joomla or testing during development, increasing the LogLevel can make it much easier to diagnose and correct problems with the system. It can also allow you to catch small problems immediately, rather than later in the life of the system when heavy usage can magnify what were minor defects. As the old saying goes — it is best to kill a monster when it is small.

The default LogLevel setting is warn. Following are the eight available settings (listed in ascending levels of verbosity):

- ❑ emerg — Only records emergency entries when system has faulted and is unusable.

- ❑ alert — Records server warnings when action should be taken immediately to prevent catastrophic failure in one part of the system.

- ❑ `crit` — Stores critical conditions that could impair the functioning of the server.
- ❑ `warn` — Records all warnings the system generates. Note that this is the default setting.
- ❑ `error` — Stores errors in system execution.
- ❑ `notice` — Records conditions that are normal and don't threaten system operations.
- ❑ `info` — Provides informational records with optimization suggestions.
- ❑ `debug` — Records all system generated messages, including the acknowledgment of execution of processes.

When the `LogLevel` is set, the log will store messages from that level, as well as all messages from the higher critical levels above it. The messages from the `notice` level are always logged, regardless of the `LogLevel` setting. For a deployment server, it is recommended that a minimum of `crit` level logging be set.

When set to `warn`, a log entry might appear like this:

```
[Sat Nov 18 08:16:04 2006] [error] [client 127.0.0.1] File does not exist:
C:/Program Files/Apache Software Foundation/Apache2.2/htdocs/AVE, referer:
http://www.yahoo.com/
```

There is also the `LogFormat` directive that can be used to customize the logged entry format. Look in the Apache manual for complete instructions regarding this directive's use.

The directive that determines the location and name of the error log is named, appropriately, `ErrorLog`. One handy capability of the `ErrorLog` directive is the ability to have any log entries routed to a remote server. You might want the log on a remote server if you want to centralize all of the log information of multiple servers in a single place for analysis. Having the log at a remote location also prevents hackers, if they gain access to your main server, from erasing the log of their actions.

To have the log sent to a remote server, you need only specify a remote syslog server in the directive like this:

```
ErrorLog syslog:logwarehouse
```

This will send the log entries to a server called `logwarehouse`. For information on setting up the server to receive the error log messages, check out the Wikipedia article on the syslog standard:

```
http://en.wikipedia.org/wiki/Syslog
```

ServerRoot Directive

The `ServerRoot` directive holds the configuration for the root directory of the Web server. On a Linux machine, this directive would likely be set like this:

```
ServerRoot "/usr/local/apache"
```

On the Windows platform, it would likely be set to something like this:

```
ServerRoot "C:/Program Files/Apache Software Foundation/Apache2.2"
```

This value will be appended to all paths that are not fully qualified. If error logs are not being written to the proper place, or configuration files are not available for access, check the value of this directive.

Other httpd.conf Directives

While the previous sections detailed the most important directives to get you started, there are many others that are relevant to Joomla configuration. Note that many suggested configuration sets for features such as languages, SSL, user directories, and so on, can be found in the /defaults folder within the /conf folder of the server. You can look at the included .conf files to see the configuration sets of directives that will best help you set up the system to provide a particular group of features.

Table 2-1 contains a list of important directives and a general description of each. You will find all of these directives in your configuration file. The proper settings for each will be dependent on your deployment needs.

Table 2-1: Important Apache Server Directives

Directive	Description
AccessFileName	Sets the name of the configuration file.
AddCharset charset extension [extension] ...	Maps files with the extension specified to a character set.
AddDefaultCharset On|Off|charset	Adds a default character set to be used with MIME type text/plain or text/HTML.
AddLanguage	Sets a map between a file extension and a language.
AllowCONNECT	Sets the ports that may accept connections through the proxy.
AllowOverride	Determines the directive types that are allowed in an .htaccess file.
CacheDefaultExpire	Holds the default duration that a document will be kept in the cache if no expiration is set for the file.
CharsetDefault	Determines the default character set.
CookieExpires	Holds the expiration time in seconds for a tracking cookie.
CustomLog	Sets a custom log file and the format to be used by the log.
DefaultLanguage	Defines the MIME tag default language for a visitor.

Continued

Table 2-1: Important Apache Server Directives *(continued)*

Directive	Description
Deny	Controls the hosts that are denied access to the Web server. This directive can be tremendously useful when fending off a hacker's attack, or limiting connections from unauthorized or unfriendly visitors.
DocumentRoot	Holds the path of the root directory that will be served to requestors. Most often, this directive specifies the path to the `htdoc` folder that holds the Joomla installation. The setting for this directive may appear as `C:/Program Files/Apache Software Foundation/Apache2.2/htdocs` on the Windows platform.
ErrorDocument	Specifies the error document that will be returned to the visitor in case of error. Note that the Joomla system overrides this operator and returns Joomla error pages. These Joomla error pages may, in turn, be overridden by a specified template to transmit custom error pages to the users.
ErrorLog	Specifies the path of the error file where error entries are logged.
Header	Used to set an HTTP response header.
HeaderName	Holds the name of the file to be inserted at the top of a directory listing if the `Header` directive is set.
IdentityCheck	Enables or disables the logging of visitor information provided by the request in the form of RFC 1413 identity.
KeepAlive	Enables or disables persistent connections/sessions.
KeepAliveTimeout	Determines the length of time before persistent connections/sessions will time out.
LanguagePriority	Holds the precedence of language variants if language is not specified by the requestor.
Listen	Custom-specifies the IP addresses and ports where the server listens. Also see the `ServerName` directive.
MaxKeepAliveRequests	Holds the number of requests allowed by a persistent connection. The default setting is `100`.

Table 2-1: Important Apache Server Directives *(continued)*

Directive	Description
Script	Configures a Common Gateway Interface (CGI) script for execution on the receipt of a particular message. If PHP will be run through CGI, this should be configured properly.
ScriptLog	Only useful if you're running PHP as a CGI execution. In that case, this directive sets the location of the CGI script error log file.
ServerAdmin	When messages are sent from the server to a client, this email address is included. It can be useful for a Joomla administrator to configure this setting so that requests and reports from users may be received by the administrator.
ServerName	Name of host and port to be used by the server. The default setting is ServerName localhost:80. If you are running multiple servers on the same machine (Apache and IIS, for example), this directive can be used to change the port that the Apache server uses to listen for requests.
TimeOut	Amount of time server will attempt operation before a failure timeout. The default setting is 300 seconds.
TraceEnable	Sets the trace behavior. The default condition is on.
TransferLog	Holds the location of the transfer log.
UserDir	Specifies user-specific directories. If your server will be hosting multiple users with various Joomla installations, user directories can be added here.
VirtualDocumentRoot	The root of the virtual document. This directive can be important if you are setting up a multi-host system to run Joomla.
VirtualDocumentRootIP	The IP number of the virtual document.

Log Files

The Apache log files can be your best friend when it comes to monitoring your Web server. Although there are some Joomla extensions that can record site statistics, their use is not recommended because of the decrease in server performance. Therefore, if you want to monitor your closely traffic, you must do it through the actual Web server log files. There are three primary types of log files: access, error, and install.

Monitoring these log files can help you do the following:

❑   *Balance traffic* — If your Web site becomes popular, it is very important that you understand the stress load that will be placed on the server. You should know the peak hours, as well as the hours when there is little activity. In special circumstances (following an event reported by the media), you may receive the mixed blessing of a flood of traffic. In these extreme circumstances, you may choose to shut down processor-intensive services (such as the search function) until the storm has passed. With the slow times, you'll definitely want the opportunity to back up your site.

❑   *Examine your user base* — The log files can generate a huge amount of information that can be extremely useful to a system administrator. Wouldn't you like to know the percentage split of the type of browsers that visitors are using? It's often surprising. What if half of your traffic comes from the Netherlands? Wouldn't that be important to the future focus of your content? And wouldn't it also be useful to know which Web site is sending all the Netherlands traffic in your direction? These are just a few of the questions you'll be able to answer by taking a serious look at the log files.

❑   *See what errors have occurred* — You need to know if one of the server modules isn't loading properly, or if the server is generating errors when it attempts a particular function. The error logs can provide vital debugging information to get the server running properly, and ensure that it stays that way.

❑   *Watch for hacks and system attacks* — The Web is like the old Wild West, and there are very few rules in place. In the 1970s, the United States had minor problems with teenage hackers breaking into computer systems to play around. Nowadays, the venue for hacking is global, and the hackers often have less benign motives. The log files can often reveal a pattern of access, particularly when a hacker is using a piece of software such as a bot that indicates your system is under attack. Once you know an attack is being attempted, there are a great number of remedies you can apply — right down to blocking the IP address that the hacker is using. But you can't stop anything if you don't know it's happening, and examining the logs can often provide an early warning that your system is in play.

After you install Apache and run it for a short time, check out the /logs directory at the Apache directory root. You will see the three main log files here. Take a look at each file with a standard text editor so that you will be familiar with them. As you progress through this book, you will return to these logs to understand the adjustment and maintenance of your Joomla site.

Modules and Extensions Folders

The /modules and /extensions folders contain all of the Apache plug-ins that allow the Web server to interact with other software, including PHP. For a Joomla installation, you're unlikely to modify these folders. However, if you experience a problem or begin having some strange results, it is often a good idea to check the version numbers of the individual modules to determine if there is an upgraded version available.

On the Linux platform, you can generally find the version of a module or extension using the file command like this:

```
file mod_authn_dbm.so
```

On the Windows platform, you can check the version numbers of each extension or module simply enough by looking at the version tab on the properties of the file, as shown in Figure 2-8. You can do a search on the Web or the Apache Web site (www.apache.org) to see if other users are having difficulty with the version of plug-in installed on your system. If you post a question regarding your problem, be sure to include the version numbers of the plug-ins that you're using so that responders can accurately assess your situation.

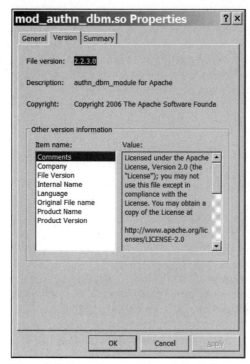

Figure 2-8: If you have problems, check the versions of the files in the modules and ext folders.

Not all modules located in these folders are active. You can use directives in the httpd.conf file to individually activate or disable a plug-in. Note that additional modules not included with the core install are available for download here:

```
http://modules.apache.org/
```

htdocs Folder

By default, all of your Web content is stored in this directory. You have to be particularly careful on the security settings that you allow for the /htdocs folder. Since hhtdocs files have execution privileges for PHP code, if a hacker can find a way to place custom code or a virus into this directory, the potential for mischief is significant. Chapter 14 discusses the best methods of configuring this folder for security.

Configuring PHP

PHP is much easier to configure than Apache, but it can also present many more security dangers. Since PHP is actually a code execution engine, you must be sure that it is properly configured so that there are no security holes. If compromised, a hacker can potentially not only gain access to confidential information and delete existing content but also set up the platform to execute a program that performs additional mischief.

> *For Joomla to operate properly, your Web server should be running a version of PHP that is 4.3.0 or greater. Before you begin installation (particularly on a remote server), check the PHP version to avoid any compatibility problems.*

Common hacker tricks including setting up a false user interface to collect personal information from your Web site visitors (and sending the data to themselves), creating an infection vector for the distribution of viruses, initiating denial-of-service attacks originating from your server, and even attempting email spam origination.

One of the simplest ways of determining current PHP settings is to use the `phpinfo()` code line that you used to check whether PHP was operating in the first place. A file with the single line that reads `<?php phpinfo(); ?>` will display the configuration screen shown in Figure 2-9.

Scrolling down to the Configuration section, you can see all the current directives and their settings. Further down are individual sections for each plug-in — many showing their version numbers for easy reference. Additionally, the PHP Variables section near the bottom will show you the values of existing PHP variables, which can be useful both in understanding the system and tracking down possible bugs.

If you are doing a manual compile of PHP to use with Joomla, there are three necessary support libraries that you must include: MySQL, Zlib, and XML. Without these libraries in the compile, Joomla will be unable to execute properly.

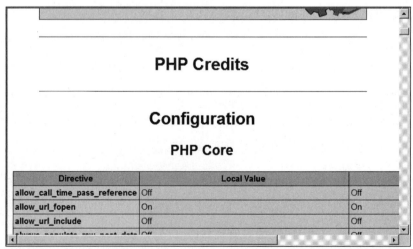

Figure 2-9: The phpinfo() command will display the complete PHP settings in the Configuration section.

The following PHP settings are checked by the Joomla system as it is loaded and the recommended settings are:

❏ Safe Mode — Set `safe_mode` to `Off`.

❏ Display Errors — Set `display_errors` to `On` (only on a staging server).

❏ File Uploads — Set `file_uploads` to `On`.

❏ Magic Quotes GPC — Set `magic_quotes_gpc` to `On`.

❏ Magic Quotes Runtime — Set `magic_quotes_runtime` to `Off`.

❏ Output Buffering — Set `output_buffering` to `Off`.

❏ Session auto start — Set `session.auto_start` to `Off`.

❏ Register Globals — Set `register_globals` to `Off` in the Joomla `globals.php` file.

❏ Register Globals Emulation — Set `RG_EMULATION` to `Off ()` in the Joomla `globals.php` file.

❏ Zlib compression — Set `zlib.output_compression` to `On`.

You should also have the Joomla file `configuration.php` in a directory with Writeable permissions so that you can make changes to the Joomla system setting from within the Administrator interface. The Session save path should also be writable; otherwise, a number of Joomla errors will occur. By modifying the PHP directives, you can change the location of objects such as the Session path.

PHP Directives

There are many PHP settings, but not all are directly relevant to a Joomla installation. Many settings you will never need, so this chapter only details the most important ones to a Joomla user. Of the directives listed that are critical to a Joomla user, the one that changes the error reporting display is the most important.

Modifying PHP Error Reporting

To allow PHP to display errors (very helpful, especially when debugging a template or new extension), you can modify the `display_errors` setting in the `php.ini` file. To turn on `display_errors`, use a line like this:

```
display_errors = On
```

By default, this directive is set to `Off` to prevent hackers from obtaining extra information about the back-end of the Web site. In fact, the errors will still be written into the Apache error log file as long as the following directive is set:

```
log_errors = On
```

By default, `log_errors` is set to `On`. However, especially when you are debugging a file and clicking the Refresh button in the browser, it is inconvenient to constantly reopen the error log to see if the problem is resolved. It is much easier to see the error information displayed inline in the browser window with the presentation generated by the code before the error occurred.

> *You should turn off the* display_errors *functionality on all deployment servers. The error information can reveal database settings, path names, server names, server addresses, and a variety of other sensitive information that can be used against your server.*

As with Apache, you can set the verbosity of the error reporting. You can use the following settings:

- ❑ E_ALL — Include all errors and warnings except E_STRICT errors.
- ❑ E_ERROR — Include fatal run-time errors.
- ❑ E_RECOVERABLE_ERROR — Include nearly fatal run-time errors.
- ❑ E_WARNING — Include run-time warnings.
- ❑ E_PARSE — Include compile-time parse errors.
- ❑ E_NOTICE — Include run-time notices.
- ❑ E_STRICT — Include run-time notices that suggest code changes to ensure forward compatibility with future PHP versions.
- ❑ E_CORE_ERROR — Include fatal errors that occur during initial startup.
- ❑ E_CORE_WARNING — Include startup warnings.
- ❑ E_COMPILE_ERROR — Include fatal compile-time errors.
- ❑ E_COMPILE_WARNING — Include compile-time warnings.
- ❑ E_USER_ERROR — Include user-generated error messages.
- ❑ E_USER_WARNING — Include user-generated warning messages.
- ❑ E_USER_NOTICE — Include user-generated notice messages.

By default, error reporting is set to E_ALL, but you can modify it to also include E_STRICT warnings by using the OR (|) operator like this:

```
error_reporting = E_ALL|E_NOTICE
```

To include all errors, yet exclude a particular category of error, by using the AND (&) and NOT (~) operators directive like this:

```
error_reporting = E_ALL & ~E_USER_NOTICE
```

You may not understand how important error reporting can be to Joomla users until you run into a situation that you can't understand. For example, you may get a blank screen when trying to access Joomla with no indication that there is even a problem. When the errors are displayed, you can immediately begin to track down the problem.

On first install, the blank screen is most likely a session path problem. With errors turned on (or you can look in the error log), you'll see an error like this:

```
Warning: session_start() [function.session-start]:
open(C:\DOCUME~1\danny\LOCALS~1\Temp\php\upload\sess_61p0kg4fu0fho3lvagt3je8d74,
O_RDWR) failed: No such file or directory (2) in C:\Program Files\Apache Software
Foundation\Apache2.2\htdocs\libraries\joomla\environment\session.php on line 234
```

The error states that the server can't start a session because there was "no such file or directory." This most likely means that your PHP server is not set up correctly to access a directory where it has read and write permissions.

Open the `php.ini` file, and search for the `session.save_path` directive. You may find that the path to this file is inaccessible to the Web server. Modifying this directive to a path within the Web server directory will most likely cure the problem on a staging server. On a deployment server, you should use the tools provided by your ISP to modify the permissions to reach the desired folder.

On the Windows platform, the original directive path reads as follows:

```
session.save_path="C:\DOCUME~1\danny\LOCALS~1\Temp\php\upload"
```

To solve the problem, simply create a folder named `php_sessions` that is located inside the Web root directory and point the PHP server to that directory. After creating the new directory, change the session path directive to read as follows (all on one line):

```
session.save_path="C:/Program Files/Apache Software
    Foundation/Apache2.2/htdocs/php_sessions"
```

For a remote Linux install, you may have to change the Linux PHP parameter from the following:

```
session.save_path = /var/php_sessions
```

Set it to a `php_sessions` folder where you have the top-level access:

```
session.save_path = /billcat/ws/b1833/pow.dan/php_sessions
```

Reboot the Apache server and Joomla should work now! From this simple example, you can see how displaying errors can help your problem solving so that you're not left in the dark. This directive is just the tip of the iceberg for configuring PHP.

Important PHP Settings

Table 2-2 shows an abbreviated list of PHP directives that are important to Joomla execution. While the first column displays the directive itself, the second column shows either the possible settings or the type of setting that can be used. The third column contains a brief description of the function of the directive.

Before you begin changing any of the PHP settings, you should make a quick backup of the `php.ini` file so that you can always return to the original settings. Since the `.ini` file is a simple text file, it won't take up much room on your local drive, and you may choose to make a new backup for every major alteration.

Once you begin making changes to the PHP directives, remember that you must reboot the Apache or IIS servers for the changes to take affect. These directives are initialized when the PHP service is booted, so restarting the Web server will read the new directives.

As an alternative to making a backup of the `.ini`, you can simply make the current directive setting line a comment with a semicolon (;) character at the beginning of the line. Then you can put in the new directive on the next line.

Chapter 2: The Finer Points of Installation and Configuration

Table 2-2: Important PHP Settings

Directive	Settings	Description
doc_root	String	Determines the directory where all PHP scripts will be executed. Best for Joomla execution if left empty.
expose_php	On/Off	Disables the response header broadcast that PHP is available for execution on the server. In most deployment situations, this setting defaults to Off.
extension_dir	String	Sets the directory where PHP extensions and modules are loaded from. If you're having problems with a module such as MySQL, check this directive to determine where it is pointing.
file_uploads	On/Off	Determines whether PHP will support file uploads. For many functions in the Joomla system, including uploads for templates, extensions, and images, should be set to On.
include_path	String	Specifies a list of directories where the require/include functions look for files.
ksmagic_quotes_gpc	On/Off	Determines whether single and double quotation marks, backslashes, and null characters are automatically encoded or escaped. Joomla recommends this setting to On, although some installers set it to Off.
magic_quotes_runtime	On/Off	Determines whether single and double quotation marks, backslashes, and null characters located in an external resource are automatically encoded or escaped. Joomla recommends this setting be Off.
max_execution_time	Integer	Sets the maximum time limit in seconds that a PHP script can execute. A setting of 0 disables the maximum limit. By default, this is set to 30 seconds. If you have a Joomla extension that takes a great deal of time to retrieve remote information, for example, you may need to increase this value.
max_input_time	Integer	Sets the maximum time limit in seconds that a process can parse input parameters. This time also governs how long the system will wait for an upload to complete. By default, it is set to 60 seconds, so if you are expecting uploads to take longer, you will have to change this parameter.

Table 2-2: Important PHP Settings *(continued)*

Directive	Settings	Description
memory_limit	Integer	Sets the memory limit.
safe_mode	On/Off	Limits functionality in a shared-server environment (particularly with remote hosting ISPs). Some of the functions disabled by safe mode include file execution (beyond PHP files), chmod (for changing directory and file permissions), the system() function, and so on. If this option is set on your remote server, many of the limited options are still available via custom provider interfaces (although not to your PHP programs). Check with your ISP for details.
upload_max_filesize	String	Sets the maximum size, in megabytes, that is allowed as an uploaded file. The default is set to 2M for 2MB.
upload_tmp_dir	String	Sets the path of the temporary directory where uploaded files are first held.
user_dir	String	The base name of the directory used on user's home directory for PHP files (for example, public_html).
zlib.output_compression	On/Off/ integer	Sets the ability to enable zlib compression. If this setting is configured to off, the option in Joomla cannot be activated.
zlib.output_handler	String	Defines an alternate compression library if the standard library is not available. By default, this is set to null to use the standard library.

If you're changing the directive for a reason, I would suggest adding an additional line comment describing the reason for the change. When you configure your next server, you can simply reference the existing .ini file and have a lot better idea of what settings you should choose.

Configuring MySQL

MySQL is blessedly simple to get running initially. The real opportunity lies in tuning the performance to provide the fastest response to Joomla system requests. There are many parameters in MySQL that allow you to specify exactly how sessions and memory are used. You can even load-balance MySQL across several servers if your site were to become extremely popular.

Configuring MySQL properly has more to do with monitoring actual usage than predicting bottlenecks. The most common barriers to optimum MySQL performance occur in local drive seeks, reads, and writes. It is only by watching the actual usage patterns that you will be able to determine how best to modify your system.

MySQL Setup

The setup of MySQL is at the same time the simplest and the most complicated of the servers used by Joomla. I have never had a MySQL installation fail on a fresh system, while I have had problems at one time or another with the stable release of all the others. That said, there can be problems getting MySQL to communicate effectively with the other servers — PHP most notoriously.

Activating the Path Parameter on Windows

On the Windows platform, if you execute Joomla and it shows that MySQL isn't active, be sure that you've rebooted your system since installing PHP. To correctly access PHP extensions, the Path variable must be set to make the PHP directory available. PHP automatically adds the path to the Path setting. However, the Path variable is only read and activated at boot time, so any changes to the variable are not active until the system has been rebooted after installation.

You can check to make sure that the Path variable is set properly by going to Control Panel ⇨ System and clicking on the Advanced tab. Click on Environment Variables at the bottom of the tab, and you can look at the Path variable in the System Variables list box.

> *This Path string is generally fairly long, so when I need to examine or edit it, I select the variable, and click the Edit button, which will display the field in a text box. The entire path string will be selected, so use Ctrl+C to copy it to the Clipboard. Then paste the string into an editor like Notepad where you examine it and make changes more easily.*

Verify that the path to your PHP directory is found in the string. If it is missing, you can change the Path string by simply adding a semicolon (;) after the last entry and then typing the PHP path. Reboot the machine and try again. That corrects the problem in a majority of cases.

Database Connectivity with MySQL 5

Once you've moved past the precheck stage of Joomla, you may get to the Database Configuration screen and begin to have problems. You may enter the correct MySQL server address, username, and password, and still the system notifies you that it "can't connect." In these circumstances, you probably have MySQL 5 installed and are using the default version 5 of the password security.

There are two methods of remedying this problem. You can turn off the new-style passwords for the entire MySQL system, or you can set an individual user password to use the old-style authentication. If you're using MySQL for applications other than Joomla, I would recommend you configure an individual password to use the old-style authentication.

To set a password to the MySQL version 4.1 authentication type, execute the MySQL command line utility. At the mysql> prompt, enter the following line, substituting joomlaAdmin for your existing username and mypassword for the password you want to use:

```
SET PASSWORD FOR 'joomlaAdmin' = OLD_PASSWORD('password');
```

The system will respond with a statement that 0 rows are affected, but the command should set up the authentication properly. Execute the Database Connectivity login again, and Joomla should now be able to connect to the system.

To change the entire MySQL authentication procedure, open the MySQL Administrator application and click the Startup Variables button. Select the Security tab and scroll down until you see the "Use old passwords" option. Check the box to the left of the option. To activate the old passwords authentication, click on the Service Control button and restart the MySQL server.

Strict Mode and Data Insert Problems

With the database connectivity working, your MySQL problems may be over — or maybe not. In Joomla, when attempting to install the sample data, if you have display errors turned on or you check the Apache log file, you may see an error such as this:

```
SQL=BLOB/TEXT column 'comments' can't have a default value: …
```

This type of error indicates that you are probably running MySQL in strict mode. That means that either STRICT_TRANS_TABLES or STRICT_ALL_TABLES is enabled. The strict options make it so that a single error writing a record will result in the entire operation being canceled.

From the MySQL Administrator application, you open the Startup Variables pane, select the Advanced tab, and check the SQL Mode option, as shown in Figure 2-10. If either of the strict modes is stored in the text box, you can simply clear the checkbox to deactivate the option and click the Apply Changes button at the bottom of the screen.

Since this is a startup option, it will not be activated until you either restart the MySQL services (under the Service Control pane), or reboot your machine.

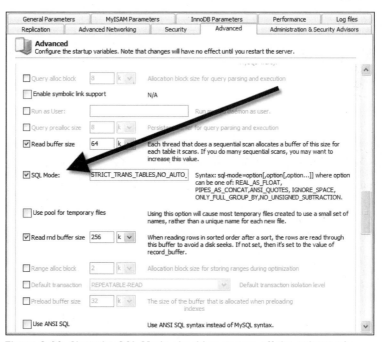

Figure 2-10: Clear the SQL Mode checkbox to turn off the strict mode.

MySQL Administration

The MySQL setup is handled primarily by the Joomla system itself. However, to really understand how the system is working, you must examine the database objects that Joomla constructs. The best way to do that is to download the MySQL Administrator application. It isn't installed natively with the MySQL server. It is free, however, and you can download it as part of the MySQL GUI Tools from the Web site at `http://dev.mysql.com`.

When you execute the application, you'll be presented with a general status screen, as shown in Figure 2-11, which will display the general parameters of the current installation. Along the left side of the screen, you can see the various function icons such as Service Control (functions to start, stop, and restart the MySQL server), Startup Variables (configuration parameters for MySQL execution), and so on.

As an administrator, you will spend most of your time working in the Catalogs area available from the last button of the left selection pane. If you click on the Catalogs button, the pane below will fill with a listing of the schemata of the databases currently available on the MySQL setup. If you click on the Joomla database listed in the pane (in this case, `joomla15`), all of the tables of the database will be displayed in the pane to the right, as shown in Figure 2-12.

You've already seen two configuration switches in the Startup Variables that can eliminate problems when executing Joomla. However, by using the Joomla data in MySQL in the manner you would approach a database, there are more powerful possibilities.

Figure 2-11: The MySQL Administrator provides an easy GUI interface to MySQL management.

You may want the ability to query a Joomla table for any reporting data you might need. For example, there is no native way in Joomla to obtain a summary all of the content items in your Joomla database that don't have a meta-description and are, therefore, indexed poorly by search engines. To find these items, you only need to do a query of the `metadesc` field of the `jos_content` table and display all of the articles that have an empty field.

Select the Joomla database in the MySQL Administrator application, and right-click on the `jos_content` table. When the context menu is displayed, select the Edit Table Data option, as shown in Figure 2-13. A window will be displayed showing all of the data currently in the table.

Notice that the top of the window displays a query like this:

```
SELECT * FROM `joomla`.`jos_content`
```

That general query displays all of the records in the `jos_content` table. You can use a simple SQL `WHERE` clause to filter the content to display only the records you want. Add a `WHERE` clause to return only records with a blank `metadesc` field like this:

```
SELECT * FROM `joomla`.`jos_content` WHERE metadesc = ""
```

When you click on the Execute button to run the query, the window will display only those records that have no meta-description. Under the File menu, you can export the result set to a number of file formats (including XML, HTML, CSV, and Excel), so you can use the report as a checklist to add the necessary descriptions to the flagged items.

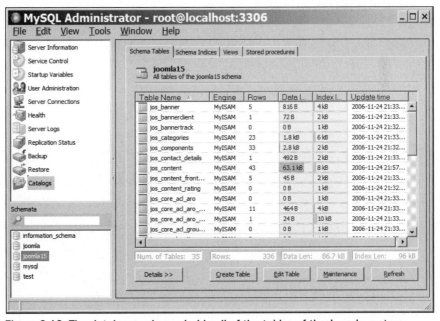

Figure 2-12: The database schema holds all of the tables of the Joomla system.

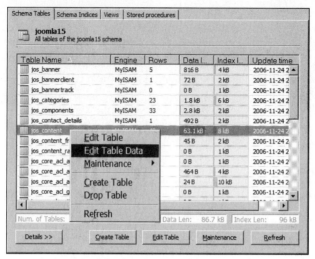

Figure 2-13: Select the Edit Table Data from the context menu.

Resetting a MySQL User Password

No user besides the administrator should ever have access to the user table. The user table holds the privileges and user data, so anyone who has access to this table essentially has control over the entire system. However, if you are the Joomla administrator and you installed MySQL long ago, you may not need to access it for quite some time. That may lead to the embarrassing situation of your forgetting the MySQL password.

If you have forgotten a password for a MySQL login, while there is no method for recovering the password, you can reset it. This technique will work even for the root or administrator password, so be careful to use it only on systems where you have permission. Create a text file, enter the following line, and save the file as resetpwd.txt at the root directory:

```
SET PASSWORD FOR 'root'@'localhost' = PASSWORD('password');
```

On the Linux platform, you can execute the file with a command like this:

```
mysql_safe -init-file = ~/resetpwd.txt &
```

On a Windows system, execute the following line at the command prompt:

```
C:\mysql\bin\mysqld-nt  - init-file=C:\resetpwd.txt
```

After the password reset, be sure to delete the resetpwd.txt file because you don't want something so potentially dangerous to remain on your local drive where some hacker might find a way to execute it.

Configuring Joomla

You probably already have a good deal of experience configuring Joomla to meet your needs. However, you may have overlooked some of the less obvious features that can dramatically change how well the site can be operated.

If you have problems with your Joomla install, you can simply copy over the files. Be sure also to delete `configuration.php` because this file is created by the Joomla installer and tells the system that it has already been installed and configured. If this file isn't found in the Joomla directory, the installer will execute automatically.

configuration.php

Although the Joomla development team recommends that you make all administrative changes from within the Administrator interface, there are some times when direct modification is more advantageous. If you are administering multiple Joomla sites, it is possible to write a macro to make batch changes to the multiple configuration files that would be tedious to accomplish through the GUI interface.

The central configuration data for Joomla is contained in the `configuration.php` file. All of the Joomla settings are contained within a PHP class called `JConfig`. If you open the configuration settings file in your text editor, you'll see the file begins with the class definition like this:

```
class JConfig {
```

The file is then divided into various portions. `Site Settings` is the first section of parameter values. It will look something like this in your editor:

```
        /* Site Settings */
        var $offline = '0';
        var $offline_message = 'This site is down for maintenance.<br /> Please check
back again soon.';
        var $sitename = 'Joomla!';                  // Name of Joomla site
        var $editor = 'tinymce';
        var $list_limit = '20';
        var $legacy = '0';
```

Note that the configuration file included here is in a pre-install state. Your configuration file should match the parameters that you've already set.

The `Database` configuration section will look like this:

```
        var $dbtype = 'mysql';
        var $host = 'localhost';
        var $user = '';                             // MySQL username
        var $password = '';
        var $db = '';
        var $dbprefix = 'jos_';
```

The `Server Settings` configuration section will look like this:

```
        //Change this to something more secure
        var $secret = 'FBVtigIl51ApEU4H';
        var $gzip = '0';
        var $lifetime = '900';          // Session timeout value
        var $error_reporting = '-1';
        var $helpurl = 'http://help.joomla.org';
        var $xmlrpc_server = '0';
        var $ftp_host = '';
        var $ftp_port = '';
```

```
        var $ftp_user = '';
        var $ftp_pass = '';
        var $ftp_root = '';
        var $ftp_enable = '';
        var $tmp_path = '/tmp';
        var $log_path = '/var/logs';
```

The Locale Settings configuration section will look like this:

```
        var $lang_site = 'en-GB';
        var $lang_administrator = 'en-GB';
        var $language = 'en-GB';
        var $lang = 'english';
        var $offset = '0';
        var $offset_user = '0';
```

The Mail Settings configuration section will look like this:

```
        var $mailer = 'mail';
        var $mailfrom = '';
        var $fromname = '';
        var $sendmail = '/usr/sbin/sendmail';
        var $smtpauth = '0';
        var $smtpuser = '';
        var $smtppass = '';
        var $smtphost = 'localhost';
```

The Cache Settings configuration section will look like this:

```
        var $caching = '0';
        var $caching_tmpl = '0';
        var $caching_page = '0';
        var $cachetime = '900';
```

The Debug Settings configuration section will look like this:

```
        var $debug      = '0';
        var $debug_db    = '0';
        var $debug_lang = '0';
```

The Meta Settings configuration for the site will look like this:

```
        var $MetaDesc = 'Joomla! - the dynamic portal engine';
        var $MetaKeys = 'joomla, Joomla';
        var $MetaTitle = '1';
        var $MetaAuthor = '1';
```

The Statistics Settings configuration section will look like this:

```
        var $enable_stats = '0';
        var $enable_log_items = '0';
        var $enable_log_searches = '0';
```

The `Search-Engine-Optimization (SEO) Settings` configuration section will look like this:

```
        var $sef = '0';
```

The `Feed Settings` configuration section will look like this:

```
        var $feed_limit   = 10;
        var $feed_summary = 0;
    }
    ?>
```

Be sure to make a backup of your settings file before making any changes. If a change of setting renders Joomla inoperative, you can restore the system by pulling the backup copy and putting it in place. Also ensure that you don't store the backup file in the directory path of your Web server. For example, if you name the backup of `configuration.php` as `configuration.backup`, if a hacker accesses the URL with that filename, it will not be recognized as a file type and the Web server will simply output it as plain text — exposing private information.

Resetting a Joomla User Password

Joomla passwords are often forgotten by users, and the Joomla Administrator interface allows the system admin to reset a user password. However, if you have ever had occasion when you've forgotten an administrator password, you know the frustration of being locked out of your own system. While I was writing this book, I myself had a hard drive crash and had yet to change the Joomla-generated random password of numbers and letters. Needless to say, I couldn't remember the password that I had recorded in a file that was lost in the crash.

Each password in Joomla is stored as a MD5 hash value, so you won't be able to recover the lost password. However, you can reset the password by accessing the table that holds all of the user information.

Message-Digest algorithm 5 (MD5) is a security algorithm that will take a string input and generate a fixed size output number. It is an Internet standard described in RFC 1321.

The length of the number for MD5 is a 128-bit (generally a 32-character hexadecimal number) hash code. Security algorithms of this type are worked so that a small change in the string input (such as the addition of an extra letter) produces a very large change in the output hash. Hash codes are generally secure because of the massive amounts of processing that would be required to decipher the initial string given only the code. However, there are more secure algorithms (such as SHA-1) that Joomla may use in the future.

To begin, you will need to execute the MySQL Administrator application. If you're using an online application such as phpMyAdmin, you will be able to perform essentially the same steps.

Begin by loading the MySQL Administrator utility. You will need to select the `jos_users` table in the Joomla database. Note that if the Joomla database is properly secured, you will need administrator or root privileges to access the `jos_users` table. If you don't have these permissions, check with the system administrator to either reset the password for you or give you the necessary access.

If you right-click the mouse, the context menu will give you the option of Edit Table Data, as shown in Figure 2-14.

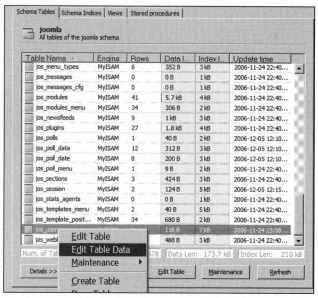

Figure 2-14: Select the Edit Table Data option on the jos_users table.

The table editor should open and display all of the current Joomla users. In my case, I needed to reset the admin password, so I went to the row for the admin user. Scroll to the right until you see the column labeled "password." That column will display the MD5 hash of the current password.

Select the field for editing. On the Windows platform, that means pressing the F2 key. You will now need to enter the MD5 hash of a known password. Enter this hash, which represents the actual word *password*:

```
5f4dcc3b5aa765d61d8327deb882cf99
```

When you've finished entering this long string, click on the Apply Changes tab at the bottom of the screen, as shown in Figure 2-15.

Now you can log into the account by typing the appropriate user name and the word *password* as the password. Be sure to go immediately to the User Manager and change the password to a new one that is more secure.

If you don't have easy access to MySQL Administrator, or if you would prefer to use the MySQL command line, the reset can be performed from there. To perform the password reset, enter the following command:

```
UPDATE jos_users SET password='5f4dcc3b5aa765d61d8327deb882cf99' WHERE
name='admin';
```

Be sure to substitute the user account you wish to use in place of the admin text in the presented code. This code will replace the current password value with the hash for the word "password."

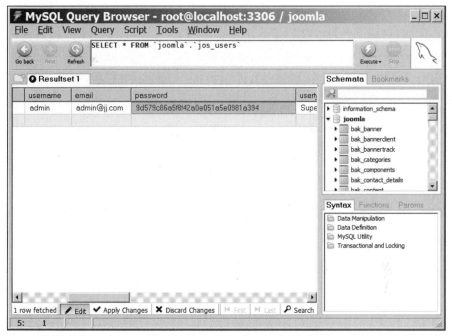

Figure 2-15: Enter a known MD5 hash code and save the field change back to the table.

Now that you can see how easy it would be for a hacker to gain access to your Joomla system, it is critical that you secure your MySQL installation against outside attack. Be sure to follow the security guideline suggestions in Chapter 14.

Staging Servers and Deployment Servers

While this chapter has primarily described general configuration, all Joomla servers should not be configured the same way. When you are doing your initial site construction and later development, you should have a *development* or *staging server* where you can freely install extensions, make rough changes to the system, and have full debugging information reported for the fastest resolution to problems. The staging server generally has little in the way of security to allow the broadest access and testing.

When the site is ready for real-world use, it is then transferred to the *deployment server*. The deployment server may be a remote Web host (such as `SiteGround.com`), or it may be a machine different from the staging server that has all the proper security configurations in place. Deployment servers are also called *production servers*.

For a staging setup, you want to receive the most information available, including error explanations, performance metrics, and login reports. In contrast, in a deployment environment, this type of monitoring exacts a tremendous performance penalty. Logging and debugging routines use a significant amount of processing resources, which have no place in a deployment system. Further, the debugging information provided should be hidden, since it can be used by hackers to locate penetration points in your system.

On the Windows OS, there is a Joomla option that can be very useful for testing purposes — particularly if you want to evaluate a prerelease or beta version of Joomla. This option, a Joomla Standalone Server (JSAS), is a self-contained version of Apache server, PHP, MySQL, and Joomla that doesn't require actual server configuration. In fact, JSAS allows you to install multiple separate sites on a single server and manage them through a single interface. You can download the JSAS from `jsas` `.joomlasolutions.com`.

Staging Server Setup

Joomla doesn't have a formal debugging structure, so most debugging occurs through a variety of error displays, strategically located print statements, and examination of error logs. In most cases, before deployment of Joomla, you will want to configure your server for the maximum amount of error reporting. When the system "goes live," you will need to turn off these options because they potentially give hackers information that can be used against your site, and the debugging systems create extra overhead that can negatively impact the performance of the server.

Because Joomla (and most PHP applications) is developed with a *make change, refresh browser, alter change, try again* methodology, the more information supplied by the server when an error is encountered, the easier it will be to locate and correct the problems.

Error codes (provided they accurately reflect the problem encountered) can be the most useful tool in debugging a Joomla application. The PHP messages are particularly helpful in that they describe the problem and cite the line number and file where the error occurred. A typical component error would appear like this:

```
Notice: Use of undefined constant kasjda - assumed 'kasjda' in
    C:\Program Files\Apache Software Foundation\Apache2.2\htdocs\components\
    com_content\content.php on line 32
```

Web servers (whether Apache or Microsoft Internet Information Server) keep extensive error logs that record problems encountered by the server. These logs can be invaluable for study to locate both problems that could fault the server, and also smaller bugs that, while not halting the application, prevent it from functioning as desired. For example, if Joomla intends to write a poll result into the MySQL database, but cannot find the proper table, an error may be generated unseen by the administrator. The log, however, will show the failed SQL insert. By examining the log, you can correct these small errors.

Deployment Server Setup

Once you have thoroughly configured and tested your Joomla system, you will want to make it available to the world of the Internet. The needs of a deployment server are very different to those of the staging server. With a deployment server, you are concerned primarily with security and performance. Many settings that are perfect for debugging can provide potentially compromising information about your Joomla system to hackers.

Additionally, most of these configurations that help you to find problems in your system will also slow down its ability to quickly serve Web pages. By streamlining the configuration, you can obtain substantial performance increases.

Default Accounts and Passwords

You should systematically check and change all of the default accounts and passwords on the system. When a hacker tries to breach a system, those accounts and passwords are known points of entry and as such, will often be the first place to try.

Default accounts and passwords include the following:

❑   *MySQL* — The *root* user is generally the superadministrator of the server. Many default installations leave the password to the account blank. Be sure to change the default password. You might also consider creating a different superadministrator account and limiting the capabilities of the root.

❑   *Joomla* — The default superadministrator account for Joomla is named *admin*. Consider changing the user name to *jadmin* or something of the sort so that a hacker's first guess will not render half of the username/password pair.

MySQL includes fairly robust security, but even the access path for MySQL access by Joomla is stored in plain-text files on the Joomla server. Therefore, you should change as many possible variables from the defaults to minimize the possibility of educated guesses that may lead to the penetration of your system.

> **Realize that any example password settings used in this book should be changed as well. This is a published work and, as such, publicly available. The accounts and passwords in this book may at some point be added to the standard hacker password dictionaries for automated testing. At a minimum, be sure that any passwords you use from this book are changed before your site is deployed.**

Error messages can provide clues to the internal structure of your Web site, including folders, databases, tables, and so on. While messages are critical for debugging on a staging server, on a deployment server, they give a potential window into your system. Therefore, make certain that any display of errors is minimized for your final deployment installation.

Summary

Joomla installation and configuration can often seem straightforward until you run into a problem. This chapter has provided an overview of the ways to install and configure Joomla by doing the following:

❑   Understanding the configuration settings of the Apache server through the `httpd.conf` file and the various directives that can help you streamline your Joomla installation.

❑   Improving the performance of the server by modifying the debugging and logging settings. By increasing the amount of logged information, you can more accurately determine the source of problems and potential problems.

❑   Refining the PHP installation by changing settings in the `PHP.ini` file. Changing the PHP settings can prevent timeouts and help maximize security.

❑   Examining a comprehensive MySQL installation that can help you use the data stored in your database for everything from reporting to a custom password reset.

❑   Adopting a staging server so that comprehensive testing and debugging of a Joomla site is possible without exposing the system to the slings and arrows of the outside world.

❑   Upgrading the staging server installation to a full deployment configuration.

Fine-tuning the configuration of a Joomla site includes much more than streamlining the server performance. The visual aspects of a site presentation can be a key factor in representing a Joomla site as a professional and substantial information portal. Chapter 3 will help you create an attractive custom template that you can use as a foundation for creating your own templates in the future.

3

Developing Custom Templates

Joomla's ability to use templates is one of the key reasons for its widespread adoption. A site that appears mediocre can be transformed into a fantastic Web presence with the five-minute installation of a professional template. In fact, a flourishing segment of the Joomla market is the commercial template market. There are literally dozens of companies offering templates for sale. Many of the sites use a monthly subscription model, where a subscriber may download any template available there. This model ensures that new templates are always needed to keep the subscribers interested.

In this chapter, you'll learn to create a template from scratch and use stylesheets to provide comprehensive layout features. Most free templates include only a single page that's used throughout the site. For a more professional presentation, you'll learn how to create a template family where multiple stylesheets are used together to provide a cohesive image or brand for a Web site.

Before you begin creating templates, it may be useful to review the structure of one. Since the general structure varies little from template to template, a thorough understanding of template organization can make designing your own templates, or editing existing ones, substantially easier.

Template Structure

Joomla templates can be made up of a any number of files and folders, but their standardized structure allows Joomla to treat templates generically. That makes it possible to switch the look-and-feel of a Joomla site by simply selecting an alternate template. As long as a template includes a place for component display and a few typical module positions, it can be used interchangeably with most other templates.

Therefore, you will need to know the folders that hold a template (often the root folder, the \css folder, and the \images folder) and the minimum files required for proper display (index.php, template.css, and templateDetails.xml). There are also several optional files (parameters.ini and template_thumbnail.png) that make it easier to manage a template. Since you may only have experience with templates from the user side, your study should begin by looking at how the Joomla system organizes each template.

Files and Folders

All user templates installed on a Joomla site are stored in the \templates directory, which is located at the root directory of a Joomla site. The \templates folder holds a single folder for each template installed on the system. The name of the folder must exactly match the name of the template, and the template system is case-sensitive. For example, the template rhuk_milkyway must be contained in the \rhuk_milkyway folder.

While it is possible for a template to consist of only a single file (index.php), even a bare-bones template would likely include a minimum of four files (index.php, template.css, templateDetails.xml, and banner.jpg). Most templates contain many more files, including additional stylesheets, a variety of images, and formatting graphics (such as rounded corners, spacers, and so on).

Each primary file performs a particular function:

- ❏ index.php — Provides the central logic of the template, including any module and component display. Also, any client-side JavaScript used by the site for user interaction is likely referenced in this file. Unfortunately, many templates include layout code in this file as well, such as multi-column tables, images, and text formatting. Stylesheets are a better place for layout and presentation selections.

- ❏ template.css — Supplies the styles for the fonts, colors, positioning, images, and other presentation aspects of the template. Since the CSS technology is supported by all browsers of significant market share, the stylesheets held in this file can provide everything from column definition to list formatting.

- ❏ templateDetails.xml — Holds the meta-information about the template itself that is used by the Joomla Administrator interface for installation and maintenance. Settings held in the file include a list of all files that make up the template, author and publication information, and parameters that are available for user modification through the Administrator interface.

- ❏ banner.fff — Although not absolutely necessary, most templates provide a central header graphic that gives the template its hallmark appearance. For commercial templates, this graphic is generally constructed such that the purchaser can overlay it with a business logo, organizational trademark, or site name to make it appear as if the graphics were custom-designed. This file is typically stored in either JPG or PNG format (which replaces the fff extension characters).

Traditionally, two folders are stored within each template folder and hold the template.css and the banner.fff files:

- ❏ \css — Holds one or more of the CSS files that are used by the template. At a minimum, the template.css file is generally located here.

- ❏ \images — Contains all of the image files used by the template. The banner.fff file will likely be stored in this directory. For most templates, a number of small graphics files used for layout formatting are also stored here.

Nearly all the Joomla templates that you will study will feature at least these basic files and folders. The Joomla system can readily address any template that is stored following these basic structural settings. In fact, unlike modules and components that must be installed through the Administrator interface (so certain settings can be written into the Joomla database), a template that is simply copied into the \templates folder will be available for system use.

Often templates will also include two other optional folders:

❑   \html — Holds template files that are used to override the core output of the Joomla system. For more information, see the section "Core Output Override Templates" later in the chapter.

❑   \javascript — Contains all of the JavaScript code files used by the template.

Templates are generally distributed in a either a .zip or .tarball archive that contains all files and the relative location of the files within their subfolders. Joomla uses the PHP Zlib to uncompress a .zip template archive uploaded via the Extension Install/Uninstall screen. The extracted files and folders are placed in a template folder with name matching the template. Most important of these files is the index.php file that contains all of the primary template logic.

Template Logic: The Index File

The index.php file is the central template file, and the only file absolutely necessary for the template to be used by the Joomla CMS. The index.php file is a combination of HTML and PHP code. The HTML generally provides the structured text elements that link to individual stylesheets for formatted presentation. The PHP code makes calls to the Joomla Framework to populate the page with the necessary content extracted from the database. The simplest index.php would look something like this:

```
<html>
<head>
    <jdoc:include type="head" />
</head>

<body>
    <h1>Hello World!</h1>
</body>
</html>
```

While this HTML hardly complies with World Wide Web Consortium (W3C) standard, it will execute and display the Hello World greeting through the Joomla system. Note that this template, in its simplicity, will display no content. The Joomla function call (held in the <jdoc> tag) only display writes header information, if available. Later in the chapter, you'll create a template that is a little more complicated than this one that displays a couple of modules and a component.

This template is stripped down so you can see that there are a few "requirements" at a bare minimum for a template file to function. In fact, even the Joomla directive could be removed and the template would still work. However, Joomla directives provide most of the power to a template, so they are worthy of closer study.

Joomla Execution Statements

Joomla operates directly with the PHP language and the Joomla application itself is a framework of PHP classes. By addressing some of the Joomla objects such as JDocument and JDocumentHTML in your template code, you can render output of modules and components, as well as retrieve information about the current execution environment.

Using JDocument Objects

The function you used in the basic template called the `include` method of the `jdoc` object. The `JDocument` class (accessed through the `jdoc` object) is the class that you will spend most of your time calling. There is one primary function or method within `jdoc` that is used within a template: `include`.

You already saw the *include* method used in the Hello World template. It was executed with a `jdoc` statement like this:

```
<jdoc:include type="head" />
```

This statement executed the *include* method in the `jdoc` object to return all of the header information for the current Joomla page. You can also use an `include` call to request any system messages for display. Code to render the system messages would look like this:

```
<jdoc:include type="message" />
```

It is most common, however, to use an `include` to insert the HTML code for a Joomla module. For example, to include the output of the `top` module (which usually displays the site banner), you would use a statement like this:

```
<jdoc:include type="modules" name="top" style="xhtml" />
```

When not using one of these `jdoc` directives, you'll generally be using standard PHP statements. PHP is a robust language with everything from execution control structures to object-oriented programming (OOP) capabilities. If you don't know PHP, but understand general programming, you should still be able to comprehend most of the examples in this book. Nonetheless, I would recommend you pick up a copy of *Beginning PHP5, Apache, and MySQL Web Development* (Indianapolis: Wiley, 2005) to gain a complete understanding of the PHP language.

> **Older versions of Joomla used a template language processor called** `patTemplate` **to supplement Joomla directives. In newer versions of Joomla, however,** `patTemplate` **has been discarded because of the reduced server performance and the increased learning curve caused by use of the template engine. Pure PHP can be compiled for much faster performance — if template code isn't used. Further, the template engine forced developers to learn PHP and the template engine for control functions (such as loops), rather than simply using PHP alone.**

Using the $this Object Variable

One of the common PHP directives you will use is the `$this` statement. The `$this` statement provides an object reference to the object it is executing within. In the case of a Joomla template, `$this` provides a reference to the `JDocumentHTML` object. There are a number of properties that you can read from the

JDocumentHTML object that are useful in coding. For example, to display the language selected for the template display, the `language` property or variable can be output like this:

```php
<?php echo $this->language;?>
```

Following are other properties of the JDocumentHTML object that can be retrieved through the `$this` reference:

- ❑ `direction` — The reading direction of left-to-right (stored as `ltr`), right-left (stored as `rtl`), and so on.

- ❑ `template` — Holds the template directory path.

- ❑ `title` — Contains the document title.

- ❑ `description` — Holds the document description (from the HTML metadata).

- ❑ `link` — Contains the document's base URL.

- ❑ `language` — Contains the document's language setting such as English (stored as `en`).

When writing a template, JDocumentHTML also has several useful methods that can be called through the `$this` operator. For example, the `countModules()` method will help you determine if, on the current page, there are any modules within a template reference. To count the number of instances of a single module, you can execute a function like this:

```php
$this->countModules('user1');
```

You can use the function to count the instances of multiple modules like this:

```php
$this->countModules('user1 + user2');
```

You can even add some Boolean logic when executing the method, such as the following:

```php
$this->countModules('user1 and user2');
$this->countModules('user1 or user2');
```

The following code checks to ensure that there are some modules in the `top` area and displays a place-holder if there are no modules found:

```php
<?php if($this->countModules('top')) : ?>
    <jdoc:include type="modules" name="top"  />
<?php else : ?>
    <img src='placeholder.gif'>
<?php endif; ?>
```

Accessing Template Parameters

A template can also change its presentation or functionality based on template parameters that can be set within the Administrator interface (see the section "Template Variables: The Parameters File" later in this chapter). The default template included with the system lets the administrator configure whether the component will be displayed via the `showComponent` parameter. Code within the template then reads the parameter and determines whether it will be displayed like this:

```php
<?php if($this->params->get('showComponent')) : ?>
    <jdoc:include type="component" />
<?php endif; ?>
```

Keep in mind that the `$this` operator will access the object context within which it is executing. Therefore, if you add a `$this` reference within a component, an entirely different object will be returned than the same object reference executed within a template.

To prevent anyone (most specifically hackers) from attempting to execute Joomla code outside of the Joomla system, you should include the following line before any executable code:

```php
defined('_JEXEC') or die('No access available');
```

This code will make sure that the _JEXEC variable is defined and, if not, will post an access limitation message. This statement is very important for Joomla security. Breaches into Joomla systems have been recorded for code execution pages (such as template files) that do not include this directive.

A Primitive index.php

A primitive example of all the coding described so far would look like this:

```php
<?php
defined('_JEXEC') or die('Restricted access');
?>
<?xml version="1.0" encoding="utf-8"?>
<html xmlns="http://www.w3.org/1999/xhtml" xml:lang=" <?php
        echo $this->language;
    ?>" lang="<?php
        echo $this->language;
    ?>" dir="<?php echo $this->direction; ?>" >

<head>
    <jdoc:include type="head" />
</head>

<body>
    <jdoc:include type="message" />
    <h1>Hello World!</h1>
    <?php if($this->countModules('top')) : ?>
        <jdoc:include type="modules" name="top"  />
    <?php else : ?>
        <img src='placeholder.gif'>
    <?php endif; ?>
    <?php if($this->params->get('showComponent')) : ?>
        <jdoc:include type="component" />
    <?php endif; ?>
</body>
</html>
```

This template code would begin by checking to make sure it was executing within the Joomla framework and stop executing if it weren't. Next, it outputs the `language` and `dir` attributes for the `<html>` tag. The `jdoc head` information is included in the header section. The body of the HTML output begins with any system messages output by Joomla (there typically aren't any). After the Hello World! greeting, the module output for the `top` position is included if there is any. If not, a placeholder GIF is output. Finally, the template parameter `showComponent` is tested and, if set to `True`, the component output is rendered.

While this code will not execute as-is (at a minimum you need an installer to create the `showComponent` parameter), it should give you a better idea of a template's structure than the stripped-down Hello World! template from earlier.

Template Presentation: The CSS File

After the `index.php` file, the second most important item in most templates is the CSS file. Templates can use one or more CSS files to govern the colors, fonts, and font attributes that will be used for display. If a template is perfectly made for your needs, but you would rather have red than green for the link text, you only need to modify the CSS to obtain the look you want.

When Joomla was upgraded to version 1.5, the team greatly expanded the flexibility of the user interface by allowing multiple CSS files where initially all styles had to be held in a single file. The Joomla team also strove to separate (as much as possible) program logic from presentation. By making that division increasingly clear, the look-and-feel of a site can be edited or even swapped out with a different template without affecting underlying code that processes a shopping cart or records a poll result in the database.

CSS plays a large role separating the presentation from program logic. Everything from fonts to table cell border colors can be defined in a CSS file. The HTML file need only to point to the CSS file to inherit the looks specified within it.

To create an effective template, you must be able to accurately position items on the page. Within a module's boundaries, the CSS parameters are used to determine spacing, as well as relative and float position. The methods and rules that are used by the CSS can help you to make text appear any way you want.

> When creating a CSS, you must take into account how it will be displayed in various browsers. You should have at least two browsers installed on your development machine. Whatever your platform, Mozilla Firefox should be one of them. It is currently the most popular cross-platform browser. If you're not using the Windows OS, be sure to test your page with Internet Explorer (preferably with versions 6 and 7) on Windows. Regardless of your personal feelings about the OS, a majority of your visitors will likely be using this browser. Browsers are constantly evolving, so be sure to test your site template often.

There may be one or more CSS files used by a template. In fact, multiple CSS files may be used on the same page. When a style overlaps (has the same name) as a style defined in an earlier CSS file, the latter style *overrides* the existing style.

In-line and Block Element Types

There are two types of positioning elements that can be defined in a CSS file: *in-line* and *block*. *In-line* elements appear as if they were text in the flow of the layout and are included in tags such as `<B>`, `<I>`, or `<SPAN>`. *Block elements* define a concrete area such as a `<P>`, `<TR>`, `<DIV>`, or `<TABLE>`. These two types should be used appropriately when you are designing the entries for your CSS file.

To add a stylesheet file reference to a template, the following two lines should appear somewhere in the header of the `index.php` file:

```
<link rel="stylesheet" href="templates/_system/css/general.css"
    type="text/css" />
<link rel="stylesheet" href="templates/<?php echo
    $this->template ?>/css/template.css" type="text/css" />
```

The first line loads the baseline styles provided with the Joomla system. The baseline file includes stylesheets that define the look of the foundation HTML elements such as the `<body>` tag. The second line uses the reference to construct an absolute path to the main stylesheet file of the template (traditionally named `template.css`).

Default Styles

To create a proper stylesheet for use within Joomla, you must use the names of the styles that Joomla provides. For example, when Joomla generates output for a component, it will include references to particular styles. The title of a component (see Figure 3-1) is defined using the `componentheading` style.

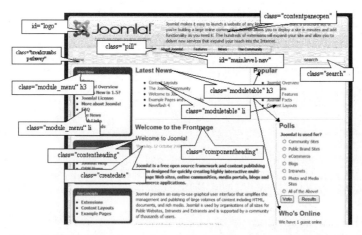

Figure 3-1: The title of a module during standard output is defined by the componentheading style.

If you were to include the following style definition in your stylesheet, the component heading would now be displayed with a single pixel bottom border and the text would be colored red:

```
.componentheading {
    color: red;
    border-bottom: 1px solid white;
}
```

There are a number of other styles that you might not even recognize on a page display because they remain undefined and, therefore, invisible. The `article_separator` style is a good example because many templates never create a definition for it, so it doesn't appear when the page is displayed. A simple style definition could add a 2-pixel green separator between articles, as shown here:

```
.article_separator {
    margin: 10px 0;
    border: 2px solid #00FF00;
}
```

In Joomla, there are a large number of default styles for output. Many of them are used in the templates provided in the default Joomla installation. Figure 3-1 shows the screen displayed by the default template, and I have labeled a number of the styles so you can see where they are used.

The styles included in the default CSS files can be generally divided into three categories: content, administration, and extensions. For content, the following stylesheets apply:

- article_separator
- author
- content_email
- content_rating
- content_vote
- contentdescription
- contentpagetitle
- contentpane
- contenttoc
- created-date
- intro
- title
- modifydate
- small
- smalldark

For administration, you can override these styles:

- adminform
- clr
- date
- input
- inputbox
- outline

- ❑ pagenav
- ❑ pagenav_next
- ❑ pagenav_prev
- ❑ pagenavbar
- ❑ pagenavcounter
- ❑ pathway

For extensions, you can override these styles:

- ❑ bannerfooter
- ❑ bannergroup
- ❑ bannerheader
- ❑ banneritem
- ❑ blog
- ❑ blog_more
- ❑ blogsection
- ❑ button
- ❑ buttonheading
- ❑ latestnews
- ❑ loclink
- ❑ message
- ❑ metadata
- ❑ module
- ❑ newsfeed
- ❑ pollstableborder
- ❑ read
- ❑ searchintro
- ❑ sections
- ❑ sectiontable_footer
- ❑ sectiontableentry
- ❑ sectiontablefooter
- ❑ sectiontableheader
- ❑ sublevel
- ❑ wrapper

You don't need to define all of these styles. Generally, for a template, you will at a minimum want to define a `body` style that will determine how all undesignated text within the body of the page will appear. Any text that is set to appear in a style that is undefined will simply default to the `body` style. The *body* style definition will probably appear as the first style in your CSS file, like this:

```
.body {
    font: 0.7em/1.5 Verdana, Arial, Helvetica, sans-serif;
}
```

By using the `body` style as a foundation for the basic font definition, you shouldn't need to even specify font sizes within the `index.php` file — all of the presentation can be kept in the stylesheet. In fact, it is a good idea to locate references to your images inside the stylesheet.

Incorporating Images in the CSS

Putting image references within a CSS file can be useful, but also problematic. You must avoid making the stylesheets so specific that they can't be used for general articles. At the same time, some important images can be incorporated into the CSS file to centralize the image references. If an image needs to be changed because of a change in site theme, the single reference in the CSS can be altered and all subsequent site visitors will see the new image.

With all that to consider, there is a more technical consideration: relative URL description. The URL path will need to be referenced so that the image is found by the browser. In the case of a template, you know that the `images` directory is at the same level as the `css` directory. Therefore, to access an image from the `css` folder, the reference will have to move the directory pointer up one directory and then into the `images` folder, like this:

```
background: url(../images/bottomleft.gif)
```

Template Metadata: The TemplateDetails File

Every template needs a metadata file that tells the Joomla system the basic authorship information (name of the template, author, copyright, and so on), the files that make up the template, and any parameters that will be available for configuration through the Administrator interface.

Listing 3-1 shows a standard details metadata file. Two extra linefeeds separate the four portions of the file.

Listing 3-1: A standard details file generally has three sections: authorship parameters, file directory, and parameters.

```xml
<?xml version="1.0" encoding="utf-8"?>
<install version="1.5" type="template">
    <name>Three Columns template</name>
    <description>
    Two CSS columns in the Joomla world.
    </description>

    <files>
            <filename>index.php</filename>
            <filename>templateDetails.xml</filename>
```

```
            <filename>images/LSlogo.jpg</filename>
            <filename>css/template.css</filename>
        </files>

        <positions>
            <position>left</position>
            <position>right</position>
        </positions>

        <param name="showComponent" type="radio" default="1"
            label="Show Component" description="Show component output">
            <option value="0">No</option>
            <option value="1">Yes</option>
        </param>

    </install>
```

The first section contains the authorship information. Except for the name of the template, the other fields in this section are optional. The Joomla interface will simply display them as `unknown` if they are left out of the file.

The second section is far more critical. It contains a table of contents or directory of the files used by the template. This file/folder is used by the installer to extract the archived files and place them in the proper folders. This list isn't referenced after the initial installation until the administrator uninstalls the template.

The third section shows the module positions that the template will display. Note that the positions denoted in this section of the file are merely for user reference — the system doesn't use them to allocate position items in the user interface.

The fourth section describes any parameters used by the template. *Parameters* are variables that may be configured through the Administrator interface that affect the operation of the template. Most often, parameters are used to configure all administrative setting of presentation variables, such as the template background color settings. The current setting values are stored in the parameter file that is described in the next section.

Template Variables: The Parameters File

The `templateDetails` file can contain template parameters that change the functioning of a template. As part of the default Joomla template, a `showComponent` parameter is included to give the Administrator the option of turning off the display of the main component (so no articles are displayed). Parameters are stored in the file `params.ini` located in the folder of each template. In the case of the default template, the file consists of a single line showing the parameter setting:

```
showComponent=1
```

Since the parameters are stored in standard INI format, any text editor may be used to read or write the values. However, it is best to use the Template Manager, which presents the parameters in the template user interface, as shown in Figure 3-2.

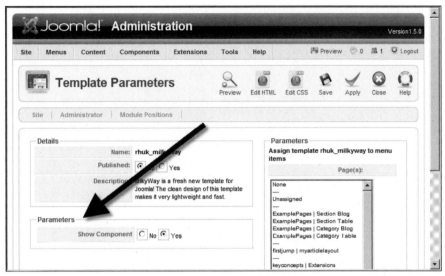

Figure 3-2: Configure parameters by selecting the template in the Template Manager.

Template parameters are most often used to allow selection of presentation options such as setting the foundation color for a color scheme, determining the number of columns in a layout, modifying the widths of page columns, and so on. Parameters make a template user-friendly because the user can make changes to the template's function without having to edit the template file.

Parameters can be accessed from within the template by using code such as `$this->params->get('showComponent')`, as shown earlier. Parameters are an excellent way to make your template more flexible.

Template Graphics: The Images Folder

Any images used by the template are generally stored in the `images` folder. Common images include the central site banner, image spacers, images to provide rounded corners to display blocks, custom bullet points, and pointer arrows. The number of graphic files used by a template will vary greatly.

Template Thumbnail

In the Administrator interface, when the Template Manager is displayed, a user can move the mouse cursor over any of the installed templates and, if available, a small thumbnail graphic will be displayed in a pop-up window showing a sample of the template.

Most templates only include the template image area, as shown in see Figure 3-3, so you should use an image editing program such as Adobe Photoshop or the free, open source GNU Image Manipulation Program, or Gimp (`www.gimp.org`), to crop off any toolbars, scrollbars, or other user-interface display features that don't represent part of the template.

**Figure 3-3: The template_
thumbnail.png file should be
around 200 × 150 pixels in size.**

The image should be named `template_thumbnail.png` and stored in the root directory of the specific template. Joomla will look for the file there, not in a subdirectory such as the `images` folder. To create a thumbnail graphic, you will need to take a screenshot of your template and then shrink it to approximately 200 ¥ 150 pixels. Taking a screenshot will vary depending on your operating system.

On the Windows platform, you can use the Print Screen key (generally labeled PrtSc on the keyboard), which will place an image on the clipboard. Holding down the Alt key while pressing the Print Screen key will capture only the active window, rather than the entire screen. Once the image is on the clipboard, paste it into your image-manipulation program of choice.

If you are doing a lot of template work, you might consider looking at the commercial application SnagIt (`www.techsmith.com/snagit.asp`). It provides excellent snapshot features, including in-program cropping and resizing.

On a Macintosh, you can take a snapshot that is saved to the local drive by pressing the Shift+Apple+3 keys simultaneously. To capture only part of the screen, the Command (Apple)+Shift+4 combination will activate a crosshairs cursor that can be used to select a rectangular portion of the screen. Mac OS also includes a utility called Grab that has a number of screen capture options. It is located under Applications ➪ Utility.

On the Linux platform, there are a variety of available programs. If you're running the XWindows interface, you can get the open source xvidcap (`http://sourceforge.net/projects/xvidcap/`). For those running GTK+, the open source Gsnapshot (`http://sourceforge.net/projects/gsnapshot/`) is available for download.

When you have the file captured, you will need to use an image editing program to resize it and save it in the PNG format. Save it in your `template` directory with the name `template_thumbnail.png`, and the Joomla Administrator interface will automatically display it when you do a mouse-over of the template name in the Template Manager.

Creating a Three-Column Template

Templates are rarely constructed from scratch. Instead, most designers take a boilerplate template and add to it to construct a new template. In this section, you'll create a three-column boilerplate template that you can use as a foundation for all of your later templates.

You'll be making extensive use of CSS for both the layout and the presentation. If you have any experience with CSS, you already know that it is implemented in many different ways by many different browsers. Most particularly, Internet Explorer 6 violates or fails to implement many of the standard functions of the CSS standard.

This has led the Joomla developers to include a special CSS file titled `ieonly.css` with their templates. With the release of Internet Explorer 7, most of these problems have been corrected, yet the installed based of version 6 will be with us for many years to come. Therefore, if you see some CSS code that seems contradictory, it is probably extra code to make the template compatible with various browsers.

> *I have tried to include enough CSS code and special cases to take care of most compatibilities with the most popular current browsers. However, if the template displays strangely on your browser, I would suggest that you attempt to locate the element in the CSS that is causing the problem, and then search for a CSS bug workaround on the Internet. You will most likely find a solution there. Once implemented, it will strengthen the compatibility of your boilerplate template.*

One of the great features of Joomla is the ability of a template to use multiple stylesheets. If a site template uses only a single page with a single stylesheet file, it must be a jack-of-all-trades. Rarely does a system designer wish for every page of the site to be displayed in exactly the same manner. Rather than use multiple templates, however, it is possible for a single Joomla template to transform itself, depending on the needs of the individual page, through the use of a special CSS file.

When you are creating and debugging your stylesheets, I recommend that you use one of the browser tools that will allow you to examine style live on a page, and even modify them for testing. For Firefox, the Firebug tool (`https://addons.mozilla.org/en-US/firefox/addon/1843`) allows you to debug, edit, and monitor CSS and JavaScript executing within the browser. For Internet Explorer, go to the Microsoft Web site (`www.microsoft.com`), and search for the Internet Explorer Developer Toolbar. It is a free download that lets you explore and modify the Document Object Model (DOM) of a Web page, set stylesheet rules for various elements, validate CSS code, and much more.

Create the Template Folder and Rough Details

You will need to start the creation of any new template by creating a folder for the template to exist. I always begin my template folder names with the `tmpl` prefix so, if I see them in code or stored in a `miscellaneous` directory, I'll know the folder contains a template and not a module or other Joomla item. Since you're going to be creating a three-column template, consider naming your folder `tmplThreeCol` and placing it inside the Joomla `templates` folder.

If you're going to be developing your template on a staging server (recommended), the path to your template may be something like this:

```
C:\Program Files\Apache Software Foundation\Apache2.2\htdocs\templates\tmplThreeCol
```

To take care of all of the housekeeping at once, create two folders inside your template folder: `css` and `images`. By the time you've completed the template, you'll have multiple stylesheet files in the `css` directory and graphic images of the site logo and the rounded corners for section display in the `images` folder.

You will need a basic `templateDetails.xml` file to test your template during development. Joomla uses this file to provide information and allow selection of the template within the Template Manager. Enter the following code and save it as `templateDetails.xml` in the root directory of your template:

```xml
<?xml version="1.0" encoding="utf-8"?>
<install version="1.5" type="template">
    <name>Three Column template</name>
    <description>
    Foundation template for a three column display.
```

```
        </description>
        <files>
                <filename>index.php</filename>
                <filename>templateDetails.xml</filename>
        </files>
            <positions>
                <position>user1</position>
                <position>right</position>
            </positions>
    </install>
```

With the basic structures in place, you're ready to begin work on template logic itself. That begins by creating a prototype index file.

Creating the index.php

The initial index.php file will be very primitive, so you can get it up and running quickly. It will display three columns, each presenting a different part of the user interface. For a default Joomla installation, the template will display the front page, as shown in Figure 3-4. Each column has a border so that you can most easily see what is encapsulated. To keep things as simple as possible, the template won't even use a separate CSS file for styles — they'll be embedded in the header section of the file.

If you've deployed Joomla already, you know that a single page is made up of a number of panels called *modules*. Each module can contain a menu, an article, a poll, or any number of other content display components. A site template can contain a number of modules that can be hidden or visible, depending on the settings of the page. By displaying or hiding modules, a site template can transform itself to flesh out numerous areas within the Web site.

Figure 3-4: The Joomla front page displayed with the foundation three-column template.

To have a good understanding of module layout, just imagine a standard newspaper where the logo of the paper runs across the top, the table of contents sits in a box at the bottom, and the rest of the page is divided into the various other panels. These panels may contain the text of an op-ed column, display ads, classified advertisements, weather charts, or just about anything else.

Joomla modules operate in the same fashion. You can define the page by putting various modules into the panel space. The most basic module will simply display the text contents of an article. A more advanced module might offer a poll of fashion questions and allow the user to submit a ballot for "Yes, skirts are shorter this season than last," for example. A dynamic display module might display a stock ticker.

In the basic three-column layout, the left column will show the `user1` module, which contains the latest news menu. The center column will hold the component that displays the article content. The right column will have the `right` module, which, in the case of the default installation, will show the user poll. If you open the template in the Template Manager and click on the Preview button, the preview will show the template and label the modules used by the template, as shown in Figure 3-5.

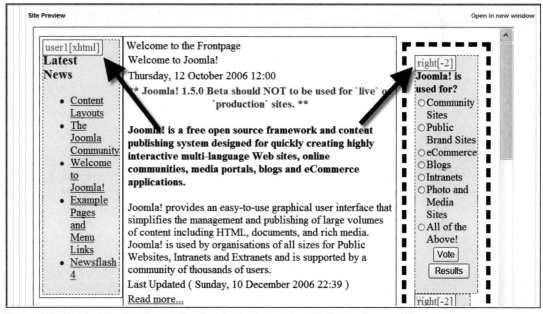

Figure 3-5: Clicking the Preview button inside the template will display the module panels.

The default install of Joomla includes the following modules: `login` module, `polling` module, `who is online` module, `syndication` module, and `search` module. All of these modules will be examined more closely in the coming chapters. In addition to the default modules, other modules can be added as extensions.

To create the Three Column template, enter the following template code and save it as `index.php` in the `template` folder:

```
<html>
<head>
```

```
<jdoc:include type="head" />
<style>
#colLeft {
 float:left;
 width:15%;
 border:1px solid black;
 padding: 5px;
}
#colCenter {
 float:left;
 width:60%;
 padding: 5px;
 border:1px solid black;
}
#colRight {
     float: left;
     width: 15%;
     margin: 10px;
     padding: 15px;
     border: 8px solid black dashed;
}
</style>
</head>

<body>

<jdoc:include type="message" />
<div id="logo"> </div>

<div id="colLeft">
     <jdoc:include type="modules" name="left" style="xhtml" />
     <div class="ArticleFooter"><p> </p> </div>
</div>

<div id="colCenter">
     <jdoc:include type="component"  />
</div>

<div id="colRight">
     <jdoc:include type="modules" name="right" style="xhtml" />
     <div class="ArticleFooter"><p> </p></div>
</div>

<jdoc:include type="modules" name="debug" />
</body>
</html>
```

The template should now be ready for testing! Open the Template Manager, and you should see the Three Column template listed. Select the radio button to the left of the template and click the Default button, and you should see the default star appear in the row of the new template, as shown in Figure 3-6.

With the basic functionality of the template working properly, it is time to refine the presentation. For example, most professional templates have a much more sophisticated look to them than three simple columns. To ensure a professional layout for the template, sections with rounded corners will go a long way toward making a stylish Joomla site.

Figure 3-6: Set the Three Column template as the default template.

Create Rounded Corners Stylesheet

To have a template that displays content within rounded corners, most of the work occurs in the stylesheet. First, you will need to put the styles in a separate sheet. Replace the `<style>` and `</style>` tags, as well as everything between them, with the following:

```
<link rel="stylesheet" href="templates/_system/css/general.css" type="text/css" />
<link rel="stylesheet" href="templates/<?php echo $this->template
    ?>/css/template.css" type="text/css" />
```

These two directives will load in the stylesheets from external files. The first directive loads the Joomla default system styles. The second directive will load the stylesheet you will create in a moment. Notice the PHP code that reads the *template* property of the `$this` variable. That command will output the directory path to the current template so that the system can find the proper CSS.

Enter the following code into your text editor, and save it with the filename `template.css` in the `css` folder of the Three Column template:

```
/* Template Styles for the three column template */

/* Define the columns for layout with no visible borders */
#colLeft { float: left; width: 15%; padding: 5px;}
#colCenter { float: left; width: 60%; padding: 5px; }
#colRight { float: left; width: 15%; padding: 5px; }

/* Set the default font for body text */
Body {
```

```
    font-family: Tahoma,Helvetica,Arial,sans-serif;
    font-size: 0.7em/1.5;
}

/* Display the organizational logo */
#logo {
    width: 110%; height: 100px;
    margin-left: -10px;
    background: url(../images/banner.png) left no-repeat;
    border: 1px solid #244223 ;
    padding: 20px;
}

/* Create the first div that shows the top-left rounded corner */
.moduletable, .moduletable_menu {
    margin-top: 10px;
  background: #999     url(../images/topleft.gif)
  top left no-repeat;
  width:90%;
}

/* Display the top-right rounded corner */
div.moduletable h3, .moduletable_menu h3,   {
  background: url(../images/topright.gif)
  top right no-repeat;
  padding:10px;
  border-bottom: 1px solid #fff;
  margin:0;
         color: #FFFFFF;
}

/* Align the poll question correctly */
.moduletable table {
  margin-top:-1em;
}

/* Set the poll question parameters */
.poll td {
    font-size: 80%;
  margin-left:5px;
  padding-left:0px;
  margin-right:5px;
  margin-top:0em;
  padding-top:-10px;
}

.latestnews, .mainmenu, .keyconcepts, .othermenu {
  background:  #ccc
  top right repeat-y;
  margin-left:5px;
  padding-left:0px;
  margin-right:5px;
```

```
    margin-top:0em;
}

div.moduletable li, .mainmenu li, .keyconcepts li, .othermenu li {
    background:  #ccc
    top right repeat-y;
     margin-left: 1.5em;
  /*margin-top:-2em;*/
    padding:5px;
    font-size: 80%;


    }

.ArticleFooter {
    background: url(../images/bottomleft.gif);
    bottom left no-repeat;
    /*clear: both;*/
    margin: -14px 0px 0px 0px;
}

.ArticleFooter p {
    background: url(../images/bottomright.gif);
    bottom right no-repeat;
    display:block;
    clear: both;
    padding: 0 15px 15px 15px;
    margin:-0.8em 0 0 0;
    }
```

This set of styles is much more complicated than the original three styles that were included in the original index.php file. The embedded comment text explains the use of each style. Note that most of the styles are ones that override basic Joomla styles. The modules output the content using various styles, such as moduletable and contentheading. By overriding these styles, you can control how the content will be displayed.

Creating the Rounded Corner Graphics

Embedded in the style definitions, four graphics files were called: topleft.gif, topright.gif, bottomleft.gif, and bottomright.gif. These are the rounded-corner graphics that you need to construct or have constructed for you. What follows is a short tutorial that describes how they may be created in Adobe Photoshop. The steps will be almost identical for other graphic programs such as Gimp.

Begin by creating a new canvas that is 100 ¥ 100 pixels using the RGB color model. Instead of the traditional white background, though, select a transparent background, as shown in Figure 3-7. You're going to make transparent corners so that color of the columns can be controlled by the stylesheet (instead of having to construct different corners for each color you might choose).

The checkerboard grid should be displayed to show there is nothing currently on the canvas. Under the Edit menu, select the Fill... option, and the fill dialog box will be displayed. For the fill color, select White, as shown in Figure 3-8, and click the OK button. The canvas should now appear as a white surface.

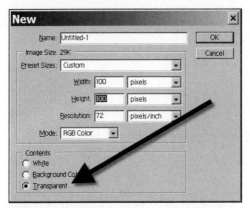

Figure 3-7: Select a transparent background for the image.

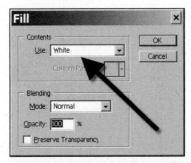

Figure 3-8: Select White for the fill color.

You will need to draw a rounded rectangle. Select the rounded rectangle tool and then you will have to modify several options in the toolbar. The first option shown in Figure 3-9 is to set the drawing type to fill pixels. Next, make sure that the rounded rectangle tool is selected. At the far right, uncheck the Anti-aliased option so the borders will be crisp. You want to draw a black rounded rectangle, so you can click on the Default Foreground and Background Colors button on the palette. Finally, increase the zoom to 400 percent and draw the rounded rectangle so that it fills the box.

From the palette, choose the Magic Wand tool and turn off the Anti-aliased option, as shown in Figure 3-10. Click in the rounded rectangle, and press the Delete key. You should now have a canvas that is mostly checkerboard (showing the transparency) and four white rounded corners. Note that for this template, you'll be using a white background. If you want to change the background color, you'll need to create new corners that match the background.

Using the standard rectangular selection tool, select just the top-left corner. Under the Image menu, select the Crop option and you should have a cropped corner, as shown in Figure 3-11. Save this first graphic with the filename of `topleft.gif`, and store it inside the `images` folder of the template.

Figure 3-9: Set all of the necessary options and then draw the rounded rectangle to fill the box.

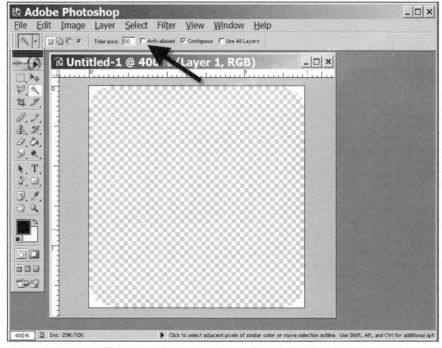

Figure 3-10: Turn off the anti-alias option for the Magic Wand tool.

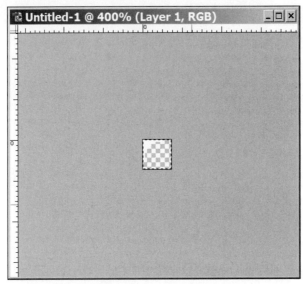

Figure 3-11: Crop the image to the top-left corner.

To create the other three corners, you need only to flip the image and resave it. Using the Rotate Canvas submenu of the Image menu, select the Flip Horizontal option and save the file as `topright.gif`. Then flip the image vertically and save as `bottomright.gif`. Finally, flip the image horizontally again and save it as `bottomleft.gif`. Your template is almost complete, but don't close your image program just yet.

Creating a Banner Graphic

You will need a banner graphic for the site to display your logo and site name. Describing how you will create this logo is beyond the scope of this book. One quick method to create a simple text-based logo is to use the Script-Fu macros included in the default Gimp install. Under the Xtns ⇨ Script-Fu ⇨ Logos, you will find a list of almost two dozen different scripts that will allow you to enter a text field and specify basic colors before the miniature program executes, and creates a logo that is simple but professional in appearance.

For this template, you should make the banner image at least 800 pixels wide (so that it stretches across the top of the page) and around 150 pixels tall. Once complete, save it as `logo.png` inside of the template's `\images` folder.

Changing the Module

Although the poll module is included in the default setup, most Web sites do not feature a poll on the front page. Therefore, although this module is selected to display on the front page, in this section you'll unpublish it and replace it with the `Latest News` module, which will be more desirable for most Web sites.

A Joomla page is made up of the modules displayed by a template. Joomla 1.5 offers a much cleaner method of seeing the module reference locations in the using the Preview option. In the Template Manager, click on the name of template to display the Template Parameters screen. Click the Preview button to display a preview of the selected template with all the module positions labeled on the screen.

When you define a template, it is good practice to use default module position names so that users will be able to easily select modules used by the template. Therefore, before you define your template module positions, select one of the default templates and examine the preview screen. You will be able to see the most common module positions names that you should duplicate in your own template.

In the Joomla Administrator interface, go into the Module Manager. Scroll down until you see the Polls module. Click on the Publish check icon so that it will toggle to the red X to show it is unpublished, as shown in Figure 3-12.

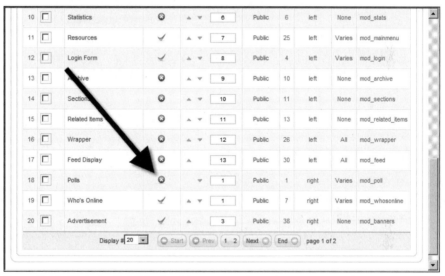

Figure 3-12: Click the Publish check icon to toggle poll to be unpublished.

Instead of the poll, you might want the Latest News module to appear in the template. Find the Latest News module in the list and click on its title to open the editing screen. Make sure it is published, and on the front page, then select the position right, as shown in Figure 3-13. Click the Apply button to save the position setting.

Any module can be put into position by simply selecting the position from the list. If you look below the details pane on the screen, you will see that there are many parameters that you may modify to set the module in the fashion you want. If you view the home page right now, you should see the Latest News module appear in the top-right corner, as shown in Figure 3-14.

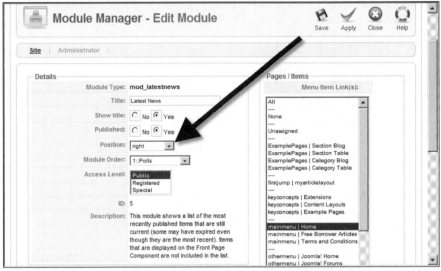

Figure 3-13: Set the position to right so the Latest News will appear in that column.

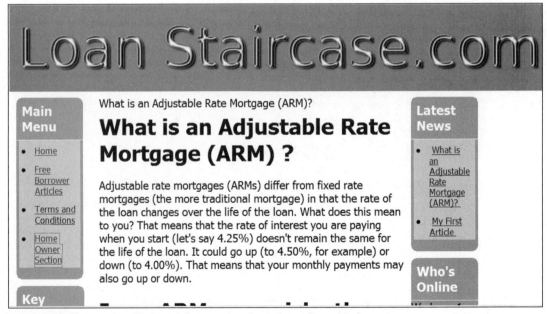

Figure 3-14: The newly added module appears where the poll used to be.

Custom CSS for Components

A great feature provided by Joomla is the ability to use a custom CSS for component display (center column) when you select a particular menu, or even for a particular article. On one level, this means that

CSS files with special color schemes can define each portion of the system. For example, a real estate site might use deep blues for the Refinancing portion of the site but use bright greens for the Sale portion.

You can create a variation on the default template styles and assign it to a specific menu. Go to the Three Column `template` folder, and open the `template.css` file. Add the following code to the bottom of the file and save it:

```
.componentheading_blue, .contentpane_blue {
    color: blue;
}
```

To make a menu reference this custom CSS file, open the Menu Manager in the Administrator interface. Click on the Menu Items icon for the type of menu that you want to assign a custom stylesheet, as shown in Figure 3-15. In this case, let's select the Main Menu, because any menu items added there will appear on the top-left side of the page when the template is displayed.

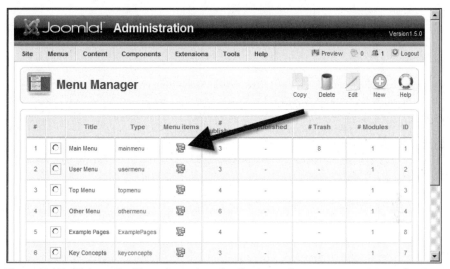

Figure 3-15: Click on the Menu items icon for the type of menu you want to assign to a custom template.

Click on the New icon to create a new menu. The screen will display a hierarchical list of the available types. Click on the Articles item to expand the possible selections. You want to create a menu that will display all of the articles in a particular section, so click on the Standard Section Layout item, as shown in Figure 3-16. The screen should now show the New Menu Item screen and allow you to set the parameters of the item.

Give the menu a name, and in the Menu Item Parameters pane to the right, select a Section to display in the list. Expand the Advanced parameters pane that appears below the Menu Item Parameters pane. In the field entitled Page Class Suffix, enter the suffix **_blue**, as shown in Figure 3-17, and click the Save button. When you view the page, the display items of the component will be presented in the color blue.

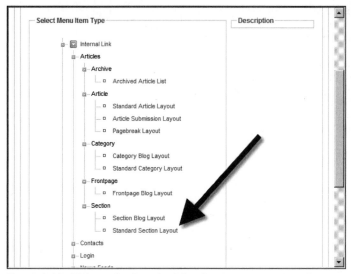

Figure 3-16: Click on the Standard Section Layout to select that menu type.

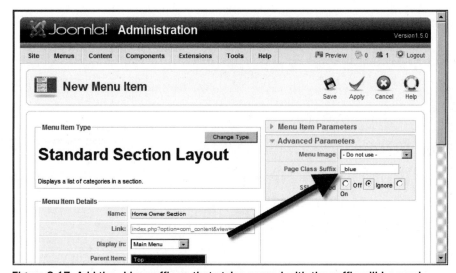

Figure 3-17. Add the _blue suffix so that styles named with the suffix will be used for this menu.

Creating the Details File for Distribution

Your template is almost complete! However, before you distribute it, you will want to polish your details file to include extra authorship details and licensing information. When complete, the details file should look something like this:

```
<?xml version="1.0" encoding="utf-8"?>
<install version="1.5" type="template">
```

```
<name>Three Column template</name>
<version>1.0</version>
<creationDate>1/20/07</creationDate>
<author>Dan Rahmel</author>
<authorEmail>admin@joomlajumpstart.com</authorEmail>
<authorUrl>http://www.joomlajumpstart.com</authorUrl>
<copyright></copyright>
<license>GNU/GPL</license>
<description>
Foundation template for a three column display.
</description>
<files>
        <filename>index.php</filename>
        <filename>templateDetails.xml</filename>
        <filename>params.ini</filename>
        <filename>images/mw_joomla_logo.png</filename>
        <filename>css/index.html</filename>
        <filename>css/template.css</filename>
</files>
    <positions>
        <position>left</position>
        <position>right</position>
    </positions>
<params>
    <param name="showComponent" type="radio" default="1"
     label="Show Component"
    description="Show/Hide the component output">
        <option value="0">No</option>
        <option value="1">Yes</option>
    </param>
</params>
</install>
```

If you now zip the entire folder and name the archive to exactly match the name of the template, you will be able to distribute the template for others to install. To give away your custom templates, the Joomla Hut (www.joomlahut.com) allows for uploads of free templates.

Advanced Template Techniques

The CSS is a key component of the Joomla template system. Not only can multiple CSS files be used with every template but a custom CSS file can be specified with a granular level down to individual articles. Even more importantly to a Joomla practitioner are the features available within a CSS.

If you do a simple survey of most CSS files, you'll find that their authors only use the most basic features available. CSS is bursting with attributes that can be used to polish the presentation of a Web site. The great news is that nearly all of the various attributes in the CSS specification are supported by all popular browsers.

In this section, you'll learn about some of the features that can make your template display stand out from other sites. You'll see how positioning can be used to locate text over an image. You'll learn the best practices about locating image references in the CSS file itself, and how to specify a CSS file for a specific article or target platform (such as cell phone or PDA).

Using a Template Family with CSS

Templates within Joomla can be designed such that all of the pages on the site use the same template or, alternately, a different template can be made for each Category and Section, so that articles will be displayed with the templates that match their categorization. For the remainder of this book, single site templates will be called *templates*, and the set of templates selected by the article categorization will be known as a *template family*.

How you design a template versus a template family requires different organization and planning. In contrast to a single template that needs to be a Swiss army knife for the entire site, a template family can be organized so that the front page sets the stylistic tone (in color, organization, and font selections), and the child templates will reinforce the site identity.

A template family can be thought of almost like a brand identity. With Coca-Cola, all the other spin-offs of the brand (Diet Coke, Cherry Coke, and so on) use similar design elements so that even a casual observer can see the relationship.

Once you have several templates of your site designed, you can assign them to different portions of the site through the Template Manager, as shown in Figure 3-18. In this example, the green-hued template has been assigned to display for all of the Key Concepts content.

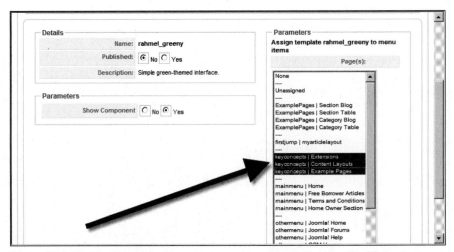

Figure 3-18: Use the Template Manager to assign a template to particular content.

favicon.ico

Templates can include a `favicon.ico` (for *favorites icon*) file at the template root. This file holds a small graphic (16 ¥ 16) icon that, if referenced in the `index.php` file, will be displayed in the address bar of a Web browser (see Figure 3-19) and also to the left of the site name in a bookmark list. If stored at the root directory of a Web server, most browsers will read the `favicon.ico` file automatically.

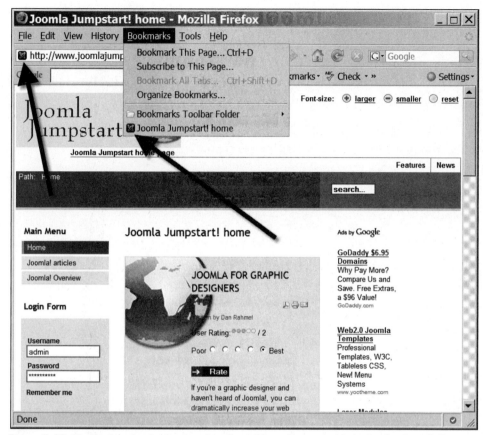

Figure 3-19: The favicon.ico is displayed in the address bar and also in the bookmark list.

To reference the file in a template, use code such as the following in the *<head>* section of the index.php file of your template:

```
<link rel="shortcut icon" href="http://example.com/favicon.ico"
    type="image/vnd.microsoft.icon" />
<link rel="icon" href="http://example.com/favicon.ico"
    type="image/vnd.microsoft.icon" />
```

The two different link references are provided for different browser versions that look for the alternate rel attribute values. Newer browsers support icons stored as GIF or PNG files and can even load animated graphics in these formats.

You don't need to include this code if your Joomla template includes the standard header include *<jdoc:include type="head" />*, because Joomla will automatically include the favorites icon link reference code.

```
<link rel="shortcut icon" href="templates/<?php echo $this->template
?>/favicon.ico" type="image/vnd.microsoft.icon" />
```

To save an image in the ICO format, you can download a free Photoshop plug-in here:

```
http://www.telegraphics.com.au/sw/#icoformat
```

There is also an .ico paint Web application you can use here:

```
http://www.favicon.cc
```

GIMP can save to the .ico format natively. To make such an icon with GIMP, simply create a 16 × 16 image and save it as a Microsoft Windows Icon (.ico) file.

Core Output Override Templates

Although beyond the scope of this chapter, it is worth mentioning that extensions (components, modules, and so on) can have their own templates to determine their particular look and feel. Generally, these templates are stored within a subfolder named \tmpl that exists in the folder of the specific component. The Joomla system was designed so that a site template can override the template used by any extension for customized look-and-feel. You can include a folder named \html in your template folder. Inside this folder can be subfolders of any specific extension types you want to override (such as \com_contact, \com_weblinks, \mod_poll, and \mod_search). For a sample of how this override feature can work, look in the \html folder of the \beez template included with the default installation.

Generally, however, it is enough to override the stylesheets of a component to have it match the selected template. There is an easy method of ensuring your template modifies all of the major styles of a site to match your interface appearance. Use your browser to access a page that features all of the components, modules, and other user interface elements.

Once the page is displayed, use the View Source option to display the HTML of the page. If you work through the HTML source, you will see the entire CSS id and class definitions that are used for the display. Now that you know the names and functions of all of the stylesheets, you can override them in your own template.

Creating a Cell Phone–Centric CSS

These days, there are a growing number of people surfing the Web through their cell phones. With the tremendous popularity of the Tungsten and Treo PDA phones, it's reasonable to assume that such Web access will become increasingly common. Sites ensuring that such visitors have a pleasant browsing experience will capture a larger audience and, if a commercial site, be better able to monetize traffic.

Joomla, by insisting most of the display settings exist within a CSS file, is the perfect platform to provide cell phone–specific templates that cater to the small viewing area and compressed navigation area.

As of this writing, the following are the most popular mobile browsers:

❑   *Pocket Internet Explorer* — All Windows-based PDAs (often called Pocket PCs) include this browser by default.

- ❑   *Opera* — Likely the most popular third-party browser (available whether included with the mobile device or not).

- ❑   *NetFront* — Popular browser, especially on the now-defunct Sony Clie line. The Blazer browser was built from the NetFront foundation.·

- ❑   *Blazer* — Popular browser included on the Tungsten and Treo PDA lines.

- ❑   *Minimo* — Open source browser based on the Mozilla Firefox engine

There are many other custom browser implementations (OpenWave, Series 60, and others) and, with the rapidly evolving mobile search market, more are surely on the way. The good news is that your Joomla site doesn't need to be designed to address each browser separately.

A normal CSS file-embedding link looks like this:

```
<link rel="stylesheet" type="text/css" href="MyCSS.css" />
```

There is a new attribute tag called *media* that is supported by most mobile browsers. In the `media` tag, you can specify the CSS to be used, depending on the viewing platform. The three widely accepted settings for this tag are: `screen`, `print`, and `handheld`. Therefore, your template can contain CSS links to the various file references.

To supply CSS files for each media type, you can include the following reference in your template:

```
<link rel="stylesheet" type="text/css" media="screen" href="screen.css" />
<link rel="stylesheet" type="text/css" media="print" href="print.css" />
<link rel="stylesheet" type="text/css" media="handheld" href="mobile.css" />
```

The `screen` media type can contain a reference to your standard CSS file. The `print` media type may strip away banners, columns, and navigation items not useful to the printed page. Often, this CSS will be · identical to the normal CSS, except that the styles for nonprinting items will have the `visible` attribute set to `false`.

> As of this writing, the Pocket Internet Explorer browser frustratingly uses both the `screen` and `handheld` media styles to display the Web page on a mobile device. However, the desktop version of Internet Explorer 6 (the most popular browser installed) doesn't display the `handheld` media styles. Therefore, one approach to compatibility with IE would be to make sure that the `screen` CSS file reference precedes the `handheld` reference. Then, you can ensure that each style in the `screen` CSS is overridden (has an identically named style) in the `handheld` CSS. Therefore, on desktop machines, the `handheld` file will be ignored, but Pocket IE browsers will read the `screen` file and then override the styles with those found in the `handheld` CSS.

The `handheld media` type is the CSS that will be used by mobile devices that support it. As of this writing, most mobile devices that have been successfully tested were able to use the CSS specified with the `handheld` attribute. The following browsers have been tested: Blazer (on Treo), Opera (on Nokia), and Pocket Internet Explorer (on iPAQ). Unfortunately, a number of those tested did not support the attribute (most notably Netfront 3.1). However, moving into the future, the standard will probably be embraced by all new browsers.

Defining the Handheld CSS

If you are going to include a `handheld` alternative CSS, you will need some guidelines. It is impossible to simply include a default CSS, because each template will use different styles to achieve the particular visual presentation results that are required. Therefore, here are some general guidelines to keep in mind when designing a `handheld` CSS:

❑ *Set the margins to 0* — For body tags, use a line such as `margin: 0 0 0 0;` to set the margins to 0 so that the text will use the maximum amount of screen area.

❑ *Set the border width to 0* — For tables and `div` sections, use a line such as `border-width: 0 0 0 0;` to eliminate any border around cells.

❑ *Set the line height to 1em* — Rather than using presentation formatting line spacing (which won't appear as desired on the mobile device anyway), use a line like `line-height: 1em;` to standardize the line height.

Using these guidelines, you can modify the template included with the default Joomla install. Create a new stylesheet in the `css` folder that has a name of `mobile.css`, and enter the following code:

```
Body {
    margin: 0.0em 0 0 0;
    line-height: 1em;
    padding: 0 0 0 0.2em;
    font-size: 100%;
    line-height: 1em;
    color: black;
    border-width: 0;
}


h1, h2, h3, h4, h5, h6 {
    line-height: 1em;
    font-size: 100%;
    font-weight: bold;
}

p, ul, ol, li, dt, dd {
    line-height: 1em;
}

.moduletable, .moduletable_menu, div.moduletable h3,
.moduletable_menu h3, .poll td {
        font-size: 100%;
        font-weight: bold;
}
```

Add the CSS link included for the `handheld` type to your `index.php`, and the site template will automatically select the `mobile.css` when necessary. This CSS will make all of the text the same size and will bold the headings and the special Joomla styles.

Converting a Mambo or Joomla 1.0 Template

Mambo and Joomla 1.0 have interchangeable templates. Because of their popularity over a period of five years, there are thousands of templates available. Joomla 1.5 can use templates from the older systems but must be set to "Legacy mode" in the Global Configuration screen. Unfortunately, using legacy mode sacrifices all of the efficiencies and features available in the new version of Joomla.

Fortunately, converting a template in most cases is not a difficult process. Nearly all of the system calls in the older Joomla/Mambo templates have a parallel function in the new Joomla. The most obvious is `mosCountModules`, which has been replaced by the `$this->countModules` function.

The `<jdoc:include ... />` elements have replaced the `mosLoadModules` functions. Also, while the global parameters still exist, they have been deprecated, so future versions of Joomla will probably eliminate them. Therefore, it is best to avoid them if possible.

In Mambo or older versions of Joomla, if the editor was needed on a page, you had to load it manually. This is no longer the case because the editor loads automatically if needed.

> One technology that has been jettisoned in the new Joomla is the `patTemplate`. The `patTemplate` plug-in automated many of the complex tasks that made template generation difficult in the past. Chiefly for performance reasons, `patTemplate` has been phased out of the new Joomla framework. Therefore, if you have a template that makes extensive use of `patTemplate`, conversion of the template will present many more obstacles than a standard template.

Summary

You now have the knowledge and understanding to design a template from scratch. There are many facets to the template, including a variety of stylesheet considerations. This chapter has provided an overview of how this book will help you to do the following:

❑   Create a template from scratch that uses stylesheets to provide a multi-column presentation.

❑   Add impressive graphical touches to make your template appear professional.

❑   Refine the template to be customized to different browsers so that CSS incompatibilities will not hamper the displaying of your site.

❑   Conform to recommended accessibility standards to allow everyone access to your Web site.

❑   Use stylesheets to customize the Web presentation to a display platform such as a PDA or cell phone.

Creating your own template is only the tip of the iceberg when it comes to customizing your Joomla site. Chapter 4 surveys a number of extensions that can add a tremendous amount of extra functionality to your Web site.

Adding and Modifying Available Extensions

Joomla's extensibility begins with templates (the simplest form) and ends with plug-ins (the most advanced). Between the two extremes are modules and components. Whereas templates modify the presentation of the Joomla site and plug-ins sit at the core level to control the functioning of the Joomla system, components and modules are the more familiar type of extension that adds a specific functionality (such as polls, forums, or a menu display). All three types of extensions (modules, components, and plug-ins) can add a tremendous amount of extra functionality to a Joomla system.

There are so many extensions available for Joomla that it's sometimes difficult to choose which one to use. For example, there are six different photo gallery plug-ins — each with its own strengths and weaknesses. Some have great customer support, while others have a broader range of features. Sometimes choosing the right extension in a feature category boils down to testing them all.

This chapter examines some of the most robust and popular extensions available in the following areas:

- ❏ Site features
- ❏ Organization and e-commerce
- ❏ Site content
- ❏ Site interaction

This survey of extensions will demonstrate the breadth and depth of available expansion potential for Joomla. Before the actual extensions are examined, it is useful to look at the central repository for add-ons located on the main Joomla site.

Extensions Directory

The main Joomla site (www.joomla.org) keeps a directory of extensions that work with Joomla, and also provides a feedback/rating system where users can describe their experiences with the various add-ons. You can directly access the extensions directory here:

    http://extensions.joomla.org

The Joomla Extension Directory (JED) catalogs more than 1,600 extensions (as of this writing) that have been registered on the system. Each extension is filed in one of 18 categories. The home page of the directory also displays the *five most recently added* extensions and lists the *five top-rated*. Each entry in the directory contains descriptive and usage information relating to the add-on.

> *As of this writing, Joomla has been moving extensions from the Joomla! Forge site to JoomlaCode (http://joomlacode.org). This process has been going on for quite some time and still remains incomplete. If you click on an extension download link in JED and get a "file not found" error, try searching the projects on JoomlaCode to see if the extension has been relocated there. If you still can't find it, go to a search engine such as Google where you can typically locate a current version on the developer's home page.*

A typical directory entry will let you know the following information:

- ❑ *Description* — Description of the component. Often the description also contains a summary of the version history, as well as the changes to the most recent version.

- ❑ *Type of extension* — Most extensions are actually a package of more than one extension type. There are separate icons for module (red), component (green), and plug-in (purple). The icons associated with the package will indicate the type or types of extensions that it contains.

- ❑ *Home page* — The home page of the extension. If you like an extension and find it useful, this link comes in handy because you can find other extensions written by the same author.

- ❑ *Version* — Displays the latest version and when the last update of the extension occurred.

- ❑ *Developer and Email* — The name and contact email address of the developer of the extension.

- ❑ *Views* — The number of times visitors to the Web site have clicked on the extension to read the descriptive entry.

- ❑ *License* — The license related to use of the extension. Most common licenses include GNU GPL, commercial, and other open source/free license.

- ❑ *Compatibility* — The version of Joomla that is compatible with the extension. Currently, compatibility is only listed for Joomla 1.0, Joomla 1.5, or both.

- ❑ *Date added* — The first date when extension was registered with the directory.

- ❑ *User ratings & comments* — Perhaps the most useful aspect of the listing. Users can post their experiences, comments, and descriptions of various issues with the extension. You'll often find not only complements for a component's capabilities but also suggestions for installation, deployment details, or recommendations for another extension that performs the task same task — only better.

There are 18 categories of extensions used on the site, and each has its own subcategories. For ease of description, this discussion divides these categories into four rough divisions:

❑   Site features and management

❑   Organizations and e-commerce

❑   Site content

❑   Site interactivity

These divisions have been used to simplify the search process when looking for an extension that adds a particular feature to Joomla.

> *The extensions directory does include a search engine, but it is often only marginally useful in finding the feature you need. When using this search feature, you should stick with single word searches, because these seem most likely to focus the search on the desired item. Multi-word searches tend to return many entries that are unrelated to the desired capability.*

Site Features and Management

Site features and site management extensions augment the existing core features of (or add functions to) the Administrator interface. These add-ons do everything from adding more hierarchical article filing depth than categories and sections, to implementing broader search options. Because these add-ons supplement core functionality, they are often plug-in extensions.

For this area of Joomla extensions, the JED includes the following categories:

❑   *Admin Tools* — Contains extensions for the back-end Administrator interface. This category features the subcategories of Admin Interface, Backup, Data Conversion, Database Management, File Management, Reporting, Search Engine Friendly URLs, Server, Statistics, and XML.

❑   *Core Enhancements* — Upgrades for the core features of the Joomla system. This category features the subcategories of Accessibility, Cache, Categories/Sections, Credits, Group Access, Menu Systems, Multiple Sites, Security, and User Management

❑   *Searching & Indexing* — This category features the subcategories of Directory, Google, Search, and Site Map.

❑   *Languages* — Holds language supplements that increase the non-English capabilities of Joomla. This category features the following subcategories: Multi-lingual Content, and Translations for Joomla

❑   *Tools* — Lists external tools such as the Dreamweaver extension for handling Joomla sites, a Joomla desktop installer, PHP development systems, and others.

❑ · *WYSIWYG Editors* — Various content editors for the Joomla site that offer more or different features than the two editors included with the Joomla default installation.

This section examines how to add a different editor than the two editors that ship with the Joomla system.

Enabling a Different WYSIWYG Editor

Joomla includes two editors: TinyMCE and XStandard Lite. The default editor is TinyMCE, and it allows rich text content to be edited using on-screen fonts, styles (bold, italic, and so on), sizes, and so on. In this editor, an article will appear just as it does when it will be published to the site. XStandard Lite also offers WYSIWYG features, but also outputs XHTML- and strict HTML-compliant code for the article (which TinyMCE does not).

> *If no editor is selected as the default editor, all article editing will occur in plain text. Since Joomla is an HTML system, the plain text actually consists of the raw HTML code.*

TinyMCE is an editor written in JavaScript that has been tested to work effectively on a variety of browsers (Internet Explorer, Firefox, Opera, and Safari), allows for XHTML 1.0 output, supports international language packs, and can even use various themes and plug-ins (including Flash). XStandard Lite, in contrast, is a compiled plug-in, which means that it is only available at present on Windows platforms. Aside from several feature advantages of XStandard, its binary execution gives it a great performance advantage over TinyMCE.

Although these editors ship with Joomla, they are not your only choices. In fact, there are more than a dozen optional editors available for downloading that are listed on the JED. The broad range of editors offers a variety of specialty features, including personal setting profiles for each user, source code formatting, plug-in support, document management, style sheet editing, and numerous other options.

For example, you could add the JoomlaFCK extension, which has fewer features than TinyMCE or XStandard but is much smaller and quicker than the standard editors. The JoomlaFCK extension shown in Figure 4-1 is based on the FCKeditor, which was created (appropriately enough) by Frederico Caldeira Knabben. It was one of the first browser-based editors that brought complete WYSIWYG functionality without requiring a client-side installation.

JoomlaFCK consists of a single plug-in that can be added to Joomla via the Extension Manager. One of the most useful (and unique) features of JoomlaFCK is the capability to use templates to provide a foundation to the article — similar to the way Microsoft Word has templates for resumes, presentations, and so on. Templates must be stored in the editor directory that will most likely be located (from the Joomla root directory) here:

```
\plugins\editors\fckeditor
```

Templates are stored in XML format in the `fcktemplates.xml` file. There are two example templates included with the system. Here is the first simple template:

```
<Template title="Image and Title" image="template1.gif">
       <Description>One main image with a title and
    text that surround the image.</Description>
    <Html>
    <![CDATA[
       <img style="MARGIN-RIGHT: 10px" height="100"
alt="" width="100" align="left"/>
    <h3>Type the title here</h3>
    Type the text here
    ]]>
</Html>
</Template>
```

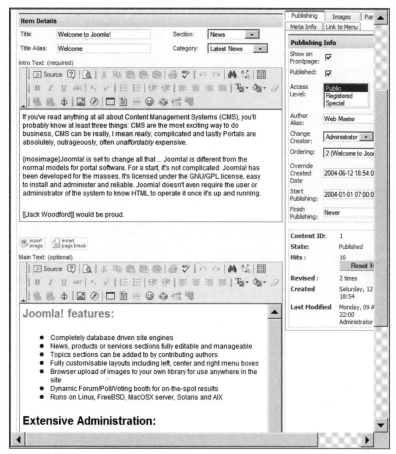

Figure 4-1: The JoomlaFCK editor has a small code footprint and executes nimbly.

You can see how simple the implementation of additional templates can be. Designing templates can be particularly useful when your site has a number of different contributors. You can standardize the way content is entered, yet provide more flexibility than would be offered by form entry. For example, if your site represented a television cooking show and you wanted to enter recipes that visitors could try at home, a recipe template could provide a way to expedite recipe entry by employees of the show.

Add a Custom Style to TinyMCE

You can add custom styles to the drop-down list of TinyMCE editor, as shown in Figure 4-2, so that contributors can use a style specific to the type of content that your site features. For example, a development site will likely have articles that feature source code. A custom style could be created to automatically render this code in the Courier font with a light gray background to separate it from the rest of the text.

TinyMCE will allow you to set a custom CSS file to be used in place of the default one. It is a good idea to simply duplicate the default CSS and add you new styles to that. You will find the default file from the root directory of your Joomla installation by following this path:

```
\plugins\editors\tinymce\jscripts\tiny_mce\themes\advanced\css\editor_content.css
```

Figure 4-2: Adding one or more styles to TinyMCE allows you to have content better customized to your site.

Copy the editor_content.css file to a different location. It is generally easiest to copy this file into the \css directory of the current template so that the styles can be matched with the wider site styles. For simplicity in this example, I copied the file to the Web server root and named it mytinymce.css.

To this file, add any styles that your site needs. I added a few styles for highlighting content with these stylesheet definitions:

```
.purplehighlighter {
    background: purple;
    color: #000000;
}

.bluehighlighter {
    background: blue;
    color: #000000;
}

.yellowhighlighter {
    background: yellow;
    color: #000000;
}
```

To have TinyMCE use your new stylesheet, you need to open the Plugin Manager in the Joomla Administrator interface. Click on Editor - TinyMCE 2.0 to display the parameters of the plug-in. In the `Custom CSS Classes` field, enter a complete URL that directs the editor to your CSS file, as shown in Figure 4-3.

On a remote server, the URL might appear like this:

```
http://www.example.com/mytinymce.css
```

Click the Save button to store the changes. When you open an article with the TinyMCE editor, the styles that you added to the file will now appear in the Styles menu.

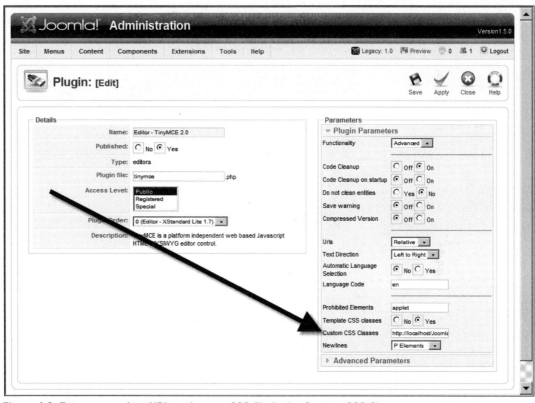

Figure 4-3: Enter a complete URL to the new CSS file in the Custom CSS Classes parameter.

Adding File Management and FTP Support

Sometimes you might need to manage your Joomla site directly from a Web interface when neither an FTP client nor FTP protocol access is possible. This can be especially true when you're using a handheld terminal or some type of public Web access (such as those offered in libraries and cafes). You can add remote file management capabilities to Joomla with the joomlaXplorer extension.

When installed, joomlaXplorer (see Figure 4-4) is available through the Administrator interface as an option listed in the Component menu. It provides access to all of the files and folders in the Web server path, and even includes a status bar displaying the amount of remaining space on the selected drive. Currently, joomlaXplorer is available in English, Dutch, German, French, Spanish, and Russian.

This extension can be used to search, edit, delete, copy, rename, archive, and unpack both files and directories. It allows uploading and downloading files through the interface or an FTP simulation. JoomlaXplorer also allows a user to change file and directory permissions using a chmod-style utility. The component is automatically restricted to use by the Joomla Super Administrator account.

The joomlaXplorer component is available for downloading here:

```
http://joomlacode.org/gf/project/joomlaxplorer/frs/
```

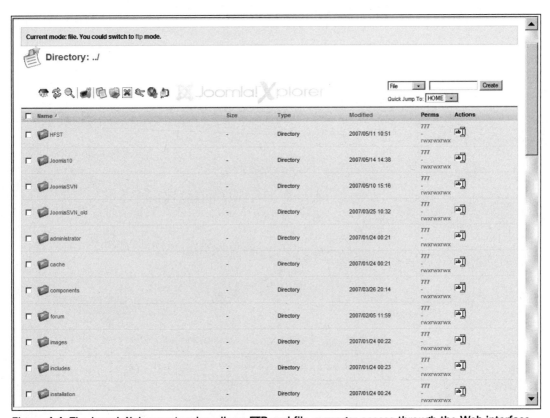

Figure 4-4: The joomlaXplorer extension allows FTP and file manager access through the Web interface.

Adding a Sitemap

Adding a sitemap is one of the best methods of ensuring that your Web site is easy to navigate. Sitemaps are often missing on smaller Web sites because, without automated sitemap creation, they are difficult and tedious to maintain. Fortunately, for Joomla users, there are many extensions that will provide this capability. They only require a small amount of time for installation and setup, and then they maintain themselves automatically and always show the most current site outline.

The most popular sitemap utility is the Joomap extension shown in Figure 4-5. Menu structure, content categories, and sections are included in the sitemap. Joomap may also output the sitemap into Google Sitemap XML format for integration with the Google system. Joomap is a simple component that can be installed in the Extension Manager and added as the last entry on the site Main Menu.

Chapter 13 provides more information on sitemaps (and Joomap). There you will find information on sitemap extensions and how they can be used to improve your site ranking.

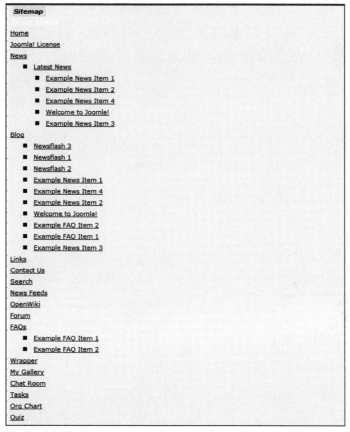

Figure 4-5: The Joomap extension will create a dynamic sitemap to show site organization.

Community Builder

Community Builder (CB) is an open source extension to Joomla that provides extensive broadening of Joomla's user management features. It is one of the most popular extensions in the Joomla world. The capabilities of CB include the following:

❏ Managed passwords and groups

❏ Avatar image for users

- ❑ Additional fields in the user profiles

- ❑ User lists

- ❑ Connection paths between users

- ❑ Custom-defined tabs

- ❑ Front-end workflow management for such processes as "Terms of Acceptance" confirmation, email messages for confirmation for activation of account, administrator notification of new applicant, and customization of email messages automatically sent to new applicants, using any field available in the user profile and formatted in either HTML or plain text

- ❑ Integration with other components such as personal mail systems (PMS), galleries, and many others

Community Builder is available here:

```
www.joomlapolis.com/
```

One of the difficulties of using CB (and also one of its advantages) is that it features a completely different login and registration system from the one included with Joomla. This means that you no longer have the single unified administration through the Joomla interface.

Structure of Community Builder

CB is made up of a Joomla extension that has its own plug-in architecture. The actual component still carries the CB's original name (comprofiler). Most of the CB features are included in three core modules that are slotted into it.

The foundation of CB is the user *login system*. It has a robust registration/login system that is extensible by an administrator. Much like an expandable contact-management system, CB allows you to add customized fields to record data unique to your needs. This user login framework is also available through an interface in the Joomla extension so that other Joomla plug-ins can access the information.

The CB login system will integrate with the following Joomla extensions (among others) so that the extensions will recognize users registered through the CB system:

- ❑ Simpleboard/JoomlaBoard

- ❑ myPMS

- ❑ Mamboblog

- ❑ Yanc tab newsletter

- ❑ zOOm Gallery

- ❑ uddeIM (private message)

- ❑ CB Gallery

❑   PHPBB bulleting board system

❑   GroupJive

When you install the CB extension, the main component page on the Administrator interface will show you the CB plug-ins that are included by default, as shown in Figure 4-6. Installation of CB plug-ins will add them to the list.

The most basic user settings screen shown in Figure 4-7 provides most of the same settings available through the Joomla registration system. This is where the similarity ends. With CB, you can not only define many other parameters through the group designation but also configure custom settings for all users.

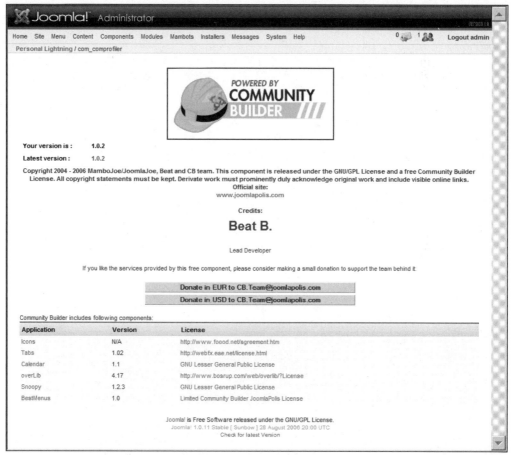

Figure 4-6: The Community Builder interface screen details which applications are installed into the CB system.

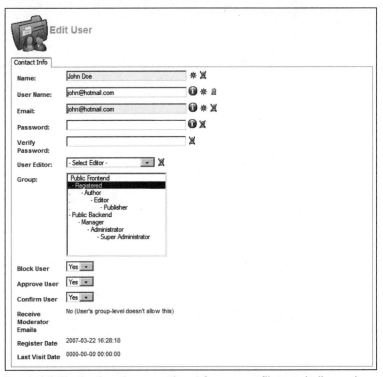

Figure 4-7: The back-end user settings of a user profile are similar to the Joomla registration system.

For user-defined fields, there are 11 field types:

- ❑ Checkbox
- ❑ Date
- ❑ Email address
- ❑ Editor text area
- ❑ Text area
- ❑ Text field
- ❑ Radio button
- ❑ Web address
- ❑ Multi-select drop-down menu
- ❑ Multi-select check box
- ❑ Fields delimiter

These types can be set up for any of the CB fields. For example, if you wanted to allow users to add their preferences for the CMS type to their profiles, you could add a *multi-select drop-down menu* field to the user profiles. By accessing the Field Management screen under the Community Builder menu, you could add such a field, as shown in Figure 4-8.

After you save the field, you must publish it. Once published, if you return to the user profile screen that was shown in Figure 4-7, you will see that your new field is added to the user profile. The power of being able to customize the user profile (even including "required" fields) allows the tailoring of a Joomla site to collect critical visitor information.

You may have noticed in Figure 4-7 that all of the user information for this screen appeared on a single tab titled Contact Info. You may also have noticed that when the new field was created, it was selected to appear on that tab. CB can add a variety of other tabs, not only to provide user information collection but even to interface with other extensions to profile-by-user features such as a user blog.

All tabs available through the user profile are displayed in the Tab Manager, as shown in Figure 4-9. From this manager, you can edit the name of the tab, its position, and the display type. If it is a particular type of tab (such as a menu tab), you will see an additional pane that displays extra parameters.

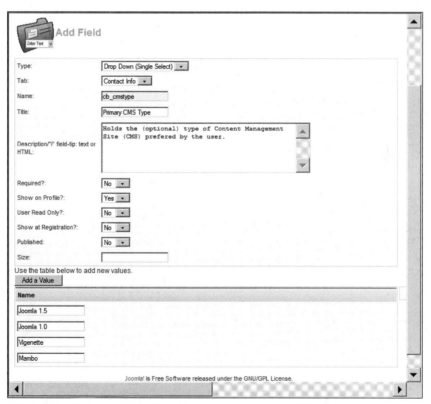

Figure 4-8: Add a new field where the user can specify a CMS preference.

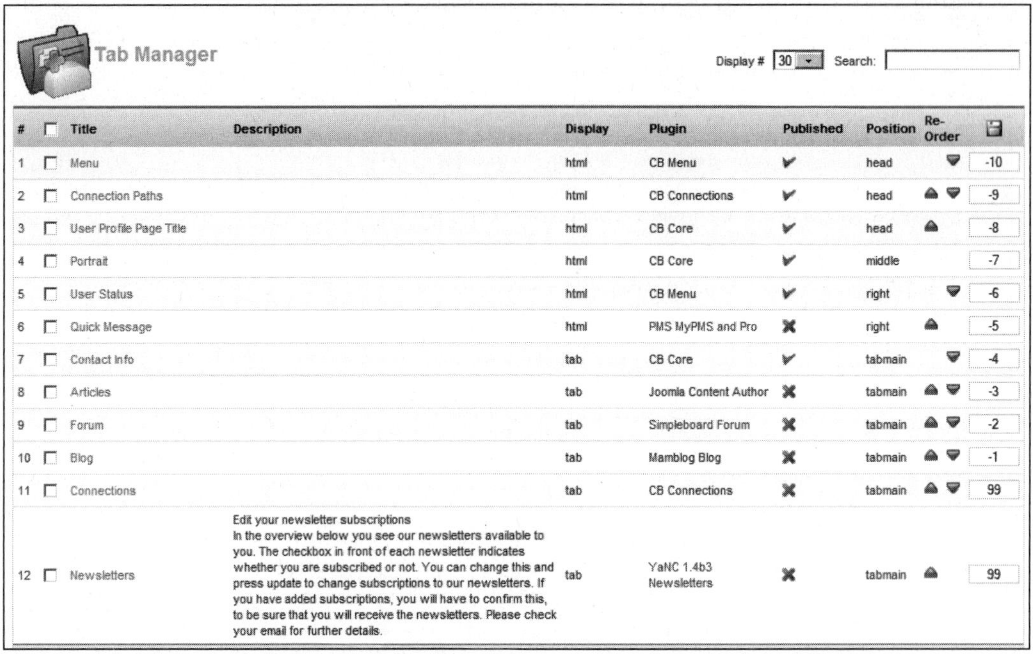

#		Title	Description	Display	Plugin	Published	Position	Re-Order	
1	☐	Menu		html	CB Menu	✔	head	▼	-10
2	☐	Connection Paths		html	CB Connections	✔	head	▲ ▼	-9
3	☐	User Profile Page Title		html	CB Core	✔	head	▲	-8
4	☐	Portrait		html	CB Core	✔	middle		-7
5	☐	User Status		html	CB Menu	✔	right	▼	-6
6	☐	Quick Message		html	PMS MyPMS and Pro	✘	right	▲	-5
7	☐	Contact Info		tab	CB Core	✔	tabmain	▼	-4
8	☐	Articles		tab	Joomla Content Author	✘	tabmain	▲ ▼	-3
9	☐	Forum		tab	Simpleboard Forum	✘	tabmain	▲ ▼	-2
10	☐	Blog		tab	Mamblog Blog	✘	tabmain	▲ ▼	-1
11	☐	Connections		tab	CB Connections	✘	tabmain	▲ ▼	99
12	☐	Newsletters	Edit your newsletter subscriptions In the overview below you see our newsletters available to you. The checkbox in front of each newsletter indicates whether you are subscribed or not. You can change this and press update to change subscriptions to our newsletters. If you have added subscriptions, you will have to confirm this, to be sure that you will receive the newsletters. Please check your email for further details.	tab	YaNC 1.4b3 Newsletters	✘	tabmain	▲	99

Figure 4-9: The Tab Manager holds all of the tabs that may be added to a user profile.

CB Plug-Ins

CB has its own plug-in architecture. Many of these plug-ins will bridge the CB authentication system for use with other extensions. Figure 4-10 shows the Plugin Manager and the plug-ins of a default installation. In the Type column, some of the plug-ins are denoted as *templates* that define the various theme displays available to CB.

The *user* type plug-ins provide either core functionality or the bridge technology for interfacing with third-party Joomla extensions. You can see that the default installation includes bridges for Simpleboard Forum, Mamblog Blog, YaNC Newslettters, and PMS MyPMS/Pro. There are many other such bridge plug-ins available on the CB Web site.

User Avatar

One of the features that is key to having the visitors of your site invest themselves there is the ability to set an *avatar* (image) that represents them to the outside world. This image will be displayed in the user's profile. Although a username can be tailored to represent the user, it doesn't have the personality that can be communicated with a small image.

Image posting may also be moderated, so avatars do not appear on the site until approved. The moderation feature can be very useful for family-oriented Joomla sites, as well as providing a means to police potential copyrighted image violation.

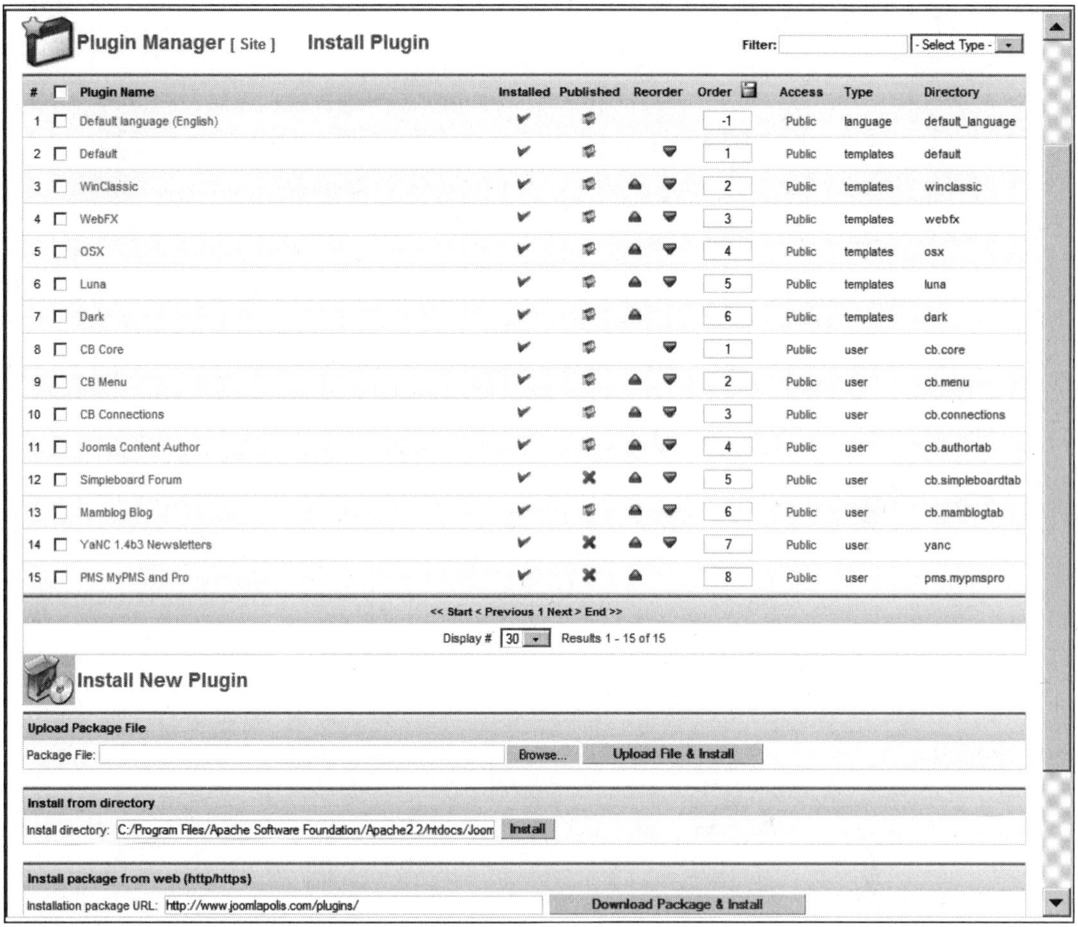

#	☐	Plugin Name	Installed	Published	Reorder	Order ⊞	Access	Type	Directory
1	☐	Default language (English)	✔	🗊		-1	Public	language	default_language
2	☐	Default	✔	🗊	▽	1	Public	templates	default
3	☐	WinClassic	✔	🗊	▲ ▽	2	Public	templates	winclassic
4	☐	WebFX	✔	🗊	▲ ▽	3	Public	templates	webfx
5	☐	OSX	✔	🗊	▲ ▽	4	Public	templates	osx
6	☐	Luna	✔	🗊	▲ ▽	5	Public	templates	luna
7	☐	Dark	✔	🗊	▲	6	Public	templates	dark
8	☐	CB Core	✔	🗊	▽	1	Public	user	cb.core
9	☐	CB Menu	✔	🗊	▲ ▽	2	Public	user	cb.menu
10	☐	CB Connections	✔	🗊	▲ ▽	3	Public	user	cb.connections
11	☐	Joomla Content Author	✔	🗊	▲ ▽	4	Public	user	cb.authortab
12	☐	Simpleboard Forum	✔	✖	▲ ▽	5	Public	user	cb.simpleboardtab
13	☐	Mamblog Blog	✔	🗊	▲ ▽	6	Public	user	cb.mamblogtab
14	☐	YaNC 1.4b3 Newsletters	✔	✖	▲ ▽	7	Public	user	yanc
15	☐	PMS MyPMS and Pro	✔	✖	▲	8	Public	user	pms.mypmspro

<< Start < Previous 1 Next > End >>

Display # [30 ▼] Results 1 - 15 of 15

Install New Plugin

Upload Package File

Package File: [   ] [Browse...] [**Upload File & Install**]

Install from directory

Install directory: [C:/Program Files/Apache Software Foundation/Apache2.2/htdocs/Joom] [Install]

Install package from web (http/https)

Installation package URL: [http://www.joomlapolis.com/plugins/] [**Download Package & Install**]

Figure 4-10: The Plugin Manager displays all of the plug-ins installed in CB.

> The concept of copyrighted images is a gray area on the Internet. Clearly, the reproduction of copyrighted content is a violation of the rights of the copyright holder and is black and white. However, many copyright holders turn a blind eye to the use of their images when no profit is sought by the use, and the presentation is not within an offensive context. Fan films have been made for years of various film franchises, and few studios actively discourage such artistic creation. If you are concerned about the legal ramifications, you should consult an attorney.

To allow a user to add an image, log in to the site where you have CB installed. When you go to your user profile, you will see an empty user icon. If you click on the item, you can select the My CB Profile item in the User Menu. From there, you can select the Update Your Image option in the Edit menu to upload an image. The image will not be displayed until it is approved through the Administrator interface.

Download and Installation

When you download CB, it is not a single file but rather a set of files that must be installed. These files include the following:

❑ comprofiler — This archive contains the actual CB component that you must install into Joomla.

❑ cblogin — The login module that must be added to your Joomla front page.

❑ mod_comprofilermoderator — Provides the workflow delegation of registration approval to individual moderators.

❑ mod_comprofileronline — Displays a list of CB members who are currently online.

You only really need to install the comprofiler component for Administrator interface control and the cblogin module to allow logging into the CB system. comprofiler was the original name of Community Builder, and you will find this denotation in many places in the back end.

If this is the first time you've run CB, you will want to access the Tools option in the CB menu. As shown in Figure 4-11, available tools provide the capabilities to install sample data, to synchronize users with the existing Joomla registration system, and to perform an integrity check on the CB databases.

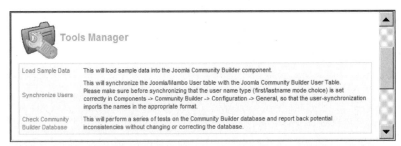

Figure 4-11: From the CB Tools page, you can install sample data, transfer existing Joomla users into CB, and check the integrity of the CB database.

Organizations and E-commerce

Extensions that relate to organizations and e-commerce often coordinate a Joomla system with outside resources (extranets, for example) to interface with affiliate programs, electronic payment systems, and other systems. These types of extensions tend to be used by organizations that need to coordinate and facilitate communication between people either in-house or in the broader Web world.

For this area of Joomla extensions, the JED includes the following categories:

❑ *Banner Ads & Affiliates* — This category features the subcategories of Advertising Banners and Classified Ads.

❑ *e-Commerce* — This category features the subcategories of Amazon, Auction, Data Interchange, Donations, Payment Systems, and Shopping Cart.

- ❏ *Extension Specific Plugin* — This category features the subcategories of AdsManager Plugins, BannersManager Plugins, Community Builder Plugins, DOCMan Plugins, ECJC Plugins, JCE Plugins, Joom!Fish Plugins, SEF Service Map Plugins, Shep2 Plugins, SOBI2 Plugins, and VirtueMart Plugins.

- ❏ *Intranet & Groupware* — This category features the subcategories of Contacts, CRM, LDAP, and Project & Task Management.

- ❏ *Vertical Markets* — This category features the subcategories of Auto & Vehicles, Boat & Yachting, Education, and Real Estate.Numerous excellent capabilities from these add-ons can turn a simple Joomla site into a professional and/or commercial Web deployment. Allowing subscriptions to content on a site, for example, is one very popular feature.

Subscription Manager

Joomla ships with the capability to limit content to a particular group, or to simply make articles invisible to all but registered users. However, there is no included granularity that lets an administrator limit content viewing to specific users, or for a limited time. Just such capabilities are provided by the Open Source Account Expiration Control & Subscription Manager (AEC) extension.

As shown in Figure 4-12, this component provides paid membership functionality to a Joomla site. The AEC extension can be integrated with other extensions (such as CB) and can communicate through payment gateways including PayPal, Authorize.net, 2Checkout, AlloPass, ViaKLIX, and others. It allows a variety of payment plans, including free trials, as well as paid, lifetime, and global free trials.

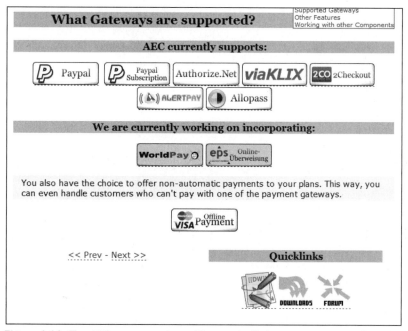

Figure 4-12: The AEC component provides controlled access to content based on a per-user subscription model.

The Administrator interface allows easy configuration of the payment options for content, as well as the external interfaces to the various payment services. It also allows you to set up the subscriptions for the various Joomla user accounts.

The developers of AEC routinely add new payment system gateways, so be sure to get the latest version. Additionally, the Web site has a forum that offers developer support. Check out the home page here:

```
www.globalnerd.org/index.php?option=com_content&task=view&id=17&Itemid=34
```

MicroShop PayPal Shopping Cart

MicroShop is a handy shopping cart extension (see Figure 4-13) that can be easily configured for adding items and final checkout. The shopping cart is fully integrated with the PayPal system for easy payment options.

The Administrator interface shown in Figure 4-14 allows setup of payment options, as well as complete order-fulfillment settings.

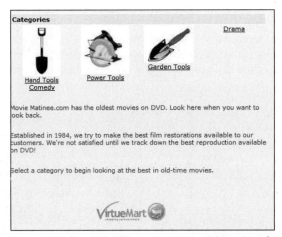

Figure 4-13: The MicroShop extension adds an interface that allows site items to be added to the shopping cart.

Project Fork Project Manager

Coordination of people on a project can be difficult and frustrating without the proper tools. Tools such as Microsoft Project or Copper are excellent for large projects, but their complexity and rigid designs limit their applicability to small and medium projects. There is a Joomla extension called Project Fork that is excellent at facilitating Web-based project management.

As shown in Figure 4-15, the Project Fork extension is a project-management tool that can handle multiple tasks and people. Since it runs under Joomla, it can be accessed anywhere a Web connection is available. Various reporting options allow a user to examine current and past performance. The extension's ability to handle documents and files associated with the project makes it into a miniature groupware application.

Figure 4-14: The MicroShop back end allows setup of payment access systems such as PayPal.

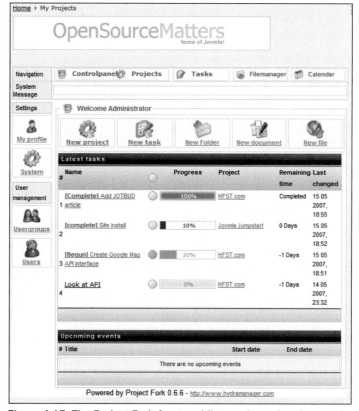

Figure 4-15: The Project Fork front end lists projects that the user is authorized to see.

New projects may be created by selecting the Projects tab and clicking on the New Project button. Once a project has been created, tasks may be assigned to the project. Each task may have a name, rich text description, status (such as canceled, complete, delayed, and so on), a start date, an end date, current progress (as a percentage), and the user who is responsible for the task. Optionally, changes to a task may automatically notify the assigned user.

Most of the project management in Project Fork (including user configuration) is possible through the front-end interface. The extension was designed in this manner because, unlike many other site-management tasks, often a particular project administrator will not need site administrator privileges. The Administrator interface provides overarching authority to configure the access privileges and manage the existing projects.

Timesheets Extension

To manage time on a project (particularly the recording of billable hours), you can use the TimeWriter extension. This extension provides an interface shown in Figure 4-16 that allows time management recording by tasks. Management can be categorized by projects and clients. Repeating tasks may be created, and time-sheet rendering can be performed.

Figure 4-16: The TimeWriter front-end allows convenient logging of all activities by project and client.

As with Project Fork, TimeWriter provides most management functions through the front-end user interface. To access these functions, simply click on the (somewhat misnamed) Reports link in the top-right corner. You'll be presented with links to the following features:

❑   Timesheet Report by Company

❑   Timesheet Report by Project

❑ Report Total Hours by Project

❑ Report Total Mileage

❑ Set User Preferences

❑ Show Vehicles

❑ Mileage Log Form

❑ Manage Companies

❑ Manage Projects

To begin, you must first create a company before you can create a project — before you can begin tracking hours. Click on the Manage Companies link to add a company definition. You can use the Manage Projects link to create a new project. Once you have created a project, you must click the Assign icon on the project list screen to assign Joomla users to the project.

The Administrator reporting capabilities allow the overall management to create weekly reports based on specified parameters. From the back-end interface, you can import Mambotastic Timesheets data.

Adding an Auction Framework to Your Site

The eBay auction Web site is one of the most popular sites on the Web. Many people actually make a living by selling products there. If you would like to be one of them, Joomla can help! There are a number of extensions available that can funnel all of the information from an eBay auction directly into your Joomla site. That means you can create a virtual store on your Joomla site that can direct visitors to your eBay auction for bidding.

Most businesses rely on repeat business for their bread and butter. This applies to eBay-based businesses. By creating an auction store adjunct to your Web site, you can provide a place where regular visitors can buy goods and services.

There are several auction extensions that will literally add auction capabilities to a Joomla site. However, an auction is only effective when many buyers can bid against each other to raise the price to a profitable level. Since eBay offers the venue to reach literally millions of potential customers, and provides all of the necessary security against false bidders and so on, adding auction capabilities to a Joomla site is a poor choice for most Web masters. If you do want to add this functionality anyway, check the Auction category of the Joomla.org *Web site.*

The My EBay Store extension shown in Figure 4-17 allows you to present your eBay store through the Joomla interface. It will be dynamically updated to present real-time information about existing eBay listings. It will display all product information, product images, bidding prices, and bidding end times. It can handle more than 150 concurrently updated listings.

You can place the My EBay Store module in any panel location on the Joomla page. You can configure the location and the other settings by selecting the module in the Module Manager. The parameter display shown in Figure 4-18 holds the settings that are used to select the items for display.

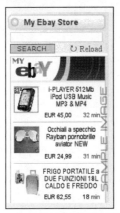

Figure 4-17: The My EBay
Store front-end allows real-time
display of existing auctions.

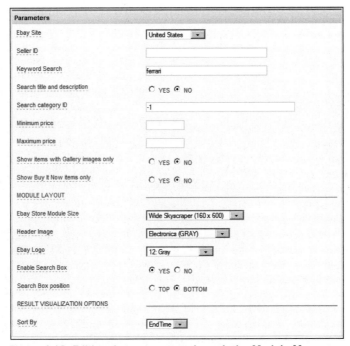

Figure 4-18: Editing the parameters through the Module Manager
allows for the setting up of product selection.

Site Content

The heart of any CMS site is the content it holds. Site content extensions allow you to expand the types of content that can be managed by Joomla to handle everything from audio podcasts to eCards to maps. There are even extensions available that can turn a Joomla site into a user-extendable wiki system.

For this area of Joomla extensions, the JED includes the following categories:

❑ *Contents & News* — Holds extensions that can import or create content beyond standard Joomla articles. This category features the subcategories of Blog, Clocks, Content Management, Custom Code, eCards, Images, Maps, News, Quiz, Ratings & Reviews, Related Items, RSS, Tips & Notes, and Weather.

❑ *Documentation* — Has extensions that allow the creation of site documentation. This category features the subcategories of Bibliography, Downloads, FAQ, Glossary & Dictionary, and Wiki.

❑ *Gallery & Multimedia* — Lists extensions that allow Joomla to host and manage various types of media. This category features the subcategories of Gallery, Podcasting, and Streaming Media.

Podcasting through Joomla

Podcasting is *the* new media. A recent Bridge Ratings study indicated that the number of people who downloaded a podcast has risen from 820,000 in 2004 to 4.8 million people in 2005. Projections for audience growth by 2010 predict adoption to reach 45 million users. According to *Business Week*, from the last six months of 2004 to the first six months of 2005, the number of podcasts published multiplied by 2500 percent.

Podcasting is the audio version of an RSS newsfeed. You may have noticed the RSS or Atom icon on your favorite news site. With the help of an application called an *aggregator*, a user can *subscribe* to a newsfeeds, which will automatically download the newest stories directly to the local desktop for later reading. RSS is the popular XML format that holds the subscription information.

A podcast generally uses an RSS file nearly identical to a newsfeed to allow podcast aggregators (or *podcatchers*) to subscribe to an audio feed. Audio files are downloaded by the aggregator (often MP3 or AAC format) into a computer or media device. You can use a computer (or more often, an MP3 player or iPod) to listen to the content. The most popular single podcasting site is Apple's iTunes Web site.

Joomla provides the capability to include a podcast on your site so that when you post audio files, they can be automatically added to the feed for subscribers to download. The PodCast Suite is a package of extensions that provide podcasting capabilities that can be downloaded here:

    www.jlleblanc.com/joomla/Articles/Podcast_Suite%2C_Version_1-1_Stable/

The PodCast Suite package includes a component, module, and plug-in that work together to provide audio podcast hosting capabilities to Joomla. The extension supports integration with Apple's iTunes. The Podcast Suite module shown in Figure 4-19 displays a link to the dynamically created RSS feed file.

The feed is generated based on the parameters set in the component presented in the Administrator interface shown in Figure 4-20. The extension will automatically look for new media in the specified folder and generate the podcast subscription directory from those items.

Unfortunately, this extension doesn't support video podcasting or *vodcasting* (video-on-demand-casting). With the tremendous growth of vodcasting, though, this oversight should be corrected soon.

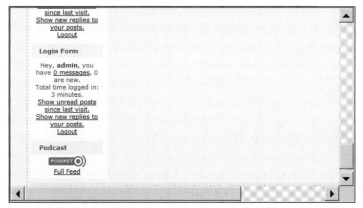

Figure 4-19: The Podcast Suite module provides a link to subscribe to the site podcast.

Providing a Picture Gallery

Picture galleries (especially those that display family photo albums) at times seem to be taking over the Web. Many jokes have been made about the huge volume of the transmission of baby pictures will eventually bring the Web to its knees. The desire to share digital pictures and the ability of geographically separated family members to share in the lives of their loved ones makes a compelling case for digital picture galleries.

Whether you want to display a professional photo portfolio or post snapshots of your daughter's first steps, Joomla can provide the solution. Joomla can host picture galleries through a number of extensions. In fact, galleries are among the most popular types of plug-ins on the Joomla system. At last count, a Google search could locate at least 50 different picture gallery extensions for Joomla, both free and commercial.

The RSGallery2 extension is the most highly rated native gallery extension and is very rich in features. It provides professional gallery and image management, integrated access control with Joomla's user registration system, and availability in almost two dozen languages.

Figure 4-20: Configuration occurs through the Administrator component of the Podcast Suite.

If you are looking to manage a large volume of digital photos, be sure to look at the Gallery2 system. It is one of the most popular gallery applications on the Web and provides many professional features. It includes automatic RSS generation, comments features, and support for many media types (not only pictures), and has shown the capability to scale on popular Web sites. Although it is a standalone PHP application, it can be included within a Joomla site by using the Gallery 2 Bridge plug-in.

The RSGallery2 extension (see Figure 4-21) is written for native-Joomla execution. The rendered HTML and CSS are standards-compliant. It also has complete support of Joomfish for language display. It can even manage Flash content! Before you install the extension, ensure that you have at least one of the popular image generation libraries (GD2, ImageMagick, or Netpbm) active on your PHP server.

Figure 4-21: The professional RSGallery2 interface makes image management a snap.

RSGallery2 has a control panel that allows access to all the configuration panels of the extension. From here, you can configure the system, upload (singly or in bulk) images, organize galleries, edit display options, or manage the image database. Additionally, the CSS editing option allows you to customize the presentation to match your current site template.

You may want to visit the RSGallery2 home page (`http://rsgallery2.net/index.php`). On the site, you can download the extension, see a demo implementation of a gallery, read or post to the forum dedicated to the extension, or learn from the tutorials available there. There are tutorials for everything from deploying the extension to building custom modules to creating a gallery template. The site also holds API documentation that details all of the classes held in the RSGallery2 framework.

Site Interactivity

To add features for user interaction, there are extensions that provide features from chat rooms to event calendars to shared recipe boxes. Interactivity is the keystone of Web sites that seek to be designated as Web 2.0. Several of the extensions are examined in Chapter 10, where Joomla is augmented to create a virtual community.

For this area of Joomla extensions, the JED includes the following categories:

❑ *Communications* — This category features the subcategories of Chat, Comments, Forum, Guest Book, Newsletter, Online Status, PMS, Polls, and Shoutbox.

❑ *Calendars* — This category features the subcategories of Events and Reservations.

❑ *Forms* — Forms capability for definition of forms that can be filled out by Joomla visitors.

❑ *Miscellaneous* — This category features the subcategories of Development Tools, Help Desk, Portfolio, Progress, Quotes, Recipes, Religion, Social Bookmarking, and Sports & Games.

Adding Comments for Posted Articles

One of the most popular new methods of creating a virtual community is the functionality for users to post their own comments regarding a particular article or blog entry. Forums can sometimes sit empty because of a lack of provocateurs who create new messages that incite others to reply. The ability to post comments in direct response to existing content can be very motivating to a user base. Almost everyone likes to add their two cents worth at one time or another.

> **Having a comments section requires quite a bit of moderation. People will post illegal content, personal attacks on each other, personal information, advertisements, profanity, obscene material, and (possibly worst of all) criticism of the site's author. Allowing comments will require you as the administrator to pay much closer attention to your site than if no feedback were allowed. Be aware that you'll have to make this extra time commitment unless you want your site to become like the Wild West with an "anything goes" mentality.**

The Joomla plug-in extension Akocomment provides users with the capability to post feedback to each article. The Akocomment extension (discussed in more detail in Chapter 10) is one of the most commonly implemented components for providing a comment interface on Joomla systems. It can handle comments in a variety of languages, including English, Chinese, and Norwegian. The most commonly adopted version of the extension is the Akocomment Tweaked Special Edition.

The Administrator interface allows complete configuration of the extension, including tabs for layout, posting, notification, reports, favored, and templates.

Guestbook

One of the features that most hobbyist Web masters want to add to their site is a guestbook. Guestbooks were one of the first interactive features to be added for Web interaction back when the Web was first getting started. They allowed visits to add comments (preferably compliments) or suggestions relating to the overall site content.

Guestbooks are still a very popular item. One of the best things about a dynamic system like Joomla is that it can automatically change the site so that things always seem new — even if you haven't updated it lately. Google uses seasonal banners to change the front page look of its site. What if your site showed a random guestbook entry as a pull quote on the front page of your site? You would have to moderate the guestbook, of course, to ensure that advertisements, spam, and obscenity didn't appear on the site. While this policing may take a small amount of work, you would have the greater dividend of always having a fresh site complement the greeting of new users.

Before you make a module that can display the pull quote, you need to select a guestbook plug-in to take user comments. See Chapter 10 for more details.

Chat Rooms through Joomla

Chat rooms can be an excellent resource for a Web site, but they can also be difficult to promote and even more difficult to manage. For most Web sites, limiting access to chat rooms to special occasions such as a guest speaker may be the wisest choice. With the number of predators and people with uncertain motives on the Web, unmonitored and unfettered chat rooms are a recipe for disaster for the Web master.

The Joomla Live Chat shown in Figure 4-22 is an administrator/user live chat for one-to-one interaction with your Web site visitors. This extension is perfect for on-site tech support. It uses Ajax technology to provide dynamic updates, and includes the features of audio alert for a session request.

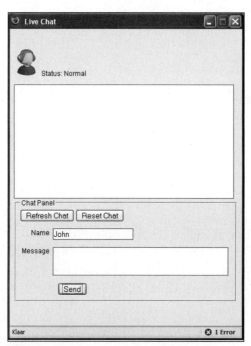

Figure 4-22: The Joomla Live Chat interface
provides a standardized look-and-feel familiar
to chat users.

Setting Up a Wiki System in Joomla

In the 1980s, Ward Cunningham invented a new method of collaboration called a *wiki*, which is a Web site where visitors can add, edit, supplement, and remove articles from an encyclopedic store. The most famous example is an online encyclopedia known as Wikipedia (www.wikipedia.org). Users of the Web site have created or contributed to more than 2 million articles currently featured there.

Within the last decade, there has been incredible growth in the wiki phenomenon, especially related to technology. The open source community, in particular, benefits from the wiki Web sites, since many of the programmers of open source applications often lack the time to document their work. A wiki created to feature a particular application (such as the FreeMind mind-mapping tool) allows passionate users to add useful information, tips, and document parts of the program that aren't self-explanatory.

Joomla is capable of hosting a wiki system through a component known as OpenWiki. OpenWiki is an extension adapted from the open source DokuWiki project (created by Andreas Gohr), which is a PHP application that provides wiki capabilities. OpenWiki is made to be fast and light, so while other wiki applications may include more features (such as the open source MediaWiki that is used for Wikipedia), OpenWiki consumes much fewer resources and provides much more responsiveness.

OpenWiki is available for download here:

    http://projects.j-prosolution.com/projects/os-projects/project-openwiki.html

Once you have installed OpenWiki, the component will display a simple starter screen. The editing permission system integrates with Joomla's ACL, so permissions for each group may be set in terms of Read, Edit, Create, Upload, and Delete.

If you click on the Edit This Page button at the top of the screen, the editor window will display the article (see Figure 4-23) using standard wiki notation. Internal links are supplied by enclosing a term in double brackets ([[ ]]) and external links are denoted with single brackets ([ ]). The buttons at the top of the editor window can be used to easily insert codes for things such as image references and heading styles.

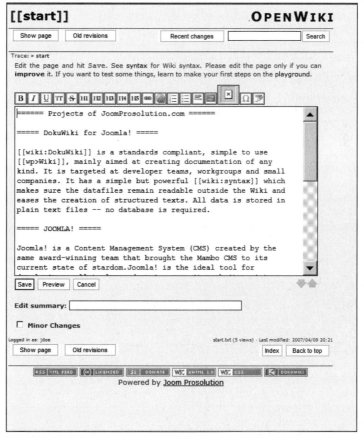

Figure 4-23: The editing screen displays standard wiki text-formatting codes.

Wiki pages are stored as standard text files in the `\pages` directory of the component, as shown here:

```
\com_openwiki\data\pages
```

Since they are stored as text files, they can be edited and manipulated by any standard text editor. This wiki extension is based on the DocBook format. *DocBook* is a markup language similar to HTML and was initially created to allow documentation of open source systems such as FreeBSD, KDE, GTK+, Gnome, and Linux. This format was made to hold content data rather than presentation information and so follows the Model-View-Controller (MVC) design pattern.

Chapter 8 provides more information on the MVC.

Since version 4, the DocBook format has adopted the conventions for storing data that are defined by XML. An example of a DocBook fragment would look like this:

```
<book id="pro_joomla">
  <title>Professional Joomla</title>
  <chapter id="chapter_1">
    <title>Chapter 1 - Introduction</title>
    <para>If you're reading this book...</para>
    <para>The method you use to master Joomla...</para>
  </chapter>
  <chapter id="chapter_2">
    <title>Chapter 2 - The Finer Points of Installation</title>
    <para>Joomla requires 4 different server technologies...</para>
  </chapter>
</book>
```

Storing the wiki information in this format allows content to be readable outside of the wiki software. That means that articles created in OpenWiki can be later reprocessed into any type of static content desired.

When changes are made to a page, the differences are stored so that previous versions may be examined. In Figure 4-24, you can see the changes made to the *main* are denoted with a plus (+) sign to the left of the text in the newer version displayed in the right column. On the screen, changes are also highlighted with a color background for easy examination.

The extension does have a number of implementation choices that can be challenging for operators who adopt this extension. Confusing to many users is the lack of a New Page button. Since all pages must be linked from another page, you must create a link in an existing page to create a new page. For example, you can add a new reference to the text of an existing article like this:

```
[[joomla_jumpstart]]
```

When the link is clicked upon, the new page creation screen is displayed, as shown in Figure 4-25.

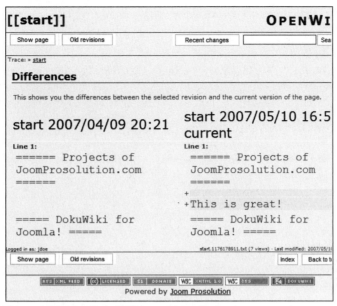

Figure 4-24: The OpenWiki extension allows you to examine differences between versions of the file.

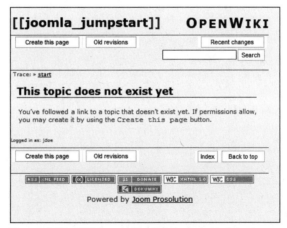

Figure 4-25: Clicking on the link to a nonexistent page will display the new topic creation page.

Following are some limitations of OpenWiki:

❑ *All documents stored in UTF-8* — Documents are only available in UTF-8 character set, regardless of the character set setting configured for the Joomla system. Therefore, some non-English language content (including other DocBook files) that use Unicode may have problems being posted into the system.

❑ *No back-end interface for administration* — Because of this, the wiki cannot be managed like a traditional Joomla extension, but must be configured through the front end.

❑ *Separate search engine* — OpenWiki content is not available for indexing by the Joomla system and, therefore, requires a separate search engine. Thus, content on the Joomla site is invisible to the wiki search, and wiki content is invisible to the Joomla search.

eWriting

The eWriting extension shown in Figure 4-26 is a wonderful add-on that allows many writing contributors to add to the Web site. This extension was created to enable sites that feature fan fiction (such as authors who want to create original romance or *Star Trek* stories) to contribute to the site. The interface allows new articles to include images and be auto-selected into categories.

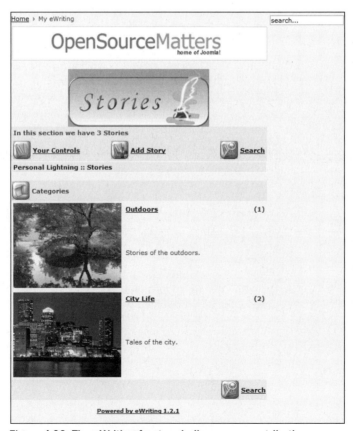

Figure 4-26: The eWriting front-end allows user contribution.

Before you can allow story posting, you must add some categories where stories can be filed. Categories are much like Joomla categories, and they may have an associated description and image.

Once categories have been created, stories may be added to the eWriting component either through the Administrator interface or directly in the front end. Stories are created as chapters and may be entered into the interface or uploaded as text files (.txt) or HTML files (.htm or .html) — although additional file types may be added in the Administrator interface.

There is also a module to show current site statistics on the front page. The Administrator interface can be used to manage the uploaded stores. The Administrator interface includes story and chapter creation. Images can be uploaded to a user gallery. The back-end interface can also be used to activate the eWriting integration with Community Builder, Joomlaboard Forum, or a Private Message System (PMS) such as Missus or MyPMSII.

The developers of eWriting also developed Missus, which provides personalized messaging on a Joomla site. Mail may be sent among Joomla users and may include attachments. You can download Missus from the eWriting Web site.

You can get a lot of great information at the eWriting home page at the following URL:

```
http://ewriting.com.ar
```

Implementing Classified Ads

Supplementing a site with classified ads can provide a great boon to your users. Although many people now think of eBay as the primary venue to sell used items, there are many Web sites such as www.photo.net that do booming business by selling to particular niche markets where the audience consists of specialists. In these niche markets, the acknowledged level of sophistication of the average site visitor can make the exchanges more lucrative.

Of course, classified advertising is hardly limited to used product selling. Service listings, event announcements, personal ads, and numerous other services are well served by a classified space. Classified business has been redefined by Web-based deployment through sites such as craigslist.

The Noah's Classifieds for Joomla extension shown in Figure 4-27 allows you to define hierarchical categories with unlimited depth, image uploads for ads, variable fields to allow advertising by category, and email notifications.

If you click on the link for Home in the Noah Classifieds menu, the menu changes and you can then click the Create New Category option. In the new category parameters, you establish that Public users may post ads, when you enter a category, the Submit Ad menu option will be displayed.

The Administrator interface, shown in Figure 4-28, allows complete configuration of the extension. The interface allows the locking of a category (so that no new ads may be placed), as well as the creation of custom fields.

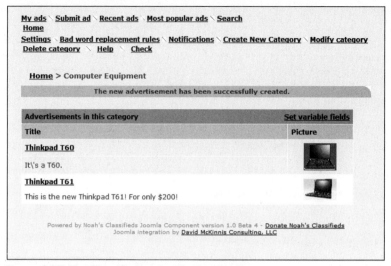

My ads \ Submit ad \ Recent ads \ Most popular ads \ Search
Home
Settings \ Bad word replacement rules \ Notifications \ Create New Category \ Modify category
Delete category \ Help \ Check

Home > Computer Equipment

The new advertisement has been successfully created.

Advertisements in this category	Set variable fields
Title	Picture
Thinkpad T60	
It\'s a T60.	
Thinkpad T61	
This is the new Thinkpad T61! For only $200!	

Powered by Noah's Classifieds Joomla Component version 1.0 Beta 4 - Donate Noah's Classifieds
Joomla integration by David McKinnis Consulting, LLC

Figure 4-27: The Classifieds extension front-end

Customize global settings	
Expiration properties	
Ad expiration in days ?	30
Number of days the user must be informed about the expiration before	5
Number of times the user is allowed to prolong his/her expired ads	5
Image upload limitations	
Maximum picture size in bytes	50000
Maximum picture width in pixels	640
Maximum picture height in pixels	480
Thumbnail width	60
Thumbnail height	60
Create thumbnails with Graphics library:	GD
Local path to graphics	

Figure 4-28: The Administrator portion of the
Classifieds package

Be sure to post a disclaimer on the classified section that explains that your site is not responsible for any transactions that occur through it. Further, state that you retain the right to delete any advertisement for any reason if the site owner believes it goes against the spirit of the site. For an excellent example of a complete legal disclaimer, check out the "Terms and Use" article on www.craigslist.org.

Adding Sports Tracking

The JoomLeague extension, shown in Figure 4-29, allows you to track sports scores for a number of different league types, including football, basketball, soccer, and so on. Statistics can be tracked for individual teams, as well as league-wide. The points system is configurable so that scoring for nearly any sport can be accommodated. You can even upload team images, including crew photos, team logos, coats of arms, and more.

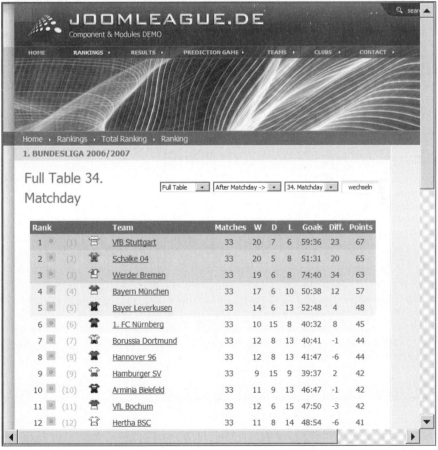

Figure 4-29: The JoomLeague extension will track and display most types of scoring information.

Tracking is organized first by projects, which essentially defines a league. Following that, teams and players are defined.

In addition to the core component that handles the tracking, the package also includes a number of display modules, including the following:

- ❏ *Events Statistic Module* — Displays an `eventtype` list for the chosen project.
- ❏ *Next Match Module* — Displays the next match of project's favorite or selected team.
- ❏ *Random Player Module* — Displays a random player of chosen project(s) and team(s).
- ❏ *Ranking Module* — Shows the actual ranking of the given project.
- ❏ *Results Module* — Shows the latest results of given project.
- ❏ *Results Tabs Module* — Uses JavaScript to display the latest results in three single tabs.
- ❏ *Team Players Module* — Displays all players of your favorite team, ordered by player positions.
- ❏ *Navigation Menu Module* — Provides a custom navigational menu to quick access to information stored in the extension. In the Administrator interface, the menu can be configured to display hyperlinks to items such as ranking and results.

The Administrator interface allows complete configuration of the tracking system. The system can track projects, clubs, teams, players, player positions, events, and even referees.

You can visit the home page for the newest version, as well as several sample configurations. Note that some of the text on the site is written in German, so speaking that language will help you get the most out of this extension. The home page can be found at the following URL:

```
www.joomleague.de
```

Adding Casino Games

One way to broaden the appeal of a Joomla site is to provide some games that users can play while online. The Joomla Casino is a set of extensions that provides baccarat, slots, video poker, roulette, and blackjack (shown in Figure 4-30) to the Joomla system. It is a game framework that is being continually extended to include new games, so by the time you read this, there may be additional games included in the extension.

When you install these games, you must first install a base component called `com_casinobase` that holds a shared library of program routines. After that component is installed, you can add one or more of the casino games. These games are also available in Flash versions for better presentation and more interactivity.

The Roulette game offers perhaps the most visually thrilling game play. These games can be addictive, so you might find Web visitors returning again and again.

Handling a Quiz

A quiz can take many forms. It might be as simple as a riddle, or as complex as a dry run for the SAT. The Quiz plug-ins for Joomla show great potential in applications of education — both formal education and self-education. Imagine an English teacher who could put a simple grammar self-test online for students to practice before the big test. Or, perhaps a tourist Web site promoting the virtues of Peru that provides a simple quiz as to the location of the largest provinces.

The Quiz 2.0 component shown in Figure 4-31 enables you to create a variety of different types of quizzes. The quiz may contain questions that are simple yes/no or true/false answers, as well as multiple choice (including a multiple selection option). The completed quiz is automatically scored, and pass or fail will be displayed based on the setting in the Administrator interface.

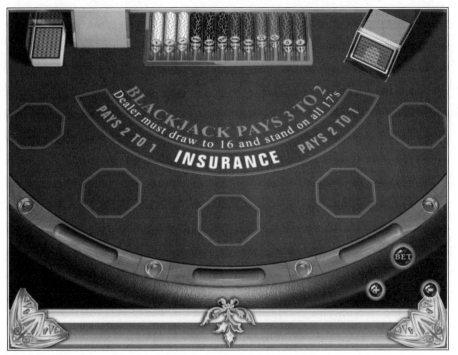

Figure 4-30: The Joomla Casino Blackjack has a beautiful user interface.

Figure 4-31: The Quiz 2.0
front end shows the currently
selected quiz.

The Quiz 2.0 Administrator interface has two options: edit quizzes and edit quiz categories. The quiz editing will let you create a new quiz or edit an existing one.

The statistics of the pass/fail, number of quizzes taken, and score ratios of quizzes are available by referencing the URL such as the following:

```
www.example.com/index.php?option=com_quiz&task=stats
```

The extension can present quizzes in multiple languages, including English, Italian, French, Danish, Norwegian, and Swedish.

Summary

Joomla extensions are one of the key reasons for the widespread adoption of the Joomla CMS. Numbering more than 1600, these extensions offer every type of feature that may be added to the Joomla system. This chapter has provided a survey of a variety of extensions that increase the Joomla capabilities by doing the following:

❑   Improving the core features of the Web site and supplementing the current Administrator interface functions with abilities such as broader search options, specialized WYSIWYG editors, Web-based file management, automated sitemap creation, and much more.

❑   Augmenting the organization and e-commerce capabilities of Joomla through extensions that provide shopping carts, subscription limitations, project management, timesheet tracking, and auction presentation.

❑   Refining the site content capabilities by allowing a Joomla site to host media such as podcasts or picture galleries.

❑   Fashioning site interactivity through commenting systems, chat, guestbooks, and even wiki capabilities.

❑   Adding sport league tracking and games to broaden a site's audience appeal.

There are hundreds of extensions available, and it is likely you can find an extension to meet most needs. However, if you need something special, or you see a feature that is not available that you want to develop, you can write your own extensions. Chapter 5 starts you down that path as it explains design development of the simplest type of extension — the module.

5

Developing Simple Extensions: Modules

While the huge library of existing Joomla extensions can fill most needs, many sites will eventually need some custom programming. This often means using a custom extension to display information in a specific fashion. Modules are the simplest form of extensions in Joomla, and they are generally either display-only or accept only minimal user input.

Modules are used in Joomla for most of the basic front page display, including the menus, the banners, the search inputs, and polls. Often, a module will provide the presentation aspects of an associated component. For example, the *search module* displays the text fields for input that is passed to the *search component* that actually runs the query. Since modules are primarily display-only, they are usually very easy to implement and deploy.

This chapter shows you how to create three modules:

❑ The first module displays a simple Hello World greeting and provides a good foundation atop which you can build nearly any type of module.

❑ The second module uses a custom table in the database to display holiday greetings. If the current day matches one of the holiday dates stored in the database, the linked greeting appears inside the module.

❑ The third module uses the infrastructure provided by the Contacts component to retrieve and display a list of custom contact information.

As you progress through the construction of these components, you will learn how to use the Joomla Administrator interface to configure a module. You will also see how a module executes within the Joomla framework. Since modules are quick and simple to construct, you can solve many of your custom development problems by generating individualized modules with the specific functionality that you need.

Creating a Hello World Module

By constructing a Joomla module in its most primitive state, the fundamentals of the module system are revealed. For that reason, you will create a module that displays a simple Hello World greeting and add it to the system. This module can be used later as a foundation on which to build other components.

To begin, you will need to create a folder to hold the module. The folder name should always match the name of the module itself. It is common practice to use the prefix mod_ to make it clear exactly what type of code is contained within the folder. Therefore, create a folder named mod_helloworld at the root of your local drive. After the modules files are created, you will need to compress this folder into an archive file for later uploading.

Within the folder, create a text file named mod_helloworld.php in your text editor and enter the following code:

```php
<?php
/**
 * @version $Id: mod_hellojoomla.php 5203 2007-03-27 01:42:10Z Danr $
 * @package Joomla
 * @copyright Copyright (C) 2007 Dan Rahmel. All rights reserved.
 * @license GNU/GPL
 * This is a simple component to display a hello greeting.
 */

// no direct access
defined( '_JEXEC' ) or die( 'Restricted access' );

echo JText::_( 'Hello World!');
```

This module only executes two lines of code. The first line should be used in all of the extensions that you create, since it ensures that the Joomla system is calling the extension and not an external agent. That can prevent hackers from potentially hijacking your add-ons and using them to do things you never intended. The second code line uses the echo command to send a greeting to the user.

Note that the echo command that displays the Hello World is not a standard text output. Instead, the underscore (_) method of the Joomla class JText is called to provide the text output. JText is a class accesses the translation services for any language packs installed to the current Joomla system. If a translation of the text sent to the underscore method is available in the language currently selected for display, that translation will be sent to the user browser.

For example, let's say that the method was passed the text "Hello." Let's also say that there was a Spanish translation for the word in the language pack and Spanish was chosen for the display language. Then the returned string would read "Hola." Therefore, if one of the installed language modules has the equivalent text of the Hello World greeting, it will appear in that language.

If the text is not found in the selected site language, the underscore method simply returns the text passed to it. Note that the method is case-insensitive and does not translate punctuation.

It is a good idea to use this class for your text printing so that if your module becomes popular, language pack creators can generate the proper native equivalents to display your extension in their target languages without the need for a custom modification to your extension.

Next, you will need to make an XML descriptor file that tells the Joomla system how to install the module. Create a new file in your text editor, enter the following code, and save the file as mod_helloworld.xml:

```
<?xml version="1.0" encoding="utf-8"?>
<install type="module" version="1.5.0">
      <name>Hello World</name>
      <author>Dan Rahmel</author>
      <creationDate>March 2007</creationDate>
      <copyright>(C) 2007 Dan Rahmel. All rights reserved.</copyright>
      <license>GNU/GPL</license>
      <authorEmail>admin@joomlajumpstart.org</authorEmail>
      <authorUrl>www.joomlajumpstart.org</authorUrl>
      <version>1.0.0</version>
      <description>Hello World module</description>
      <files>
            <filename module="mod_helloworld">mod_helloworld.php</filename>
      </files>
</install>
```

The descriptor file tells the Joomla system the "what" and "where" of the installation. In the <install> tag, the type attribute instructs Joomla that this installation holds a module. The version attribute indicates that the model is compatible with Joomla 1.5 and above. The <name> element specifies the name of the first module instance of this module type to create. The <description> element holds the text that will appear in the Extension Manager after the installation is complete. The <filename> element shows the module attribute that defines the module type from which any instances of the module will be created.

That's all you need for the Hello World module. However, unlike templates that can be simply dropped into the proper folder, modules must be registered with the Joomla system to be recognized. For that reason, you will need to create a ZIP archive that holds the modules, and then install it via the Extension Manager.

Creating the archive will vary depending on your operating system. On the Windows platform and the MacOS, you can right-click on the folder and create an archive from it. On Linux, see your manual for the best application or command line utility to create the archive.

When you register a new module, information about it is stored in the jos_modules table of the Joomla database. This table holds the name of the module, registration information, parameter settings, published status, module positioning, and module ordering. Changes to the XML file after installation will not directly affect information about the module shown in the Administrator interface (with the sole exception of the parameter definitions that continue to access the XML file). To make changes to this information, you will need to modify the Joomla table through the MySQL interface or reinstall the module.

Open the Joomla Administrator in a browser window, and go to the Extension Manager. You will need to select the Install/Uninstall option, select the module archive for upload, and click the Install button to add the module to your system. Once the process has completed, open the Module Manager and you should see your new module in the list, as shown in Figure 5-1.

The entries listed in the Module Manager are actually *module instances*. The module you created is actually known as a *module type,* which acts as a template to create one or more instances. In the far-right column of the figure, you can see that the module type for the new installation is mod_helloworld.

121

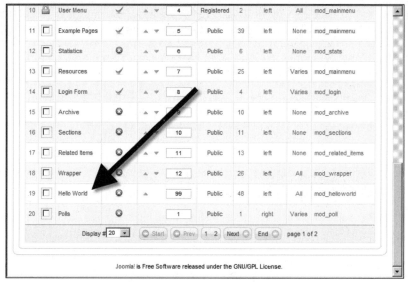

Figure 5-1: The Hello World module appears in the module list.

You could create additional instances of this or other types of modules by clicking the New button in the Module Manager and selecting the desired type. Multiple instances of a module are particularly useful if they have parameter settings that change their presentation. The mod_mainmenu module, for example, is the module type that. once the parameter has been set to connect to a particular menu, displays all of that particular menu's options.

If you open the /modules folder of your Joomla installation, you will see the new folder holding your module is installed there. If you are developing a new module, you will need to access the installed source file to modify it as you work on the project. On the Windows platform, the directory path to the new module may be similar to this:

```
C:\Program Files\Apache Software Foundation\Apache2.2
     \htdocs\modules\mod_helloworld
```

By default, new modules are unpublished. Click on the red "X" in the Published column to toggle the Hello World module to be published and available for use. Once it has been published, you will need to check the module settings to ensure that the module will appear in the place where you want it. By default, the module will appear in the left template position. That is the location where it should appear, but let's check to make sure things are set up properly.

Click on the name of the module in the Module Manager to open the module settings window. You can see that the Position setting is set to the proper location (see Figure 5-2). The Module Order setting shows that the module will appear as the third item in the panel after the Main Menu, so you will know where to look for it on the front page.

Bring up a browser window to display the front page of your Joomla site. If you look under the Main Menu listings, you should now see the greeting from your new module (see Figure 5-3). This Hello World module shows the fundamentals of module design and deployment. You can use it as the basis for more advanced modules. For now, since it doesn't provide a more useful function, you should unpublish it in the Module Manager so that it doesn't clutter your site interface.

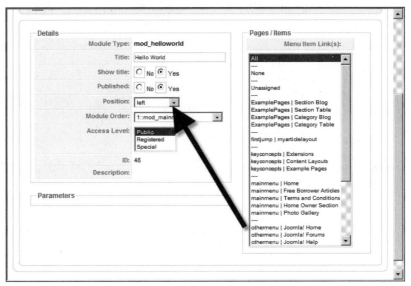

Figure 5-2: Ensure that the new module appears in the left position.

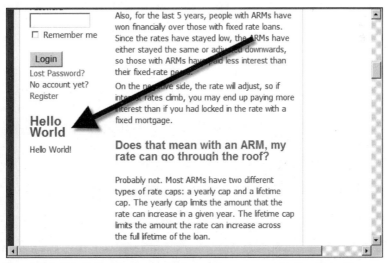

Figure 5-3: The Hello World greeting should appear under the Main Menu list in the panel.

Creating a Holiday Greetings Module

Few real-world modules are as simple as the Hello World example. Often a module requires some type of database access to read data or content from the Joomla database for display. One simple (but useful) module is a Holiday Greetings module. This module will check the current date and determine if it matches any of the holidays stored in a table. If it does, a special holiday greeting will be automatically displayed. If not, the day and date will appear in the module panel.

For this example, begin module creation the same way you did with the Hello World module, by creating a folder at the root of your local drive. Name the folder /mod_holidaygreeting. This folder will mirror the folder that will be stored in the /modules directory of the Joomla system once the module is installed.

Creating the XML Descriptor File

Create a file named mod_holidaygreeting.xml in the /mod_holidaygreeting folder and use your text editor to enter the following code:

```xml
<?xml version="1.0" encoding="utf-8"?>
<install type="module" version="1.5.0">
    <name>Holiday Greetings module</name>
    <author>Dan Rahmel</author>
    <creationDate>March 2007</creationDate>
    <copyright>(C) 2007 Dan Rahmel. All rights reserved.</copyright>
    <license>http://www.gnu.org/copyleft/gpl.html GNU/GPL</license>
    <authorEmail>admin@joomlajumpstart.org</authorEmail>
    <authorUrl>www.joomlajumpstart.org</authorUrl>
    <version>1.0.0</version>
    <description>The Holiday Greetings module will display a holiday
        greeting based on the current date. Holiday dates are stored
        within the jos_holidays table and can be augmented or
        modified through the MySQL interface.</description>
    <files>
        <filename module="mod_holidaygreeting"
            >mod_holidaygreeting.php</filename>
    </files>
    <params>
        <param name="greeting" type="text" default="Enjoy the holiday!"
            label="Greeting"
            description=
             "The text that will appear after the holiday message." />
        <param name="boldgreeting" type="radio" default="0"
            label="Bold Greeting" description=
             "Determines whether greeting will be bold or not.">
            <option value="0">No</option>
            <option value="1">Yes</option>
        </param>
    </params>
</install>
```

In contrast to the earlier descriptor file, you might notice at the bottom of the file that there are two parameters described in the <params> field. These parameters (greeting and boldgreeting) are good examples of the type of administrative settings that should be made available by most modules. Once loaded into the Joomla system, these parameters will appear for modification within the Module Manager interface. Module parameters allow an administrator to configure the module's appearance or functions without the need to modify the module's source code.

The parameters are of two different types: `text` and `radio`. The `text` parameter will accept a string up to 255 characters. The `radio` value simply stores a selection among a list of several parameters. In this case, it is a simple no (value 0) or yes (value 1) selection. These parameter selections are set in the Module Manager interface and stored in the Joomla database.

Parameters specified in the XML descriptor file can be one of up to 17 types. The Joomla system handles the display and modification code for any of these parameter styles. The other Joomla types include `category`, `editors`, `filelist`, `folderlist`, `helpsites`, `imagelist`, `languages`, `list`, `menu`, `menuitem`, `password`, `radio`, `section`, `spacer`, `text`, and `textarea`.

Creating the Module Code File

In the `/mod_holidaygreeting` folder, create a new file named `mod_holidaygreeting.php` by using your text editor to enter the following code:

```php
<?php
/**
* @version $Id: mod_holidaygreetings.php 5203 2006-09-27 02:45:14Z Danr $
* @package Joomla
* @copyright Copyright (C) 2007 Dan Rahmel. All rights reserved.
* @license GNU/GPL
* This is a module to display a holiday greeting on the proper day.
*/

// no direct access
defined( '_JEXEC' ) or die( 'Restricted access' );
?>
<div><small>
<?php
    echo JText::_( '<p>Today is ' );
    echo( date("l, F dS Y.") . '</p>' );
?>
</small></div>
<div>
<?php
    $myGreeting = $params->get('greeting', 0);
    $boldSetting = $params->get('boldgreeting', 0);
    if ($boldSetting == 1) {
        $bb = "<b>";
        $be = "</b>";
    } else {
        $bb = "";
        $be = "";
    }

    $curDay = date("d");
```

125

```
$curMonth = date("m");

$db            =& JFactory::getDBO();
$query = "SELECT *" .
              "\n FROM jos_greetings"   .
              "\n WHERE holidayMonth = " .
              intval($curMonth) . " and " .
              "holidayDay = " . intval($curDay);
$db->setQuery($query);
$holidays = $db->loadObjectList();
if(count($holidays)) {
    foreach ($holidays as $holiday) {
        echo JText::_( '<p>' . $bb .
            $holiday->greeting . $be . '</p>');
    }
    echo JText::_( '<p>' . $myGreeting . '</p>');
} else {
    echo JText::_( '<p>Welcome!</p>');
}

?>
</div>
```

This code is quite a bit more complicated than the single-line Hello World module. The code begins by outputting the text of the current day as `<small>` text. The next code section retrieves the values of the two parameters that can be set by the administrator in the Module Manager. If the `boldgreeting` parameter is set to Yes, then the variables bold begin ($bb) and bold end ($be) are set to contain the HTML tags to bold the text. Next, the current day and month are stored into variables so that they can be accessed later.

At this point, the setup is complete and the database retrieval of the holidays can begin. First, the $db variable is set to hold a reference to the current database object. Then, a variable is created to hold the query that will retrieve any greetings for the current day and month. Note that the `intval()` function is used around the values retrieved by the `date()` function. The date function returns the numbers of single-digit months such as January with a leading zero (January = 01). Since the values of months are stored as integers in the database table (January = 1), the `intval` function will shave off the prefix, if necessary, and avoid any confusion.

The query is then set in the current database object, and the `loadObjectList()` function executes the query against the database to return a list of values. The `count()` function checks if there are any holidays on the present date and, if not, displays a simple Welcome greeting. If there are greetings, it outputs each one as a paragraph and follows the list with the greeting set in the module's parameters.

When you have completed entering the code for the file, create a ZIP or TAR archive with both files. Use the Extension Manager to upload and install the ZIP archive of the component to the Joomla system. If the Holiday Greetings module is successfully installed, you will see the success page with the module instructions on it, as shown in Figure 5-4.

Before you can use the module, however, you must still create the data that the module references to retrieve the holiday dates and the greetings associated with them.

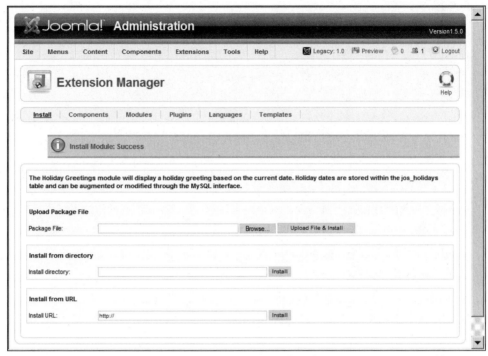

Figure 5-4: After successful installation, the description field from the XML descriptor file is displayed.

Creating the Table and Storing Sample Data

To create a database table where the greetings are stored, you can use the graphical interface of the MySQL Administrator application to set up the table quickly and easily. The table should be named jos_greetings and should have three columns: id (auto-increment primary key integer field), greeting (varchar field), holidayMonth (integer field), and holidayDay (integer field).

Alternately, you can use the following SQL code from the command line to create the table:

```
CREATE TABLE jos_greetings (
   id int(10) unsigned NOT NULL auto_increment,
   greeting varchar(45) NOT NULL,
   holidayMonth int(10) unsigned NOT NULL,
   holidayDay int(10) unsigned NOT NULL,
   PRIMARY KEY  (`id`)
);
```

Once the table has been created, populate it with a few holidays that you want to display for your users. You can right-click on the table in MySQL Administrator and select the Edit Table Data option from the context menu to add the new data. Be sure to add an entry for the current date so that you can test the module and ensure that it works properly.

127

If you want to insert the data from the command line, you can use the following SQL code, which will insert a few common holidays:

```
INSERT INTO `jos_greetings` (`id`,`greeting`,
 `holidayMonth`,`holidayDay`) VALUES
(1,'Merry Christmas!',12,25),
(2,'Happy New Year',1,1),
(3,'Happy President\'s Day!',2,19);
```

With active data in the table, install the ZIP archive of the component in the Extension Manager. If the Holiday Greetings module is successfully installed, you will see the success page with the module instructions on it.

Configuring the Module

Go to the Module Manager and click on the Holiday Greetings module. If you scroll to the lower part of the page, you will see the module parameters that you defined in the XML file, as shown in Figure 5-5. Set the greeting to any text you want and turn on the option to display the greeting in bold.

It would be helpful if the greeting appeared first in the module order at the top of the column — before any other module in the `left` position. To set the order, look at the list of modules in the Module Manager. The second drop-down menu at the top of the screen allows you to filter by module position. Select the `left` position, and you should see only those modules. In the `Order` column, click the up arrow on the Holiday Greetings module until it is located in the number 1 position, as shown in Figure 5-6. Alternately, you can enter the number **0** in the Order field and click on the small disk icon at the top of the column that represents the Save Order function.

Now that the module has been set up properly, load the front page of the site into your browser. On the left side of the page, you should see the holiday greeting, as shown in Figure 5-7.

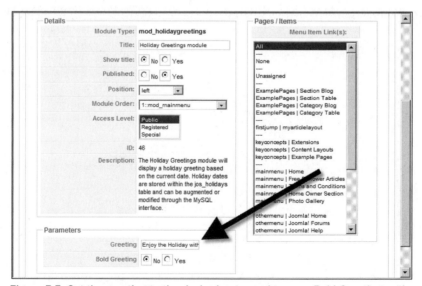

Figure 5-5: Set the greeting to the desired entry and turn on Bold Greeting option.

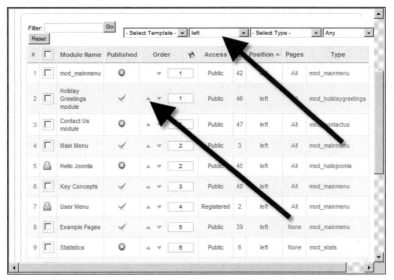

Figure 5-6: Re-order the Holiday Greetings module to the first position.

In the current implementation, the font styles for presentation are specified in the module file. It is generally preferable to specify module output using the common styles that are defined by the template CSS file (such as the `moduletable` class). If the template styles are used, the presentation formatting of the module output will match that of the rest of the site.

If you use this module on your site, you should add greetings for the day before the holiday, as well as the holiday itself. You can create a greeting entry to precede the holiday (such as a Christmas Eve entry).

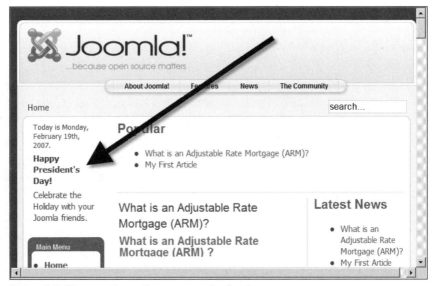

Figure 5-7: The greeting will appear on the front page.

129

Creating a Contact Us Module

Many of the utilities that are included with the Joomla system can be extended for site-specific uses. Since all of the primary data is stored in the central MySQL database, it is very easy to design extensions that can retrieve and modify the Joomla data store. In fact, the Joomla framework encapsulates database interaction to make communication easy and minimize security loopholes. Through the framework, a module can access the data store with only a few lines of code.

For example, Joomla has a built-in contact manager component that can have records linked directly to registered users. A category could be created to file certain contact records available for public access. These public contacts could be automatically retrieved and displayed in the Contact Us portion of the Web site. A custom module could display the information anywhere on the Joomla page. Updates to the contact database would be reflected automatically on the Contact Us page, since the information is drawn from the same place.

To create this type of module, you'll first need a Public category where contacts can be filed. The Contacts component has a menu area under the Components menu in the Administrator interface. Select the Categories option in this menu. The default Joomla installation includes only a single category titled Contacts.

Click on the New button to add a new category. Enter general parameters such as those shown in Figure 5-8. Make sure you set Published to Yes so that contacts can be selected into this category. Click the Save button to write the new category into the Joomla database.

Figure 5-8: Create a new public category where the public contacts will be filed.

The Contact Us module will use data access in a similar way to the Holiday Greetings module. However, in this case, the data table has already been created by the Joomla system. All of the contact information is stored in the `jos_contact_details` table. However, the information for every contact is stored in this table — not just the Public contacts that the module will display.

The module will need to query the database and obtain only the records that are in the Public category. To create this query, the module will need to know the `category id` of the Public category to display. Fortunately, the `id` is easy to obtain from the Contacts Categories screen.

After you have saved your new category, the list of categories will be displayed. In the far-right column, you should see the `category id` of the Public category, as shown in Figure 5-9. Write down this number for later when you configure the module.

To display a list of public contacts, you must file some users in the public category so that they can be displayed by the module. Use the Contacts menu option under the Contacts menu to display the current contacts user list. Either create a new user (see Figure 5-10) or select an existing user and set the category for the record to the Public one that was just created. Click the Save button to write the contact settings into the table.

With everything properly configured, the module can be implemented to use this information. Create a folder named `mod_contactus`. It will hold the module code file and the XML descriptor file for the module.

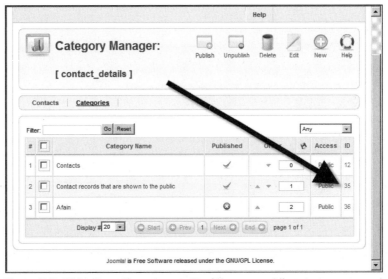

Figure 5-9: Write down the category ID of the new public category.

Figure 5-10: Create new contact and put it in the public category.

In the `mod_contactus` folder, use your text editor to create a file named `mod_contactus.php` and enter the following code:

```php
<?php
/**
 * @version $Id: mod_contactus.php 5203 2006-09-27 02:45:14Z Danr $
 * @package Joomla
 * @copyright Copyright (C) 2007 Dan Rahmel. All rights reserved.
 * @license GNU/GPL, see LICENSE.php
 * This module displays the public contact information.
 */

// no direct access
defined( '_JEXEC' ) or die( 'Restricted access' );
?>
<div style="border: 1px solid black; padding: 5px;">
<h3>Contact Us</h3>
<?php
    $publiccat = $params->get('publiccat', 0);

    $db          =& JFactory::getDBO();
    $query = "SELECT *" .
             "\n FROM jos_contact_details" .
             "\n WHERE catid = " .
             intval($publiccat);
    $db->setQuery($query);
    $contacts = $db->loadObjectList();
    if(count($contacts)) {
        foreach ($contacts as $contact) {
            echo JText::_( '<p><strong>' . $contact->name .
                ', </strong>');
```

```
                        echo JText::_( '<small>' . $contact->con_position .
                                ', </small>');
                        echo JText::_( '<small>' . $contact->telephone .
                                ', </small>');
                        echo JText::_( '<small>' . $contact->email_to .
                                '</small></p>');
                }
        } else {
                echo JText::_( '<p>Email help@mycom.com</p>');
        }

    ?>
    </div>
```

The code for the module is structured much like the code for the Holiday Greetings module. In this case, the first <div> tag has a style attribute that places a box around the module.

When executed, the module first retrieves the parameter publiccat, which will hold the value of the category id of the Public category. The module queries the database for all of the contacts stored in the jos_contact_details table that have catid column values that match the Public id. The result set is loaded into the $contacts list and processed, outputting the name, position, telephone number, and email address of that contact record. If no Public contacts are found, the email address of the help desk is published.

To complete the module, the XML descriptor file must be created. Create a file named mod_contactus .xml in the folder, and enter the following code:

```
<?xml version="1.0" encoding="utf-8"?>
<install type="module" version="1.5.0">
    <name>Contact Us module</name>
    <author>Dan Rahmel</author>
    <creationDate>March 2007</creationDate>
    <copyright>(C) 2007 Dan Rahmel. All rights reserved.</copyright>
    <license>http://www.gnu.org/copyleft/gpl.html GNU/GPL</license>
    <authorEmail>admin@joomlajumpstart.org</authorEmail>
    <authorUrl>www.joomlajumpstart.org</authorUrl>
    <version>1.0.0</version>
    <description>The Contact Us module will display the contact info
            for contacts filed in the public contacts category. Select
            the public contacts category in the Module Manager
            interface for this module.</description>
    <files>
        <filename module="mod_contactus"
            >mod_contactus.php</filename>
    </files>
    <params>
        <param name="publiccat" type="text"
            label="Public Contacts Category ID"
            description="Contact records in this category will be displayed." />
    </params>
</install>
```

You may have noticed that the `<description>` field contains configuration instructions. Since this description is displayed when the module is installed correctly, it is useful to provide the user with any configuration guidance that might be needed for the module.

For this module, there is only a single parameter: `publiccat`. This parameter is accessed by the module to create the query necessary to return the contacts filed in the Public category. If the module needed the selection of a traditional Joomla category, the parameter could be set to the type `category` and the Joomla system would automatically populate a drop-down list of available categories that could be chosen from.

Archive this folder as you have done with the previous modules, and use the Extension Manager to install it into the system. When it is successfully installed, go to the Module Manager to set the category ID that will be used by the query.

In the Module Manager, click on the Contact Us module entry to open the module parameter editing screen. In the Category ID field, enter the Public Contacts Category ID that you wrote down earlier, as shown in Figure 5-11. Click the Save button to store the parameters.

Display the front page of your site in a browser window. You should now see a list of contact information for any contact entries that are filed in the Public category, as shown in Figure 5-12. This module is an excellent technology demonstration of the ability to access the actual Joomla-stored system data. Take some time to look through the various tables in the Joomla database so that you can find the location of the data you might want to address for implementation in a module.

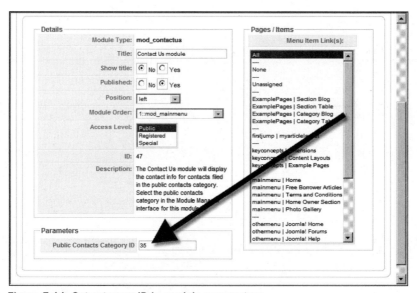

Figure 5-11: Set category ID in module parameters.

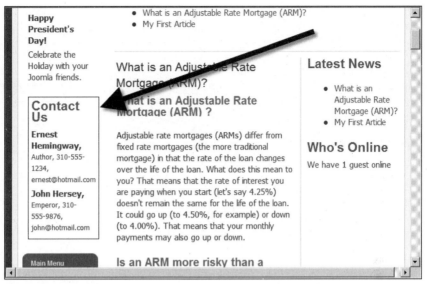

Figure 5-12: Contact information will appear on the front page.

Summary

Joomla modules provide the simplest and most straightforward method of extending Joomla with custom programming. Modules are not only easy to author but the single ZIP archive installation makes them easy to distribute. Multiple modules may appear on a single page, so nearly any small functionality that needs to be added to Joomla can be added as a module. If you need a good deal of user interaction, however, it would be best to look at creating a component such as one of those detailed in Chapter 6.

This chapter has provided an introduction to creating modules and presented the steps for the following:

❑ Creating a Hello World module that supplied a basic foundation for more complex module development.

❑ Implementing a module that accessed a custom database to retrieve holiday dates, check for holidays that match the current date, and display the associated greeting.

❑ Developing a module that adapted the existing Joomla contact component functionality to provide a custom display of public information.

Joomla modules are the simplest form of Joomla extension. In Chapter 6, you'll learn how to create a custom component. Component development will likely lie at the heart of most of your future professional Joomla programming efforts.

6

Advanced Extensions: Components

In Chapter 5, you developed a few simple extensions to grasp the basic aspects of Joomla's extensibility. You were instructed to construct the various modules with a simple text editor, since the code was rudimentary and already debugged. Professional development, however, requires far greater control of the project. For example, to develop a multi-module and component-based shopping cart application, a developer would need to coordinate multiple development files, and may need to work in conjunction with other programmers.

This chapter outlines the work process of creating an advanced Joomla extension. You will be using a professional development system (Eclipse), source code control (through Subversion), and generating project documentation (through phpDocumentor). By following this development process from beginning to end, you will have a better idea of how professional Joomla applications can be created in an enterprise situation.

Setting Up a Development System

Chapter 5 has you use any text editor to create the program files and save them in the Joomla system. The quick-and-dirty use of text files is one of the advantages of creating programs for a PHP system, since you aren't locked into the overhead and complexity of using a complete integrated development environment (IDE).

Approaching the development process by the seat of your pants is fine when you need to throw together a simple module or make a small edit. But any project that is even medium sized (as the creation of most components will be) is a job that can be simplified by using more powerful development tools. Additionally, if the project is being handled by a team of even two members, bringing professional tools to bear may be the difference between completing a project on schedule and having it drag on endlessly.

With that in mind, you'll be using two professional-grade development tools in this chapter to create the example projects. The IDE known as Eclipse has capabilities that far surpass a simple text editor. It is project-based and has a plug-in architecture that benefits Joomla development with plug-ins to support Subversion (SVN), PHP coding, XML, and HTML file definition. SVN is a source code control system that streamlines group development and makes it possible to have an excellent source code archive, even if there is only a sole developer working on the project. Using code control is essential for all but the smallest projects.

You may already be using a development system that suits your needs and have no desire to switch to something else. If so, that's fantastic. Finding a development system you like is like finding a car you like — it's a matter of personal choice. However, you should still skim the sections that detail Eclipse. You may find a new way to use your existing IDE that you haven't considered previously.

Adopting Source Code Control with SVN

Source code control (SCC) should be one of the mostly widely used technologies by software developers. Sadly, many people don't understand the advantages of SCC, and development houses often don't demand its adoption. So, it remains disregarded. Essentially, SCC is like an archivist for source code files, logging all changes made to each file. The changes saved into an archive may be later consulted and, if necessary, the older version can be restored.

One of the most popular programs for SCC or revision control is *Subversion* (SVN). SVN is a comprehensive server-and-client pair that provides local and network-based revision control for all types of development files. Several developers can work on the same project at the same time. The system handles all merges, and the system provides an interface for examining conflicts and choosing resolutions to those conflicts.

The revision control system that is slightly more popular than SVN is Concurrent Versions System (CVS). SVN was designed to become a successor to CVS because some of the design decisions made when CVS was born created inherent limitations to the system. Despite any foundational handicaps, CVS has gone through significant improvements and maintains its popularity. I use CVS for day-to-day use, primarily for historical reasons and the legacy archives that I have from past projects. However, the Joomla development is all occurring under SVN control, so Joomla developers benefit most if they adopt it for their revision control.

Here are a number of common problems you may encounter while developing an application and how SVN would solve them:

❑ Many changes have been made to a new version when it's discovered that a major feature no longer works — and you can't figure out why. With SVN, you can simply look back at the source code and see what changes were made to a section of code. If necessary, you can have the archive recreate the complete project source code of the last working version, which can then be debugged or monitored to determine the difference from the new version execution.

❑ The current machine crashes, and you don't have a recent backup. Since SVN is server-based, it's common to run it as an archival application on another machine. Committing current file changes to the archive is as simple as right-clicking on the file or folder and then activating the "check in" feature to store the changes. This convenience makes backups much more likely, even for slovenly programmers.

❑ Multiple people are working on the same project, and they need a way to coordinate the work and changes. Applications such as SVN were born out of the need for open source developers who work at different times and places but must have a consistent way of combining changes without breaking the project.

❑ A feature that was removed four months ago is needed again. You don't have to dig through system backups for the proper file, because a version has been tagged within SVN. Simply by accessing the version by name or date, the last source that included the deleted feature can be quickly and easily retrieved.

❑ The stripped-down version of this routine ran much better before all the revisions, so a developer wants to refactor a routine, starting with the initial bare-bones implementation. Retrieving an old version from SCC is painless.

❑ A company is developing a new version of an application that requires drastic changes, but the older version must still be supported with updates and bug fixes. SVN can elegantly manage what is known as a "fork" so that the new version can be created while leaving the older version in place for continued development.

These few examples provide just a handful of situations where SCC can save the day. These situations don't even touch on the potential of refining later development by allowing a historical postmortem of a project to be completed, or the legal protection afforded by a thorough record of development to defend against accusations of code theft.

Installing SVN

The SVN system can be installed in several different ways. If you prefer a command line interface, you can install the SVN core system after downloading from the following URL:

    http://subversion.tigris.org/

If you would prefer a GUI front end, you can use one of these implementations:

❑ *TortoiseSVN* — The most popular SVN implementation on the Windows operating system. TortoiseSVN (http://tortoisesvn.tigris.org) integrates with the Explorer interface so that all functions are available directly at the file/folder level through the right-click context menu in the operating system.

❑ *eSvn* — A Qt-based Subversion client can be found at http://esvn.umputun.com.

❑ *JSVN* — A proof-of-concept Java Swing client can be found at http://jsvn.alternatecomputing.com.

❑ *kdesvn* — Another SVN client for KDE can be found at www.alwins-world.de/wiki/programs/kdesvn.

❑ *psvn.el* — An SVN interface for Emacs can be found at www.xsteve.at/prg/emacs.

❑ *QSvn* — Another Qt-based SVN client can be found at http://ar.oszine.de/projects/qsvn.

❑ *RapidSVN* — A cross-platform (Linux-Win32-Mac OS X) GUI front end written in C++ using the wxWidgets framework can be found at `http://rapidsvn.tigris.org`.

❑ *SCPlugin* — A Mac OS X plug-in for the Finder can be found at `http://scplugin.tigris.org`.

❑ *SmartSVN* — A cross-platform (Linux-Mac OS X-Win32) client for SVN can be found at `www.syntevo.com/smartsvn`. This is available as a free Foundation version and as a commercial Professional version. It makes use of the SVNKit library to provide a pure Java implementation of SVN.

❑ *Subcommander* — A cross-platform (Linux-Win32-Mac OS X) GUI front end written in C++ using the Qt framework can be found at `http://subcommander.tigris.org`.

❑ *svnX* — A Mac OS X GUI front end to command line SVN can be found at `www.lachoseinteractive.net/en/community/subversion/svnx`.

❑ *tkSVN* — A Tcl/Tk-based combined SVN and CVS client can be found at `www.twobarleycorns.net/tkcvs.html`.

❑ *WorkBench* — Cross-platform (written with wxPython and pysvn) that provides an alternative object-oriented-style Python binding for the SVN library can be found at `http://pysvn.tigris.org`.

❑ *ZigVersion* — A commercial Mac OS X SVN client can be found at `http://zigversion.com`.

❑ *Syncro* SVN Client — A cross-platform front end can be found at `www.syncrosvnclient.com`.

I recommend that you install TortoiseSVN if you're just getting started. It integrates perfectly with the Windows operating system and allows you to right-click on any file or folder to access the TortoiseSVN menu. Files can be updated and downloaded from the repository with a single click. You can download TortoiseSVN here:

```
http://tortoisesvn.tigris.org
```

The installation process is a simple three-step wizard. Once you install the application, you can right-click in any Explorer window. If you don't have any files or folders selected in an Explorer window, the first items in the File menu will provide access to all of the application functions.

Creating a SVN Repository

Any SCC system needs a repository that acts like a vault to hold the current and archival copies of the files that have been registered with the application. For a single developer, a repository can simply be created as a folder on the local drive. Once the folder is created, SVN can be selected to register it as a repository, and it immediately creates the files and folders that will be needed by the application for housekeeping of the archive.

Create a folder and name it `SVN_Repository`. This folder may be located on your local drive or, for backup possibilities, may be located on a network drive that is scheduled for automated backup. If you would prefer to set up a SVN Server, you can easily find instructions on that process on the SVN site, although the configurations (particularly in regard to security) are beyond the scope of this book.

Right-click on the folder and, from the context menu, select the TortoiseSVN ➪ Create repository here... option. You will be asked to select the repository type, as shown in Figure 6-1. Leave the default selection and click the OK button. The system should let you know that the repository was created successfully.

Because SVN may be integrated with many development systems (most particularly, Eclipse), you will be able to use this repository from within your development environment.

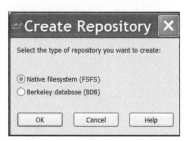

Figure 6-1: When creating a new repository, leave the default selection for the repository type.

Using Eclipse

Eclipse is a professional development system originally created by IBM before it was transferred to the open source community. Eclipse has a complete IDE, and an extension gives the system full support for PHP development. The Eclipse IDE is project-based, so all of the various files of a project can be coordinated.

There is a plug-in for the Eclipse development system called *Subclipse* that seamlessly integrates SVN version control into the development environment. With a simple right-click and menu selection within the environment, you can check in or check out files for your project.

Download EasyEclipse and Installation

Rather than downloading Eclipse and performing the necessary installation on all of the various plug-ins, it is generally a good idea to simply download the EasyEclipse for PHP distribution. This installer includes all of the key plug-ins for PHP development, including Subclipse. At the EasyEclipse Web site, you can find the installers for Windows, Mac OS X, and Linux:

```
www.easyeclipse.org
```

The package is more than 100MB, so it is best to download it using a fast connection. The installation procedure only requires two steps: accepting the license agreement and choosing the installation directory.

Configuring Eclipse

When you first run Eclipse, the application will prompt you for the location of your workspace folder. Select the "Use this as the default" option so that workspace will be used in future executions.

The first time Eclipse opens, it will bring up the Welcome screen, as shown in Figure 6-2.

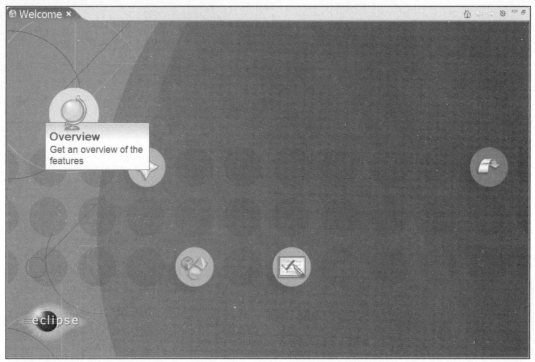

Figure 6-2: The Eclipse Welcome screen will take you through a brief tour of the interface and provides access to the complete tutorials.

Workbench Basics

In Eclipse, the development environment is called the *workbench*. The main workbench window appears as shown in Figure 6-3. The configuration of the workbench display is determined by the current *perspective*. A perspective governs which windows (or *parts*, as they are known in Eclipse terminology) are displayed and the current resources available. In the upper-right corner of the window, you can see the perspectives shortcut bar that allows switching between current perspectives, as well as opening other ones. The title bar shows which perspective is currently displayed. In this figure, the Resource perspective is being used.

You can create a new project from a variety of templates (such as Java, Static Web, PHP, XML, and so on), all of which include basic templates that cater to the type of project that is being created. The type you will be using for Joomla development will be a PHP project. Before you create a new project, it is useful for Joomla development that all project files have the security code that prevents the file from being executed outside of the Joomla framework.

To begin to familiarize yourself with Eclipse, modify the default PHP template to use the Joomla security code. Under the Window menu, select the Preferences option. The preferences are stored within a tree inside the window, as shown in Figure 6-4. Expand the PHPeclipse Web Development node, then expand the PHP node, and finally click on the Code Templates item.

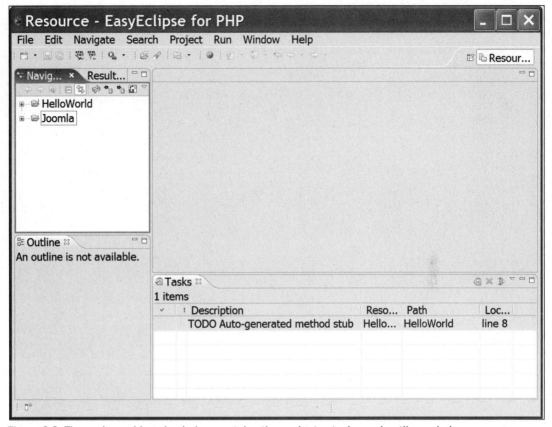

Figure 6-3: The main workbench window contains the navigator, tasks, and outlines windows.

In the right pane of the Preferences window, you can see all of the available template files for this type of project. Select the "New PHP files" item and click the Edit button. You can now add any code you want to be presented in a new file. In this case, enter the following code:

```
// no direct access
defined('_JEXEC') or die('Restricted access');
```

Click the OK button to save the changes. Now, any new PHP files created in Eclipse will automatically have run security included.

The Subclipse plug-in included with the EasyEclipse installation. If you have installed the standard Eclipse application, be sure to download and install Subclipse to give Eclipse access to the SVN functionality. Subclipse is available for download here:

```
http://subclipse.tigris.org
```

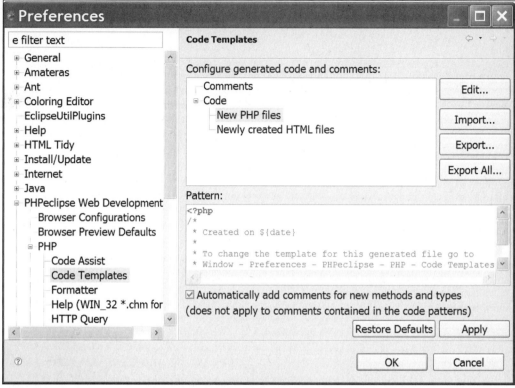

Figure 6-4: Preferences are organized under a tree structure.

Creating a Guestbook Component

A traditional Web application that will provide an excellent example of component creation is a guest-book. Guestbook extensions allow users to post comments that can be viewed by other visitors to the Web site. Most often, guestbook entries are compliments to the person that runs the system. They also may be suggestions for improvement or (hopefully rarely) criticism.

In this case, you'll learn how to create a guestbook component that features both a front end part for display of the guestbook entries and the submission form for new postings, as well as an administrative part for editing the existing entries. Most components feature both of these parts to provide a user interface for users and a way to maintain the system from the Administrator interface.

Begin by creating the Guestbook project in Eclipse. Create a new project by selecting File ⇨ New ⇨ PHP Project. When the wizard asks for a project name, set it to **com_guestbook**, as shown in Figure 6-5.

Protecting against Guestbook Spamming

Guestbook spamming is a common problem. Spammers use automated routines to locate guestbook features on Web sites and post spam links that lead to their sites. These serve two functions for the spammer: the generation of traffic if guestbook viewers click on the link and increased page ranking in the search engines because of the reference link.

This guestbook component protects against spammers by only letting registered users post to the guestbook, and using a regular expression to strip characters such as those that would allow active HTML (including links) to appear in the text of the entry.

However, if you intend to use this component to allow unregistered users to post entries, you should implement a CAPTCHA routine. The CAPTCHA will display a distorted series of numbers and letters within a graphic image and then ask the user to enter the characters into a text field for confirmation. Spam programs can't decipher the warped letters, so they are unable to post the spam.

Routines to generate a CAPTCHA (which stands for "Completely Automated Public Turing test to tell Computers and Humans Apart") image are freely available on the Web. Simply go to a search engine and enter **CAPTCHA PHP**. You will find many versions of example code. At the time of writing, one such free PHP routine is available at www.cryptographp.com.

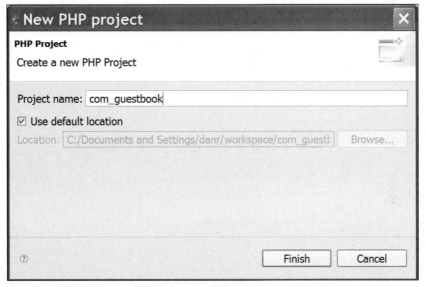

Figure 6-5: Create a new PHP Project in Eclipse, and name it com_guestbook.

The Front-End Guestbook Component

The front-end component is the display component. Since a component is a great deal more advanced than a module, a number of extensions (such as the Polls component) use a module to provide the front-end interface. However, modules can be limiting — especially if you want to allow interactive modification of data.

In the case of this guestbook component, the presentation will not only show all current entries, but below them will be a form to allow new entries, as shown in Figure 6-6. The front-end component will be accessible through a menu item.

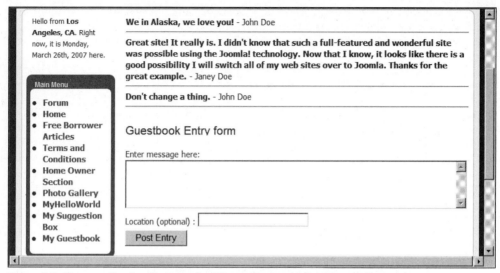

Figure 6-6: The guestbook will show all of the entries and who they are from.

As you construct the code, you may notice that all variables that are accepted (either from query string parameters or variables posted by a user) are obtained through the getVar() method, rather than through traditional PHP calls. The getVar routine provides valuable security features by scrutinizing the values submitted by the user. Hacker submissions (such as a SQL injection attack) are automatically detected and removed. Be sure to use this routine to take advantage of some of the security built into the Joomla framework.

> When a Web-based program accepts a variable from the outside world, you need to protect against a hacker using a technique called an injection attack. Most common is the SQL injection attack. In a SQL injection attack, a complete SQL statement is appended to a SQL instruction. For example, a form might accept the user input of a last name. The hacker enters a last name that reads something like "smith; Select * from PasswordTable" and submits the form. If the PHP code simply inserts the last name input into the SQL update statement, the hacker SQL code will execute and display the information in the table (in this case, a password list). For more information on this and other security concerns, see Chapter 14.

Creating the Front-End Component

Begin the coding for the project by creating the front-end component. This component will be displayed to registered users and will present all of the current guestbook entries. It will also allow the user to enter a new entry and submit it.

The component is broken into two functions: addEntry() and displayGuestbook(). The addEntry function is actually executed by the displayGuestbook function if the user enters form information and submits it. The displayGuestbook function queries the database and displays any entries it finds in the guestbook table. Following the entries, displayGuestbook includes a form that allows a user to make a new entry.

Note that the database query uses #__guestbook to reference the table name. Most likely, the table will be named jos_guestbook if the user has installed Joomla without changing the default prefix for tables. If the prefix has been changed, however, the database object will substitute the current prefix for the pound (#_) notation.

The guestbook table will not have been created the first time the component is displayed. Only after the first user posts an entry and the addEntry function is executed will the table exist on the server. Although the Create Table routine is executed each time against the MySQL server, if the table already exists on the server, the execution of the table creation command is aborted.

To create the component file, right-click in the Eclipse Navigator window on the project and select the New ⇨ PHP File option. Set the filename to guestbook.php. Enter the following code into the guestbook.php window:

```php
<?php
/**
* @version $Id: guestbook.php 5203 2007-06-15 02:45:14Z DanR $
* @copyright Copyright (C) 2007 Dan Rahmel. All rights reserved.
* @package Guestbook
* This component displays guestbook entries and allows the addition
* of entries from registered users.
*/

// no direct access
defined( '_JEXEC' ) or die( 'Restricted access' );

// Check the task parameter and execute appropriate function
switch( JRequest::getVar( 'task' )) {
    case 'add':
        addEntry();
        break;
    default:
        displayGuestbook();
        break;
}

// Process data received from form.
function addEntry()  {
    // Get reference to database object
    $db =& JFactory::getDBO();
    // Get user id for recording with entry.
    $user =& JFactory::getUser();
    $uid    = $user->get('id');


    // Get message and location from form posting values
    $fldMessage = JRequest::getVar('message') ;
    // Strip away anything that could be code, carriage returns, and so on
    $fldMessage = preg_replace("/[^a-zA-Z0-9 .?!$()\'\"]/", "", $fldMessage);
```

147

```php
        // Escape the message so it can be placed in the insert statement
        $fldMessage = "'" . $db->getEscaped($fldMessage) . "'";
        $fldLocation = "'" . $db->getEscaped(JRequest::getVar( 'location' )) . "'";
        // Obtain userIP and store with entry for security reasons
        $userIp = "'" . $_SERVER['REMOTE_ADDR'] . "'";

        $insertFields = "INSERT INTO #__guestbook " .
            "(message, created_by, location, userip) " .
            "VALUES (" . $fldMessage . "," . intval($uid) . "," .
                $fldLocation . "," . $userIp . ");";
        $db->setQuery( $insertFields, 0);
        $db->query();
        echo "<h1>Thanks for the entry!</h1>";
        echo "<a href=index.php?option=com_guestbook>" .
            "Return to guestbook</a>";
}

// Output a list of guestbook entries
function displayGuestbook() {
    $db =& JFactory::getDBO();
    // Query database and display guestbook entries
    $query = "SELECT a.message, u.name" .
    " FROM #__guestbook AS a" .
    " LEFT JOIN #__users AS u ON u.id=a.created_by" .
    " ORDER BY a.created DESC";

    $db->setQuery( $query, 0);
    // Make sure rows were returned before outputting
    if($rows = $db->loadObjectList()) {
        foreach ($rows as $row)
        {
            // Encode text to HTML formatting
            $rowMessage = htmlspecialchars($row->message, ENT_QUOTES);
            echo "<b>" . $rowMessage . "</b>";
            echo " - " . $row->name;
            // Put horizontal rules between entries
            echo "<hr />";
        }
    }
}

// Display guestbook entry form
?>
<h1 class="contentheading">Guestbook Entry form</h1>

<form id="form1" name="form1" method="post"
    action="index.php?option=com_guestbook&task=add">
  <p>Enter message here:<br />
    <textarea name="message" cols="60" rows="4" id="message"></textarea>
  </p>
  <p>
    <label>Location (optional) : </label>
    <input name="location" type="text" id="location" />
  </p>
  <p>
```

```
    <input type="submit" name="Submit" value="Post Entry" />
  </p>
</form>

<?php    } ?>
```

As soon as you've saved the file, Eclipse automatically evaluates the code contained in the file and updates the environment. For example, the Outline window on the right side of the workbench displays all functions or methods contained in the file, as shown in Figure 6-7. These outline entries act as hyperlinks, so if you click on one, the source code window will be immediately scrolled to that item. Click on the `displayGuestbook()` function. The editor window will highlight the function. Notice just to the left of the function header is a small circle with a minus (–) sign in it. If you click on the circle, the character will change to a plus (+) sign and the code will collapse as if it were the body of an outline. The ability to collapse code lines makes it convenient to manage large source files in Eclipse.

Click on the `displayGuestbook()` function. The editor window will highlight the function. Notice just to the left of the function header is a small circle with a minus (–) sign in it. If you click on the circle, the character will change to a plus (+) sign and the code will collapse as if it were the body of an outline. The ability to collapse code lines makes it convenient to manage large source files in Eclipse.

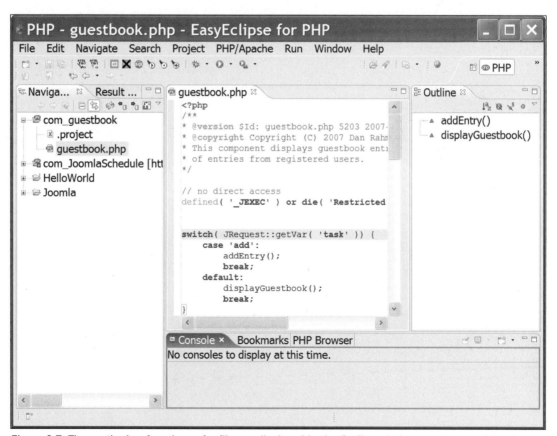

Figure 6-7: The method or functions of a file are displayed in the Outline window on the right side of the screen.

The Administrator Guestbook Editor Component

The Administrator portion of the component features three different execution paths. The `displayEntries()` function will create a display table of all the entries that exist in the guestbook table. Each entry in the table will include a link that can be used to edit that entry. Clicking on the link will recall the component, only this time with the `task` parameter of the query string is set to `edit`. That will cause the `editEntry()` function to execute and present a form with the values of the selected entry for modification. Once changes are complete and the administrator clicks the button to post the changes, the `updateEntry()` routine is executed to make the modifications to the table.

Create another new PHP File in the Eclipse interface, and name it `admin.guestbook.php`. This file will contain the administrative user interface for the component. Enter the following code:

```php
<?php
/**
 * @version $Id: guestbook.php 5203 2007-06-15 02:45:14Z DanR $
 * @copyright Copyright (C) 2007 Dan Rahmel. All rights reserved.
 * @package Guestbook
 * This component displays guestbook entries and allows the addition
 * of entries from registered users.
 */

// no direct access
defined( '_JEXEC' ) or die( 'Restricted access' );

// Check the task parameter and execute appropriate function
switch( JRequest::getVar( 'task' )) {
    case 'edit':
        editEntry();
        break;
    case 'update':
        updateEntry();
        break;
    default:
        displayEntries();
        break;
}

// Record data received from form posting
function updateEntry()  {
    // Set title in Administrator interface
    JMenuBar::title( JText::_( 'Update Guestbook Entry' ), 'addedit.png' );

    // Get reference to database object
    $db =& JFactory::getDBO();

    // Retrieve data from form
    $fldMessage = "'" . $db->getEscaped(JRequest::getVar('message')) . "'";
    $fldLocation = "'" . $db->getEscaped(JRequest::getVar( 'location' )) . "'";
    $fldID = "'" . $db->getEscaped(JRequest::getVar( 'id' )) . "'";

    // Record updates to jos_guestbook table
    $insertFields = "UPDATE #__guestbook " .
```

```
                " SET message=" . $fldMessage . ", " .
                " location=" . $fldLocation .
                " WHERE id = " . $fldID ;
        $db->setQuery( $insertFields, 0);
        $db->query();
        echo "<h3>Field updated!</h3>";
        echo "<a href='index.php?option=com_guestbook'>Return to guestbook list</a>";
    }


    // Display edit list of all guestbook entries
    function displayEntries() {
        // Set title in Administrator interface
        JMenuBar::title( JText::_( 'Guestbook Entries' ), 'addedit.png' );

        // Query database for guestbook entries
        $db =& JFactory::getDBO();
        $query = "SELECT a.id, a.message,a.created,a.created_by, u.name" .
        " FROM #__guestbook AS a" .
        " LEFT JOIN #__users AS u ON u.id=a.created_by" .
        " ORDER BY created DESC";
        $db->setQuery( $query, 0, 10 );
        $rows = $db->loadObjectList();
?>
<table class="adminlist">
<tr>
    <td class="title" width=10%>
        <strong><?php echo JText::_( 'EntryID' ); ?></strong>
    </td>
    <td class="title" width=50%>
        <strong><?php echo JText::_( 'Entry' ); ?></strong>
    </td>
    <td class="title" width=10%>
        <strong><?php echo JText::_( 'Created' ); ?></strong>
    </td>
    <td class="title" width=10%>
        <strong><?php echo JText::_( 'Created by' ); ?></strong>
    </td>
</tr>

<?php
    foreach ($rows as $row) {
        $link = 'index.php?option=com_guestbook&task=edit&id='. $row->id;
        // Truncate row message for display
        $rowMessage = $row->message;
        if(strlen($rowMessage) > 100) {
            $rowMessage = substr($rowMessage, 0, 100) . "...";
        }
        echo "<tr>" .
            "<td>" . $row->id . "</td>" .
            "<td><a href=" . $link . ">" . $rowMessage . "</a></td>" .
            "<td>" . $row->created . "</td>" .
            "<td>" . $row->name . "</td>" .
            "</tr>";
    }
```

```
            echo "</table>";
            echo "<h3>Click on an entry link in the table to edit entry.</h3>";
    }

    function editEntry() {
            JMenuBar::title( JText::_( 'Guestbook Entry Editor' ), 'addedit.png' );

            $db =& JFactory::getDBO();
            $query = "SELECT a.id, a.message,a.created,a.created_by,a.location" .
            " FROM #__guestbook AS a" .
            " WHERE a.id = " . JRequest::getVar( 'id' );
            $db->setQuery( $query, 0, 10 );
            If($rows = $db->loadObjectList()) {
    ?>

    <form id="form1" name="form1" method="post"
    action="index.php?option=com_guestbook&task=update">
      <p>Enter message here:<br />
        <textarea name="message" cols="60" rows="4" id="message"><?php
        echo $rows[0]->message;
        ?></textarea>
      </p>
      <p>
        <label>Location (optional) : </label>
        <input name="location" type="text" id="location"
        value='<?php echo $rows[0]->location; ?>'
        />
        <input name="id" type="hidden" id="id"
        value='<?php echo $rows[0]->id; ?>'
        />
      </p>
      <p>
        <input type="submit" name="Submit" value="Record Changes" />
      </p>
    </form>

    <?php }      } ?>
```

Save the file, and you will notice the same postprocessing will occur to file the Outline window.

The XML Descriptor

The descriptor file for this component is more complicated than the simple one created for the Hello World component. This component has both front-end and Administrator files to install.

Since the Eclipse interface doesn't have a default new XML file selection, choose the File ➪ New ➪ File selection. When the New File window appears, enter **guestbook.xml** as the filename. Enter the following XML data code:

```
<?xml version="1.0" encoding="utf-8"?>
<install version="1.5.0" type="component">
      <name>Guestbook</name>
      <author>Dan Rahmel</author>
```

```
<version>1.0.0</version>
<description>Presents a guestbook and lists all of the current entries
along with an entry form at the bottom for registered user
additions.</description>
<files>
        <filename component="com_guestbook">
                guestbook.php</filename>
</files>
<install>
        <sql>
                <file driver="mysql" charset="utf8">install.sql</file>
        </sql>
</install>

<uninstall>
        <sql>
                <file driver="mysql" charset="utf8">uninstall.sql</file>
        </sql>
</uninstall>
<administration>
        <menu>Guestbook</menu>
        <files>
                <filename component="admin.guestbook">
                admin.guestbook.php</filename>
                <filename>install.sql</filename>
                <filename>uninstall.sql</filename>
        </files>
</administration>

</install>
```

When you save this file, the Outline window will update to show the entire XML schema, as shown in Figure 6-8. Clicking on any of the elements of the schema will highlight that element in the editor window. Eclipse understands the XML format, so if you right-click in the editor window, the context menu provides an option titled Validate. Selecting this option will validate the formatting of the XML and flag errors in the file with small red icons in the left margin.

This XML descriptor file is different from previous descriptors in that it references two SQL script files to create the guestbook table on install, and remove it when the component is uninstalled. You will need to create these two files that will be included in the package.

Create a new file called install.sql, and enter the following code:

```
CREATE TABLE IF NOT EXISTS `#__guestbook`
        (`id` INTEGER UNSIGNED NOT NULL AUTO_INCREMENT,
        `message` text NOT NULL, `created_by` INTEGER UNSIGNED NOT NULL,
        `location` VARCHAR(45), `created` TIMESTAMP NOT NULL,
        `userip` VARCHAR(16), PRIMARY KEY(`id`))
```

Create another new file called uninstall.sql, and enter the following code:

```
DROP TABLE IF EXISTS `#__guestbook`
```

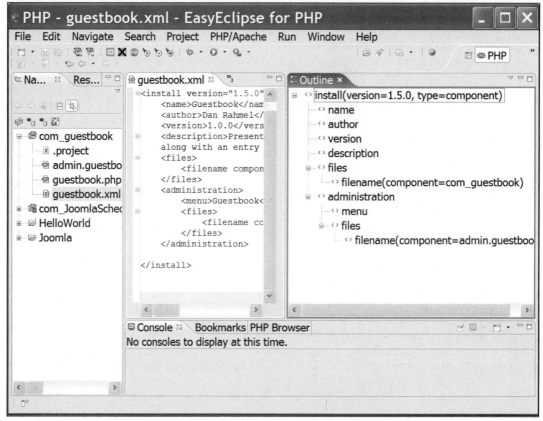

Figure 6-8: The XML schema of the file is displayed in the Outline window.

Adding the Component to the SVN Repository

To add the project to the repository that you created earlier, right-click on the project and, from the context menu, select the Team ⇨ Share Project... option. You will be presented with a window that allows selection of either a CVS or SVN repository. Select the SVN option, and click the Next button.

Select the "Create a new repository location" option, and click the Next button. You will be prompted for the URL of the location of the repository. As of this writing, there was no Browse button available, so you will have to enter the path by hand.

Once complete, your project will be archived in the repository. You can right-click on the individual files to store changes. You can also set a version tag when you have made comprehensive enough changes to warrant it.

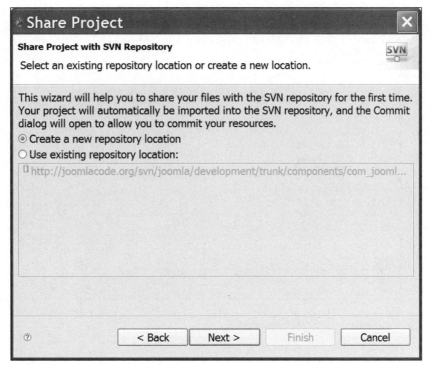

Share Project

Share Project with SVN Repository   SVN

Select an existing repository location or create a new location.

This wizard will help you to share your files with the SVN repository for the first time. Your project will automatically be imported into the SVN repository, and the Commit dialog will open to allow you to commit your resources.

◉ Create a new repository location

○ Use existing repository location:

☐ http://joomlacode.org/svn/joomla/development/trunk/components/com_jooml...

| ② | < Back | Next > | Finish | Cancel |

Figure 6-9: Select the "Create a new repository location" to point Eclipse at your repository.

Archiving the Component

Your project is now ready for archiving and installing on the Joomla system. Eclipse can create the archive file for you! In the Navigator window, right-click on the com_guestbook project, and select the Export... option. The Export options window will be displayed, as shown in Figure 6-10. Expand the General category, select the Archive File option, and click the Next button.

The Archive file option box will display a number of different settings that can be used in creating the archive. In the file selection box, you should see your project checked in the left pane and all of the files selected in the right pane. Unless you want to deselect the project file for inclusion in the archive (it won't hurt anything if it is there), the default selections are fine.

Leave the default selections of "Save in zip format" and "Create directory structure for files." In the "To archive file" text box, enter or browse to a path on your local drive. Title the file com_guestbook.zip, and click the Finish button. Eclipse will create the archive file and store it on the local drive.

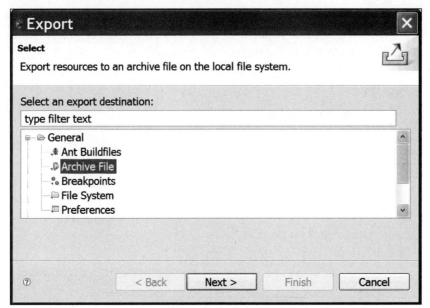

Figure 6-10: The Export options window provides the Archive selection to create a ZIP archive of all the project files.

Installing the Guestbook Component

Open the Extension Manager in the Joomla Administrator interface, and install the file. The archive created by Eclipse is properly formatted for the Joomla framework to place all the files into their proper locations. One file will be placed in the `components` folder, while the XML descriptor and the Administrator interface component will be placed in the `administrator\components` folder. In the future, you can edit them in these folders to support live development where testing code only requires a browser refresh.

When the Extension Manager informs you that the installation has succeeded, you should be able to see the Guestbook entry in the Components menu, as shown in Figure 6-11. You don't need to access it right now, since there are no guestbook entries to manage.

Create a menu item to the `Guestbook` control on the Main Menu. When the component list is presented for the new menu item, you should see the `Guestbook` item. Select `Guestbook`, and when the parameter screen is displayed, name the menu entry `My Guestbook`. For security reasons, be sure to set the menu so it will only be displayed to Registered users, as shown in Figure 6-12.

To try the guestbook, open a browser window and click on the `My Guestbook` link. There will be no entries, so only the entry form will be displayed. Enter a message in the guestbook as shown in Figure 6-13, and click the Post Entry button to send it into the system.

The guestbook will acknowledge your entry and provide a return link. Click the return link, and you should see the guestbook entries. With some entries in the `jos_guestbook` table, return to the Administrator interface. Select the Guestbook option from the Components menu. You'll see a row for each entry in the guestbook, as shown in Figure 6-14.

Figure 6-11: The Components menu will display the Guestbook entry that provides access to the guestbook administrative interface.

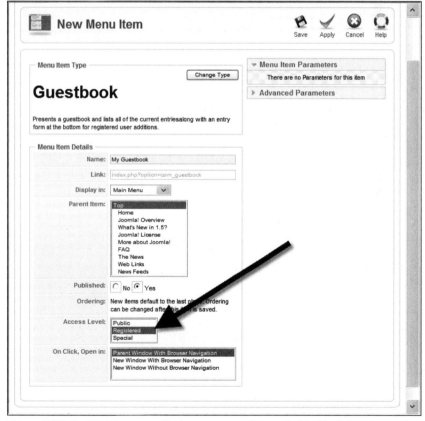

Figure 6-12: Restrict the users that may access the control to Registered users to prevent spammers from abusing the guestbook.

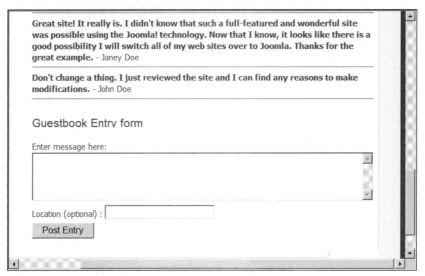

Figure 6-13: Enter a message in the guestbook form.

Each row of the table has the first 200 characters of the entry displayed as a link. Clicking on the link will take you to the edit form for that entry, as shown in Figure 6-15.

Any changes to the entry can be posted back into the database by clicking on the Record Changes button. For both security and convenience, nearly all characters beyond alphanumeric and basic punctuation are stripped from the entry when the user enters it through the front-end form. No such protection occurs through the Administrator interface form. It is possible that the Administrator will want to add any number of extras, so that functionality is left intact for those with administrative access.

The guestbook component has both a front-end and administrative interface, creates a custom table to store data, and accesses the data source for a variety of different activities (query, insert, and update). These features make it the perfect foundation from which you can build other database-centric components.

Guestbook Entries

EntryID	Entry	Created	Created by
1	We in Alaska, we love you! The scenery up here is wonderful, but so is looking at your site.	2007-03-27 11:41:15	John Doe
3	Don't change a thing. I just reviewed the site and I can find any reasons to make modifications.	2007-03-27 11:39:08	John Doe
2	Great site! It really is. I didn't know that such a full-featured and wonderful site was possible us...	2007-03-26 22:20:47	Janey Doe

Click on an entry link in the table to edit entry.

Figure 6-14: In the administrative interface, the guestbook will list all of the available entries.

Figure 6-15: Selecting a link from the table will display the editing form for that entry.

Using phpDocumentor

One of the aspects of development that programmers spend the least time executing is creating documentation. It can be a tedious process not only to create documentation but also to keep it up to date as the development progresses and the application evolves. A lack of documentation, however, can mean that the code is difficult to manage in the present and to maintain in the future.

To minimize this problem, the phpDocumentor was created. An open source application, phpDocumentor allows developers to place basic documentation and application structuring information directly in the source code itself. The Documentor can access all of the source code files and harvests the information to generate documentation. The program can output the documentation in a variety of formats, including HTML, PDF, CHM (compiled HTML), and XML.

Since the generation of the documentation is automated, it is possible to simply execute phpDocumentor at any time to create accurate, up-to-the-minute documentation of the current project. That means that the documentation can be kept current, and poorly documented portions of the code can be seen instantly in the overview (and, thus, targeted for supplementing).

Installation

Installing phpDocumentor on your Web server is extremely easy. The program doesn't need any database access or rendering technology, so any Web server that can execute PHP code can use it.

First, you will need to download the archive of the latest version from SourceForge. You'll find the link at the phpDocumentor site here:

```
http://www.phpdoc.org
```

All you need to do is extract the files and folders into a folder on the Web server. Be sure that you don't locate it in a place that can be addressed by the public Internet, since it is not a secure application. On my staging server, I placed the files in a folder called `phpdoc` at the root of the Web server. To access the administrative interface, just enter a URL such as the following:

```
http://localhost/phpdoc
```

The Web interface displays a Welcome screen with a number of menus (Introduction, Config, Files, Output, and so on). It also displays the working directory and the current status of the application. Generally, the status will read "Awaiting your command."

In this chapter, you'll be using phpDocumentor through the Web interface. However, it can also be executed using the command line interface. If you choose to use it through the command line, you might use the Pear installer, which makes the setup much simpler.

Adding DocBlocks to Source Code

You may have noticed that the source code in this book usually begins with a C++-style comment block that looks something like this:

```
/**
 *
 */
```

These comment sections are called *DocBlocks* and are harvested by phpDocumentor for inclusion in the code documentation. For complete documentation, one DocBlock should precede each element, including functions, classes, methods, and procedures.

The documentation is organized according to *packages*. A package is a conceptual grouping of classes, methods, and functions. You can explicitly define the package location of an element by using the `@package` tag. Within a master package, subpackages may also be defined with the `@subpackage` tag. Here is an example of some Joomla source code that is placed into the `Joomla` package and the `Content` subpackage:

```
/**
 * @package Joomla
 * @subpackage Content
 */
class TOOLBAR_content
{
      function _EDIT()
      {
```

To see how all of this works, you can execute phpDocumentor on Joomla itself, since it has the necessary DocBlocks to create basic documentation. Before you do, however, create a directory on your Web server to store the documentation files. The application generates numerous HTML files, so it's best to keep them centralized within a folder.

Joomla regularly updates the complete output of phpDocumentor for the Joomla framework. You can access it on the web at `http://api.joomla.org`.

Open the phpDocumentor Web interface, and click on the Output tab link at the top of the page. The first field is labeled Target and specifies the directory where the parsed files will be written. Enter the directory path for the folder that you created a moment ago.

Click on the Files tab link to configure the files that will be parsed by the program. The `includes` directory of the Joomla system contains numerous classes that have DocBlocks. Enter a path to this folder, which, on the Windows platform, may look something like this:

```
C:\Program Files\Apache Software Foundation\Apache2.2\htdocs\includes
```

To begin the process, click on the Create (new window) button. It may be a few minutes before the window is displayed, since Joomla has a great deal of code that must be processed. When complete, the status output of the documentation process will be presented. This window is very helpful when you have just begun using phpDocumentor because it will contain a list of errors or problems that occurred during the compilation.

Open the directory where the documentation was output, and open the `index.html` in a browser window. You will see a breakdown of the Joomla files contained in the `includes` directory. In the left column, there are links to each of the packages defined in the files, followed by a list of files documented, and, finally, the classes found within the packages.

In the classes section, click on the `JSite` link. You will see the class overview, as well as a list of methods for the class. The file contains class details (including comments from the development team), a breakdown of each class variable and method, and class constants.

Any development project can benefit greatly from having good programmer-level documentation. The few extra moments required to add this information to a file will reap significant rewards when later development is attempted. Be sure to read the phpDocumentor instructions because there are many other features such as the ability to include/exclude information for multiple versions of the documentation (one for developers and another for users, for example) and the functionality to include separate documentation files so source code can remain clean of extensive commentary.

Summary

Components are perhaps the most common type of extension in Joomla because they have extensive display capabilities and the capability to include an administrative interface. By using an advanced development system such as Eclipse, coupled with the capabilities of SVN, you can create components by doing the following:

❑ Customizing the default Eclipse templates to include any necessary foundation code.

❑ Defining both a front-end and administrator interface for the functionality desired.

❑ Archiving past versions of your source files with the source code control available through the SVN interface available to Eclipse.

❑   Refining the guestbook interface to include any other form items.

❑   Upgrading the guestbook administrative interface to further integrate with the Joomla framework.

❑   Rendering documentation using comments included in the source code and then processing the
files using phpDocumentor.

The components you created in this chapter provide traditional Web interaction. The flowering of the
coordination of a number of technologies known as Ajax lies at the heart of the new interactive Web
dubbed Web 2.0. In Chapter 7, you will use Ajax technology to create a Joomla application that uses
asynchronous access for dynamic user interaction.

7

Joomla! and Ajax

Ajax (which stands for Asynchronous JavaScript and XML) combines a powerful set of technologies for Web 2.0 sites. Using Ajax technology, you can make the user experience far more interactive than previous Web site implementations. In the past, changes to parameters or the selection of buttons on a Web page required the changes be sent back to the Web server for an update. The browser would have to wait for the entire modified page to be returned to display the revisions. Using that process, user interaction with a Web application was fairly clunky.

In a Web application designed with Ajax, near-immediate interaction is possible. User-interface requests such as changing the sort order of a table by clicking on the column headings can be handled on the client with little delay. If the interaction involves requesting additional information (such as help text on a line item), rather than requesting an update of the entire page, Ajax technology allows small amounts of data to be exchanged with the server. Updates can happen dynamically, so the entire Web page doesn't need to be reloaded.

Joomla has incorporated functionality that promotes Ajax technology. A Joomla site can support Ajax background information exchange for a more dynamic and responsive user experience.

Structure of Ajax

Contrary to all of the press regarding the recent birth of Ajax, it is not a new technology. Instead, it is a method of using existing technologies that is nearly ubiquitous to accomplish greater user interaction than in the past. An Ajax system combines the existing Web technologies of HTML, Cascading Style Sheets (CSS), JavaScript, Document Object Model (DOM), XML, and Extensible Stylesheet Language Transformation (XSLT). JavaScript code is executed on the user browser, and it communicates with the Web server in the background. Information can be sent and retrieved, and can be formatted dynamically for displaying in the browser window.

A very simple and increasingly common application of Ajax is the mouse-over pop-up information window such as the one used by Netflix (Figure 7-1). If the user moves the mouse cursor over the title or picture of a product, a pop-up window displays the associated information and images. In the case of Netflix, the information might include a picture of the movie box cover, a summary of the plot, the rating, starring actors, and so on.

The information displayed in the small window is not embedded in the Web page source. Rather than slowing the initial page downloading with lots of information the user will never mouse over, only the basic page is sent with the necessary logic to draw the pop-up and retrieve the information from the server. When the mouse over occurs, JavaScript code activates to query the server for the new information, and then populates the pop-up window with the new information.

For this Ajax magic to happen, a number of pieces of technology must work in conjunction. The browser must be capable of running JavaScript to detect user events and place a request to the server. The server must be able to respond with the specifically formatted information that matches the JavaScript request. JavaScript code must be able to receive the new information, process it, and format it for display via the browser's DOM.

While this may seem like a daunting number of functions, most of the technology is extensively deployed. The two dominant browsers, Internet Explorer (IE) and Mozilla Firefox, have included the features to perform the necessary client-side execution for the last several versions. That means that a large majority of existing browsers can execute Ajax content. On the server side, Joomla has included in the JDocument framework the necessary options so that the Joomla server can respond to an Ajax request through a custom component.

Figure 7-1: The Netflix Web site retrieves the movie information for the pop-up window dynamically.

Simple Ajax Component

An Ajax system can become complicated very quickly. There are many pieces to the puzzle, so it is easy to get lost at the beginning. Therefore, a beginning demonstration of rudimentary Ajax technology will be useful. This example will essentially provide a "Hello World" style Ajax pop-up to illuminate how the various pieces of the puzzle fit together.

The demonstration will consist of a single Web page that has a bordered paragraph with the text "My Product." When the mouse cursor passes over the paragraph, JavaScript executes a query to a Joomla server for a component. That returns a simple message regarding the inventory status of the product. The received message is displayed in an alert box, as shown in Figure 7-2.

This primitive example supplies a skeleton of a Joomla Ajax solution that you'll soon extend to provide a more substantial Ajax solution. However, it will include all of the most important pieces that will mirror the structure of advanced Ajax applications.

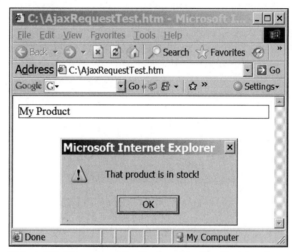

Figure 7-2: The message displayed in the alert box has been dynamically requested and received from a Joomla component.

Creating the Component

The first piece in the application is the Joomla component. A Joomla component can be directly queried so that it will provide output without any menus or the other user-interface items that usually surround it. Therefore, the component only must output a single line of text that the Ajax application will display.

Begin by creating a folder \com_productinfo on your local drive. Inside the folder, create a file productinfo.php and enter the following code:

```php
<?php
// no direct access
defined( '_JEXEC' ) or die( 'Restricted access' );

echo 'That product is in stock!';
?>
```

You will need a XML descriptor file to allow Joomla to install the component. Create a file called productinfo.xml and enter the following code:

```xml
<?xml version="1.0" encoding="utf-8"?>
<install version="1.5.0" type="component">
    <name>ProductInfo</name>
    <version>1.5.0</version>
    <description>Product Info component for Ajax queries</description>
    <files>
        <filename component="com_productinfo">productinfo.php</filename>
    </files>
</install>
```

Archive the folder containing the two files as com_productinfo.zip and use the Extension Manager to install it into the Joomla system. You can test the component by performing a direct URL query by typing the following address into your browser:

```
http://localhost/index.php?option=com_productinfo&format=raw
```

If the component is working properly, you will see the single line of text output by the component in the browser window, as shown in Figure 7-3. If you view the source of the window, the HTML code will show nothing except the exact text. By setting the format to raw (the second query parameter), Joomla executes the specified component and returns only the output that it has generated. This method is exactly how the Ajax Web page requests information for display.

Figure 7-3: The component will display the product's stocking status in plain text.

Creating the Ajax Web Page

The Ajax Web page will call upon the component for the product information and then display this information in an alert window. This file will be more complicated because it includes three steps of the Ajax process: user interaction, information request, and information receive/display.

The user interaction consists of a simple onMouseOver event that will be constructed to execute a JavaScript function. In this case, the event will be set up to activate when the user places the mouse cursor within the area specified by a paragraph or <p> tag.

The information request involves executing the displayAjax() function and passing it the URL that will provide the requested information. This function will open an XML request object (data is primarily exchanged using XML) and send a request to the URL that was passed to it.

The displayAjax function first creates an XML request object. As with most browser code, the execution must detect the browser where it is being executed, and then use logic specific for that one. The IE browser both pioneered the XML request interface (through an ActiveX object) and then violated the standard by not implementing the common interface. While this has been resolved in the later versions of IE (post IE-6), the code must take into account the large number of older IE browsers in use.

Once created, the code sets the XML request object's event return function to handle the results, opens the connection, and sends the request. When it sends that request, it will pass a function pointer to indicate the routine to execute when the request is complete. Remember that *the first A in Ajax stands for asynchronous*, so the rest of the Web page can continue functioning without waiting for the request to be answered.

When the displayReturn() function is activated, it first checks the returned information. The request might have timed-out or been given some other error. The function makes sure there is a valid message, and then displays the message in an alert box.

To see Ajax in action, enter the following code into a text editor, save it as AjaxRequestTest.html, and open it in your browser:

```
<!DOCTYPE html PUBLIC "-//W3C//DTD XHTML 1.0 Strict//EN"
    "http://www.w3.org/TR/xhtml1/DTD/xhtml1-strict.dtd">
<html xmlns="http://www.w3.org/1999/xhtml">
<head>
<meta http-equiv="Content-Type" content="text/html; charset=UTF-8" />
<script type="text/javascript" language="javascript">

// Create XML request variable
var myRequest = false;

function displayAjax(myURL) {
    // Clear myRequest
    myRequest = false;

    // For browsers: Safari, Firefox, etc. use one XML model
    if (window.XMLHttpRequest) {
```

```
            myRequest = new XMLHttpRequest();
            if (myRequest.overrideMimeType) {
                myRequest.overrideMimeType('text/xml');
            }
        } else if (window.ActiveXObject) {
            // For browsers: IE, version 6 and before, use another model
            try {
                myRequest = new
                    ActiveXObject("Msxml2.XMLHTTP");
            } catch (e) {
                try {
                    myRequest = new
                        ActiveXObject("Microsoft.XMLHTTP");
                } catch (e) {}
            }
        }

        // Make sure the request object is valid
        if (!myRequest) {
            alert('Error: Cannot create XMLHTTP object');
            return false;
        }

        // Link to display function activated when result returned
        myRequest.onreadystatechange = displayReturn;
        // Open the URL request
        myRequest.open('GET', myURL, true);
        // Send request
        myRequest.send(null);
    }

    function displayReturn() {
        // Check to make sure result came through, 4=complete
        if (myRequest.readyState == 4) {
            // Check HTTP status code
            if (myRequest.status == 200) {
                // Display the responseText
                        alert(myRequest.responseText);
            } else {
                alert('There was a problem with the request.');
            }
        }
    }
</script>
</head>
<body>

<p style="border:1px solid black;"
    onmouseover=
    "displayAjax('http://localhost/index.php?option=com_productinfo&format=raw')">
    My Product
        </p>
    </body>
</html>
```

Place this file at the root directory of your Joomla server to execute it. Note that the URL in the `displayAjax()` function code currently points to the server activated on `localhost`. Change the URL to your site URL if you are running the file on a remote server. . When you move the mouse cursor over the paragraph, the message will be displayed in an alert. That wasn't so bad, was it?

With Firefox, the cross-site scripting attack protection will prevent the code from executing on a local drive. When you try to access the page, you will receive an error such as "`Error: uncaught exception: Permission denied to call method XMLHttpRequest.open`" and the browser will refuse to display the page. Simply transfer the file to your Web server and access it there to have Firefox display it.

With a basic implementation complete, it is time to provide a more complex example. Most real-world Ajax solutions require a combination of dynamic content generation and Ajax interactive technology to allow more information to be retrieved from the same system. In the next sample, you'll create an entire Joomla-based Ajax system.

Creating a Server-Query Component

Using that basic application as a foundation, you'll need to augment the component to make it a truly useful data-retrieval black box. The server-query component presented here will provide the same functionality as the pop-up shown on the Netflix site, but it will return Joomla article content instead of film information. Under this implementation, when the user moves the mouse cursor over an article title displayed by the custom component, a small pop-up window will display the article title and the first 200 characters of the article text.

While this application is not especially useful itself, it can be readily adapted to almost any use. It will demonstrate how to request a dataset from a Joomla component that, once received by the client browser, can be displayed in a pop-up window. This can be applicable to almost any type of site — from an e-commerce solution where extra product display information is presented to the user, to an email application where new messages can be downloaded without the need to refresh a page.

Creating the Component

Begin by duplicating the `\com_productinfo` folder and naming the copy `\com_articleinfo`. Rename the `productinfo.php` and `productinfo.xml` to read `articleinfo.php` and `articleinfo.xml`, respectively. In the `articleinfo.php`, change the code to match the following:

```php
<?php
/**
 * @version $Id: com_articleinfo.php 5203 2007-07-27 01:45:14Z DanR $
 * This component will process a request parameter 'articlenum'
 * to query the article database and return the title and
 * article text in XML format.
 *
 */
    // no direct access
    defined( '_JEXEC' ) or die( 'Restricted access' );

    // Get request ID from query string variable
```

```php
$articleNum = intval(JRequest::getVar( 'articlenum' ));
// Define default values if query fails
$articleTitle = "Error";
$articleBody = "Error";

// Get instance of database object
$db =& JFactory::getDBO();
// Create query to return id, title, and text of article
$query = "SELECT a.id, a.title,a.introtext  \n" .
    " FROM #__content AS a \n" .
    " WHERE a.id =" . $articleNum . "\n";
$db->setQuery( $query, 0);
// Execute query
if ($rows = $db->loadObjectList()) {
    // Get first row returned
    $row = $rows[0];
    // Load article title and text into variables
    $articleTitle = $row->title;
    $articleBody = $row->introtext;
    // Strip all the HTML from the article text
    $articleBody = strip_tags($articleBody);
    // Strip all non-alpha, numeric, or punctuation
    $articleBody = preg_replace(
        "/[^a-zA-Z0-9 .?!$()\'\"]/", "", $articleBody);
    // If length is > 200, truncate length
    if(strlen($articleBody) > 200) {
        $articleBody = substr($articleBody, 0, 200);
    }
}
// Return XML of article title and article text
echo "<article><title>" . $articleTitle . "</title><body>" .
    $articleBody . "</body></article>";
?>
```

Once you've completed that code, change the XML descriptor file to point to the new code file and name the component. Don't forget to modify the component attribute in the filename tag. I've forgotten before, and when you try to install, Joomla informs you that the component is already installed!

Create an archive of the folder containing the two files named com_articleinfo.zip, and use the Extension Manager to install it into the Joomla system. While you're in the Administrator interface, go to the Article Manager and write down the Article ID of an existing article. You'll see the Article ID values in the main article list in the column titled ID.

Open a Web browser window and enter the following URL:

```
http://localhost/index.php?option=com_articleinfo&format=raw&articlenum=36
```

Modify the URL to match your server URL and change the articlenum parameter value on the end to reflect the Article ID number you found in the Article Manager. The browser should display the first 200 characters of the body of the article. Pretty cool, eh? Now that the code works, you can take a close look at it to see how it actually functions.

Accepting the Query Request

The first portion of the component performs general setup functions and receives the Article ID sent by the request. In the code, the `JRequest::getVar()` method is called to obtain the value sent in the query string and then places it in the `$articlenum` variable. The `getVar()` method actually executes several functions. Most importantly, it can receive parameter values from all of the different passing methods (`GET`, `POST`, and so on). So, whether your component needs to obtain information from a query string or a form posting or elsewhere, it can look for the parameter using this single method.

Also very important, the method will perform basic processing on the value to strip what may be a SQL injection attack (see the section, "Security Risks," later in this chapter) or other hacker attempt. This provides a very important security layer function, so it is best to use this method rather than grabbing the input yourself through a PHP function.

Just in case something slipped through the `getVar()` method, the `intval()` function converts the value to an integer rendering anything passed to a harmless number. After the `$articlenum` variable is set, the `$articleTitle` and `$articleBody` are set to default values.

Querying the MySQL Database

The query uses the standard `getDBO()` method to obtain a database object reference. The query string is constructed to return only the ID, title, and `introtext` (which contains the article body) from the database. Note that the FROM statement uses the reference #__content instead of a specific table reference such as `jos_content`. When the query is executed, Joomla will automatically replace the pound sign (#) and underscores with the necessary table prefixes. This frees the developer from the need to determine the user-configured prefix.

The query is then set and executed. If the object list contains at least one row, the routing processes the record. First, a `$row` reference is created to the first object in the `$rows` array. If there are more records returned by the query, the code will simply ignore them.

The routine will need to pass back the information in plain text, so the function calls that follow strip any HTML tags and then non-alpha characters (that will make the pop-up fault). After the content is stripped down to only the basic alphabetic, numeric, and punctuation characters, the string is truncated to a maximum of 200 characters. Since Ajax is supposed to be fast and interactive, it is good to attempt to minimize the amount of information that is returned to the requesting client.

Returning XML Output

Since only two pieces of information are needed by the client (the title and article summary), there is no need to create a complicated XML model. The `echo` statement constructs a simple XML tree with a parent element of `article` that contains a `title` field and a `body` field. If multiple records were to be returned, they could easily be encapsulated within a parent `articles` element.

That's it! The component receives the requested record in a query string, takes the requested `articleID` and searches the database for that article, renders down the information to basic plain text, and sends it back in a rudimentary XML tree. The module will be more complicated, because it needs to handle three parts of the Ajax relation: user-interface interaction, Ajax request, and information display.

Creating the Ajax Module

For the module that will display returned Ajax information, you're going to perform the best sort of code reuse. Joomla is overflowing with routines and objects that can be addressed and used within your own Joomla extensions. In this case, rather than implementing a pop-up window from scratch, the code will use the pop-up routine already used by the Joomla system for display.

Joomla includes an excellent pop-up window routine that allows everything from customizing color to setting the display location configuration. The JavaScript routine is overLIB, written by Erik Bosrup (www.bosrup.com/web/overlib), who has graciously allowed it to be included in the Joomla installation. You can visit his Web site for the latest version if you're going to implement it outside of Joomla.

To use it within Joomla, you need add only a single line:

```
<script type="text/javascript" src="includes/js/overlib_mini.js"></script>
```

From this reference, you can see the code is stored in the /includes/js/ directory. You should take a look at the code when you have some spare time so that you can see all of the parameters and features it includes.

Creating the Module Folder and XML File

For your module, create a folder named mod_articleajax. In the folder, create a file named mod_articleajax.xml and enter the following code:

```
<?xml version="1.0" encoding="utf-8"?>
<install type="module" version="1.5.0">
      <name>Article Ajax</name>
      <version>1.5.0</version>
      <description>This module will display links to 5 current articles. <p />
          Each link has an onMouseOver event to activate an
          Ajax routine to retrieve article information from
          com_articleinfo.
      </description>
      <files>
          <filename module="mod_articleajax">mod_articleajax.php</filename>
      </files>
</install>
```

This code is the simplest XML descriptor file. You will be able to expand it to include other files and parameters if you want to enhance the application.

Creating mod_articleajax

Create a file within the folder called mod_articleajax.php and enter the following code:

```
<?php
/**
* @version $Id: mod_articleajax.php 5203 2007-07-27 01:45:14Z DanR $
* This module will display links to 5 current articles.
* Each link has an onMouseOver event to activate an
* Ajax routine to retrieve article information from
```

```
 * com_articleinfo.
 */
?>
<script type="text/javascript" src="includes/js/overlib_mini.js"></script>
<script type="text/javascript">
     // Create XML request variable
     var myRequest = false;

function displayAjax(tempArticleID) {
     // Setup component query URL
     var myURL =
      'http://localhost/index.php?option=com_articleinfo&format=raw&articlenum='
      + tempArticleID;
     // Clear myRequest
     myRequest = false;

     // For browsers: Safari, Firefox, etc. use one XML model
     if (window.XMLHttpRequest) {
         myRequest = new XMLHttpRequest();
         if (myRequest.overrideMimeType) {
             myRequest.overrideMimeType('text/xml');
         }
     } else if (window.ActiveXObject) {
         // For browsers: IE, version 6 and before, use another model
         try {
             myRequest = new ActiveXObject("Msxml2.XMLHTTP");
         } catch (e) {
             try {
                 myRequest = new ActiveXObject("Microsoft.XMLHTTP");
             } catch (e) {}
         }
     }

     // Make sure the request object is valid
     if (!myRequest) {
         overlib('Error: Cannot create XMLHTTP object');
         return false;
     }

     // Link to display function activated when result returned
     myRequest.onreadystatechange = displayReturn;
     // Open the URL request
     myRequest.open('GET', myURL, true);
     // Send request
     myRequest.send(null);
}

function displayReturn() {
     // Check to make sure result came through, 4=complete
     if (myRequest.readyState == 4) {
         // Check HTTP status code
         if (myRequest.status == 200) {
             // Get head XML object
             var article =
```

```
myRequest.responseXML.getElementsByTagName('article');
            // Get title and body elements
            myTitle =
article[0].getElementsByTagName('title')[0].firstChild.nodeValue;
            myBody =
article[0].getElementsByTagName('body')[0].firstChild.nodeValue;
            // Display in popup window
            overlib(myBody,CAPTION,myTitle,BELOW,RIGHT);
        } else {
            // Problem, popup an error
            overlib('There was a problem with the request.',
                CAPTION,'Retrieval Error',BELOW,RIGHT);
        }
    }
}
</script>

<small>Ajax enabled module</small><br />

<?php
    // no direct access
    defined( '_JEXEC' ) or die( 'Restricted access' );

    // Define local variables
    $db =& JFactory::getDBO();
    $user =& JFactory::getUser();
    $userId = (int) $user->get('id');

    // Define date parameters to ensure articles are available
    $nullDate    = $db->getNullDate();
    $now         = date('Y-m-d H:i:s', time());

    // Create search string to display only published articles
    $where = 'a.state = 1' .
        " AND (a.publish_up = '" . $nullDate .
        "' OR a.publish_up <= '" . $now . "')" .
        " AND ( a.publish_down = '" . $nullDate .
        "' OR a.publish_down >= '" . $now . "')";

    // Create query
    $query = "SELECT a.id, a.title  \n" .
        " FROM #__content AS a \n" .
        " WHERE " . $where . "\n" .
        " AND a.access <= " . $userId;

    // Execute query to return a maximum of 5 records
    $db->setQuery( $query, 0,5);
    if ($rows = $db->loadObjectList()) {
        // Process each article row
        foreach ( $rows as $row )
        {
            // Process article title
            $artTitle = JText::_($row->title);
```

```
                        // Create mouseover event to call displayAjax function
                        echo "<span onmouseover=displayAjax(" . $row->id . ");
        onmouseout=nd(); >";
                        // Create link for the current article
                        echo "<a href=index.php?option=com_content&view=article&id=" .
                            $row->id . "&Itemid=44>" . $artTitle . "</a><br /></span>\n";
                }
        }
        // Display error message if db retrieval failed.
        echo $db->getErrorMsg();
    ?>
```

As with the earlier Ajax code, if you are not running this file on a `localhost` Web server, you will need to modify the URL that is used in the `displayAjax()` function.

Once you have the entire code ready, package the module in an archive named `mod_articleajax.zip` and use the Extension Manager to install it. If you keep the module position set to left, it will appear in the main window.

Open a browser window, and access the main page of your site. When the mouse cursor is moved over each of the links, a pop-up window will appear that shows the title and the first 200 characters of the contents of the article, as shown in Figure 7-4. As you can see, Ajax adds a great deal of instantaneous feedback to a user interface.

With the power of this simple example, you most likely want to get started creating your own Ajax solutions. This code, however, is quite a bit more complex than the component. You'll need to review it closely to fully understand the function.

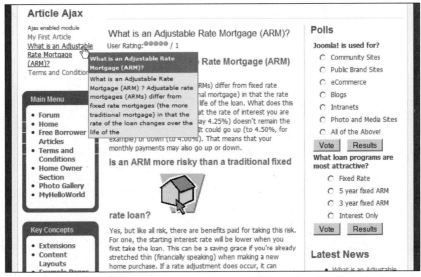

Figure 7-4: The title and first 200 characters of each article will appear in the pop-up window.

Pop-Up Window

The module code begins with the `script` statement needed to add the `overLIB` functionality to the module. With the `overLIB` library available, a call to the `overLIB()` function will display the pop-up window. There are a great number of parameters that you may set to control the window display, including height, window, color, window location, and text handling.

Requestor Functions

The `displayAjax()` and `displayReturn()` functions follow the `script` statement for the `overLIB` library. The `displayAjax` function is nearly identical to the one used earlier in the simple product info example. The only significant change is the argument passed to the function. Instead of accepting a URL, the function requires the `articleID`, from which it creates the URL to access the `com_articleinfo` component.

In contrast to `displayAjax()`, the heart of the `displayReturn()` function is much different. Instead of simply retrieving text from the component (using the `responseText` object), the new code accesses the `responseXML` object to gain access to the XML data object tree. The code first creates a reference to the `article` element. It then retrieves the values of the `title` and `body` elements, using the `nodeValue` property.

The text from these elements is used to call the `overLIB()` function, submitting them as body text and a caption for the presentation. That's all that is needed for the retrieval portion of the Ajax module.

The user-interface portion is slightly more complex because the Joomla database must be accessed to retrieve the appropriate article references.

Finding Articles in the Joomla Database

The article code cannot simply grab the current article titles and put them in the module display. Since the code is directly addressing the article contents table, complete access to unpublished and unauthorized content is possible. The code needs to protect against making secure content available.

Therefore, after references to the database, user, and user ID are created, the necessary date variables are set for the search. The `$nullDate` value will be used to search for articles that have no expiration date. The `$now` variable will allow the display to be limited to articles already available, not those with a publication date that exists in the future.

The `$where` statement of the query is constructed to ensure that the article is formally published and that its publication lies within the present time period. The `Where` clause is then added to the `$query` variable, which only requests the article ID and title columns. For the module, only the table of contents entries need be displayed, so there is no reason to retrieve unnecessary data.

Finally, the `setQuery()` method is used to execute the query and retrieve five records or less. It could retrieve all of the articles, but then the height of the module display might take up too much screen space. Better to limit the query by record size or data.

The record set that is returned by the query is processed. For each record, a `<span>` is created that contains an `onMouseOver` event. From the code, you can see the code that is output into the HTML page calls the `displayAjax()` function and has the Article ID of the current record hard-coded. If you were to examine the source code of the page once it was displayed in the browser, you would find that each `onMouseOver` event coding contains its own Article ID. It also contains code for the `onMouseOut` event to hide any window displayed.

Contained within the HTML `span` is a custom link for the current row's article. The link is generated to access the standard `com_content` component to display the article, and the Article ID is passed through the `id` parameter. The link name is the title retrieved from the row.

Finally, if any error messages were generated by the database retrieval, they would be displayed below the module output.

You should now have a very good grasp of implementing an Ajax solution on the Joomla CMS platform. This basic foundation can be extended in nearly any direction to create further Ajax interactivity.

Ajax Disadvantages

Given the exciting nature of the Ajax technology, it is easy for developers to overlook the shortcomings. Aside from the complexity that Ajax can add to a Web development project, there are a number of very real problems that will be encountered as Ajax use grows:

- ❑ Ajax Search Engine Optimized (SEO) invisibility
- ❑ Information harvesting
- ❑ Possible security risks

Ajax SEO Invisibility

Since Ajax has begun to spread like wildfire, entire sites are using Ajax for everything from menu display to core information presentation. While it is easy to get caught up in the excitement of a new technology, it is important to recognize where that technology can be best applied. So far, the best uses have been for dynamic user-interface widgets for everything from Netflix to Google Maps.

However, all of the content that is displayed by the Ajax widgets is *invisible to search engines*. A search engine spider will not execute the code contained in an Ajax JavaScript link. Therefore, while the pop-up content may appear slick and inviting to your users, a search engine will be blind to it.

Make certain that any content you use for Ajax is also present somewhere else on the site using traditional HTML. Using this method, your site will not look empty to the search engine spider. Further, to make sure your site is SEO, be sure to have your central site content in HTML prominent on the central pages. If the content is presented by Ajax and simply included in a low-ranked part of the site for completeness, your search engine ranking will suffer.

Information Harvesting

Most Ajax requests are directly querying for formatted data that is returned to the browser. You have to be careful to prevent unauthorized access and also shield yourself against potential hackers. Most Ajax applications will make a request to your system that you supply with formatted data from within your data stores. This information may be important price/stocking records, or even proprietary company data. With the data returned in XML format, it would take little time or effort for your competitors to author an information harvesting program that simply makes request after request to your Ajax component until all the information it can provide is stored safely in a rogue database.

There are a few ways to guard against this type of information harvesting, but the easiest is to ensure that the requests are not sent with a simple sequential ID number. If you have products numbered 1 through 50, use some other method of ID request so that a harvesting application can't simply loop through the sequence to gain the requested information.

Security Risks

The other danger lies in the potential for a SQL injection attack. In an injection attack, the hacker simply tacks on a full SQL query to the request string. If the receiving program simply passes the parameter received from the request directly to the database, a great deal of private information can be exposed.

Fortunately, Joomla has built-in routines such as `getVar()` to prevent most of the potentially harmful code from getting through. Be sure to think twice before you decide to circumvent the Joomla security routines because they offer a great deal of tried-and-tested security technology.

Summary

Adding Ajax to your Joomla site can bring it up to the cutting edge of Web 2.0 implementation. Implementing the technologies (HTML, XML, JavaScript, and so on) that need to operate in concert for an Ajax application can be frustrating but very rewarding when the site is finally deployed. This chapter has provided an overview of implementing Ajax within Joomla by doing the following:

❑   Explaining how the Ajax technologies work together and can be implemented by Joomla.

❑   Refining your understanding of components, including the capability of a component to output in raw format.

❑   Creating a simple Ajax application so that the rudimentary framework could be understood.

❑   Improving the performance of the server by modifying the debugging and logging settings.

❑   Upgrading that component to a more robust pop-up window application that demonstrates the best in functionality that Ajax has to offer.

❑   Adopting a conservative view of where Ajax can be best applied and what disadvantages the new technology may present.

Ajax implementation can be fairly complicated conceptually. As part of a larger development project, implementation can be downright confusing. A conceptual development tool called *design patterns* can help you organize application development to minimize bugs and maximize the knowledge gained from past projects. Chapter 8 examines how design patterns can be applied to Joomla development.

8

Design Patterns and Joomla!

Joomla is an object-oriented application. The Joomla framework has been developed as a series of classes that work together to provide the content management system (CMS) functionality. Developing for Joomla effectively requires that certain object-oriented concepts be understood and adopted. One of these concepts is the use of design patterns for development. *Design patterns* are essentially conceptual models that direct the way new object-oriented programming is approached.

Design patterns are models that have been refined over many projects so that, if properly matched to the problem that you are trying to solve, can supply a proven effective methodology to solving that problem. Adoption of effective design patterns means that development schedules are easier to keep, maintenance of the system is cheaper, communication about the evolving system is clearer, and new developers will have an easier time programming the system. By following a design pattern, a developer essential avoids reinventing the wheel every time a new project is started.

Since Erich Gamma, Richard Helm, Ralph Johnson, and John Vlissides pioneered work in this field in the early 1990s, there have been many comprehensive explanations written. The original (and perhaps most important) book on the subject, *Design Patterns: Elements of Reusable Object-Oriented Software* (Boston: Addison-Wesley, 1995), laid the foundations for many of the patterns that are used up to the present day — including those you see in Joomla.

This chapter introduces the basic concepts of design patterns and, since the Joomla team has adopted them in the CMS design, describes how some of them apply to Joomla. When you understand the design philosophy behind Joomla, you will not only be able to build more effective Joomla extensions, you will also better recognize how the framework itself can be addressed, examined, and used.

Design Patterns

Design patterns are object-oriented development outlines that reflect the fundamental aims and process of a development cycle. Design patterns are made to address a specific development problem and provide a pattern for how to reach the solution.

A pattern generally documented with the following information:

❑ *Name and classification* — The name of the pattern and the general classification that will tell the type of pattern. Typically, the classification is one of the three primary types: creational, structural, or behavioral.

❑ *Problem* — Describes the problem that the pattern is designed to solve.

❑ *Solution* — Details the solution to the problem, including general conceptual models, processes, and objects involved.

❑ *Hypothesis* — General description of what the pattern does, and how it will solve the problem.

❑ *Concrete example* — A tangible example of how the pattern was used to solve a problem.

❑ *Applicability* — Where the problem can be effectively applied, as well as the solution's limitations.

❑ *Consequences* — The trade-offs of adopting the pattern and the dependencies created by the pattern's adoption.

❑ *Implementation tips* — General advice for usage of the pattern.

It is important to note that design patterns are neither perfect nor meant to create dogma that must be rigidly applied. Design patterns are guides, and generally the closer you stick to the pattern, the more advantages promised by the pattern will be reaped. However, practical considerations such as performance often intrude on strict adoption of a pattern.

Design patterns can be overkill if a project is very small. There is no easy way to determine the right size for when a pattern should be used. A general rule of thumb may be that if the project requires three or more developers now or in the future, then the design patterns will be worth implementing.

Individual developers, while not reaping the huge number of benefits from the practice of implementing patterns, may want to use them anyway for good habits so that use of them will become routine. That way, if the project expands, the best practices will already be in place.

Identify what benefits each pattern will provide, but don't slavishly abide by the pattern if it makes implementation impossible. The design patterns were made to streamline development, not inflexibly encase it in ivory tower commandments that require vast sacrifice to adopt.

Three Primary Categories of Patterns

To organize design patterns, the originators of the system divided them into three types:

❑ Creational

❑ Structural

❑ Behavioral

Each of these categories represents a type of solitary pattern that can be used for good programming pattern definition.

Creational Patterns

Patterns that are classified as *creational* relate to the mechanisms of the creation of objects. It might seem like object creation is straightforward and mostly handled by the system. However, managed object creation can provide many benefits, such as streamlined upgrades or better resource sharing — particularly in a large system.

In many programming systems, creation of new objects is performed simply by calling the programming language's object creation function. However, there are many applications that can reap benefits by introducing a middleware application to handle object creation.

For example, database abstract layer (DAL) technology (such as PEAR DAL, PDO, and ADOdb) forms a middle layer between an application as a data source so that a programmer can write database access code that addresses the DAL, and the application can talk to any database back-end the DAL supports.

To make a connection, rather than creating a connection object directly, the application requests a connection object from the DAL. With this method, the DAL can perform connection pooling, so connections that have been created but released from the originating process can simply be handed to the new requestor, rather than creating a new connection from scratch. This creational pattern conserves precious server resources and, since the DAL handles the creation of connection objects directly, it can handle many of the special case problems of addressing particular data sources.

This is one real-world example of a creational pattern. Patterns held in the creational pattern category include abstract factory, factory method, builder, lazy initialization, object pool, prototype, and singleton. These pattern definitions specifically detail some of the processes that are needed by an application. The three most common creational patterns used by Joomla are the abstract factory pattern (which was used in this example), singleton pattern, and builder pattern.

Abstract Factory Pattern

One creational pattern is the *abstract factory pattern* whereby a factory class is constructed that accepts object creation requests and returns an instance of the specified class. If the object creation were to be coded into every aspect of the system, then a change in object class would require a rewrite and recompile of the system to allow the new class to be used.

A good example of using the abstract factory pattern is an encryption system. Imagine that there is a class called `EncryptionA` that provides routines to encrypt data for storage into a database. For this design pattern, an abstract factory could be created called `EncryptionObject` that would be called to obtain an instance of an `EncryptionA` object.

Now, imagine that time passes, and a flaw is found in the method used by `EncryptionA`. Therefore, a new class is created, called `EncryptionB`, that is more secure. To upgrade a system designed using the abstract factory pattern, only the `EncryptionObject` needs to be changed to respond to object requests with an `EncryptionB` object. If the `EncryptionA` object creation had been hard-coded into each program that needed encryption, large portions of the system would need to be upgraded and recompiled to use the new object. When `EncryptionC` is invented, without following the design pattern, another systemwide upgrade and recompile would be necessary.

Singleton Pattern

The *singleton pattern* is a creational pattern used by Joomla classes — particularly for database access. In database applications, there is a great deal of overhead spent opening and closing database connections. To minimize this performance problem, the singleton pattern uses a single object to hold the database connection. The object is accessed by methods that need to address the connection to the database. Rather than creating new connections each time, the object will return a handle to the existing database connection.

In Joomla, a query to the database object is performed like this:

```
$db =& JFactory::getDBO();
$query = "SELECT *" .
  "\n FROM jos_messages"   .
  "\n WHERE messageMonth = " .
  intval($curMonth);
$db->setQuery($query);
$myRows = $db->loadObjectList();
```

Using the object reference supplied by the `getDBO()` function allows the singleton connection of the current `JFactory` object to be reused.

Builder Pattern

The *builder pattern* is applied when conversions are necessary. The builder is actually a sort of plug-in for the parent class that is called the *director*. The director processes a file or input stream and parses it down to individual elements. Each element is sent to a builder, which returns a formatted output of the type that the builder was made to create.

Take the example of an XML processor class that is a director. It works through the XML tree and sends each tag and element to be processed by a builder class. The function of the builder class will depend on what it was designed to render. One builder may return a comma-delimited row for each element sent to it. Another builder may output SQL code to write the data of the elements into a database. In the builder pattern, each builder can be constructed independently of the director.

An example of the use of the builder pattern in Joomla would be the handler routines for the various user-configurable parameters of a module. These parameters are modifiable through the Module Manager in the Administrator interface of the Joomla system. To see the code that handles the various parameter types (`text`, `textarea`, `radio button`, `filelist`, and so on), open the `element` directory, which should have a path something like this:

```
\htdocs\libraries\joomla\html\parameter\element
```

This folder will contain a number of PHP files, one for each type of module parameter (such as `filelist.php`, `imagelist.php`, `password.php`, and so on). The director part of the Joomla framework loads the module parameters list and then calls the individual builder files to render the appropriate the appropriate HTML code back to the browser.

Structural Patterns

Structural patterns are related to the organization and process of a class. Classes within the framework that are organized around these patterns have specific inheritance characteristics. These patterns seek to simplify (as much as possible) the relationships between entities (or classes).

Patterns held in the structural patterns category include adapter, aggregate, bridge, composite, container, decorator, extensibility or framework, façade, flyweight, proxy, pipes and filters, private class data, and wrapper. The most common patterns used by Joomla include the adapter pattern and the bridge pattern.

Adapter Pattern

The *adapter pattern* is used to allow one interface to use another, otherwise incompatible, interface. This pattern is used by Joomla bridge components that allow a technology such as the Simple Machines Forum to interoperate with the Joomla system. The bridge component provides a two-way adapter so that the incompatible systems can communicate.

Bridge Pattern

The *bridge pattern* is used to abstract implementation by providing a standardized interface. The most common example of a bridge pattern is a generic printer system. The printer system feeds information through a standardized interface to any number of drivers. Since the output interface is abstracted, the user can switch printer drivers without reimplementation of the system's printer output.

An example of this pattern can be seen in the output type setting of a Joomla component. The type requested might be HTML, raw, text, and so on. These individual implementer classes will output in their various formats.

Behavioral Patterns

Behavioral patterns relate to the communication behavior of a class and its objects. These patterns seek to simplify and increase the flexibility of communications between entities.

Patterns held in the behavioral patterns category include chain of responsibility, command, interpreter, iterator, mediator, memento, observer, state, strategy, template, visitor, single-serving visitor, and hierarchical visitor. The most common patterns used by Joomla include the observer pattern, the chain-of-responsibility pattern, and the strategy pattern.

Observer Pattern

In the *observer pattern*, an object called the *observable object* is the common point for notifying other objects of a change in parameters. Each observer object registers itself with the observable object. When there is a change to the object that the observable represents, it notifies all registered observers.

A simple example is an auto-player on a USB system. Imagine an observable object created that watched the USB chain of devices. One of the observer objects registered with the observable is DVD player software. When a change occurs in the USB chain (such as a DVD inserted into a drive), all of the observers are notified. The DVD player observer would receive the notification of the change, determine whether a DVD movie was inserted, and automatically play the disc if set to do so.

Joomla uses the observer pattern for plug-in handling. Each plug-in registers with the Joomla system for the types of events that it might handle. When such an event occurs, the observable (Joomla) notifies the observer (plug-in) that a change has taken place.

Chain-of-Responsibility Pattern

Joomla plug-ins also comply with the *chain-of-responsibility pattern*. This pattern indicates that when an event occurs, that event is passed through a set of handlers. These handlers may be observers for the observer pattern. In the observer pattern, the observers are notified and no further behavior is expected from either the observer or the observable. In contrast, the chain-of-responsibility pattern queries the handlers as it makes each notification. If the observer acknowledges that it will handle the current event, the process stops, and no further observers are notified.

In a Joomla system, a plug-in may notify the system that it will handle the generated event, and the processing is handed off to the extension. Thereafter, no other action is performed by Joomla for that event.

Strategy Pattern

In the *strategy pattern*, an algorithm is encapsulated within an object. That way, algorithms can be swapped, depending on the need to upgrade or reimplement without changing anything but the object passed for the algorithm activated. This strategy is commonly used for algorithms such as authentication and encryption/ decryption.

This pattern is often used with the *factory patterns*. When the algorithm is changed, the new object is assigned within the factory to be passed to objects requesting one of those types.

Concurrency Patterns

While not part of the original Gang of Four patterns, *concurrency patterns* have become important, and will increase in importance. Within database specialist circles, concurrency is perhaps the primary problem. A typical large organization database system has potentially thousands of users attempting to access and modify the same data at the same time.

A typical airline ticket agent at an airport must determine whether he or she can sell a ticket or make a reservation for a particular flight at the moment a customer stands before them. The system must take into account when all flights that may be arriving, the current booking on a flight, what connecting flights (perhaps from other airlines) will use seats on the current flight, and even the predicted percentage of those who will not show up. All told, the program must take into account numerous instantaneous variables given the current availabilities and the ability to book a flight.

While this example is far from most Joomla uses (that don't have large-scale concurrent operations), more immediate examples such as two people (an editor and a chief editor) modifying the same article at the same time is extremely relevant. Joomla is a CMS, which means that at the most primitive level, it is likely that a contributor may be attempting to supplement an article at the same time a technical editor is editing for accuracy at the same time another editor is editing the grammar.

Therefore, examining a few concurrency patterns is important to understanding the uses these patterns have for managing concurrency conflict, now and in the future.

Architectural Patterns

Architectural patterns are not specified in the original Gang of Four selection of patterns, but they are perhaps the most relevant to Joomla developers. These patterns present a general system architectural overview, showing how an entire software system might be created.

Most popular among these patterns is the *client-server pattern*. In the client-server pattern, a client executes a large amount of the processor-intensive calculations on the desktop platform, and communicates with the server for centralized database access. The client-server pattern allocates the majority of client interaction processing to the client (desktop machine), while the major data store occurs on the server, as shown in Figure 8-1.

In early Web development, the server-based pattern meant that all core processing occurred on the server. A simple Web browser could be used to access a server-based application. All data and program logic existed on the server, and the browser was used for simple display.

The new Ajax technologies described in Chapter 7 cut a middle road between the client-server pattern and the server-based pattern. While the application itself is server-based, the browser downloads a certain amount of logic to the client for execution (generally as JavaScript). Therefore, processing such as data validation and individual data process retrieval is performed on the client via execution code that is downloaded from the server.

While in the past Joomla has performed mostly under the server-based pattern, with the increasing adoption of the client-server pattern, Joomla is moving into the world of Web 2.0.

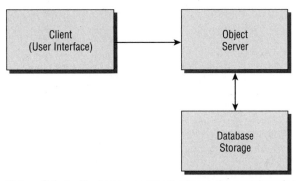

Figure 8-1: A client-server pattern places the user-interface processing on the client and the data coordination on the server.

Server-Based Pattern

Joomla is the essence of a server-based system. The client (browser) executes very little or no code. The server handles all queries, the presentation, and most code execution. Except for the article content editing (through TinyMCE, for example), all of the site processing occurs on the Web server (through PHP code), and the formatted page is then distributed to the Web browser.

Server-based patterns have perhaps the longest history in computer science. These go back to the punch cards that were fed into a central processor that then output the results, to the UNIX interfaces of the 1970s and 1980s, where dumb terminals were used to submit a process to the server and all execution occurred on the server platform.

While the client-server pattern took precedence in the era following the growth of the UNIX platform, the Web-based application interface temporarily returned the focus of the computer world to the server-based pattern. Many companies during the dot-com boom in the 1990s predicted that the server-based pattern would retake the position of the principal deployment model in the computer world. Poor server performance, discontinuous connections, and underpowered clients rendered this model unlikely. However, the widespread adoption of high-speed connections and powerful client devices has made the client-execution pattern likely to become a dominant pattern of the future.

Client-Execution Pattern

In the *client-execution pattern*, code is downloaded from the server that will perform the most interactive functions on the client. Instead of performing validation on the server (such as making sure a ZIP code is accurate), the downloaded client code will query the server without an entire browser-page reload. If the ZIP code is invalid, the client code will prompt the user for further clarification. The ZIP code databases are generally large (about 8.5MB), making a database of ZIP codes impractical for client downloading.

However, by allowing client process querying (without the entire page update) on the entered ZIP code, the application can be as responsive as a common client-server implementation that includes the ZIP code database on the local drive.

Google has attempted to seize on this new pattern with a challenge to Microsoft's desktop application dominance with a suite known as Google Apps Premier Edition. This application suite uses the server platform for data storage and distribution, while harnessing the client's processing power to allow very interactive user-interface conventions.

Model-View-Controller Pattern

The most important design patterns to Joomla are three design patterns (*Observer*, *Composite*, and *Strategy*) that are combined into the *Model-View-Controller* (MVC) *pattern*. The pattern seeks to break an application into three separate conceptual areas so that each can be developed as separately as possible from the others so that changes to one part have a minimum impact on the other parts.

In this pattern, each conceptual area represents a clear layer in the application:

❑ *Model* — The logic or actual execution code of the application.

❑ *View* — The presentation of graphics of text of the application.

❑ *Controller* — The user interaction of the application including processing events.

If you think of these three areas in general terms in relation to Joomla, the Model would be the PHP and database code that executes on the Web server that is part of the Joomla framework. The View would be the template that determines how article content is displayed. The Controller would be the menu event system and extensions such as the search module that sends user requests into the Joomla model for processing.

With Joomla, templates provide an easy-to-understand representation of the advantages of keeping the three parts independent. Selecting a new template in the Template Manager can completely redefine the appearance of a Web site. If the Model and View were merged (as they have been in most past applications), the look-and-feel could be changed only with a great deal of custom programming.

Likewise, separating the user interface or Controller from the Model allows many ways for the user to interact with the application. In a simple example, the Controller might allow both a drop-down menu and a command key to activate the same function in the Model. Even more advanced would be a command line user interface or a graphical user interface (these two Controllers are available for MySQL) that allow the users to interact with the system using whichever method they prefer.

On a Web site, a separate Controller may come in the form of alternate text attributes for graphic menus and links that allow a vision-impaired person to navigate the graphical site. With accessibility functionality, a Web site can be accessed with a text-based browser (and through the text, a voice-based browser), and the Model can be controlled to retrieve article content.

Operating systems have been struggling for years to adopt the MVC model so that they could change their user interface based on the user's desire. One of the trade-offs of using MVC is that performance suffers. Since the separation means that each portion of the application is treated like a black box, information must be funneled from one layer to another — making optimization difficult. Partial adoption of the MVC model is one reason that operating systems have come a long way in enabling users to change the theme or view of the operating system, depending on user preferences. The lack of complete MVC adoption means that it is still difficult to make Mac OS look and feel like Windows Vista, or vice versa.

Like these operating systems, Joomla does not yet completely embrace this model. The templates themselves have a fair amount of PHP code logic (the Model) in them for proper execution. Likewise, the Controller aspects of modules are fairly tightly bound to their display (the View). As stated earlier, however, design patterns are an ideal to strive toward, not a straightjacket that requires all-or-nothing compliance.

While the implementation of the MVC model is not yet in perfect compliance with the pattern, the Joomla class framework is formally defined by an object for each portion of the model:

❑   `JModel` — The class that acts as a factory for the model portion of the Joomla framework.

❑   `JView` — The class that acts as a factory for the presentation display portion of the Joomla framework.

❑   `JController` — The class that acts as a factory for the controller portion of the Joomla framework.

MVC for Joomla Components

Within the Joomla system, it is components that are likely to be the most important places for a developer to implement the MVC pattern. Joomla components will often have all three of the layers of the pattern, while modules generally lack Controller aspects and plug-ins may only include Model logic.

In this section, you will use the MVC pattern to create a simple Hello World MVC component. Implementing this component will not only provide a good basic demonstration of how design patterns can be used in Joomla development, but it will hopefully also provide the impetus for you to begin looking at design patterns for possible solutions before you begin application implementation.

Components in Joomla lend themselves to the MVC pattern in that the three parts of the model can be located in separate files. A Joomla component that embraces the MVC pattern will need to be divided into the three parts of the pattern:

- ❑ *Model* — The `hellomvc.php` file will hold the core logic of the component.
- ❑ *View* — The `view.html.php` file will contain the presentation rendering logic.
- ❑ *Controller* — The `controller.php` file will handle all of the user interaction.

Begin by creating a folder called `\com_hellomvc`. Within this main folder, create the following directories:

```
\com_hellomvc\controllers
\com_hellomvc\models
\com_hellomvc\views
```

The Model File: mvc.php

In this example component file, you can see the controller extension addressed, while the system will automatically reference a default view unless instructed. Enter the following code and save it as `hellomvc.php` in the `\com_hellomvc` directory:

```php
<?php
/**
 * @version        $Id: hellomvc.php 7122 2007-06-21 11:52:29Z danr $
 * @package        hellomvc
 */

/* Make sure this is not direct access */
defined('_JEXEC') or die('Restricted access');

/* Load the main controller */
require_once (JPATH_COMPONENT.DS.'controller.php');

/* If controller variable is present, load component's controller. */
if($controller = JRequest::getVar('controller')) {
    require_once (JPATH_COMPONENT . DS . 'controllers' .
        DS.$controller . '.php');
}

/* Create an instance of the controller */
$classname = 'HelloMVCcontroller'.ucfirst($controller);
$controller = new $classname( );

/* Execute the request */
$controller->execute(JRequest::getCmd('task'));
$controller->redirect();

?>
```

Because of the MVC division, the design of the Model or code for the component does not have to be concerned with the presentation or user interface interaction with the Web visitor. That allows the core logic to be refined by professional developers separate from the categories of work traditionally associated with graphic artists and Web designers.

The View Files

In this example View file, you can see the controller and interface portions of the extension addressed. Enter the following code, and save it as `view.html.php` in the `\hellomvc\view\hellomvc` folder:

```php
<?php
/**
* @version          $Id: hellomvc.php 7122 2007-06-21 11:52:29Z danr $
* @package          hellomvc
*/

/* Make sure this is not direct access */
defined('_JEXEC') or die('Restricted access');

/* Import the view class */
jimport( 'joomla.application.component.view');

class HelloMvcViewHelloMvc extends JView
{
    function display($tpl = null)
    {
        /* Display our greeting */
        echo "<h1>Hello MVC!</h1>";
    }
}
?>
```

If possible, the View aspect of any component should adopt the presentation of the selected Joomla component. Thanks to the comprehensiveness of the Joomla core template CSS, there are a large number of stylesheet selections that can be cited through `class` or `id` references by the View interface. By adopting these stylesheets, the View presentation can be automatically synchronized with the styles chosen by the user through the current template.

The `display()` method is automatically called when a display request to the class is invoked. As you can see, it can be modified without affecting either the Model or the Controller.

The Controller File: controller.php

Since the Controller does not handle any user interaction in this example, it must incorporate only the `display()` method to make the presentation. By calling the `JController::display()` method, most of the housekeeping for the presentation is handled automatically.

You will notice that this Controller functions under the observer pattern described earlier by extending the `JController` class. The code for the Controller should be saved in the `site` directory with a filename of `controller.php`:

```php
<?php
/**
* @version          $Id: hellomvc.php 7122 2007-06-21 11:52:29Z danr $
* @package          hellomvc
*/

/* Make sure this is not direct access */
```

```
defined('_JEXEC') or die('Restricted access');

/* Import the controller class */
jimport('joomla.application.component.controller');


/* Extend the JController class */
class HelloMVCcontroller extends JController
{
    /* If request is for display of a view, call parent method
    *   so the view can be rendered.
    */
    function display()
    {
        parent::display();
    }
}

?>
```

Once you address a menu to this component, the presentation will appear as if you used no design pattern within the implementation. However, when you attempt to upgrade the component or seek to further integrate the presentation of the component with the currently selected template, the advantages of using the MVC pattern will immediately become apparent. Instead of compromising the core code of the extension with special exceptions to follow the desired presentation, only the presentation layer will need to be modified, which will minimize potential execution errors.

Any changes to the basic algorithms held in the Model portion will not affect the layout. The layout may be custom-chosen by the client, but the developer of the core Model code will not have to worry about these considerations.

Even more encouraging, the interface can be freely expanded without jeopardizing the functioning of the application. The addition of such user interface niceties as a pop-up calendar or an interactive spell-checker will have no effect on the functioning of the core aspects of the component.

The Descriptor File: hellomvc.xml

Enter the following code and save it as hellomvc.xml in the root of the component folder:

```
<?xml version="1.0" encoding="utf-8"?>
<install type="component" version="1.5.0">
    <name>HelloMVC</name>
    <version>1.5.0</version>
    <description>Hello World example of an MVC component.</description>

    <files>
        <filename component="hellomvc">hellomvc.php</filename>
        <filename>index.html</filename>
        <filename>controller.php</filename>
        <filename>views/index.html</filename>
        <filename>views/hellomvc/index.html</filename>
        <filename>views/hellomvc/view.html.php</filename>
```

```
    </files>
    <administration>
        <menu>HelloMVC</menu>
        <files>
        <filename component="hellomvc">hellomvc.php</filename>
        <filename>index.html</filename>
        <filename>controller.php</filename>
        <filename>views/index.html</filename>
        <filename>views/hellomvc/index.html</filename>
        <filename>views/hellomvc/view.html.php</filename>
        </files>
    </administration>
</install>
```

Now, package the component in an archive named com_hellomvc.zip, and use the Extension Manager to install it into your Joomla system. If you connect a menu to reference the component and click on it, the greeting will been displayed as shown in Figure 8-2.

This is a very primitive example and only shows a glimmer of what can be accomplished using the MVC model. For example, the controllers and models folders were created but unused, since this component only had a single model and a single controller. Likewise, only a single view was placed in the \views folder, whereas a standard component would have a different view for each task sent to it (such as displaylist, edit, newentry, and so on). Since the component has been stripped down to its very essence, you now understand the foundations of how this style of programming is performed.

If you now study the components that ship with the Joomla system (all of which use this structure), you will be able to adapt this Hello MVC implementation to nearly any type of component.

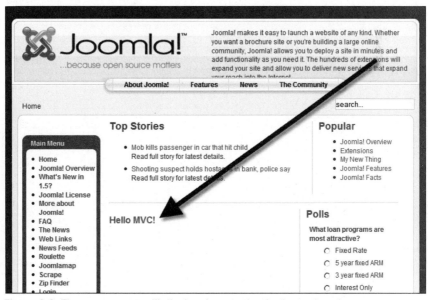

Figure 8-2: The component will display the greeting in the main column.

Summary

Design patterns have become increasingly important to developers as they face problems of increasing sophistication. By creating a documented library of successful implementation designs, the opportunity exists to minimize cost and schedule overruns that are common in the information technology industry.

More than ever, these patterns can be applied to subsystems such as extensions that are made to work with the Joomla framework. In this chapter, you learned how to apply design patterns by doing the following:

❑   Understanding the Joomla implementation and object framework.

❑   Using existing Joomla modules, components, and plug-ins to increase system capability.

❑   Designing extensions that follow effective patterns for best-case implementation.

❑   Evaluating existing system in terms of patterns so that the functionality of architectures such as Ajax could be understood within the evolution of networked systems.

Design patterns should help you to reuse the best methods of programming to develop any type of Joomla extension. In Chapter 9, you'll learn to create a plug-in that processes text for the Joomla system. For that plug-in, you will be able to see several of the patterns at work.

9

Hooking into the Joomla! Foundation: Plug-Ins

You have already created modules and components, so now it's time to tackle the final Joomla programming extension: the plug-in. While a module is primarily for presentation and a component is chiefly for user interaction, plug-ins sit at the lowest level of the system and can modify core Joomla functionality. In this chapter, you will create a simple Hello World plug-in, and then proceed to a far more complex plug-in that intercepts article content after Joomla has rendered it and make modifications to the page before it is sent to the visitor's browser.

After you've created and tested this pair of plug-ins, together with your previous comprehension of module and component programming, you will definitely be considered an advanced Joomla extension developer. The overview of the Joomla programming framework will complete your education. The framework is the actual skeleton of the Joomla CMS; it is made up of all classes that, once you understand them, you can leverage in direct use.

Joomla Plug-In Overview

Unlike modules that are all stored in the `\modules` folder or components that all exist in the `\components` folder, plug-ins are categorized and grouped within folders that define their categories. For example, plug-ins that provide search functionality are stored in the `\plugins\search` folder, while content plug-ins exist in the `\plugins\content` folder.

In the Plugin Manager, the category of plug-in is generally displayed in two places: as a prefix to the plug-in name and in the `Type` column. As shown in Figure 9-1, the name of each plug-in is preceded by the type. For example, the LDAP plug-in displays a name of "Authentication - LDAP." The type of plug-in defines how the extension will be treated by the system.

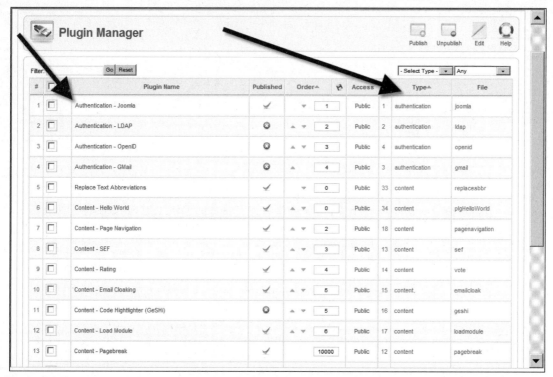

Figure 9-1: The category of the plug-in is shown in the Type column and added as a prefix to the plug-in name.

The eight different types of plug-ins include the following:

❑ *Authentication* — Provides user authentication functionality so that additional methods may be added. Some of the authentication plug-ins included with Joomla are LDAP, OpenID, GMail, and Joomla.

❑ *Content* — Allows content to be modified after it is retrieved from the database and before it is sent to the user. This allows content to be modified (for applications such as email address cloaking to prevent spam) or supplemented with additional information (such as item rating, user comments, and page navigation features).

❑ *Editor* — For content editors such as TinyMCE and XStandard Lite.

❑ *Editor button* — These plug-ins extend the capabilities of the content editor with buttons that add functions such as the ability to insert an image or a page break. In previous versions of Joomla, this type of plug-in was called an *editor-xtd*.

❑ *Search* — Used to add search capabilities for a particular item type such as content, sections, contacts, Web links, newsfeeds, or categories.

❑ *System* — Interfaces with the core Joomla system functions and allows control and modification over foundation tasks such as publishing, unpublishing, and even installation.

❏ *User* — Used to synchronize a user database with another user privilege system such as Gallery2, Simple Machines Forum, and so on.

❏ *XML-RPC* — Receives events directed through the XML Remote Procedure Call (RPC) communication protocol.

The creation of a plug-in entails creating a class that extends the `JPlugin` master class. Within the new class, functions are defined that match the names of the Joomla events. The code within these methods accepts the call of a trigger when that event occurs. For example, if you included a method called `onAfterInitialise()` in your plug-in definition, the code in the method would be executed every time a page was requested from the Joomla system, before the Joomla system started and began any processing.

Grouping the plug-ins into these type categories is more than just a semantic designation. The definition of the plug-in type determines the primary events that are available to that plug-in. However, some events (especially system events) can cross plug-in type boundaries. For that reason, the events themselves are divided into the following four generalized categories:

❏ Content

❏ Editor

❏ System and search

❏ User

These event categories limit the events that may be used by a given plug-in type, although most system events can be registered with any plug-in type.

Content Events

Content plug-ins are generally designed to make modifications to the content of the page before it is sent to the browser. For example, the Email Cloaking extension searches the page for all email addresses that are displayed by the page (or found in a hyperlink) and replaces them with an anti-spam version provided by the `JHTMLEmail::cloak` routine. The plug-in you'll be creating in this chapter is similar in that it searches for abbreviations/initials/acronyms and replaces them with the words represented by the shortened characters.

For content type plug-ins, the following are the six available events:

❏ `onBeforeDisplay` — Triggered just before content rendering has begun. The framework has been loaded and the page initialized.

❏ `onAfterDisplay` — Activated after content rendering is complete.

❏ `onPrepareContent` — Activated after the content has been rendered by the Joomla system but before it has been sent to the browser. This event is the most commonly used by plug-ins that are made to modify content. The current content is passed as a reference in the `article` parameter, so modifications made to the parameter will directly affect the content sent to the user browser. The `params` parameter holds an array of parameters relevant to the view, and the `limitstart` parameter holds an integer value of the "page" that the content represents.

❏ onAfterDisplayTitle — Triggered after the title text is generated and before the body of the content is rendered. Functions registered for this event should return an array of string values, and each string will be added to the output string. This event is useful if you want to create an extension that shows a current user rating of an article.

❏ onBeforeDisplayContent — Activated directly before the content is rendered. Functions registered for this event should return an array of string values, and each string will be added to the output string. This event is particularly useful if you need to output custom styles for content presentation.

❏ onAfterDisplayContent — Triggered immediately after article content is rendered. Functions registered for this event should return an array of string values, and each string will be added to the output string. This event is useful if you want to add a user comments system to display comments related to the given article.

By extending the JPlugin master class to define a plug-in of the content type, you can create functions within the class definition that can be triggered by these events and execute content modification code.

Editor Events

The core editor events apply to plug-ins that provide editor functionality (such as TinyMCE or XStandard Lite). Joomla editor core events include the following:

❏ onInit — Fires when the editor plug-in should be initialized. No parameters are passed to this event function.

❏ onDisplay — Triggers when the editor should be displayed. Passes the name of the editor as the only argument.

❏ onGetContent — Activates after the editing content is received. Passes the name of the editor as the only argument.

❏ onSetContent — Triggers just before the editor sets the new content. Passes the name of the editor as the only argument.

❏ onSave — Activates before the saving of content takes place.

❏ onCustomEditorButton — This event can be used to take advantage of custom editor buttons such as Image, Pagebreak, and Readmore buttons that come standard with the Joomla installation.

❏ onGetInsertMethod — Used by an editor plug-in to add a jInsertEditorText JavaScript function to the script declarations for an output document.

System and Search Events

System events trigger when global systemwide events occur. Function definitions for these events can be included with any of the plug-in types. Following are the five different system events:

❏ onAfterInitialise — This event is triggered when a browser makes a request of the Joomla system to display a page. It activates after the framework has been loaded and the application initialize function has been called but before any page output has been generated. This function is most useful when intercepting a task (the task type can be read from the query string parameters) and performing some preprocessing. For example, a plug-in could intercept the `save` task and before the save processing writes over the article content in that database, a backup could be made of the existing article that is stored in the database.

❑ `onAfterRoute` — This event is triggered when a browser makes a request of the Joomla system to display a page. It activates after the framework has been loaded and initialized, and after the router has parsed the route (to the desired component) and stored the request parameters in the `JRequest` object.

❑ `onAfterDispatch` — Triggered after the framework is loaded and startup functions initialized, and the content is rendered to the buffer. When code for this event is called, the application has already been mapped to a component.

❑ `onAfterRender` — This event is triggered when a browser makes a request of the Joomla system to display a page. It activates after the framework has been loaded and initialized and the rendered output has been stored in the `JResponse` object.

❑ `onSearch` — Triggered when a search has been requested.

❑ `onSearchAreas` — Triggered by the system to request from search plug-ins what "areas" each plug-in covers.

❑ `onGetWebServices` — Allows for implementing introspection by plug-ins. *Introspection* is a programming technique whereby an object can be queried about its API and functions. In this case, if a plug-in implements this trigger, it can provide the function names implemented in the plug-in, a `doc-string` with a human readable description of the plug-in, and a signature array holding the types of the method's parameters. This is used primarily by XML-RPC plug-ins.

User Events

There are two different sets of user events: the authentication events and the administrative user account events. Authentication events occur with plug-ins that are installed for the front end of the system, while administrative events handle the user account modifications that occur on the backend.

The user events related to the user accounts include triggers for the logging in and out of users. The following events are triggered when user authorization occurs:

❑ `onLoginUser` — Triggered after user has been authenticated against the username and password table in the Joomla database. If this function (or the trigger of any other plug-in that is registered for this event) returns a `False` value, then Joomla will consider the authentication as failed.

❑ `onLogoutUser` — Activated when user is attempting to log out. If this function returns a `False` value, then Joomla will consider the logout as failed.

❑ `onAuthenticate` — Triggered when all plug-ins have confirmed authentication and an array of login credentials is passed with `JAuthenticateResponse` objects holding the results from each plug-in.

❑ `onAuthenticateFailure` — Activated every time an authentication request is failed by a plug-in.

The events that are triggered when user management is occurring in the Administrator interface include the following:

- ❑ onBeforeStoreUser — Triggered before a user modification is written into the jos_users table.

- ❑ onAfterStoreUser — Activated after a user modification is written into the jos_users table.

- ❑ onBeforeDeleteUser — Triggered before a user record is deleted from the jos_users table.

- ❑ onAfterDeleteUser — Activated after a user record is deleted from the jos_users table.

Hello World Plug-In

Events are difficult to understand until you see them handled by a real plug-in. With that in mind, you will now create a simple Joomla Hello World! plug-in. This extension will be activated when the onAfterDisplayTitle event is triggered. Functions that handle this event are called for a piece of content as it is rendered. The execution of the event code occurs after the title has been output but before any of the article content has been rendered.

For the Hello World! plug-in, a greeting will be inserted between the title of each article and its content, as shown in Figure 9-2. When the onAfterDisplayTitle event is activated, the event function accepts a return value of HTML text that is appended to the content directly after the title. In the case of this plug-in, it is a simple matter of returning the greeting string.

Much like modules and components, you will need to create an XML descriptor file to inform the installer of the particulars of the plug-in, and a code file that holds the actual plug-in execution code.

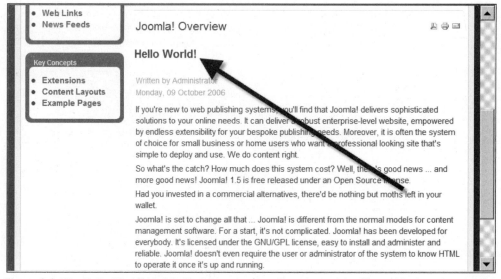

Figure 9-2: The Hello World! plug-in inserts a greeting after the article title and before the content.

Create the XML Descriptor File

Begin by creating the XML descriptor file in your text editor or development IDE, naming it `plgHelloWorld.xml` and entering the following code:

```
<?xml version="1.0" encoding="iso-8859-1"?>
<install version="1.5" type="plugin" group="content">
    <name>Content - Hello World</name>
    <author>Dan Rahmel</author>
    <creationDate>July 2007</creationDate>
    <authorEmail>admin@joomlajumpstart.com</authorEmail>
    <authorUrl>www.joomlajumpstart.com</authorUrl>
    <version>1.0</version>
    <description>Adds a Hello World greeting after the title of each
article.</description>
    <files>
        <filename plugin="plgHelloWorld">plgHelloWorld.php</filename>
    </files>
</install>
```

This XML file is very similar to the ones you've created for previous extensions. However, there are a few parameter settings that are specific to plug-in definition. Notice that the `<install>` tag has two attributes that denote the extension as a plug-in: the `type` and the `group`. The `type`, set to `plugin`, is straightforward enough. The `group` parameter must be set to the plug-in group enumerated earlier in the chapter (content, user, search, authentication, and so on). The plug-in files will be stored in the folder that is designated for that group.

The other item that you should pay close attention to and properly set is the `plugin` attribute for the `<filename>` tag. This name should match the name of the file for the plug-in — minus the file extension. When the plug-in is activated by the event trigger, it will search for the filename using the value in this attribute that is written into (at the time of plug-in installation) the `element` field of the `jos_plugins` table at run time. If it cannot find the file, the event code will not be executed.

Create the Plug-In Code

With the XML descriptor file stored on your local drive, use your editor to create another file in the same directory, naming it `plgHelloWorld.php` and entering the following code:

```php
<?php
/**
* @version          $Id: plgHelloWorld.php 6138 2007-07-02 03:44:18Z danr $
* @package          plgHelloWorld
*/

// no direct access
defined( '_JEXEC' ) or die( 'Restricted access' );

class plgContentHelloWorld extends JPlugin {
    // PHP4 compatible constructor
    function plgContentHelloWorld( & $subject ) {
        parent::__construct( $subject );
```

```
        }

        // Name function same as event so it will be called.
        function onAfterDisplayTitle(& $article, & $params, $limitstart=0) {
            $myOutput = "<h4>Hello World!</h4>";
            return $myOutput;
        }
    }

    // Instantiate the plug-in with an instance of the event dispatcher
    $myPlugin =& new plgContentHelloWorld( JEventDispatcher::getInstance() );

    ?>
```

You can see from the code that a new class called `plgContentHelloWorld` is defined as an extension of the `JPlugin` abstract class. The constructor is first defined as a function with a name that matches the class name. In this case, for PHP 4 compatibility, the constructor simply executes the constructor of the parent base class.

The `onAfterDisplayTitle()` event function definition comes next. When this event occurs, it will pass three parameters that provide read-only access to the content of the article from which the event was triggered. Since this is a simple greeting program, you can ignore those parameters for the moment. Instead, the plug-in simply defines the `"Hello World!"` string and passes it back to the calling function, using the `return` statement. That's it.

Take both the XML file and the PHP file and compress them into an archive (either ZIP or Tarball). From the Extension Manager, install the file in the system. By default, newly installed plug-ins are listed as unpublished. Go to the PlugIn Manager and publish the extension (which you will find under the name "Content - Hello World") to activate it.

If you browse to the main page, you should see the greeting between the title and the content of each article. That was pretty easy, wasn't it? The next plug-in will be a bit more complicated, and will actually perform a real function. For now, return to the PlugIn Manager and unpublish the Hello World plug-in so that it won't clutter up your system.

> *If you activated the plug-in, but saw no greeting when you looked at a Joomla article, there are two likely possible solutions. You may be looking at the articles summaries on the front page, and the `onAfterDisplayTitle` event isn't thrown there. Click on the Read More link or the title itself, and you will likely see the greeting when the entire article is displayed. Alternately, you may have the* Show Introduction *setting turned off either as a global setting or for the particular article. In the Article Manager of the Administrator interface, click on the Preferences button. Set the* Show Intro Text *option to* Show. *Alternately, you can edit the article itself, and, in the Advanced Parameters, set the* Intro Text *parameter to* Show.

Text Abbreviation Replacement Plug-In

The largest number of plug-ins are developed to modify the existing article content in some way before it is broadcast to the client browser. The plug-in may censor profanity, modify email addresses to prevent spam-bot harvesting, add keyword linking like Google Adsense, truncate an article for nonregistered users, and so on. Therefore, it would be most helpful to understand how such a content-modification extension can be created.

The Text Abbreviation Replacement plug-in you'll construct will scan an article for text abbreviations or acronyms and replace them with the words that the characters represent. For example, a poster might enter text in an article or chat setting and use the abbreviation "IMO," which stands for *In My Opinion*. The plug-in will intercept content retrieved from the Joomla database and expand these abbreviations before the article is sent to the browser. Since no changes are made to the database, the actual content remains intact.

While this plug-in may not solve a widespread problem, it will demonstrate all of the key implementation details of the Joomla plug-in system and provide an ideal foundation for development of other similar plug-ins. In fact, most common Joomla content extensions (censoring profanity, modifying email addresses, and so on) could easily be created with only a few changes to the Text Abbreviation Replacement plug-in.

Before you create the extension, produce a new article that contains some of the text abbreviations in the Article Manager. The body of the article I created reads like this:

```
I think the pink limo is great IMO, AFAIK, but IAC your image posting is definitely
NSFW and I have a POS or I would be ROTFL.
```

Not only does this text include a number of abbreviations, it also demonstrates the capabilities of the control to recognize and replace only the abbreviations — not the matching string of letters when they appear in other words. For example, the word `limo` includes the "IMO" characters of the abbreviation and `posting` includes the letters "POS." If the plug-in used a simple search and replace, the letters that match the abbreviation would be found in these words and replaced, destroying the text of the message. The plug-in should be programmed to avoid such mistakes.

When this document is displayed on the front page without the plug-in, the text appears exactly as entered (see Figure 9-3).

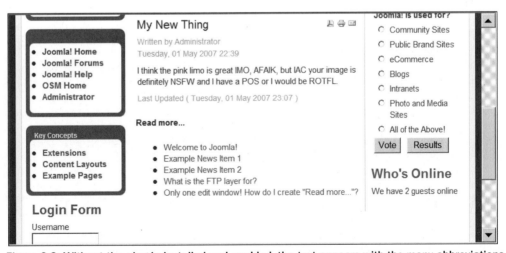

Figure 9-3: Without the plug-in installed and enabled, the text appears with the many abbreviations.

Once you have created and activated the plug-in, the abbreviations will be replaced with the phrases they represent, and the article will read much closer to English (see Figure 9-4).

To create this plug-in, you're going to again hook into the event structure for a content type component. The method of modifying content for this extension will be mirrored for other content event triggers.

Figure 9-4: Once the plug-in is enabled, it will replace the abbreviations before the text is sent to the browser.

XML Descriptor Code

Begin by creating the XML descriptor file in your text editor or development IDE, naming it `replaceabbr.xml` and entering the following code:

```
<?xml version="1.0" encoding="iso-8859-1"?>
<install version="1.5" type="plugin" group="content">
    <name>Content - Replace Text Abbreviations</name>
    <author>Dan Rahmel</author>
    <creationDate>July 2007</creationDate>
    <authorEmail>admin@joomlajumpstart.com</authorEmail>
    <authorUrl>www.joomlajumpstart.com</authorUrl>
    <version>1.0</version>
    <description>Replaces text abbreviations with the phrases they
represent.</description>
    <files>
        <filename plugin="replaceabbr">replaceabbr.php</filename>
    </files>
    <params>
        <param name="replace_limit" type="text" size="5" default="50"
label="Search Limit" description="Number of search items to return"/>
    </params>
</install>
```

The `<name>` tag can be set to anything, but Joomla naming conventions recommend placing a prefix denoting the group (in this case, "Content -") before the general plug-in name. The extension will work if you ignore this convention, but the naming practice allows faster identification of group type within the Administrator interface.

In the `<filename>` tag, the name of the plug-in is set with the `plugin` attribute. In this plug-in, the `plugin` attribute is even more important than in the Hello World! extension. You'll need to use this name later to access the plug-in's parameters. For this plug-in, a single parameter of `replace_limit` is included. The necessity of using this parameter in the Replace Abbreviation plug-in is dubious, but including a parameter provides a good demonstration of parameter configuration access.

Plug-In Code

With the XML descriptor file stored on your local drive, use your editor to create another file in the same directory, naming it `replaceabbr.php` and entering the following code:

```php
<?php
/**
* @version          $Id: replaceabbr.php 6138 2007-07-02 03:44:18Z danr $
* @package          ReplaceAbbr
*/

// no direct access
defined( '_JEXEC' ) or die( 'Restricted access' );

class plgContentReplaceabbr extends JPlugin {
    // PHP4 compatible constructor
    function plgContentReplaceabbr( & $subject ) {
        parent::__construct( $subject );
    }

    // Name function same as event so it will be called.
    function onPrepareContent(&$article, &$params, $limitstart=0) {
        // Get the parameters in case we need them in a later plug-in
        $plugin =& JPluginHelper::getPlugin('content', 'replaceabbr');
        $pluginParams = new JParameter( $plugin->params );
        $num =1;
        if (!$pluginParams->get('replace_limit', 1)) {
            $num = $pluginParams->get('replace_limit', 1);
        }

        if ( !JString::strpos( $article->text, '{replaceabbr=off}' ) === false )
        {
            $article->text = str_replace( '{replaceabbr=off}',
                    '', $article->text );
            return true;
        }

        $article->text =$this->replaceAbbrStr($article->text, $num);
        return true;
    }
```

```
    function replaceAbbrStr($myStr, $num) {
        // Create an array of text abbreviations
        $abbr=array( "@TEOTD","2G2BT",
            "ROTFL", "IMO",
            "AFAIK","NSFW",
            "BFF", "BF",
            "ATM","DIY",
            "IAC","IMO",
            "IMHO","OTOH",
            "POS","RTFM",
            "TGIF","TMI"
            );

        // Create a matching array of the phrases the words represent.
        // These are coded two per line so they are more human readable
        // making it easier to match them up to the above array.
        $actual=array("at the end of the day", "too good to be true",
            "rolling on the floor laughing","in my opinion",
            "as far as I know","not safe for work",
            "best friends forever","boyfriend",
            "at the moment ","do it yourself",
            "in any case","in my opinion",
            "in my humble opinion","on the other hand",
            "parent over shoulder","read the freakin manual",
            "thank goodness it's Friday","too much information"
            );

        // Add the regular expression notation to the abbreviations in the
        // array so the strings will only be matched if they are found as
        // lone words. Also make search case insensitive.
        for($i=0;$i < sizeof($abbr);$i++) {
            $abbr[$i] = "/\\b" . $abbr[$i] . "\\b/i";
        }

        // Do a regular expression replace
        $myStr = preg_replace ( $abbr, $actual, $myStr, $num);
        // Return altered string
        return $myStr;
    }
}

$myPlugin =& new plgContentReplaceabbr( JEventDispatcher::getInstance() );

?>
```

This extension is quite a bit more complicated than the earlier Hello World! plug-in. It begins the same with an extension of the JPlugin class, only this time named plgContentReplaceabbr.

This plug-in is triggered by the onPrepareContent event. This event is triggered after the Joomla system has prepared all of the article content, but before it is sent to the browser. You can see that this event receives three parameters: $article, $params, and $limitstart. The first two parameters are passed as references, so the function can modify the actual data — as this extension will do. The

`$limitstart` parameter holds the value of the current "page" of content, which is not relevant to this implementation.

This plug-in has a parameter (named `replace_limit`) that needs to be retrieved. Using the `JPluginHelper::getPlugin`, a reference to the plug-in is retrieved. From that, the plug-in parameters are retrieved and the value of the parameter is placed in the `$num` variable.

Before the plug-in does any processing, it needs to check if the content holds a manual override that will signal the plug-in to ignore this article. The override is denoted in the article with the text that reads `{replaceabbr=off}`. This is not any type of `patTemplate` directive or any formal declaration — I've just made it up for this extension to allow manual control for particular articles without disabling the entire plug-in. If the override is encountered, the override text is eliminated from the article content and the return statement aborts further plug-in processing.

If no override is found, the `$article->text` (which holds the current article) is passed to the `replaceAbbrStr` function for processing. The value returned by that function replaces the original content of the `$article->text` variable, and execution control returns to the system.

The `replaceAbbrStr` function is an ordinary PHP function that uses the two arrays with the regular expression function called `preg_replace` to replace the instances. The first statement of the function defines an array of the abbreviation values to be replaced. I have placed them two per line so that they are easy to maintain and coordinate with the second array. The second array (`$actual`) holds each complete phrase that will replace the element it parallels in the first array.

Before the replacement begins, the regular expression characters need to be added to the strings of the first array. This regular expression begins with a forward slash (`/`) delimiter to encapsulate the expression. The `\\b` is really only a `\b` command, but needs the preceding backslash for an escape character to formally include the second backslash in the string. The `\b` command tells the regular expression processor to only match if this is the beginning of a word (meaning the character preceding it is white space or punctuation).

Next, the abbreviation string is concatenated and this is followed by another `\b` to ensure that the expression ends on a word boundary. The final delimiter slash (`/`) is followed by the `i` directive telling the regular expression engine to perform a case-insensitive search.

> *If you're not already familiar with regular expression text processing, you should remedy this oversight in your education. Regular expressions are tremendously powerful for text processing and can save you huge amounts of time and energy. Check out the excellent tutorials at* `www.regular-expressions.info/php.html`.

Finally, the `preg_replace` function is called, passing the array of abbreviations (`$abbr`), the matching list of replacement values (`$actual`), the string to be processed (`$myStr`), and the number of replacements to make (`$num`). If the number of replacements is set to `-1` (the default), then all of the matching occurrences are replaced. The string returned by the expression engine should contain all of the replacement values, and is passed back to the calling routine.

From this small sample plug-in, I'm certain you can understand the power available through this extension system. You probably also now understand how the plug-ins integrate into the very foundation of the Joomla Framework and control many aspects of the core execution.

Joomla Framework Access

Now that you possess the skills to program all three types of extensions (modules, components, and plug-ins), your development will probably require that you integrate any extension you create with the Joomla system. This means understanding how Joomla functions on an execution level, and likely being able to make calls to the Joomla framework.

The complete Joomla framework is divided into a sizable number of packages, most of which are represented in an actual Joomla installation with a folder dedicated to the source files:

❑ *Application Package* — JApplication and related libraries are implemented as a factory class (see Chapter 8 for this design pattern). The four classes extended from this package (JInstallation, JModel, JSite, and JAdministrator) make up the Joomla CMS application. Also included are the Data Access Object (DAO) libraries, including the abstract JModel class that is extended to create the classes JModelCategory, JModelComponent, JModelMenu, JModelModule, JModelPlugins, JModelSection, JModelSession, and JModelUser. It is located in the \libraries\joomla directory.

❑ *Cache Package* — Cache libraries implemented as an abstract class that is extended by caching handlers. Includes the adapters JCacheCallback, JCacheView, JCacheOutput, and JCachePage.

❑ *Base Package* — The common package houses the base classes such as JObject, which is extended to create the classes JObservable and JTree. It is located in the \libraries\joomla\base directory.

❑ *Client Package* — Connector libraries such as FTP (JFTP class) and LDAP (JLDAP class) clients. This package is located in the \libraries\joomla\client directory.

❑ *Database Package* — JDatabase and related libraries provide the database connector functionality. Classes extend the JDatabase class to provide database access. Currently, only the JDatabaseMySQL and JDatabaseMySQLi classes exist, but connectors for Oracle and Microsoft SQL Server are planned in the future. The JSimpleRecordSet class is used for database interaction. This package is located in the \libraries\joomla\database directory.

❑ *Document Package* — Libraries for building and rendering pages featuring the JDocument abstract class. The JDocumentHTML class used to render HTML pages is an extension of the JDocument class. This package is located in the \libraries\joomla\document directory.

❑ *Environment Package* — Libraries for interacting with the user including classes for JResponse, JRequest, JBrowser, and JURI (which parses the URI). This package is located in the \libraries\joomla\environment directory.

❑ *Event Package* — Handles the Joomla events with classes that include JEventDispatcher, which extends JObservable (found in the Base Package); JPluginHelper; JEventHandler, which extends JObserver; and JPlugin, which extends JEventHandler. This package is located in the \libraries\joomla\event directory.

❑ *Filesystem Package* — Libraries for interacting with the file system, including classes for JArchive, JFile, JFolder, and JPath. The file management routines are used primarily for uploads of media, extensions, and languages. This package is located in the \libraries\joomla\filesystem directory.

❑ *Filter Package* — Libraries to filter input and output from any data source to prevent insertion attacks. Classes include `JInputFilter` and `JOutputFilter`. This package is located in the `\libraries\joomla\filter` directory.

❑ *i18n Package* — Internationalization libraries, including the classes `JLanguage` (singleton pattern), `JText`, and `JHelp`. This package is located in the `\libraries\joomla\i18n` directory.

❑ *Installer Package* — Libraries for installing extensions, including the abstract class `JInstaller`, which is extended to create the classes `JInstallerComponent`, `JInstallerLanguage`, `JInstallerModule`, `JInstallerPlugin`, and `JInstallerTemplate`. This package is located in the `\libraries\joomla\installer` directory.

❑ *Parameter Package* — Parameter manipulation and rendering libraries. This package is located in the `\libraries\joomla\parameter` directory.

❑ *Registry Package* — Configuration store libraries that include the classes `JRegistry`, `JRegistryFormat`, `JRegistryFormatINI`, `JRegistryFormatXML`, and `JRegistryFormatPHP`. This package is located in the `\libraries\joomla\registry` directory.

❑ *Session Package* — Library to handle a Joomla session through the `JSessionStorage` and `JSession` classes. This package is located in the `\libraries\joomla\session` directory.

❑ *Template Package* — Templating libraries that access `patTemplate`. Since Joomla is phasing out the use of `patTemplate`, it is not recommended you use classes or functions here in order to ensure future compatibility. This package is located in the `\libraries\joomla\template` directory.

❑ *User Package* — Libraries to activate, authorized, and authenticate a user login. Includes the classes `JAuthorization`; `JUserHelper`; `JAuthentication`; which extends `JObservable`; and `JUser`. This package is located in the `\libraries\joomla\user` directory.

❑ *Utilities Package* — Miscellaneous libraries, including `JError`, `JMail`, `JMailHelper`, `JProfiler`, and `JPagination`. The `JUtility` class includes the functions `sendMail()`, `sendAdminMail()`, `getHash()`, `getToken()`, `parseAttributes()`, and `isWinOS()`. Other utility functions include tools for arrays, buffers, dates, errors, functions, logs, mail, profiling, `simplexml`, and strings. This package is located in the `\libraries\joomla\utilities` directory. Email-related libraries, including the `JMail` class that is extended from the PHP class `PHPMailer`. The `JMailHelper` class provides some email utility functions, including `cleanLine()`, `cleanText()`, `cleanBody()`, `cleanSubject()`, `cleanAddress()`, and `isEmailAddress()`.

As mentioned in previous chapters, the Joomla CMS is actually an application that sits atop the general Joomla Framework. Other applications could be built using the Joomla Framework, although such development is beyond the scope of this book. Core framework development requires dedicated study of the actual Joomla source code.

There are two root classes for the Joomla framework: `JFactory` and `JVersion`. `JFactory` is a factory class used to create and return various framework objects, while the `JVersion` class holds the version information of the current installation. Although you will be unlikely to reference these classes, they sit at the most primitive level of the framework, so ground-up studies of Joomla might begin there.

Joomla CMS (JApplication) Structure

The Joomla CMS system has three faces:

❑ *Installation* — The installation portion of Joomla handles the initial installation and configuration of the Joomla system. After it performs that function during the first system setup, it is never used again.

❑ *Front end* — The front end defines the user experience. In most cases of access to the front end, the session will be read-only. Except in circumstances when an extension performs a dynamic user interaction function (such as registering a poll vote), Joomla content will be read from the MySQL server and returned as formatted Web pages to the visitor.

❑ *Back end* — The back end is used almost entirely to add and modify content. Even third-party contributors will spend little time browsing content on the back end. In comparison to front-end user access, there will be a substantially smaller amount of traffic (read or write) on the back end.

The Joomla CMS system is divided along these lines into the following three different "applications" that execute at various times and are structured after their primary functions:

❑ `JSite` — The front-end user application.

❑ `JAdministrator` — The back-end Administrator interface.

❑ `JInstallation` — The installation interface.

Each of the applications is actually a class that has been extended from the `JApplication` abstract class. Since nearly all extension development will interface with the `JSite` application, only a general overview of the `JAdministration` and `JInstallation` interfaces will be covered here.

JInstallation Application

The installation application represented by the `JInstallation` class is generally only executed once — when the Joomla system is first installed. The program files for this class can be found in the `\installation` directory. Most of the core logic for this class is found in the `\installation\ includes` directory. The `\includes` directory contains the following files:

❑ `application.php` — Initializes and activates the installation application and creates the user session.

❑ `defines.php` — Creates the global path variables used by the installer.

❑ `framework.php` — Imports the Joomla framework libraries used by the installer.

❑ `xajax.php` — Holds the Joomla Ajax code that is used to asynchronously parse the language XML files, install the sample data, verify the FTP connection, and populate the database collation list.

Other core files are located in the `\installation\installer` directory and include the following:

❑ `controller.php` — Holds the `JInstallationController` class, which is the main execution code of the installer. Handles all of the installation screen processing, including language choice, pre-installation check, GPL license agreement, database configuration, FTP configuration, and finish screen. Also contains the logic for the database creation.

- ❑ `html.php` — Holds the presentation logic that displays the screens generated by the `JInstallationController` class.

- ❑ `installer.php` — Executes the `JInstallationController` class.

- ❑ `jajax.php` — Handles the Ajax tasks using the routines found in `xajax.php`.

Although you will rarely need to use any of the routines in the installer, if you are having difficulty with an installation, it may be helpful to examine the source files for the class. The source code holds the actual execution process for the installation, so unexplained errors and other problems may be explainable through the code.

Don't rely on this class to be available on a normal Joomla deployment. The `\installation` directory should be deleted after Joomla is installed on any deployment server. Therefore, it will not be available for access under ordinary circumstances.

JSite Front-End Application

The area where the execution will be most important to your studies is `JSite`. The `JSite` application provides the code that takes all of the content in the MySQL database, integrates it with a selected template, and generates the output to the user. It also handles all of the login and user-interaction functions.

As with all Joomla framework applications, the `JSite` front end begins execution with the `index.php` located in the root directory. That index loads three central files: `defines.php`, `framework.php`, and `application.php`. The main `JSite` class definition file (`application.php`) is located in the root `\includes` directory. The `index.php` file creates an instance of the `JSite` class and, after performing some setup functions (such as establishing a session and importing the `system` plug-in), executes the application.

It includes the following central functions:

- ❑ `initialize` — Initializes the user and language settings.

- ❑ `dispatch` — Provides the top-level HTML rendering, including the title, description, metadata, and JavaScript linking. It also executes the `JComponentHelper::renderComponent` method.

- ❑ `render` — Generates the main HTML display of the CMS page by first checking the format (whether HTML or feed) and then calling the render method of the `JDocument` class. After the content is rendered, the `setBody` method of the `JResponse` object is called with the generated data to provide the output.

- ❑ `login` — Checks the authentication of the username and password.

- ❑ `logout` — Calls the `logout` method of the `JApplication` class to terminate the session.

- ❑ `getPageParameters` — Retrieves the menu and the component parameters, and returns them in the array named `$params`.

- ❑ `loadConfiguration` — Uses the `JPATH_SITE` constant to locate the `configuration.php` site settings file and load the configurations it contains. When in legacy mode, also checks for the `mosConfig` file for various site settings.

- ❑ `getTemplate` — Returns the name of the selected display template for the page. If there are multiple templates for the current `menuid`, it queries the `jos_templates_menu` table to retrieve a list of them, and returns the first one in the resultset.

❑   setTemplate — Used to override the default template of the site.

❑   createPathway — Constructs a URL pathway for the various site objects such as the menu path items.

The methods of the application.php file make up the core of the CMS system. You can see by how few routines are included that a vast amount of the program logic is provided by the foundation Joomla framework.

JAdministrator Back-End Application

The JAdministrator application is located in the \administrator directory of the Joomla installation. It executes in a nearly identical fashion to the JSite application, except that it initializes the JAdministrator class instead of JSite. In addition to the administrative versions of the three central files (defines.php, framework.php, and application.php), this version of the index.php file also loads the toolbar.php file to provide the menu bar to the Administrator interface.

If you examine the \administrator directory, you'll notice that, while there are folders for administrative modules and components, there is no folder for plug-ins. The JAdministrator application executes differently from the JSite front end, which uses a single display method for all content. In contrast, the Administrator interface acts more like a series of small applications executing to produce the display. That means there isn't a single standard event structure that can be easily exposed for plug-ins to use.

Path Variables

There are a number of constant variables that Joomla code can address to determine access paths to the various Joomla folders. These include the following:

❑   JPATH_ROOT — Holds the root path to the Joomla framework.

❑   JPATH_SITE — Contains the root path of the JSite application.

❑   JPATH_ADMINISTRATOR — Holds the root path of the JAdministrator application.

❑   JPATH_INSTALLATION — Contains the root path of the JInstallation application.

❑   JPATH_BASE — Holds the path of the currently executing application. Therefore, when the JSite application is executing, this variable holds the same value as JPATH_SITE. However, while displaying the Administrator interface, the value matches JPATH_ADMINISTRATOR.

These constants are some of the few global variables that will be available in the future. Most global variables have been deprecated and will be eliminated in future Joomla versions.

Tips for Examining Joomla Source Code

Now that you know how to create every type of programmatic extension (modules, components, and plug-ins), the ability to extend the Joomla system is limited only by your programming skills and knowledge of the Joomla system. While developing add-ons, there are many times when you will not understand exactly how Joomla handles particular data or user interaction. That is where Joomla source code examination provides an ideal solution.

Since Joomla is open source, all of the source code is fully available for examination in each installation. Almost any question you would have about Joomla execution can be revealed by checking the source files.

I would highly recommend that you look through some of the code if you plan to do advanced Joomla development. It may be a little overwhelming at first, but you'll quickly come to understand how the code is organized.

The following sections provide some pointers that should help your Joomla studies. There is no substitute for opening up your text editor and making an educated examination of the source files.

Using a Directory Search Function

Whenever you have a question about how Joomla is executing, it is likely that you can find the relevant code with a simple text search. You must approach the task as a detective would — looking for clues to lead you to the final resolution. For example, imagine that you wanted to extend the types of module parameters available for editing within the Administrator interface. If you look at the Module Editing screen for any module, you see that the display of the parameters is titled "Module Parameters," as shown in Figure 9-5.

If you use an application such as jEdit that includes a directory search, you can search for that text value. Searching for the value will show you a number of different files where the term appears, as shown in Figure 9-6. If you examine the individual files, it is clear that the parameters are displayed in the admin.modules.html.php file in the com_modules directory of the Administrator installation.

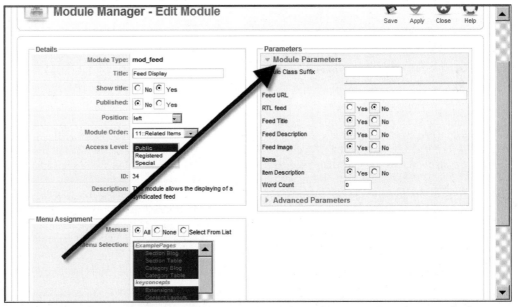

Figure 9-5: The parameters for a module use the title "Module Parameters" on the page display.

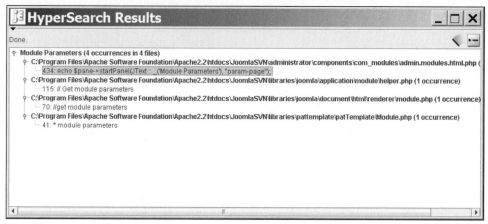

Figure 9-6: The directory search from jEdit shows the files that contain these references.

A few lines after the one that contains the search text, you will find the following code:

```
$p->render('params')
```

Another search for the text "function render" should result in the file that renders the module parameters. There are 35 files that have that function, but the following one stands out:

```
\libraries\joomla\html\parameter.php
```

In this file, the function getParams() handles the retrieval of the parameters. You can keep following the path until it reaches the level that you need. Another method of searching would entail looking in the XML descriptor files, finding a unique type of element (radio, for example), and searching for that. The files that render that element are found in (jackpot) this directory:

```
\libraries\joomla\html\parameter\element
```

You'll find the definitions for the display of all types of elements, including spacer, section, editors, category, filelist, imagelist, and so on. From there, all you need to do is trace backward to the code that executes these element renderers, and you can likely define your own!

Most Joomla developers will want to research and modify the CMS interface, so the best place to begin may be the \libraries\joomla folder. You can use the package descriptions discussed earlier in this chapter to understand exactly the functions stored in the various files of these libraries.

Examining com_content

Content display in the Joomla system is not embedded in the actual framework — it is processed by the com_content component. On a staging server, you will find the component at a directory something like this:

```
C:\Program Files\Apache Software Foundation\Apache2\htdocs\components\com_content
```

This component has been developed using the Model-View-Controller (MVC) design pattern described in Chapter 8. By examining the various component files (particularly `content.php`), you can learn how the content is formatted for display. The final HTML rendering of the component is handled by the `ContentViewArticle` class. You'll find that class in the `view.html.php` file in the following component folder:

```
\components\com_content\views\article\view.html.php
```

Joomla SVN: The Bleeding Edge

Whenever you are performing Joomla development on extensions (such as modules, components, or plug-ins), you should use a version control system. A version control system has a repository that stores current versions of selected program files. Members of a development team access the repository and download the current versions of the files. A user may check out a file to perform some programming on it. Any changes are then uploaded back into the version control system, where they are integrated into the whole project. However, the old version of the file is archived in the repository in case changes need to be rolled back or an older version is needed.

The Joomla development team uses the Subversion (SVN) version control application to manage development. They have made the Joomla repository open for read-only access to the public. You can access the SVN repository of Joomla and download up-to-the-moment versions of Joomla if you wish. First, you need to install SVN. See Chapter 6 for information on SVN application availability and installation.

Once you have SVN installed, you must create a folder where the downloading of the source files will occur. On my staging server, I always keep a `JoomlaSVN` directory stored in the root directory of my Apache directory. Therefore, I have a folder with a path like this:

```
C:\Program Files\Apache Software Foundation\Apache2.2\htdocs\JoomlaSVN
```

Once the folder is created, you must set it up to retrieve the files from the repository. For TortoiseSVN on Windows, you can simply right-click on the folder and select the SVN Checkout option. The checkout window will be displayed as shown in Figure 9-7. For the URL of the repository, enter **http://joomlacode.org/svn/joomla/development/trunk** and click the OK button.

For the username, enter **anonymous** and leave the password blank. The SVN client will contact the repository and download all of the Joomla source files to the directory. This may take a little time for the first download because the system needs to check out more than 3000 files. You can now use this Joomla version like any other.

To update the files at a later time, you only have to right-click on the folder again and select the SVN Update option. The application will contact the main repository and only update the files that have been changed. A window will display the update's progress (see Figure 9-8). When complete, the label under the list box will report how many bytes were transferred, as well as the files that were merged, added, deleted, and updated.

Updating your folder will not write over other files that you have stored there, or erase the Joomla database. If you have run the Joomla installation, added extensions, adjusted configuration settings, or made any other changes that don't directly affect the source files, the update will be transparent. The only files that are overwritten are those found in the repository, which are transferred to your folder.

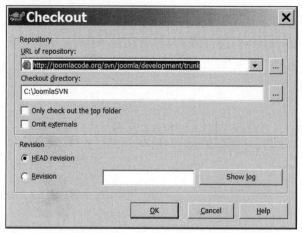

Figure 9-7: You can set up the checkout of the current version of Joomla through this TortoiseSVN window.

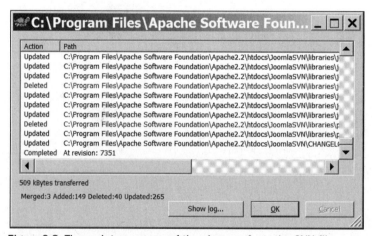

Figure 9-8: The update progress of the changes from the SVN file repository are displayed in the status window.

Downloading a version of Joomla into a local folder via SVN will create a folder named .svn at each level of the project hierarchy. In each folder are a large number of control files that track the versioning of the project. *Do not delete* these folders if you want to do another download update at a later time. They are needed for SVN to know which files on your local drive need to be updated and which files are current.

The files contained in the .svn folders are small but numerous. If you want to upload to an FTP site the version found in your local folder, all of these files will make the process take almost 10 times longer than usual. Therefore, before you perform the upload, use SVN to export the project files to another folder. Only the project files will be transferred, and not the version control folders. In Tortoise SVN, you need only right-click on the project folder and select the TortoiseSVN ⇨ Export... option.

Since the SVN update does not update the Joomla database in any way; that means changes to the development version of the database (and the code that accesses it) may result in code that faults on your system once the update is complete. In this situation, the Joomla execution will start generating database errors when trying to access the altered schema. The easiest way to get your system functioning again is to delete or rename the `configuration.php` *at the root directory and re-run the installer. It will create a backup version of existing tables if you want to manually copy over content or extension settings.*

There is a repository available for Joomla version 1.0.x here:

```
http://joomlacode.org/svn/joomla/development/releases/1.0
```

The repository for the modules for Joomla 1.x (which contains historical snapshot releases and experimental development branches) can be found here:

```
http://joomlacode.org/svn/joomla/development
```

These repositories use the same login procedure as the central Joomla trunk development.

Summary

Joomla plug-ins allows execution code to be activated by events at the very core of the Joomla system. These extensions can do everything from intercept content for modification to providing additional forms of user authentication. Once you understand how to create plug-ins, you will have reached a point where you can develop all three types of Joomla extensions, since you've previously learned about modules and components. You can use this knowledge together with a foundation understanding of the Joomla framework to create almost any custom Joomla system you can imagine.

This chapter has provided an overview of the Joomla plug-in and framework architecture by doing the following:

❑   Introducing the eight types of plug-ins the Joomla system uses.

❑   Explaining the four categories of events that a plug-in may be registered to handle if triggered by the system.

❑   Creating a Hello World! plug-in that is activated by the `onAfterDisplayTitle()` event to add a Hello World! greeting between each article's title and body content.

❑   Developing a Text Abbreviation Replacement plug-in that intercepts article content and replaces common abbreviations with the phrases that they represent.

❑   Examining the various packages of the Joomla framework for greater knowledge and utilization of the Joomla programming system.

❑   Teaching you useful guidelines that will aid you in the direct examination and comprehension of the Joomla source code.

Now that you have explored under the surface of Joomla execution, it is time to return to the aspects of Web site deployment that will make your Joomla development worthwhile. In Chapter 10, you will implement existing extensions to add interactive community features to your site.

10

Building Joomla! Communities

In the world of Web 2.0, *interactivity* and *community* are the watchwords. Organizations have learned that establishing a *virtual community* (that is, an online community), while difficult, is essential to thriving in the new marketplace. By adding community technology to a Web site, visitors are encouraged to add their voices to the interaction between the site content and other visitors. Communication occurs through a variety of site features, including chat rooms, forums, personal pages, guestbooks, polls, commenting systems, social networking, event calendars, and wiki systems.

Whether the virtual community is a loose gathering of participants (such as consumers entering product reviews on the target Web site) or the intensive daily use of MySpace, the rewards are significant in terms of traffic and site ranking. The development of Joomla itself is a success story in terms of creating a sustained online community that has fostered a thriving forum (`forum.joomla.org`), an active user-contribution directory with visitor commenting (`extensions.joomla.org`), and a high-volume, user-submitted site directory (`www.joomla.org/content/blogcategory/35/69`). Joomla wouldn't be thriving without the embrace of the community technologies by the system user.

Fostering an online community or social network takes careful deployment and the coordination of many different pieces of technology. Unlike a traditional static Web site, a virtual community accepts input rather than simply outputting stored pages. This means a whole new set of challenges from configuring data sources to accepting and storing submitted data to the extra administration (both automated and manual) required to control the flow and efficacy of new content.

Fortunately, Joomla not only has the technology to create a thriving community, but it also minimizes the difficulties of implementing this functionality. In this chapter, you will learn an approach to planning a virtual community all the way through implementation using existing free Joomla extensions.

As of this writing, some of the extensions described in this chapter have not yet been upgraded to work with Joomla 1.5. I hope by the time you read this, all of the add-ons will be available in their version 1.5 incarnations. If the extension you want to use is not yet upgraded, look in the Joomla extensions directory (`extensions.joomla.org`) and it is very likely you will find a substitute extension that will perform the same functions.

Because virtual communities require a large amount of maintenance time, it is useful to take a conservative approach to deployment. The extensible nature of the Joomla system is perfect for such an incremental deployment. In most cases, you can add an extension that provides a specific community capability in less than 10 minutes. If the feature is not popular on the site, or if you're not satisfied with the options it provides, you can use the Extension Manager to uninstall or unpublish it in seconds. Without Joomla, most Web sites would require a great deal of custom programming to integrate these considerable features into a system.

Some of the extensions used in creating an online community have already been introduced in Chapter 4, so they will only be briefly reviewed here to describe their place in the community setup. A variety of other extensions will be presented to offer a representative sample of the types of features that can be added to the Joomla system. All of the extensions covered in this chapter are available for free. When there is a particularly well-known commercial extension to provide a specific functionality, that product will be cited.

For each extension demonstrated, a URL is provided where it can be found as of this writing. However, projects tend to change and move around. All of the cited extensions are included in the directory that you will find in the Joomla extensions directory. So, if the Web address denoted in this book is no longer valid, you should be able to locate the current download location in the directory.

Planning a Virtual Community

Creating a virtual community is somewhat like making a movie. Before a single camera starts to roll, there is an entire process of preproduction ensuring that the actors are properly cast, the equipment is rented and functioning, the script is in place, and the department heads know what type of movie they are trying to make. If any of these areas are neglected, from the first day of shooting, the movie will stumble forward, and a vast amount of time and energy will likely be wasted.

Likewise, a virtual community is expensive in time to launch, difficult to attract visitors/contributors, and poorly planned execution will make even a promising start fizzle into a disappointment. Although Joomla makes the deployment of the features simple, proper planning even for an incremental deployment is critical for site success. By being deliberate in your planning and construction of the new community site, you will minimize the chances of hard-won users becoming frustrated with a poorly working or confusing rollout and leaving your site forever. The creation and deployment may be divided into roughly three stages.

Three Stages of a Virtual Community

Virtual communities are unlike most traditional Web deployments (such as a static site or online store) in that they derive their value from the intercommunication of a large user base. Under any circumstances, gathering this large number of users can take quite a bit of time. The creation of a virtual community is typically a gradual process, and a visitor surge does not provide the benefits it would on a traditional site. If your Web site was suddenly flooded with a million users overnight, it is unlikely that the site could retain those users for more than a short period of time. Furthermore, the first experience of these new visitors would be empty content and slow performance. Growth for virtual communities is organic because the community slowly discovers what the group has to offer.

Given the unique nature of virtual community deployment and expansion, it may be helpful to look at a "roadmap" of development so that you can maintain your direction as you navigate the sometimes frustrating terrain. The deployment procedure can best be separated into three stages:

❑   Development/testing

❑   Launching/gathering

❑   Redefinition/maturity

Nearly all successful virtual communities follow these paths, so certain landmarks can be identified.

Stage 1: Development and Testing

When the idea of creating a virtual community is first examined, you should have a preconception of the type of community that you want to create. Joomla makes it easy for you to use a local deployment to experiment with various features to decide what type of site you want to create. Using this hands-on approach while answering the following questions will give you a clear idea of the site concept:

❑   *Will the community be commercial or hobbyist?* — This makes a greater difference than you might imagine. The answer to this question will determine the audience that you are seeking for the site. For example, a commercial community that focuses on Product A will be unlikely to gain the contributions of users of competitive Products B and C. However, a hobbyist site catering to all the products of that category may not have the necessary focus to attract advertising dollars for vendors of add-on offerings for Product A. Additionally, hobbyist Web sites have much looser standards in terms of vulgarity and off-topic communication, since they don't have to answer to a sponsoring company or advertising clients.

❑   *Do you have an agenda of the topics discussed?* — Many failed virtual communities have no skeleton upon which content can grow. Like a trellis that guides climbing plants to extend upward and thrive, a topic agenda is a good place to begin planning. With an effective agenda, visitors can be guided into their area of desire.

❑   *Will the virtual community be a supplement to a Web site or the main attraction?* — Since virtual communities require a great deal of time and maintenance, many sites add them as minor additions, instead of making them the centerpiece of the site. This strategy provides advantages of progressive introduction of the community technology, and allows you to build on the existing visitor base. However, it is unlikely to produce MySpace-like success that is encouraged when the site's reason for existence is community.

With the general concept outlined, development can begin. Most virtual communities use preexisting software (such as the extensions described in this chapter), so development generally is a small part of the project's time budget. Once the software is set up and configured, the framework developed during the planning stages can be input. This might include creating categories, providing foundation documents and terms of service, and setting up the security login structure.

Testing should be done with a load-testing and performance tool so that the limits of the current deployment can be understood. Be sure to read the sections in Chapter 11 on load testing and load balancing. These tools, while important to a normal Joomla site, are critical for determining the capacity of your virtual site so that you can judge the upper size limits of your community on the current server setup.

It is a further good idea to personally recruit some users, in the area you want to target, to the virtual community for an informal test. With Joomla's registered user display options, you can limit access of the new community features to only those who will be helpful in figuring out the deployment. If your site targets teenagers, find some who can try the site and give you their input. For a site focused on high-tech professionals, ask not only for their opinions of your community but also for recommendations of other communities that they visit so that you can have some idea of the types of sites already pulling in that audience.

Stage 2: Launch and Gathering

The time of launching a Joomla virtual community is exciting, but it can often be disheartening. There are usually far fewer visitors than were expected, and those who do arrive are more likely to look around or "lurk" than contribute content or join in a discussion. While the low traffic levels may seem bad at the time, for most sites, this period is actually of great advantage.

As in most arenas, 10 percent of the people will do 90 percent of the work. The launch will help you locate contributors who will take ownership responsibility for the site. As the first people in the door, you can make them feel like they are extremely important to the direction of the site (which they are) and that they are, in a sense, cofounders of the community.

In the beginning, you will need to reach out to those who make even the smallest contribution. Someone who makes a single comment on an article or posts the first message to a forum deserves at least a personal email of thanks from the people running the site. Ensure that you take the time to make these early adopters feel appreciated, because they will reward you by contributing more to the site. You may even reward contributors with giveaways, extra site privileges, or title status (such as site tester, advanced user, featured contributor, and so on).

Many proponents of virtual communities have likened the care and maintenance of the community to caring for a garden. New seeds must be planted, trees pruned, and weeds rooted out. It is in adolescence that the tasks of gardener are most needed, but also most tedious. The "bloom has left the rose," as the saying goes, and what was exciting and new at the beginning has become more labor and tedium. Like the difficulty of any adolescence, however, it is during this time when a virtual community truly decides what it will become in the future.

Stage 3: Redefinition and Maturity

As the virtual community begins gaining strength, a Joomla web master must examine the site to see if a redefinition is required. For example, a site may have been envisioned as a place for joggers to exchange information about running shoes, but if a huge majority of visitors exchange information on the most scenic routes to run, a redefinition of the site may be in order. You may even want to change the look of the site to better reflect the content, which is an easy task given Joomla's template interface. Perhaps a site theme that communicated solid professionalism needs to be softened to warm friendliness given the community interaction — or vice versa.

To refocus the site on another topic does not mean abandoning the initial topic (although it may). Rather, it most often means that priorities and resources are redeployed to the areas that reflect visitor interest. In the example of the running shoe site, redefinition might include adding a photo gallery extension to the site that would allow users to post pictures of the most scenic routes. Additionally, the site might include a category breakdown by geography, where visitors could suggest their routes by area.

There is no simple litmus test to determine when a site must be redefined, yet it is helpful to have specific milestones to indicate when the redefinition evaluation should occur. For example, set a calendar date or choose a Web traffic threshold that will trigger the reevaluation of the site. You will need to dedicate enough time to examining the logs and looking at contributor interests that you can make a thorough examination of the direction of the community.

Once you have survived redefinition, solidified your community, and have many regular visitors/ contributors, that is the time to evaluate how to better serve your virtual community. At this point, you have a clear understanding of your most frequent visitors and most reliable contributors. You can determine how best to add value to their experiences and, if the site is commercial, monetize the traffic. To make this determination, there are a number of areas to examine, including the following:

❑   *Ancillary topics or products* — If your site focuses on running shoes, can you also provide information related to the larger areas of fitness? Or, maybe you could provide general information on living an upscale lifestyle. Ensure that the new additions are sideline features. A virtual community can destroy itself by becoming too general, or by watering down the reasons people came in the first place. A successful site for professional joggers does not want to be flooded with newbie visitors who don't know the difference between a half marathon and a marathon.

❑   *Special group activities and offers* — Like the collective bargaining power of a union, any significant group of people working in concert wields a great deal of power. This power can be used in a great number of ways, including organizing a conference, supporting a fund-raising drive, creating a group purchase for discounted rates, or starting a letter-writing campaign to a regional politician. Think in terms of both what could benefit members of the group (such as a high-volume purchase of a product) and what can benefit the community itself (such as a fund-raising drive for a faster server). Using Joomla extensions such as forums or guestbooks, you can determine if there is interest in such a program.

❑   *Targeted advertising* — Most sites sport some type of advertising through banner ads or affiliate programs for click-through sales of products. With Joomla's Banner component, setting up a custom ad campaign is a snap and sometimes Joomla users overwhelm their visitors with marketing. Each Web page offers only so much space for advertising before the marketing becomes unattractive and begins to deter visitors from returning. Evaluate the ads on your site in terms of both attractiveness and revenue generation. If an affiliate-provided banner slows the loading of your page and represents little actual revenue, would the site benefit by eliminating that ad? If a small ad generates a great deal of revenue, perhaps that ad should be moved to a place of greater prominence. In addition to examining the affiliates you already have, it would also be wise to look around to see if new vendors have opportunities that might fit better with your site goals.

Understanding the Importance of Stability and Regularity

For a traditional Web site, stability is important. For a virtual community, it is critical. If a virtual community is serving its purpose, it has become a place where visitors come to connect with others. Any downtime for the site will frustrate users who will feel cut off from one another. If the site regularly experiences service disruption, many users will reach a point where they will simply refuse to return.

Almost as important as keeping users happy is meeting posted deadlines. If the site declares that there will be new content every Tuesday, there *must be* new content every Tuesday. The Internet is full of abandoned Web sites or "ghost pages" stating that an update will be made in the next week — with a date that is years old. If you risk making infrequent updates to your virtual community, ensure that you post no scheduling claims so that your credibility will not be diminished.

> *Joomla has a great feature to protect against missed publication deadlines: a begin publication date. For each article, you may specify when it will be published (as well as a date when the content will stop appearing). If your schedule is uncertain, do yourself a favor and generate a number of content pieces before you announce a Web site feature such as a newsletter or column. You can then post all of these articles to the system at once and stagger the publication dates. Not only will you be several dates ahead (thus preventing any publication delays), but events such as a family emergency will not affect your Web site's appearance of regularity.*

Why You Should Create a Virtual Community

With all of the difficulties in running a virtual community (mostly in added workload and time), it might seem to be a questionable undertaking. This is not the case. I am not trying to discourage the adoption of virtual community technologies but simply make you aware of some of the challenges in their deployment.

The greater your knowledge of the challenges before you attempt to create a virtual community, the greater the likelihood that you will be prepared for the difficulties and overcome them. A poorly implemented community is much more likely to be a failure than a poorly implemented Web site. The Web site will still garner visitors looking for the information it contains, while a failed online community will be like a ghost town with few tourists.

Despite any disadvantages to creating a community, the benefits are substantial:

❑ *Creation of a growing audience* — Over the long term, a virtual community will grow itself. If the community achieves the momentum of MySpace.com or YouTube.com, that will mean literally millions of Web visitors and contributors. Your community does not have to reach these stellar heights to be successful. But, like them, if your community reaches a critical mass, you may see exponential growth.

❑ *Long site visits* — In contrast to the quick-stop nature of most Web visits, a virtual community will have visitors that stay on the site for hours at a time. That not only provides a great opportunity to gain site loyalty but also maximizes advertising impressions. There is an old sales precept that customers must encounter a product seven times before they will feel comfortable enough to buy it. Long site visits promote exactly this type of repeated exposure.

❑ *Group marketing opportunities* — Since the contributors themselves will outline their interests through the content that is communicated on the site, there are many opportunities to precisely target offers to visitors. This is especially true when a sale on a directly relevant product or

service occurs. Bringing the opportunity to the attention of the group may further the site's reputation of being immediate and relevant to the subject area.

❑ *Direct feedback* — Unlike a traditional Web site, where only by watching the log statistics can
you learn about visitor activity, in a virtual community, you will be able to obtain direct feedback from others interested in your topic area and your site.

❑ *Concentration of specific knowledge* — Most virtual communities provide a very high level of specific information and help. The people who converge on an online meeting place typically have
a high level of expertise (or are seeking to attain these skills), so the information generated by
such a community actually creates a gold mine of specific information for a topic area.

❑ *Loyalty of visitors* — A traditional Web site has very limited sticking power. If the Web master stops
providing the desired information, the site will quickly decline and visitors will stay away. In contrast, once a community is established, the site will perpetuate itself for a long time on its own.

❑ *Community service* — Whatever the focus of the community, a virtual community is largely a
social "good." Most virtual communities bring together people of similar interests and help
them share information.

Technology of a Virtual Community

A community site is not created by a single technology. In fact, there are a large number of different types
of Joomla extensions that allow dynamic interaction among users on a site, including the following:

❑ Guestbook

❑ Chat

❑ Forum/message boards

❑ Polls

❑ Comments

❑ Social networking

❑ Event calendar

❑ Wiki systems

These technologies can be mixed and matched to the best effect on the site. Joomla supplies a perfect host
for these features, since it plays a unifying role in administration and often common login. The extensions
that are particularly database-intensive (such as forums/message boards) require close monitoring so that
the database server can be tuned for maximum performance.

A virtual community will be a "work in progress," so don't be afraid to add a technology that you may
remove later because of disuse. If enough users complain about the absence of a feature that seemed to
be unpopular, you may be able to refine it during a redeployment phase so that it will provide what the
visitors have been seeking.

The following sections will introduce one or more Joomla extensions for each of the community technology areas: guestbook, chat, forums/messageboards, polls, comments, social networking, event calendar,
and wiki systems. In my testing, I found no conflicts where installation of one extension would interfere
with installation of another. Therefore, you can freely mix and match the applications as necessary.

Guestbook

A *guestbook* is one of the oldest forms of Web interaction. It allows visitors to post commentary and compliments on the contents of the board. (You created a small guestbook application in Chapter 6.) Although a guestbook has little implementation cost in terms of time and energy, it also inspires the least community spirit. Therefore, a guestbook is a better addition to a traditional Web site than it is a feature used with most community sites.

The two most popular guestbook extensions for Joomla are Easybook and Jambook. Since a guestbook is fairly simple in both conception and implementation, these extensions provide very similar features. Your choice will likely be dependent on which extension most appropriately compliments the visual aspect of your site.

Easybook

As you can see in Figure 10-1, Easybook is an excellent simple guestbook component. One of the best features of the component is the extensive anti-spam protection such as CAPTCHA (Completely Automated Public Turing Test to Tell Computers and Humans Apart) image generation, live email address confirmation checking, and automated word filter. The word filter list can be defined through the Administrator interface of the component and configured to automatically send an email to the administrator if someone attempts to post an item on the prohibited word list. Easybook can also be set to ping the supplied email server of the poster and ignore the post if the server isn't valid.

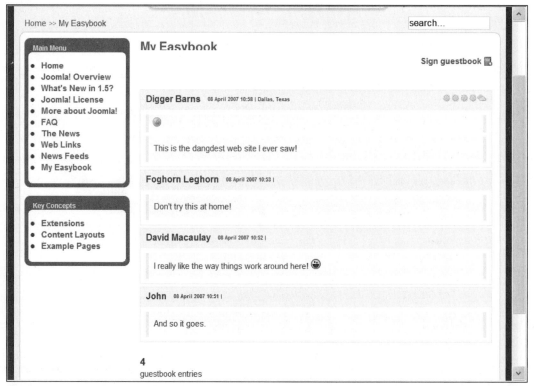

Figure 10-1: The Easybook entry display can display as little (such as a simple poster name) or as much (such as email, ICQ, Web site) as the Administrator chooses to allow.

Easybook supports BBCode (bulletin board code) for rich text entry (bold, italic, and so on). Entries can be limited to registered users, or anonymous posting can be allowed. Pictures and smilies may also be included in an entry if permitted by the administrator. Easybook can be set to automatically send a thank-you email to users when they've added a guestbook entry.

The extensive Easybook Administrator interface allows posters to include many fields (such as their Web page, ICQ, and so on) and gives the Administrator complete control over which of this information is displayed with the entry list (see Figure 10-2). The email notification options allow administrators to receive new entries by email, which can be modified, published, commented on, deleted, or withheld via the email! The component can also import archived guestbook entries that were created with the Akobook component.

The component is compatible with Simple Machine Forum (SMF) Bridge component (see the section "Simple Machines Forum (SMF)" later in this chapter for more information on this component). It is also available in a large number of languages, including German, Dutch, Simplified Chinese, Italian, Russian, Greek, Spanish, French, Norwegian, and Danish.

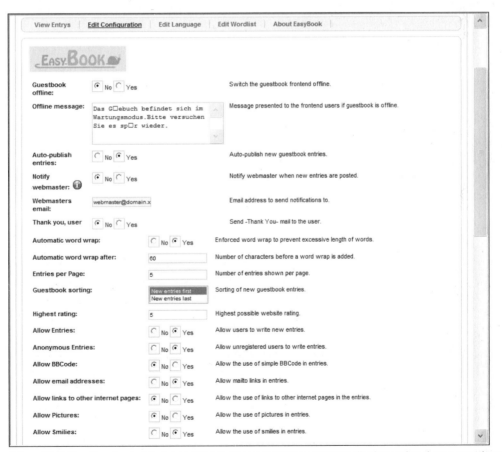

Figure 10-2: The Easybook Administrator interfaces provides extensive display and anti-spam settings.

To install Easybook, download the ZIP archive here:

```
http://joomlacode.org/gf/project/easyjoomla/frs/
```

Extract the `readme` and the component archive from the downloaded file. The component is configured to display natively in German. To change it to default to English, you will need to use the English XML descriptor file and recreate the component archive. To perform the English modification, extract all of the files from the archive. You need to rename the `easybook.xml` to `easybook.xmlde`, then rename `easybook.xmlen` to `easybook.xml`. When that is complete, simply create a new archive that contains all of the component files.

After you have used the Extension Manager to install the component, you'll need to create a front-end menu component through the Menu Manager. New entries can be added through the Administrator interface or on the front end. When you click the link to add a new entry, the Easybook entry screen will be displayed (see Figure 10-3). `Your Name` and `Your Email` are the only two required fields. The figure shows that the entry also records the poster's IP address for security and tracking.

While EasyBook is a very popular guestbook with straightforward installation and configuration, some sites need a guestbook that provides more control over presentation. Jambook supplies that control with a custom templating system.

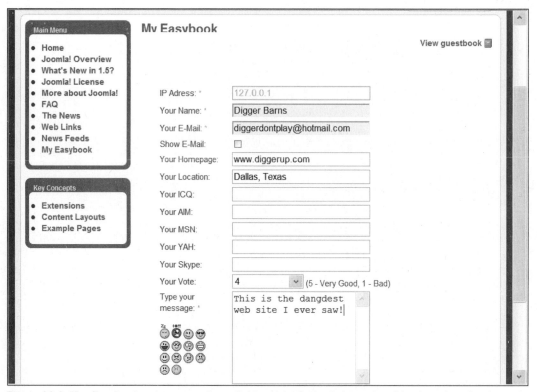

Figure 10-3: The Easybook entry screen is available via both the front end and back end, and only requires the Your Name and Your Email fields for submission.

Jambook

Jambook (see Figure 10-4) is one of the most popular guestbook components because of the focus on spam protection, the capability to import AkoBook entries, and its robust Administrator interface. Jambook includes a powerful templating system that allows you to modify all aspects of the HTML presentation of the front end. The presentation templates are editable through the Joomla Administrator interface, so you can customize this component to match your site template.

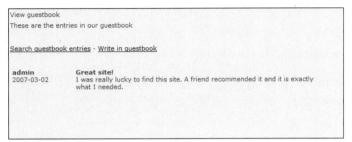

Figure 10-4: The Jambook front end provides entry display and search capabilities.

Some of the numerous security features include the following:

❏ CAPTCHA image generation

❏ IP blacklist to prevent abusers from posting

❏ Integration with the Joomla login and registration system

❏ Administrator email notification of new postings

❏ Configurable HTML stripping from messages

❏ Email address cloaking

❏ Flood protection

❏ Editable list of HTML tags that may be used in an entry post

If you have been using Easybook in the past, Jambook can import entries from that application. For new entries, Jambook can be configured to either use the currently selected WYSIWYG Joomla editor or a plain-text entry box if no rich text is permitted. A Preview button allows a visitor to see the rendering of the post before submission. Users registered in the Joomla system can edit their entries for a limited amount of time specified in the Administrator interface. The component even includes technology to prevent double-posting — a very common problem with inexperienced guestbook visitors.

Jambook supports a number of languages, including English, German, French, Portuguese, Serbian (Latin charset), Norwegian, and Polish. It also provides a simple search engine so guests can query the entries for particular text. You can download the Jambook extension here:

```
www.jxdevelopment.com/jambook
```

As shown in Figure 10-5, the Administrator interface for Jambook is incredibly full-featured for a simple component. Not only can all entries be edited or deleted, but the HTML templates can be modified to suit the desired guestbook presentation.

The default installation includes the following templates available for editing the presentation of the component:

❏ *Show* — Display for a single Jambook entry

❏ *List* — Defines how the entry list will be presented

❏ *List empty* — Display of list when no entries have been made

❏ *List item* — Presentation logic called to render each item in the entry list

❏ *Edit item* — Display for the entry editing

❏ *Thankyou* — Presentation screen displayed after user has successfully submitted an entry

❏ *Search* — Defines how the search page will be rendered

❏ *Preview* — Presentation of the preview of a new entry

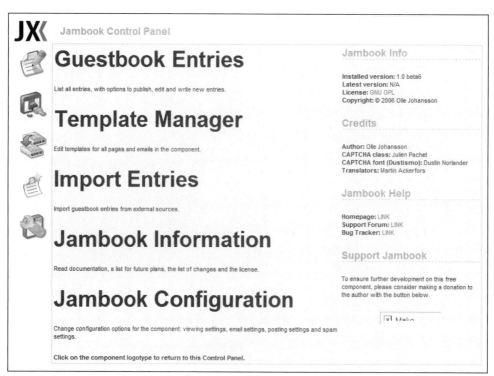

Figure 10-5: Jambook control panel provides all Administrator capabilities.

The documentation for the component (including directions for editing the templates) can be accessed from the Administrator interface of the component.

> *Jambook uses TrueType in GD2 capabilities to generate the CAPTCHA image. Therefore, TrueType support must be available to the PHP system for message posting to work correctly. PHP5 supports TrueType native, but if you are running PHP4, you may need to install an additional module.*

Chat

Online chat can mean anything from a traditional direct chat room interface to the newer Shoutbox implementations that add instant messaging (IM) capabilities to a site. In recent years, chat features have gained a somewhat dubious reputation because of their use by predators who seek to lure underage participants. Not a week goes by without some news feature or investigative piece airing on television that describes some villain using a chat room for bad purposes.

While a huge majority of chat rooms are certainly not dens of iniquity, the problem is significant enough that you should give it serious consideration before adding these capabilities to your site. The immediate interactive nature of an online chat makes it much more likely to be abused than other technologies where interaction is non-instantaneous and, the interaction is generally posted for the entire world to see.

You should also know about the legal implications if a bad person were to use your site for some form of crime. See the section "Legal Liabilities" later in the chapter for more detailed information on this aspect of running a site.

BlastChat

BlastChat (see Figure 10-6) is an Ajax-based component that provides chat services via a remote server (the BlastChat server). Since your server is only used for the connection initiation, none of your site resources or bandwidth is used when chat services are provided through this extension. The BlastChat site claims that more than 14,000 Web sites are using this chat technology. In addition to the basic chat component, a module is included that provides a who-is-online list, as well as a hypertext link that will connect to a profile of the users.

You can download the BlastChat package here:

```
www.blastchat.com
```

Installation of the component and modules is performed in the standard manner through the Extension Manager. After you install the BlastChat component, you can use the Joomla Administrator interface to create a BlastChat account. Open the Configuration screen in the Joomla Administrator interface by selecting that option under the BlastChat submenu displayed by the Components menu. You need to create an account with the BlastChat server before chat functionality is available for your site. A free registration can be configured through this screen.

Once you are registered with the BlastChat server, you must log in and set up the server registration for your Web site, as shown in Figure 10-7. With the registration, your Joomla site may also be entered into the BlastChat centralized chat directory, so your site may gain increased traffic as a result.

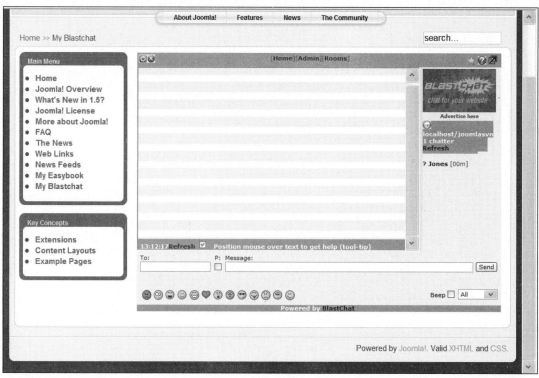

Figure 10-6: BlastChat uses Ajax technology to update the chat entries without requiring a page update.

BlastChat uses Ajax to retrieve any chat entries. It simply displays the text in the chat area rather than requiring a complete HTTP update of the Web page. In the component administration screen, you can set the display parameter of the chat area, including `Width`, `Height`, `Detached Width`, `Detached Height`, `Frame Border`, `Margin Width`, and `Margin Height`. For presentation, the extension uses the styles defined by the current template for display so that it will appear to be integrated with your Web site.

The administrator of the chat room has complete control over the interaction, including the capability to:

❑   Send public messages (to individual users and rooms)

❑   Kick users out of a room

❑   Ban users from a room or multiple rooms

❑   Set ban duration

❑   Ban based on IP address

❑   Assign moderator privileges to other users

The BlastChat interface is written in JavaScript and has been tested to work on Firefox (versions 1 and 2), Internet Explorer (versions 6 and 7), Opera (versions 8 and 9), and Netscape 8.1. It is also compatible with Joomfish and can use any language supported by that extension, including right-to-left text.

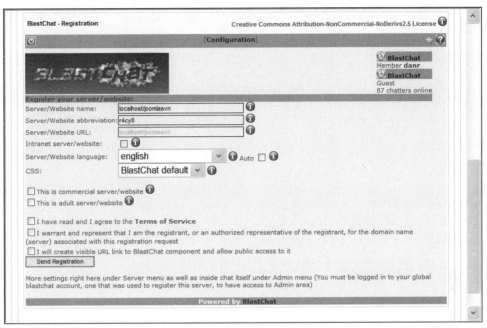

Figure 10-7: The BlastChat server configuration will determine how the chat environment is presented.

utChat

The utChat component shown in Figure 10-8 is an extension that encapsulates the PhpFreeChat script so that it appears within the Joomla interface. Ajax technology is used to refresh the display without requiring a complete page refresh. utChat is a simple, multilingual chat implementation that uses very few server resources.

You can download the utChat extension here:

    www.utopiart.com/telechargement/index.php

Install utChat components through the Extension Manager, and then create a menu item to access it on the front end. The utChat component doesn't use the Joomla database to store messages and nicknames, but rather saves all chat messages in a simple filing system. PhpFreeChat (and, therefore, utChat) includes the following features:

❑   Multiple chat rooms

❑   Private messages between members

❑   Administrator moderation (including the ability to kick out or even ban a chat user)

❑   Presentation modifiable through Cascading Style Sheets (CSS) styles

❑   Support of any language that can be stored and displayed using UTF-8 character encoding

❑   Rich text chat support that includes smilies and style selection through BBCode

❑   A custom plug-in system that allows modification of data storage (for example, for writing into a database server)

By default, utChat doesn't come configured for a default language. Once you have installed the component, select the utChat option under the Components menu in the Joomla Administrator interface. A text editor will be displayed to allow editing of the current parameter settings, as shown in Figure 10-9. These settings are stored in the form of PHP code that is executed directly by the extension.

Add the following parameter setting line to set the language used to be United States English:

```
$utparams['language'] = 'en_US';
```

For complete documentation on utChat (phpFreeChat), go to the following Web site:

```
www.phpFreeChat.net
```

Figure 10-8: The utChat component uses the PhpFreeChat script foundation to provide Joomla with chat services.

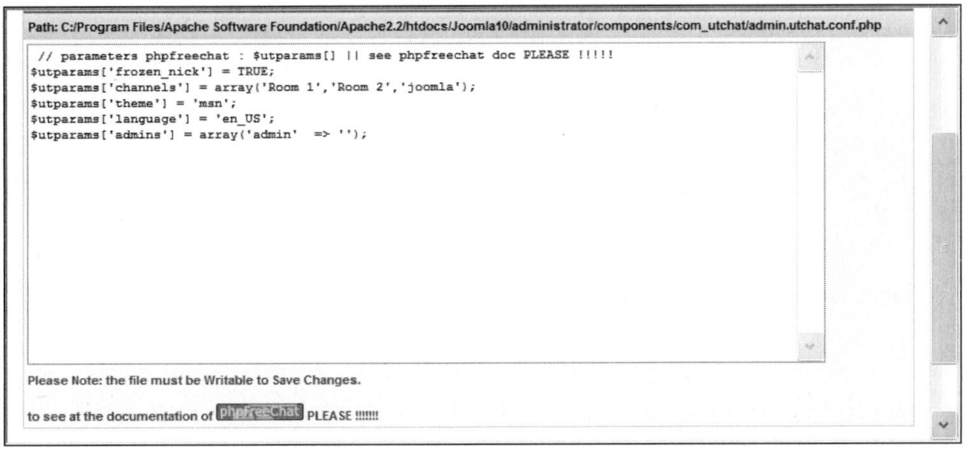

```
Path: C:/Program Files/Apache Software Foundation/Apache2.2/htdocs/Joomla10/administrator/components/com_utchat/admin.utchat.conf.php

    // parameters phpfreechat : $utparams[] || see phpfreechat doc PLEASE !!!!!
$utparams['frozen_nick'] = TRUE;
$utparams['channels'] = array('Room 1','Room 2','joomla');
$utparams['theme'] = 'msn';
$utparams['language'] = 'en_US';
$utparams['admins'] = array('admin'   => '');
```

Please Note: the file must be Writable to Save Changes.

to see at the documentation of phpfreeChat PLEASE !!!!!!

Figure 10-9: The utChat configuration parameters are stored as PHP code that is executed by the system.

Forums and Message Boards

Forums are extremely popular methods of product support for both commercial and Open Source applications. In fact, the Joomla community thrives because of the forums (forum.joomla.org) that cater to both Joomla Web masters and Joomla developers. This forum uses the Simple Machines Forum (SMF) application to provide message-posting services.

Message boards predate the Web in the form of an electronic Bulletin Board System (BBS), the most popular among them probably being *The Well*. When the Internet began to grow, the Usenet "distributed Internet discussion system" gained prominence. Now, Web-based forums can be easily incorporated into an existing Web site or Joomla system.

Simple Machines Forum (SMF)

The Simple Machines Forum (SMF) is the forum component (see Figure 10-10) that is used for a message board on the central Joomla site (www.joomla.org), so it has proven its ability to sustain great amounts of traffic and continue to perform well. The application is available in more than 20 languages, including English, Albanian, Arabic, Swedish, Catalan, Persian, Chinese, Finnish, Greek, Japanese, Turkish, Portuguese, French, Dutch, Spanish, German, Hungarian, Hebrew, Bulgarian, Italian, Thai, Polish, Russian, Norwegian, and Romanian.

SMF is not an extension. It is a separately developed PHP forum application that is used on many sites including forum.joomla.org. Instead of running outside of Joomla, however, you can bridge SMF into your Joomla system with a special component. Since SMF has its own plug-in architecture, there are a large number of extensions available, including ones to add a gallery, spam filter, search-engine optimization (SEO) features, Shoutbox, advertising management, and many other features.

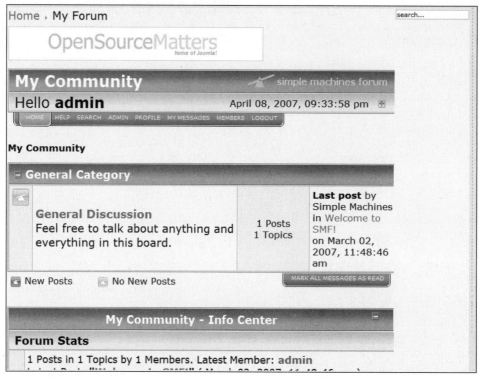

Figure 10-10: The SMF front end, although displayed within the Joomla interface, has a number of themes that determine its presentation.

SMF must be installed separately from Joomla. You can download the forum application here:

```
www.simplemachines.org
```

For integration into a Joomla system, you should install SMF within the Joomla directory hierarchy. One effective method is to create a directory called \forum at the root of the Joomla directory and place the SMF files there. The SMF installation is performed much like Joomla installation by pointing your browser at the directory containing the SMF files. A wizard installer will guide you through the process.

Once SMF is installed, you need the SMF Bridge to allow it to execute within the Joomla site. You can download the Joomla bridge component here:

```
www.simplemachines.org/download/?bridges
```

Note that there are a number of different extensions that offer a bridge between SMF and Joomla. Each of these extensions has advantages and disadvantages. You should stick with SMF Bridge because it is the official extension put out by the SMF development group and is, therefore, likely to be the most compatible.

Once you install the component, you must configure it to address the SMF installation through the Joomla Administrator interface. Use the bridge entry in the Joomla Administrator interface Components menu to display the configuration screen shown in Figure 10-11. The "Path to SMF" parameter is the most important, since it must be set correctly before the bridge will function. This is an absolute path and should be set accordingly.

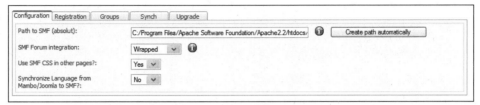

Figure 10-11: SMF Bridge back end displays for configuration settings including the "Path to SMF."

Fireboard

In contrast to the SMF application's separation from Joomla, the Fireboard (now merged with the Joomlaboard extension) extension shown in Figure 10-12 was developed specifically for use with Joomla, so it requires no encapsulation or bridge component. Its integration with Joomla is substantial — specifically in regard to presentation and user permissions. It communicates directly with the Access Control List (ACL) used by Joomla to govern user access privileges.

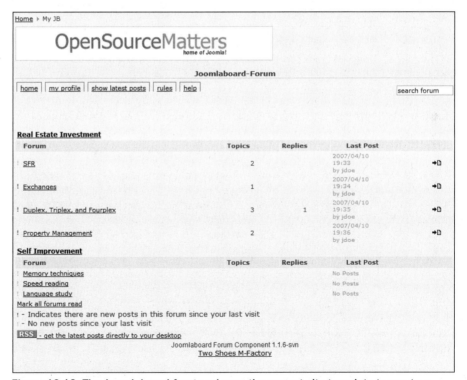

Figure 10-12: The Joomlaboard front end uses the current site template to create a compatible presentation.

Fireboard offers the following forum features:

❑ Unlimited definition of categories and subcategories

❑ Multilingual support

❑ Templating system on par with SMF

❑ Sidebar features such as forum spotlights, forum highlights, forum announcements, latest messages, and latest threads

❑ User-customizable favorite threads

❑ Joomlaboard import

❑ Custom plug-in architecture that allows the addition of features such as Joomap integration, Google sitemap generation, Joom!Fish support, commenting system, and others

❑ Output for RSS feed or PDF document creation

❑ Integration with Community Builder user profile system

❑ Support for personal messaging systems, including ClexusPM and Uddeim

You can download the Joomlaboard component and related modules at the following Web site:

```
www.bestofjoomla.org
```

After you download the component, you can install it using the traditional procedure through the Extension Manager. Then connect a menu item in the Menu Manager to the Fireboard component. The Web site also provides Joomla modules that add features such as a user template chooser, a latest subjects Ajax display, a Fireboard Administrator interface quick icon, a top user and last user display, forum statistics, and more.

Once installed, you must first add categories and then forums to allow for user access. The Joomlaboard Control Panel shown in Figure 10-13 provides access to all of the extension's functions. Clicking the Forum Administration button will take you to the screen where you can add new categories.

When you click the New button, the category creation screen will be displayed. Leave the item level set to Top Level, and create a category such as Real Estate Investment. Save that category, and create a new one. This time, open the drop-down list for item level and you'll see the category you just created. Select this item and then enter a forum title. The forum you create will now allow users to enter messages into it.

Polls

Once a virtual community is already established, *polls* can be a great addition. Few visitors will come to a site simply to vote in or see the results of a poll. However, once a community has begun to solidify, a poll can be an excellent method of allowing users to see the opinions of other site participants. A poll can also provide the site Web master with important feedback on the opinions of the community on a variety of topics — including the views on the site itself.

Joomla, of course, has a polling system incorporated into the default installation. In Figure 10-14, you can see the poll displayed on a generic front page.

Figure 10-13: The Fireboard Control Panel provides access the configuration, user management, uploads, and forum administration.

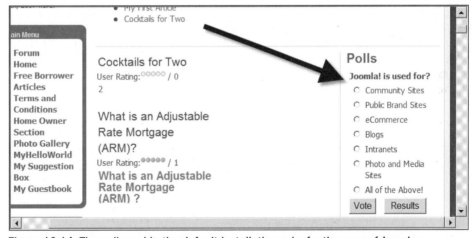

Figure 10-14: The poll used in the default installation asks for the uses of Joomla.

A number of poll extensions provide a great deal more flexibility and functionality than the core extension. In fact, a poll module is included with the SMF that you may have installed earlier.

You add an SMF poll to a message forum by clicking the Add Poll button within the SMF Administrator interface. The poll definition screen will be displayed, as shown in Figure 10-15. You can add any number of poll options, set the poll execution, and add an explanation message describing the reason for the poll.

From the SMF Administrator page, you can configure all of the possible parameters and capabilities of the poll setup.

One of the advantages of starting polls in SMF is their close proximity to subjects of discussion. Since you are trying to foster an involved community on your Joomla site, what could be better than allowing poll feedback in the same area where an online discussion on the topic of contention is taking place?

Polls created in SMF appear as if they were messages within the forum (see Figure 10-16) where they were created. When the user clicks on the poll entry, it displays the voting form to allow for vote submission instead of message text. Note that in order to vote in a poll, visitors must have cookies enabled in their browsers, since the polling module records a cookie to prevent multiple voting by a single user on the same poll.

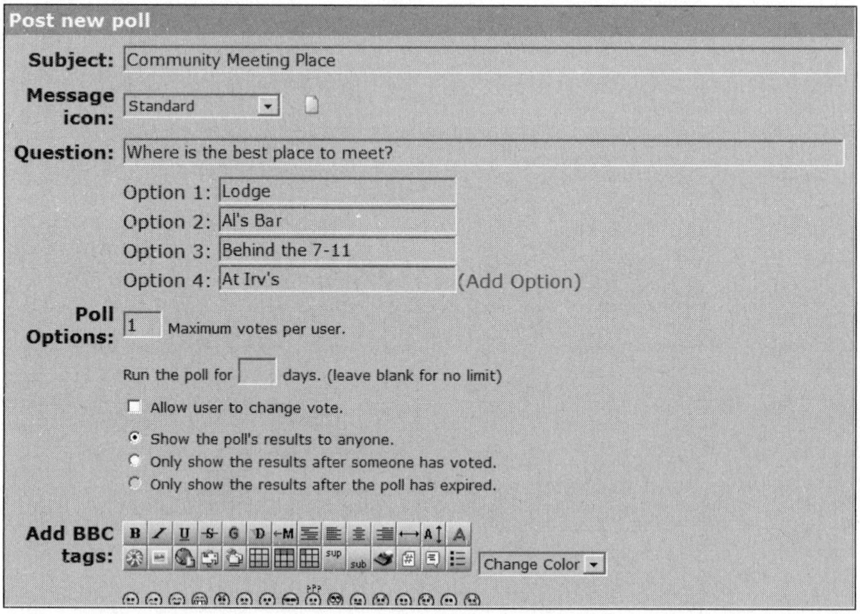

Figure 10-15: Adding an SMF Poll is as simple as adding a new forum message.

Comments

Comments are a particularly effective method of community building. They don't require the blank-slate topic generation of a message board, and yet they allow people to post their comments and share their views about a specific content item on the site. The number of successful sites that feature comment capabilities is almost uncountable. Some sites (such as epinions.com) don't even produce much original content — the majority of the site is dedicated to user opinions. This is actually becoming a common feature on all large sites. Some sites that have the comment feature include Ain't It Cool News, Target, Macy's, The Superficial, and TMZ. By implementing AkoComment or !JoomlaComment extensions on your Joomla site, you can allow visitors to provide their comments to any article. Enabling commenting capability on your site does more than provide an open forum for constructive criticism. It allows visitors to supplement the content of an article with additional information and hyperlinks.

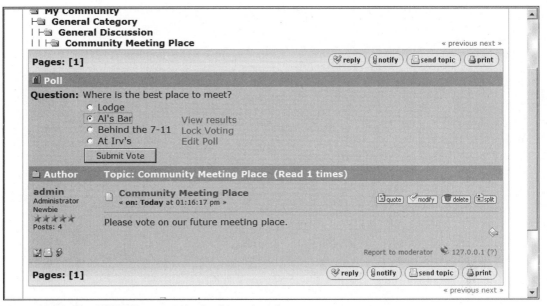

Figure 10-16: The SMF Poll appears in the forum interface.

AkoComment Tweaked Special Edition 1.4.6

One of the most popular comment engines is the AkoComment extension. All of its display is provided through CSS layout, which gives the Web master complete control over the comment appearance. The AkoComment extension provides the following features:

❑ Rich text commenting system

❑ Generation of RSS feed of posted comments

❑ Administrator notification of new comment posting

❑ Support of numerous display templates for custom presentation

❑ Configuration settings to limit the number of comments per article

❑ Delay setting for same user comment posting

❑ Optional user notification of follow-up comments

❑ CAPTCHA image generation to prevent spamming

❑ Integration with the Community Builder user profile

It supports a large number of languages, including English, Brazilian/Portuguese, Chinese, Czech, Finnish, French, German, Greek, Hungarian, Indonesian, Italian, Norwegian, Polish, Russian, Slovak, Spanish, and Turkish. The entry screen allows the email and homepage for the comment to be entered (see Figure 10-17), and the administrator can configure whether these items are displayed with the posting.

AkoComment supports rich text formatting through Bulletin Board Code (BBCode), a lightweight markup language similar to HTML. Codes are placed between two brackets such as [b] for bold, [i] for italic, and `[u]` for underline. The component also supports bulleted lists, smilies, and any language available in the Joomla system.

You can download AkoComment here:

    www.visualclinic.fr

The AkoComment package to be installed is made up of a plug-in (`bot_akocomment_SE.zip`), a component (`com_akocomment_SE.zip`), and two modules (`mod_ac_lastcomments.zip` and `mod_ac_mostfavoured.zip`). The plug-in displays the `"Comments (x)"` link below each article with the letter x representing the number of available comments. Clicking on the link will display the component

The administrative interface shown in Figure 10-18 allows complete control over layout and posting. It also provides reporting capabilities so that users can send a message to the Joomla Administrator over offensive or questionable comments.

AkoComment allows nearly all aspects of the commenting system display to be configured either through various parameter settings or selection of a presentation template. Display parameters include `Autolimit num of comments to display`, `Num of comments per page`, `Show favoured link`, `Show quote this article in website link`, `Show hits/views`, `Show print link`, `Show send Email link`, `Show read more link`, and `Character to separate each link`. The templates may be selected to use various stylesheets or to perform the layout in an HTML table.

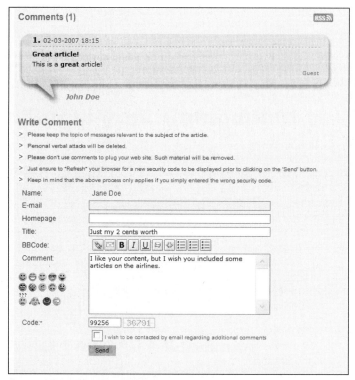

Figure 10-17: The AkoComment display appears both professional and friendly at the same time.

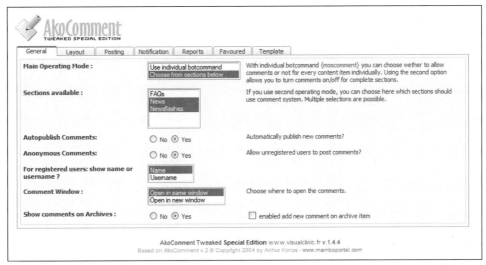

Figure 10-18: The AkoComment administrative interface allows configuration of the posting display and process.

!JoomlaComment

The !JoomlaComment component shown in Figure 10-19 provides excellent Ajax-based comment functionality. It allows importing existing comments from AkoComment.

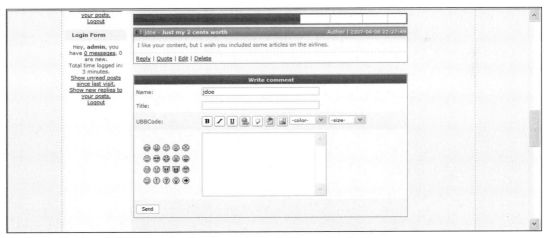

Figure 10-19: !JoomlaComment front end provides a clean presentation.

The !JoomlaComment extension includes the following features:

❏ Ajax interaction so that the commenting interface doesn't require a separate page display

❏ Picture support

- ❑ User avatars

- ❑ Quoting of other comments

- ❑ Rich text formatting with smilies through BBCode

- ❑ Integration with Community Builder profiles and avatars

- ❑ Multilingual support of languages such as English, Slovak, Czech, Italian, German, Norwegian, Spanish, Turkish, Greek, Hungarian, Persian, Bulgarian, Macedonian, Dutch, Brazilian, and Portuguese

Like most robust user-entry components, !JoomlaComment has anti-spamming features, including the following:

- ❑ CAPTCHA image generation

- ❑ User banning

- ❑ Word censorship

- ❑ Comment length limitations

You can download !JoomlaComment at the following Web site:

```
http://cavovweb.ca.funpic.de/index.php?option=com_content&
task=blogsection&id=5&Itemid=29
```

The !JoomlaComment component is installed through the Extension Manager like most components. Unlike most components, the Administrator interface for the component handles the installation of the plug-in that adds a commenting section at the bottom of each article.

The Administrator interface shown in Figure 10-20 provides configuration of all component settings via three tabs: General, Layout, and Security. General settings include enabling Ajax technology, exclusion of commenting on particular sections and categories, use of BBCode, date format, and various notification settings. The Layout tab lets you choose from several different templates, set nested comments, the permissible length of the comments, and the activation of a Read On feature. The Security tab allows setup of all security features from CAPTCHA to IP address logging. Very useful is the editable word substitution feature that will replace words (mostly swear words in the included setting) with censored words.

Social Networking

Though the most popular example is MySpace.com, *social networking* pages can be anything from a "my favorite movies" list to a display section for family recipes. It is a way of classifying and sharing list of bookmarks and through these lists the contents that they point toward. With a social network, the host site allows sharing content lists with other users through links or email.

In a social network, users create lists of Internet bookmarks that they find interesting or useful. Bookmarks are generally categorized or associated with given tags so that they can be searched and sorted. Other people can access their lists and often rank the usefulness of the link or the list itself. Often, these lists of bookmarks are published as an RSS feed so that interested parties can view the latest bookmarks for a given list.

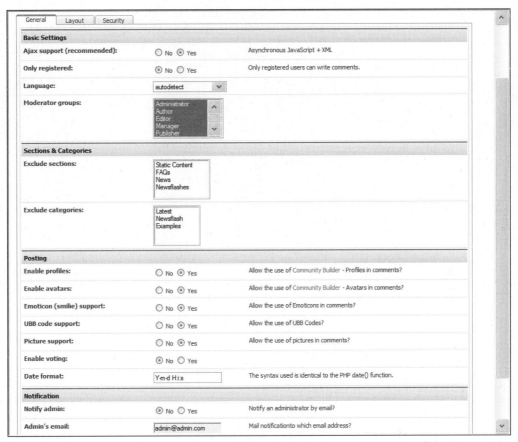

Figure 10-20: The !JoomlaComment administrative interface allows configuration of the comment entry and display screens.

Joomla's article structure makes it a perfect host for content that can be linked to by others. Several extensions provide interfaces to the various social networking sites so that a user needs only to click on an icon to add an article on your site to a bookmark list. One of the most popular social networking extensions for Joomla is SocialBookmarkerBot.

SocialBookmarkerBot v1.3.2

To encourage social linking to content on a Joomla site, you can add the SocialBookmarkerBot extension, which creates a row of buttons at the bottom of each page of content, as shown in Figure 10-21. These buttons provide support for social bookmarking through sites such as BlinkBits, Blinklist, Blogmarks, BlogMemes, Del.icio.us, Digg, Facebook, Fark, FeedMeLinks, Furl, Google Bookmarks, Ma.gnolia, Netscape, Netvouz, Newsline, PlugIM, RawSugar, Reddit, Shadows, Simpy, Slashdot, Smarking, Spurl, Squidoo, StumbleUpon, Tailrank and linkaGoGo, Technorati, Windows Live, Wists, and Yahoo! Bookmarks.

Figure 10-21: The Social Bookmarker provides a setup of buttons that allows bookmarks to be shared with other users.

Advanced smart buttons for the sites Digg, Del.icio.us, and Reddit can be displayed at the top-right or top-left of each article. The buttons may be set to appear when a user is viewing the full article or only when displaying the summary. The display panel can be configured to appear at the top, bottom, or both sides; show all buttons; or show no buttons. The extension also shaves off any user ID information and display location information for links submitted by the buttons so that the hyperlinks are "permalink" URLs (that is, URLs that remain valid regardless of whether the article is shown on the front page or elsewhere on the site).

The Digg button displayed on the right side of the article only functions if the Search Engine Friendly (SEF) URLs option is enabled on the Global Configuration screen of the Joomla system. An error is generated by JavaScript code retrieved from the Digg.com *server if the SEF option is not turned on.*

You can download SocialBookmarkerBot at the following URL:

    www.patrickswesey.com/applications/socialbookmarkerbot

Install this plug-in through the Extension Manager and publish it. Once published, the button panel will automatically display on all articles on the site. Use the Plugin Manager in the Joomla Administrator interface to configure the button display options.

Event Calendar

An *event calendar* is a perfect way to offer a centralized place for people interested in a topic area to find out about events related to it. It also bridges an online community to physical meetings and interaction.

The event calendar extensions available to Joomla users are simple yet well-implemented. The Events Calendar (JEvents) extension allows great flexibility in display and categorization. JCalPro provides more control over repeating events and scheduling.

*If you don't want to host the event calendar on your Web site, the Google Calendar (*www.google.com/calendar*) is a free service that will host an event calendar for you. You can use the Joomla Wrapper module to include it in your Web site. The Google Calendar even includes automatic event reminders that can notify (either through email or mobile phone messages) people who subscribed to the calendar.*

Events Calendar (JEvents) Extension

The Events Calendar extension shown in Figure 10-22 (also known as JEvents) provides easy management for shared events. Not only does the extension allow an essentially unlimited number of events, but it also provides complete event repetition settings (daily, monthly, and yearly). Events can be filed and sorted by user-definable categories.

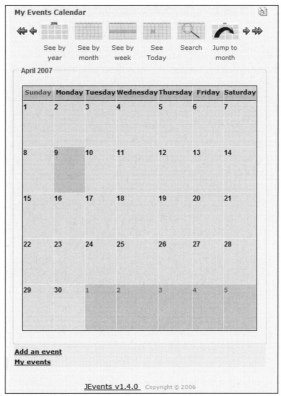

Figure 10-22: The Events Calendar (JEvents) provides a straightforward display.

The complete Events Calendar (JEvents) package consists of a number of components, modules, and plug-ins, including the following:

❑ *Events Calendar component* — The main component for calendar display

❑ *Administrator component* — The administrative component for system configuration

❑ *Events Calendar visual calendar module* — A small, quick-display calendar for places such as the front page of a Joomla site

❑ *Latest/Upcoming list module* — Lists the latest upcoming events that are entered into the event database

❑ *Events Legend module* — Displays the legend for symbols displayed in the event calendar

❑ *Search plug-in* — Provides search capabilities for the events in the calendar

❑ *Event Report plug-in* — Provides for automatic linking to event reports or photo galleries of the event once it has been completed

Before any events can be added, you must create a category by using the Add Category screen shown in Figure 10-23 in the Administrator interface of the JEvents component. After you save the category, be

245

sure to publish it because categories are unpublished by default. After you have created a category, you can begin inserting events.

The entry of an event (see Figure 10-24) is performed from the front end of the JEvents interface. A new event creation allows a subject line, a category selection, and a complete description. Optional fields include location, contact information, and any extra comment information that should be provided for the event. Text included in any of these fields is searched by the Search component, so be sure that you enter important keywords so that users can find events related to their interests.

If you return to the configuration screen in the Administrator interface, it shown in Figure 10-25 enables you to have complete control over event presentation, access, and editing permissions. It also allows the editing of the CSS that is used for display of the events. This CSS may be modified to more appropriately match your currently selected site template.

You can download JEvents at:

    joomlacode.org/gf/projects/jevents

Install the component through the Extension Manager as you would install any other component. To add the JEvents calendar to the front end of the site, create a menu item that connects to the component.

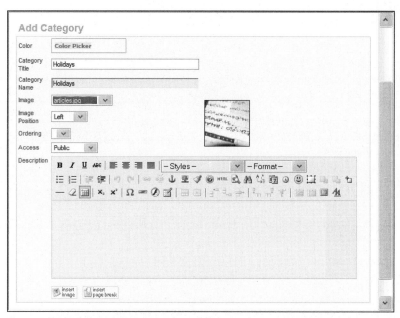

Figure 10-23: Before events can be entered, categories such as Holidays must be created to organize them.

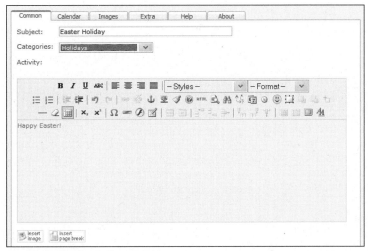

Figure 10-24: The Add Event screen organizes all of the information relating to an event in separate tabs.

Figure 10-25: The Administrator configuration provides configuration and reporting capabilities.

JCalPro

One of the most attractive event calendars is the JCalPro extension shown in Figure 10-26. It can display in a number of different styles that can match the look-and-feel of your Joomla site. All display is CSS-based for easy Web master modification. Event additions use the Joomla editor for complete rich text capabilities. The security is integrated with Joomla security to allow specified permissions for private event categories and managed event creation. Modules are available for a mini-calendar and latest events.

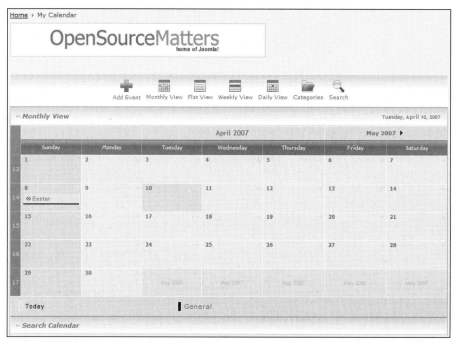

Figure 10-26: The JCalPro interface presents an excellent front end that is customizable through templates.

JCalPro includes the following features:

❏   Daily, weekly, monthly, and by-category calendar views

❏   Integration with Joomla categories, including the display permissions system

❏   A rendered calendar that is W3C valid XHTML- and CSS-compliant

❏   Content that is integrated with standard Joomla site search features

❏   The use of a Joomla WYSIWYG editor to allow event definitions to be included as rich text

❏   The capability to schedule events by minutes

❏   The capability to import of Extcalendar event and category data

❏   Latest Events module for current events display

❏   Multilingual support through the Joomla language system

❏   Administrator notification of newly added events

❑   Support of recurring, all day, and multi-day events

❑   Email support for user notification of events

You can download JCalPro at:

```
http://dev.anything-digital.com
```

Install the component through the Extension Manager as you would install any other component. To add the JEvents calendar to the front end of the site, create a menu item that connects to the component.

Wiki Systems

One of the most interesting interactive technologies (and perhaps the fastest growing) is the *wiki* system. Under a wiki system, users post contributions, and then subsequent visitors can edit or augment this content. The most famous example is Wikipedia, which is a user-generated encyclopedia. Any user can post a new entry, and then the system will track changes made by the users.

Although Joomla operates as a CMS and can readily accept new content from contributors, it was not designed to allow a large number of people to make minor changes or modifications to content — exactly the functionality provided by a wiki. There are several good offerings of Joomla extensions that add wiki capabilities to Joomla, including OpenWiki and WikiBot.

OpenWiki

OpenWiki (see Figure 10-27) provides a bridge to encapsulate the PHP application DokuWiki within the Joomla system. It features a complete ACL implementation that builds on the Joomla ACL for groups such as `Super Administrator`, `Administrator`, `Manager`, `Author`, `Registered`, and `Public`. ACL permissions include create, edit, read, upload, and delete.

OpenWiki has a number of useful features, including the following:

❑   Simple, standard wiki syntax for article formatting

❑   Unlimited page revisions with diff support to show colorized differences between past revisions

❑   Rich text support, including image embedding

❑   Optional CamelCase support

❑   Automatic index generation with full text search capabilities

❑   Quickbuttons and access keys for fast editing

❑   Breadcrumbs link tree for easy navigation

❑   Spam blacklist

❑   Designation of read-only pages

❑   Support for more than 30 languages

❑   CSS templates that allow customization of presentation

❑   Custom plug-in architecture (with more than 100 plug-ins already available)

❑   Generation of RSS feed for content

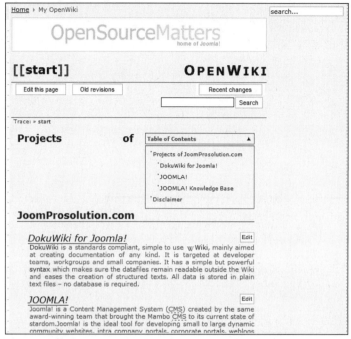

Figure 10-27: The OpenWiki interface encapsulates the DokuWiki PHP application for use within the Joomla system.

You can download OpenWiki here:

```
http://projects.j-prosolution.com/projects/os-projects/project-openwiki.html
```

Install the component through the Extension Manager as you would install any other component. To add the JEvents calendar to the front end of the site, create a menu item that connects to the component. The component is self-contained, so all interaction and administration occurs of the underlying DokuWiki itself occurs through the front end. Configuration of the OpenWiki hosting is performed through the component's administrative interface.

> DokuWiki, upon which OpenWicki is based, doesn't write the wiki entries into a database for dynamic creation of content. Instead, the pages are generated as static files. Therefore, to use OpenWiki, the application must have write permissions within the site directory structure. It relies primarily on the `fwrite()` **and** `fopen()` PHP methods, so be sure to establish if these are activated on your Web server before you attempt installation.

In the Joomla Administrator interface, you can open the OpenWiki Configuration Settings screen shown in Figure 10-28 through the OpenWiki option in the Components menu. The interface allows you to set up not only the permissions but also the parameters for content creation.

Figure 10-28: The OpenWiki Configuration Settings screen

WikiBot

WikiBot bridges Joomla with the free encyclopedia Wikipedia. Words can be tagged in Joomla content to link to related articles in the encyclopedia. This tool makes it extremely convenient to bridge content on your Joomla site to the large Wikipedia database.

You can download the WikiBot here:

    www.theinevitabledossier.com/wikibot.html

Install the plug-in through the Extension Manager as you would install any other plug-in. You will need to publish the WikiBot to enable it for automatic handling of article content.

WikiBot performs completely in the background to the Joomla site. Simply add the necessary tags directly into the body of a standard Joomla article. Words are tagged the same way they are cited in a Wiki by enclosing them in double square brackets like `[[these words]]`. WikiBot supports international language tagging. Additionally, links within articles are possible with `[[article|linkname]]` notation. Placing the double brackets around text in a content article will display a Wikipedia link when the page is viewed.

Words tagged with the double brackets do not appear as links in the preview window but only when viewed through the front end.

Deploying a Virtual Community

If you've planned the community thoroughly, deploying it should not be difficult. The technology provided by Joomla extensions makes for a simple plug-in implementation. However, you should also consider the management responsibilities, including legal liability and the grooming of appropriate moderators.

Legal Liabilities

Be sure to read basic information on free speech guarantees and limits. You can find a great deal of information about this topic at the Electronic Frontier Foundation (EFF) Web site (`www.eff.org`). EFF also has information relating to the defamation and libel aspects of online content. For the online copyright liability act, check out `http://en.wikipedia.org/wiki/OCILLA`.

In regard to legal liabilities a site Web master might incur by allowing community interaction in the United States, this is a very gray area of the law at the moment. Two court cases (*Cubby Inc. v. CompuServe,*

Inc. and *Stratton Oakmont, Inc. v. Prodigy Services Co.*) came to different conclusions on the liability of a host of traffic. But most large sites have taken the rulings to indicate that if the site is actively monitored, then there is more legal risk than if the site acts strictly as a distributor of other people's content — good or bad.

To clarify the situation further, the U.S. Congress enacted Section 230 when it created the 1996 Communications Decency Act. The act provides immunity from liability when the questionable content comes from an outside source. The key provision of the act reads as follows:

> *No provider or user of an interactive computer service shall be treated as the publisher or speaker of any information provided by another information content provider.*

You can read more about Section 230 on Wikipedia (`http://en.wikipedia.org/wiki/Section_230_of_the_Communications_Decency_Act`) or the excellent Legal Notes summary (`www.rtndf.org/members/legalnotes/legalnotes900.asp`) of this and other Internet-related liability issues.

Grooming Moderators

Virtual communities are a great deal of work, and it won't be long before you would like some help on the endeavor. Communities thrive on volunteer moderators who have already shown a commitment to the Web site. Choosing moderators often takes no more effort than examining the user log. Would-be moderators will be on the site a great deal of time and will generally freely dispense information and help.

Why would someone want to volunteer his or her time with little or no pay? There are a few reasons, the simplest and most prominent one being a passion for the field that is the focus of the site. Most people feel an intrinsic need to contribute, even if it is a small amount of time to a virtual community.

Another reason someone will volunteer for a moderator position is small power. This is a most difficult problem to guard against as a site Web master. Generally, the moderator who abuses this power will do so in a way that the victim has little recourse or chance to be heard. Banning a user from the site limits the available options to describe abuses. It is a good idea to provide a direct administrator email address that is only sent to you. That way, complaints can't be filtered to show only the best messages.

Also, take complaints from users with a grain of salt. I have seen a user post on a children's forum the most foul message that included sexual references and a great deal of profanity. When banned from the site, the user complained loudly and often that *he* was the victim and his free speech rights had been violated. Therefore, with complaints that come over the transom, be sure to review each one; but approach each one logically and dispassionately.

Maintaining a Community

Directing a community is like driving a car with a dozen people squashed into the passenger seat — and each has a hand on the wheel. Communities zig this way and that, burst with magnificent growth and then stagnate, and are always vulnerable to another community with more relevant information or a better user interface.

Here are a few tips for keeping your sanity and generating steady growth of visitors and contributors:

❑ *Have site policies clearly posted* — You can't blame a users for violating a site rule if they don't know what the rules are. Prominently place your site policies so that if there is ever a question, the visitor can examine them easily. In a forum environment, this generally means entering the policy as an article itself on the system, and then making it "sticky" so that it will always appear first in the message list.

❑ *Ensure that your site is clean* — Like graffiti in a neighborhood, the longer spam is posted or flourishes on your site, the more that space will feel abandoned or unused. A Web master who is asleep at the wheel of a virtual community will soon hit a tree.

❑ *Don't launch the site until foundational content is in place* — The old saying "you never get a second chance to make a first impression" is no more true than when you launch a virtual community. With the amount of money commercial ventures are spending on their Web sites, a site *must* appear professional if it is to gain widespread acceptance. When people visit and find an empty shell of a site, they are unlikely to return, and are likely to avoid it when they come across a link. From the very first day that the site goes online, there should be enough content and (hopefully) activity to ensure that each visitor will return.

Summary

Building an effective virtual community is one of the most difficult (yet one of the most rewarding) activities in Web deployment. Since an effective virtual community requires the contributions of many Web visitors, maintaining the community can require a great deal of effort as well. Fortunately, the tools available for adoption using the Joomla system can ease both the initial deployment and the time spent in administration of the site.

This chapter has provided an overview of the ways to install and configure Joomla by providing you with the tools for the following:

❑ Understanding the advantages and disadvantages of a virtual community.

❑ Improving interaction of a Web site.

❑ Refining the site deployment plan.

❑ Creating a coherent site by melding together several community technologies.

❑ Adopting the various extensions to give the site interactive features.

❑ Deploying extensions properly for maximum throughput and minimum problems.

The more successful your Joomla site, the more important it will be to have your site fine-tuned for maximum traffic. Many users of a virtual community can be lost if the host Web site is slow or unresponsive. Chapter 11 supplies a variety of techniques and configurations that will help you to maximize the performance of your Joomla server.

11

Managing a Professional Deployment

Basic Joomla installation will get a site up and running quickly and easily, but a professional deployment may require a good deal more effort in the areas of management and administration. Although Joomla accommodates beginning users, expert users will find substantial administrative capabilities that make professional deployment possible. Additionally, the servers that the system relies on for Web serving and execution have a variety of management tools and settings.

Since an "untuned" system will never provide the performance of a tuned and refined system, spending the time to adjust all of the systems will provide great benefits. By customizing these settings to the needs of your Joomla system, you will be able to squeeze a great deal more performance out of the same hardware.

The techniques examined in this chapter can be divided into broad areas such as separating your development server from your deployment server, Joomla administration, Joomla maintenance, and fine-tuning the final deployment. Of course, these areas overlap quite a bit because they all deal with management and configuration of the Joomla server.

Development and Testing

Professional Joomla development means much more than choosing the correct IDE for coding purposes. Understanding the features of Joomla that can help you with your debugging efforts, with using the PHP tools available on the system, and with implementing automated testing routines, which all can play a significant part in creating dependable solutions.

The portions of Joomla that you've studied so far deal primarily with the Joomla system itself. However, development extends beyond Joomla to the servers that underlie the system, and utilities that can be applied to the system from the outside. By activating the reporting of Joomla's internal debugging processes, you can gain the information you need to supplement your development efforts.

Debug Settings

The Joomla Administrator interface allows you to activate a number of debugging settings to aid development on a staging server. Enabling the debugging functionality of Joomla causes the system to report information about its own execution. In the Global Configuration screen, the Debug Settings panel (see Figure 11-1) shows the options available to the developer.

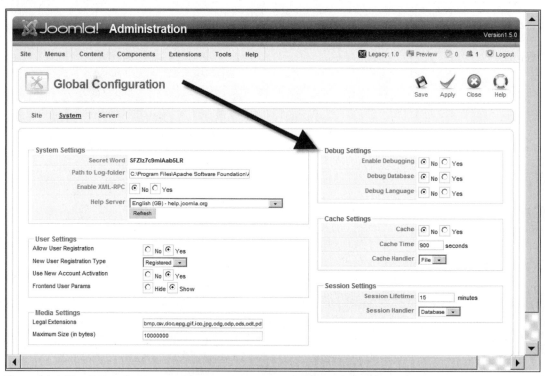

Figure 11-1: The Debug Settings can be set to aid a developer on the staging server.

The three available debugging settings include Enable Debugging, Debug Database, and Debug Language. Each of these options supplies information at the bottom of a Web page to give the developer information about system execution. Note that this debugging information is generated by the Joomla system, and it is separate from the data supplied by the PHP `display errors` command.

When active, the Enable Debugging option will display the debugging messages, as shown in Figure 11-2. These messages are divided into five sections: execution speed, memory usage, query logging, language files loaded, and untranslated strings. This information will only be displayed if the template includes the code to display the debug module. In most templates, this code will appear as `<jdoc:include type= "modules" name="debug" />`.

When the debug information is activated, the first text area displays the execution times for each logged event. The second section shows the current memory usage of the Joomla server. The sections that follow don't provide useful information until the other debugging options are activated.

When the same page is refreshed with the Debug Database option enabled, the queries to the database will be logged and displayed, as shown in Figure 11-3. This information not only helps you track down your own bugs, but it can also provide a window into the functioning of the Joomla system itself.

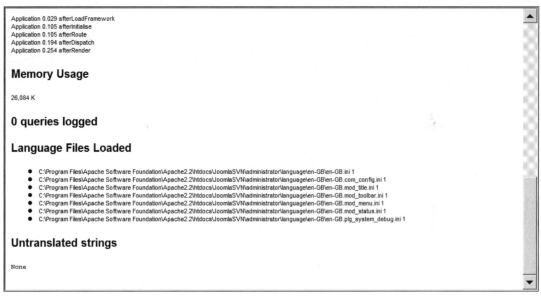

Figure 11-2: Activating the debugging information will display debugging messages.

Figure 11-3: When the Debug Database option is activated, all queries are logged and displayed with the debugging data.

The Debug Language option will display all of the text that is untranslated on the page, as shown in Figure 11-4. If you are creating a new language pack or acting as a tester for someone who is developing a new Joomla translation, this feedback provides essential information to list what remains undone.

Be sure that you don't have these settings enabled on your deployment server, or else the system may reveal information useful to hackers who may want to penetrate your system.

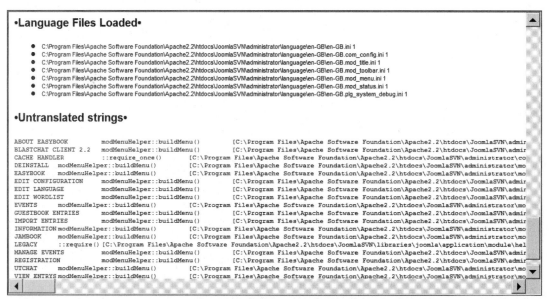

Figure 11-4: The Debug Language option will show the un-translated text on the page.

PHP Command Line Interface (CLI)

When developing Joomla extensions, you are authoring code in PHP, so tools that can aid in PHP development can help you. Rather than running code through the entire Joomla system, it is often useful to execute code snippets or files directly, rather than through the browser interface. PHP offers this capability through the PHP Command Line Interface (CLI).

You can execute PHP code directly from the PHP executable included with every install. Open a window with the operating system command line and navigate to the PHP directory (often the main Apache directory). On the Windows platform, you'll find the php.exe file that provides the CLI.

The most basic example of using the CLI would use the -r switch to execute a single line of code like this:

```
php -r "echo 'Hello World';"
```

When the code executes, it should display an execution summary and the greeting. You can also have the CLI execute a PHP file and output it to another file. If you wanted to run the file test.php and have the output rendered to the test.html file without any of the HTTP headers, you could use this command:

```
php -q test.php > test.html
```

Switch settings include the following:

- ❑   -h or -? — Display a list of all command line switches and basic descriptions of each.
- ❑   -r — Execute the single line of statements held in the string that follows.
- ❑   -v — Display the current version of PHP.
- ❑   -d — Define the value of a directive. For example, the following code will set the maximum execution time directive:

```
php -d max_execution_time=20
```

- ❑   -m — Display the list of currently loaded PHP and Zend modules.
- ❑   -i — Print out the same information rendered by the phpinfo() function call.
- ❑   -q — Do not include HTTP headers in the generated output.
- ❑   -s — Display the color highlighted version of the specified source file. This same output can be generated from within PHP with the highlight_file() function.
- ❑   -c — Used to specify the directory where the system will look for the php.ini file.
- ❑   -a — Used to put PHP into interactive mode where commands may be entered into a PHP prompt for immediate execution (not available on Windows).

Using direct PHP execution can be a great way to test simple code executions. If you are running on a UNIX-based operating system, the interactive mode using the -a switch is one of the most helpful tools for performing fast PHP test execution with immediate feedback of results.

Automated Testing

Testing on a staging server involves troubleshooting, interoperability, and unit test checks. Testing is an important step in development and one that is often neglected in a rush to release. As professional development has matured, however, there have been an increasing number of automated testing applications that take much of the arduousness and scattershot effectiveness out of performing analysis.

Page Validation

There are several aspects of Joomla development that should be tested before deployment, including HTML and XHTML compliance, link checking, script validation, and accessibility validation. A number of free online services will analyze a Web page and generate reports describing problems and possible improvements.

Many Web applications such as Adobe Dreamweaver and Microsoft Expression Web will perform page validation, but most Joomla developers are creating solutions inside a development system such as Eclipse. Web Page Valet (http://valet.webthing.com/page) is a Web application that will validate a Web page for any errors in HTML markup. Errors are referenced by line numbers, and a numbered list of the targeted page is included at the bottom of the report. For XHTML validation, try the W3C Markup Validation service at http://validator.w3.org.

For link validation, Link Valet (http://valet.webthing.com/link) will confirm the integrity of page links and report a broken link summary. There are also a number of client link checking applications, including Jenu (`http://sourceforge.net/projects/jenu`), which is written in Java and provides a multi-threaded graphical link checker.

Finally, for accessibility, try the Accessibility Valet (`http://valet.webthing.com/access/url.html`). Accessibility is more important to Web sites than making a Web site useful to the disabled (although that is a noble goal you should pursue). Search engine spiders tend to approach a Web site in much the same way as the programs used by the disabled. Therefore, a site that provides robust accessibility features is likely to also be very search-engine-friendly.

Unit Testing

Developers of most robust applications use a strategy called *unit testing* to ensure that the software under development works as desired. Unit testing works by creating a suite of tests that are executed against the system with known results.

For example, one test in a suite might call the function `add(a,b)`, which is used to add two numbers together. The unit test calls the `add` function and passes it two numbers (2 and 2, for example) and retrieves the result. If the result matches that specified for the test (4, in this case), then the function passes the unit test.

If a different result is returned, however, the test has failed, and the failure is noted in the unit test report. By creating a robust suite of such tests, any time significant changes are made to a program, unit testing may be performed on the desired code, and the developer can see any places where changes have caused unexpected results (most likely a broken function).

Unit testing has proven itself as a critical technology for group development, since it allows many developers to make changes to every part of the code. Yet, *summary unit testing* can instantly reveal problems caused by changes in disparate parts of the system. Further, it has allowed designers to rough in the outlines or *stubs* of features by creating a number of unit tests (which all fail at first) before any true coding has begun. The system designer can then assign a developer to an area of work and when the unit tests pass, that piece of the system is ready for integration into the whole.

You should create unit tests and use automated testing for all but the simplest extensions. These tests will aid you when creating version upgrades, since they allow fast extension-wide testing to ensure that new code doesn't render previously working functions inoperable.

For PHP unit testing, you can use a program called SimpleTest. It is available for free download from here:

```
www.lastcraft.com/simple_test.php
```

For commercial automated Web page testing, check out the trial version of Selenium at the following URL:

```
www.openqa.org/selenium
```

Site Deployment

Once the system has been thoroughly tested, you will need to deploy it to one or more production servers. Transition to deployment is actually one of the more problematic tasks to accomplish in the Joomla system, since there is no built-in transfer system. Therefore, making a backup may require transfer of both the data stored in the database and the files that make up the Joomla system.

Transferring to the Deployment Server

Transferring a Joomla configuration to a deployment server requires a fair number of manual tasks. There is no automated method of performing a server transfer of key aspects of the staging system (such as selected extensions), while leaving behind such things as test components and test security settings.

Since transfer between the servers is generally a manual process, it's helpful to have a transfer checklist to ensure that all necessary items are copied to the new server. Here is a basic checklist for deployment:

❑ *Extensions* — Any third-party modules, components, or plug-ins used on your staging server must be installed and configured on the production server. It is generally not a good idea to attempt to copy the extensions manually from the Joomla directories, because often the add-ons have created tables, altered configuration data, and perhaps even stored one or more Administrator interface components in the Joomla system.

❑ PHP.ini *directives* — You most likely have one or more configuration settings in the PHP.ini file that are necessary for your server configuration. Keep in mind that many PHP directives will be *different* between the staging server and the deployment server because of security and testing reasons. Most commonly, there will be PHP directives to enable PHP extensions, such as gd2 that must be set for proper Joomla application execution.

❑ *Apache* httpd.conf *directives* — Like PHP directives, most Apache directives that will need to be transferred relate to module activation to allow the same functionality on both servers.

❑ *Joomla* configuration.php — You should always back up the original configuration file on your production server so that you don't lose it when you transfer the staging configuration file to the deployment server. Also, be sure to modify the $host parameter to match the base URL address of the deployment server once the file transfer is complete.

Joomla Backup

Your staging server will likely have a good amount of data that you will want to transfer to the production server. Since all of the data is stored in the MySQL database, you can transfer exactly the data you want, but you must perform the transfer using MySQL.

The number of Joomla files you must back up on your system will depend on the number of modifications you make to the various files. For example, the simplest site would be a default installation with only the sections, categories, and article content changed through the graphical user interface. Under those circumstances, only the database and a single file must be backed up (the configuration.php file) to allow the entire site to be restored in the future.

A setup as vanilla as the one just described is fairly rare. Typically, the first thing added to a Joomla site is a new header graphic. That is followed by modifications to the template and other file changes. Therefore, to make a complete snapshot backup of the site, you must copy all of those files from the deployment server.

> Be sure that you back up all the files on the deployment server — don't use the staging server as an implicit backup. While the staging server is an important development tool, the actual site that users interact with is on the deployment server. If that fails, you want to be able to have it up and running again in the minimal amount of time. The staging server, in contrast, is usually in some state of development and may not be ready to copy to the deployment server for live use.

You can create a scheduled backup of the database using MySQL Administrator. Click on the Backup icon on the left side of the screen, and when the right pane is populated, click the New button. The backup system provides numerous options (see Figure 11-5) that can include backing up the schema, the data (including table creates and drops), and many other features.

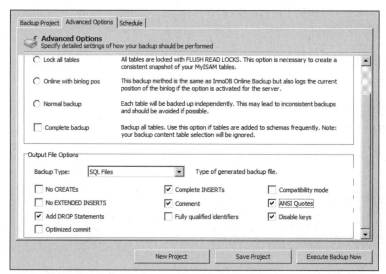

Figure 11-5: Setting a Joomla backup schedule allows you to configure many parameters.

Apache Virtual Hosts Configuration

A single Apache server can actually host multiple Web sites. For example, a single server machine could theoretically host www.disney.com and www.abc.com. Virtual hosting is extremely useful if you have an organization where you want to make one presentation to your customers (www.example.com) and another for an extranet for your suppliers (www.examplesuppliers.com).

When Apache has multi-hosting enabled, domain names are assigned to specific IP numbers. Traffic for a particular IP number is routed to a specific folder that holds the Web files for that domain. Therefore, to run multiple Joomla sites on one server, you only need to place the Joomla installations in separate folders and create a database for each installation.

The Apache directive code will look like this:

```
<VirtualHost xx.xx.xx.xxx>
ServerAlias example.com
ServerAlias *.example.com
ServerAlias alt1site.com
ServerAlias *.alt1site.com
ServerAlias http://www.alt1site.com/
ServerAlias alt2site.com
ServerAlias *.alt2site.com
ServerAlias http://www.alt2site.com/
ServerAdmin webmaster@example.com
DocumentRoot /home/example/public_html
BytesLog domlogs/example.com-bytes_log
ServerName http://www.example.com/

<IfModule mod_php4.c>
 php_admin_value open_basedir
        "/home/example:/usr/lib/php:/usr/local/lib/php:/tmp"
</IfModule>
<IfModule mod_php5.c>
 php_admin_value open_basedir
"/home/example:/usr/lib/php:/usr/local/lib/php:/tmp"
</IfModule>

User example
Group example
CustomLog /usr/local/apache/domlogs/example.com combined
ScriptAlias /cgi-bin/ /home/example/public_html/cgi-bin/
</VirtualHost>
```

This style of hosting is known as *IP-based hosting*, where multiple IP addresses are configured on a single server. There is an alternate method known as *name-based hosting* that allows many multiple virtual hosts to share the same IP address. Name-based hosting uses the `hostname` parameter in the HTTP request to determine where to route the Web communication. You can find a complete description of configuring name-based hosting on the Apache Web site (`http://httpd.apache.org/docs/1.3/vhosts/name-based.html`).

Controlling Apache from the Command Line

Apache administration on a local server is handled mostly from the command line. You can pause, restart, start, and stop the server by entering statements at the command line. For example, to restart the server, you could enter a line like this at the command line:

```
C:\Program Files\Apache\Apache2.2\bin\httpd.exe
    -w -n "Apache2.2" -k restart
```

Multi-Server Management

There will come a time where you will almost certainly need to manage multiple installations of Joomla that are located on various servers. While, as of this writing, Joomla has no method of managing these multiple sites from a single interface, there are some solutions to managing particular aspects of the servers. For example, MySQL includes a utility that lets you manage multiple instances of database servers, thereby providing access to multiple Joomla databases.

MySQL Instance Manager

The MySQL Instance Manager is a command line utility available for both UNIX-based and Windows operating systems. It reports the status of any instance of the server. It allows individual or all the servers to be started, stopped, or restarted. Through the utility, you can designate a server as *guarded* that will make the Instance Manager monitor the server and automatically restart it if a fault is detected.

All selected instances may be configured through the Manager for unified configuration. Additionally, the Instance Manager can control instances remotely, so while the Manager needs to be running on the server hosting the database, it can be accessed remotely.

PhpMyAdmin

If you are running phpMyAdmin for your MySQL site administration needs, it can be set to configure multiple MySQL servers. Management is as simple as defining a `$cfg['Servers']` array to contain the login information for all of the servers to be managed, where each entry of `$cfg['Servers']` `[$i]['host']` contains the hostname of each server.

Load Testing

To test the performance of a Web server configuration, it is a good idea to do *load testing* before deployment. Load testing is the process of placing an artificial load on the Web server (such as hundreds of simultaneous page requests) and monitoring the response. Particularly useful is placing a load far beyond the normal usage patterns to stress test the system and determine if anything breaks down.

Load testing is possible through the open source Dieseltest Load Testing Software tool shown in Figure 11-6. It can simulate multiple user types, as well as hundreds or thousands of simultaneous users on a Web site. It can also record scripts and play them back, showing results in real time. A log evaluator is included for generating result statistics for further analysis.

Dieseltest is available for download here:

```
http://sourceforge.net/projects/dieseltest
```

You can do load testing on your MySQL and Joomla applications with DB Monster, which is found here:

```
http://sourceforge.net/projects/dbmonster
```

DB Monster generates random test data for insertion in a SQL database. After the data has been inserted, you can use query-evaluation tools to determine how well your query is optimized to handle a large amount of data.

To test the MySQL configuration and database server performance in general, you can use the Database Opensource Test Suite for the Linux Test Project, which you can download here:

```
http://ltp.sourceforge.net
```

Each of these applications let you create a *load profile* where you determine the operations that will be thrown against the server for the test. Creating an effective load profile is as much of an art as a science. Steve Splaine has written an excellent article called "Modeling the Real World for Load Testing Web Sites" (www.stickyminds.com/s.asp?F=S3116_ART_2) that introduces the basic considerations of designing an effective profile.

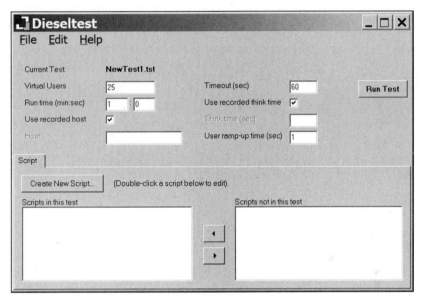

Figure 11-6: The Dieseltest application simulates users who will place a load on the server.

Load Balancing

Load balancing is the other side of the coin from load testing. When a site is extremely popular, it is likely that it will require more than a single server for purposes of redundancy (that is, in case one fails, the whole site doesn't fail) and request distribution (so that requests are split among identical servers for better performance).

Load balancing is limited on a staging server. The staging server is typically running on a local area network (LAN) and may hold all servers (Web/PHP and database) on a single machine with limited resources. When deployment occurs, most Joomla systems will be running on the Internet, executing on one or more servers. Each server will have significant memory and hard drive resources to handle the incoming Internet traffic.

You can perform some basic load balancing to see where the most obvious bottlenecks in execution might occur on the staging server. But general balancing is impossible without a system that mirrors the deployment conditions.

You can download phpLoadBalancer here:

```
http://sourceforge.net/projects/phploadbalancer
```

For larger systems, you might consider the XLB HTTP Load Balancer (XLB) (`http://sourceforge.net/projects/xlb`) or the Linux Virtual Server (`www.linuxvirtualserver.org`). These applications provide load balancing at the server level for complete scaling capability.

Internationalization

With version 1.5, Joomla has been rewritten from the ground up to embrace international deployment. One of the most challenging aspects of this redevelopment effort was the modification of the entire system to accept the UTF-8 standard so that international languages could be used effectively.

The UTF-8 character-encoding scheme saves text characters using variable-length data. One character (a simple alpha character, for example) may take up a single byte, while another character (a rare Chinese pictogram, for example) may take up to 3 bytes. Extremely rare characters may take up to 4 bytes.

This encoding scheme has advantages over Unicode, which takes up 2 bytes for every character. UTF-8 not only can store more variability (with maximum of 4 bytes), but the majority of text can be stored as a single byte. Since most Roman characters can fit within the first byte, that means for most Western language sites a lion's share of text transmitted can keep the size and storage advantages of single-byte ASCII, while providing the flexibility for non-Roman character sets that Unicode allows.

With the new revisions, the entire Joomla application has been localized. It has also been upgraded to include right-to-left (RTL) languages. Therefore, if you are deploying non-Roman languages, be sure to configure both Joomla and the MySQL database server to use the UTF-8 character-encoding method.

Automated Content Vetting

When sites allow for posting of content, there are a number of controls that must be put in place so that visitors aren't offended. Many of the tools described in Chapter 10 (including the guestbook extensions) have built-in functionality that can be used to censor curse words and general inappropriate language.

There is an extension called Foul Filter that will mask a set of administrator-defined words. It can perform the masking depending on registration status, or for all users. It will replace all listed foul words with asterisk (*) characters.

The plug-in does not change any of the content but instead intercepts the text before it is broadcast to the visiting browser, and then does the replacement at that point. This system has the advantages of not only leaving your initial content intact but also allowing a change of policy (whether new words are added for censorship or words once taboo are now permissible) to immediately display all content using the new rules.

You can find Foul Filter on the Joomla extensions site at the following URL:

```
www.girlsgonedumb.com/component/option,com_remository/Itemid,41/
func,fileinfo/id,1
```

MySQL Performance Tuning

While the execution of PHP can't be substantially accelerated through system settings, the configuration and setup of MySQL can dramatically alter the performance of the database server. Since all display content for Joomla occurs by data retrieval from the MySQL database, performance tuning of MySQL and data retrieval can provide substantial improvements in Web site responsiveness — particularly on a site with heavy traffic.

Performance tuning for MySQL goes far beyond making adjustments to the server. If your custom-built extensions query the database, how you format your tables, database interactivity, and general queries can make as much difference in responsiveness as any settings you can make to the server itself. Therefore, you should approach optimization of MySQL on two fronts: configuring the server for best performance, and configuring your application and custom data structures to maximize throughput.

Setting the Data Drive

The location of the data that MySQL addresses can be specified. If you are running your Web server on the Windows platform, there are ways that the data can be configured for the best performance. For example, if the data storage is located on a different IDE drive from the OS execution, retrieval and storage will be faster.

Selecting a Server Type

MySQL has configuration settings that can be adjusted to maximize performance given the type of MySQL access that is most common. Installed with MySQL is a utility called the MySQL Server Instance Configuration Wizard. It will help you reconfigure the MySQL installation for best performance for your deployment intentions. Execute the application and select Reconfigure Instance, followed by the Detailed Configuration setting.

The Server Type screen shown in Figure 11-7 allows you to select the types of task that this MySQL instance will be performing. Obviously, a staging server that's running multiple programs should be set to Developer Machine. The Server Machine setting will optimize MySQL for a standalone server that is running multiple servers on it. The Dedicated MySQL Server Machine setting is self-explanatory.

For the database usage setting shown in Figure 11-8, most Joomla users leave the usage setting to the default of Multifunctional Database. However, unless you're running a virtual community site with a great deal of data entry, or an e-commerce site that needs transactional integrity, the Non-Transactional Database Only option will provide better performance. For e-commerce sites where transactional integrity is critical, the Transactional Database Only setting is probably the best option.

The concurrent connections setting shown in Figure 11-9 defines the expected number of concurrent connections. For most Joomla sites, the Decision Support (DSS)/OLAP setting will be fine. Setting MYSQL to the Online Transaction Processing (OLTP) connection will use up a great deal more resources that are set aside in anticipation of the higher connection volume.

The next options for the network protocol and strict mode should be left with their default settings unless, because of firewall issues, you need to change the MySQL port number. For the default character set screen shown in Figure 11-10, leave whatever setting you used during installation, unless you want to reinstall Joomla. The character mode for the database server should be set before the Joomla installation so that the installer will be able to configure the proper database storage procedures.

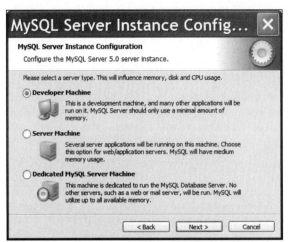

Figure 11-7: Selecting the MySQL server type will optimize memory, disk space, and cache for the execution circumstances of the database server.

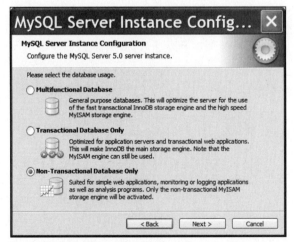

Figure 11-8: The type of database usage can be set to Multifunctional Database, Transactional Database Only, or Non-Transactional Database Only.

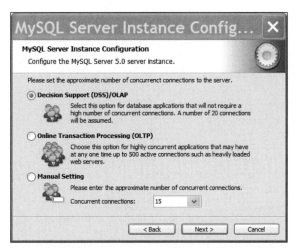

Figure 11-9: The various concurrent connections settings can optimize the MySQL server for the expected level of traffic.

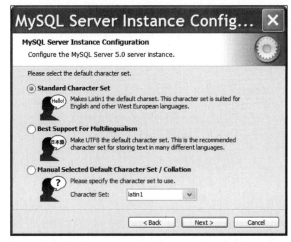

Figure 11-10: Select the Best Support for Multilingualism (UTF8) option if you are going to use many non-English languages with Joomla.

The remainder of the settings are made for personal choice and don't have much relevance to Joomla configuration. However, if you change the root password of the database server, ensure that you likewise change the password in the Joomla Administrator interface so that Joomla can log into the server.

Source of Problems

Although the Joomla development team has optimized Joomla database structures for general use, you could find that you may be able to "hack" the database to tweak a great deal more performance that caters to your needs. Additionally, tables that you create for custom extensions can gain substantially by proper application of some database guidelines.

269

Optimizing Indexes

The single most likely areas for performance problems (and the place for optimization) are the *indexes* used by database tables. In a database, data is stored unsorted. A contact record, for example, with a last name of "Smith" may be the first record in the database, while a record with the name "Abbott" could be at the very end. To output a sorted list of all the names that begin with the letter "B," a query would require the database to use a great deal of resources and processing power each time to generate such a list.

To speed database searching and sorting capabilities, the database server uses indexes that contain an indexed list of records sorted in a particular order. Each index remains stored on the database server. In the contact database example, when a request for last name records is made, the index for the last name field is accessed. Just as a book index allows a reader to jump directly to a page reference, the database can quickly find a record in the alphabetically sorted list and jump directly to that record.

Indexes must be created for any fields (or combination of fields) that the table designer will be requesting often. In Figure 11-11, the MySQL Administrator is displaying some of the indexes created for use in the Joomla database. The `jos_content` table alone has seven indexes associates with it to provide fast sorting on fields such as `access`, `catid`, `section`, and so on.

Poor indexing choices are one of the key reasons for poor database performance. If the indexes are created such that they don't accommodate the manner in which the database query is performed, they provide no speed improvements. In fact, the more indexes applied to a table, the more the write speed is slowed because the new data must be indexed for the additions or modifications.

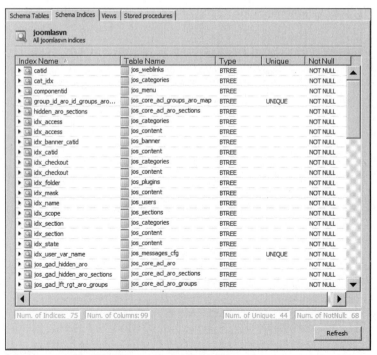

Figure 11-11: The MySQL Administrator displays the indexes associated with the Joomla database.

Use of Compound Indexes

A simple index is one that only indexes a single field — last name, for example. It is possible to create an index for multiple fields, such as last name and first name. These indexes are called *compound indexes* or *composite indexes*. For example, an index called `lastname_firstname` could be created that would index both fields.

One of the common misunderstandings that make compound indexes worthless in implementation is the ordering of the index. Compound indexes are ordered by the fields they contain. Therefore, in the `lastname_firstname` index, the last name field comes first in the index, followed by the first name. Therefore, a search on only the last name field will be able to use the index. However, a query that requests the first name field *will not* be able to use this index because of the way the index is created on the database server.

Unique Values in an Index Field

An index might seem to always improve performance, but that is not the case. The database server does a great deal of work behind the scenes to optimize query performance. One of those processes will be to determine whether a query will be optimized by an index or not.

One method it uses in determining the use of the index is to check whether more than 30 percent of the indexed field values are unique. For example, a contact database might hold an index for the `State` field. If 90 percent of the people in the database were from California, then the index would actually be counter-productive in terms of processing performance. The database server would have to check the index, determine the record that it references, load that record, and then retrieve the data. Compare that with ignoring the index, simply retrieving the record in the first place, checking the `State` field, and using the data if it matches.

Therefore, in fields or columns where there are fewer than 30 percent unique values, MySQL simply ignores the index and performs the query directly on the records. In this situation, if you were to modify the index to be a compound index (a `state_lastname` index, for example), the performance would increase dramatically if your query needed both of these pieces of information.

Since the majority of databases shift in data segmentation from initial release to maturity, the index strategy should be evaluated at regular intervals to ensure that the choices are still relevant.

Remove Redundant Indexes

Each additional index on a table lengthens the amount of time required for record storage. Additions and modifications must be sorted for each index. Therefore, any indexes that are redundant can cause a slow-down of system performance. While this might not be a problem for a traditional Joomla site, a transaction-heavy e-commerce site or a popular community forum site may see delays that can be eliminated.

The first redundancy that should be checked lies in simple indexes versus compound indexes. If a compound index has the `lastname_firstname` fields, then there is no need for a `lastname` index, since MySQL will use the compound index automatically for that field. Likewise, a `lastname_firstname_middlename` eliminates the need for a `lastname_firstname` index.

Further, especially in a team situation, indexes that perform exactly the same sort may be added over time. Be sure to eliminate any of the redundancies to improve performance.

Use the Smallest Possible Data Type

When creating a new table for a custom extension, be very careful when defining your fields or columns. There is a definite tendency to overengineer a table definition, especially after the expenditures incurred during the Y2K scare (where the years digits were stored as only two character places, which made the turning of the millennium a potentially serious problem). Nonetheless, for performance reasons, it is usually better to minimize data type sizes that make them large for unknown what-ifs in the future.

For example, if you're going to be storing the day of the year, use a SMALLINT (which has a 32,000 value range) rather than an INT (which has a range of 2 billion, but takes up double the storage space). While this savings may not seem like much, like compound interest, it adds up. Imagine this 2-byte waste per field *times* 8 fields *times* 30 user reads per session *times* 2000 visitors per hour, and you have a lot of unnecessary reads and database processing. And that's just with a 2-byte waste on one field.

Imagine in a worst-case scenario where a table is defined with a CHAR field with a length of 300 instead of a VARCHAR field. The amount of wasted data transfer can be staggering, and significantly decrease the performance of the system. Examine Table 11-1 for a list of data types you can use with MySQL and their limitations, as well as how much byte space they will occupy in the database. This table should help you determine the smallest data type that will fit in each situation.

Table 11-1: MySQL Data Types

Data Type	Description	Bytes
TINYINT	Integer values in the range -/+ 127	1
SMALLINT	Integer values in the range -/+ 32,767	2
MEDIUMINT	Integer values in the range -/+ 8,388,607	3
INT	Integer values in the range -/+ 2,147,483,647	4
BIGINT	Integer values in the range -/+ 9,223,372,036,854,775,807	8
FLOAT	Single-precision floating-point values	4
DOUBLE	Double-precision floating-point values	8
DECIMAL	Floating-point values with user-defined precision	Variable
CHAR	Fixed-length strings	Specified length up to 255 characters
VARCHAR	Variable-length strings, with a preset maximum limit	Variable (up to 65,535 characters)

Table 11-1: MySQL Data Types *(continued)*

Data Type	Description	Bytes
TEXT	Variable-length strings	Variable (up to 65,535 characters)
MEDIUMTEXT	Variable-length strings	Variable (up to 16,777,216 characters)
LONGTEXT	Variable-length strings	Variable (up to 4,294,967,295 characters)
BLOB	Binary strings	Variable (up to 65,535 bytes)
MEDIUMBLOB	Binary strings	Variable (up to 16,777,216 bytes)
LONGBLOB	Binary strings	Variable (up to 4,294,967,295 bytes)
DATE	Date values in the format yyyy-mm-dd	3
TIME	Time values in the format hh:mm:ss	3
DATETIME	Combined date and time values in the format yyyy-mm-ddhh:mm:ss	8
TIMESTAMP	Combined date and time values in the format yyyy-mm-ddhh:mm:ss	4
YEAR	Year values in the format yyyy	1
ENUM	A set of values from which the user must select one	1 or 2 bytes
SET	Values from which the user can select zero, one or more	Between 1 and 8 bytes

Keep in mind that when you create an index, the rows of the index hold more than a simple reference to the column specified — they hold the actual data for the column. Therefore, indexing a column that has a data type of `char(200)` means that every index entry will hold the size of that field. Therefore, to preserve space and minimize index processing, try to avoid indexing the larger data columns of a table.

Only Retrieve What You Need

Many beginning developers use a query like this one in their applications:

```
SELECT * FROM jos_contact_details
```

By exactly specifying the fields that are needed for the application, a query like this would take a fraction of the time and data transfer:

```
SELECT name, telephone FROM jos_contact_details
```

When creating a query, only return the columns that you need for your dataset. Don't forget that columns evaluated in your WHERE clause do not need to be returned with the resultset. That means a streamline query like this:

```
SELECT name, telephone FROM jos_contact_details WHERE postcode = '92107'
```

Use the EXPLAIN Command

One of the most effective ways of optimizing a query is through examination of the results of the EXPLAIN command. Placing the command EXPLAIN before a query will return information about the query execution instead of the resultset:

```
EXPLAIN SELECT * FROM jos_contact_details
```

Following are the columns of the data returned by the EXPLAIN statement:

❏ Select_type *column* — Describes the type of query that was executed. A value of Simple means the query did not use any unions or subqueries. Primary indicates an outermost select. Union, Dependent Union, and Union Result all performed union operations. Subquery, Dependent Subquery, Uncacheable Subquery, and Derived all use subqueries to obtain their results.

❏ Type *column* — Describes the path of execution in terms of the join type. A value of system or const indicates the table only has a single row. Other values include eq_ref, ref, ref_or_null, index_merge, unique_subquery, index_subquery, range, and index. If the column reads all, that means the full table was accessed without the use of an index.

❏ Possible_keys *column* — Details the possible indexes that MySQL can choose from to execute the query.

❏ key *column* — Indicates the index that MySQL actually chose to execute the query.

I would highly recommend that you read the "Optimizing Queries with EXPLAIN" section of the MySQL manual (http://dev.mysql.com/doc/refman/5.0/en). The EXPLAIN command will be the most powerful and useful tool you will need to optimize the performance of your queries. Pay particular attention to the Type column, as the value shown there is often the best clue on how you might optimize the search.

Profiling the Existing System

Once you've deployed your Joomla site, you shouldn't consider that you've reached the finish line. In fact, tuning the performance once you can evaluate the real loads being placed on it can generate far better results than tuning based on assumptions. MySQL makes it particularly easy to examine the performance and helps you to determine where the bottlenecks are occurring.

Profiling is the method of diagnosing a running system and determining where the bottlenecks occur. One excellent tool you can use in profiling the system is examining the *slow queries log*. The slow query log holds all of the SQL statements whose execution exceeded the time set in the long_query_time parameter. The default value of this variable is set to 10 seconds.

You can activate this log in the Startup Variables of the MySQL Administrator application. On the "Log files" tab, activate the log as shown in Figure 11-12 and provide a filename. If no filename is specified, it will default to `host_name-slow.log`. You will need to restart the MySQL server for the setting to take effect.

You can also activate the log from the command line by starting MySQL like this:

```
mysqld --log-slow-queries=joomlaSlowQLog
```

Once you have a query log, you can summarize the log from the MySQL command line with this statement:

```
mysqldumpslow <path-to-MySQL-log-files>/joomlaSlowQLog
```

The `--help` switch can be used to display all the parameters available to the `dump` command.

> *You can also obtain data on the MySQL query performance using the `myshow` module. This utility is slightly complicated to configure and use, so I would suggest you look at the home page (`http://jfontain.free.fr/myshow/myshow.htm`) and determine if it suits your needs.*

In addition to monitoring MySQL query performance, you should also profile the system in terms of overall performance. The MyTop utility (`http://jeremy.zawodny.com/mysql/mytop`) mimics the functionality of the Top utility in Linux but applies itself to monitoring the threads and overall performance of MySQL. It can be used to execute against local or remote hosts. It runs on Linux, MacOS, and Windows.

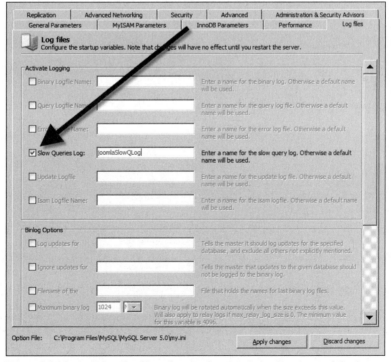

Figure 11-12: Activate the Slow Queries Log, and set the name of the log.

Administration

Joomla has made administration generally very easy. However, as a site expands, managing the existing content, user authentication, and keeping the system clear of dead or outdated data can become a real chore. There are methods for handling all of these problems, largely thanks to Joomla's embrace of open standards and compatibility with a large number of technologies.

For infrastructure-wide user authentication, Joomla is compatible with Lightweight Directory Access Protocol (LDAP) servers that can also be used to manage users on other server types. For handling old content, menus, and users, you can either use the Joomla Administrator interface or directly query the Joomla database tables using MySQL tools. Most of the Joomla maintenance on even a larger system can be accomplished without having to resort to expensive or complex system tools.

LDAP Authentication

LDAP is an implementation standard that provides ways to centralize access authorization. Instead of requiring a separate login for each of numerous systems a client might use, a single authorization contained in an LDAP directory can provide authorization to all of those systems. For example, an LDAP server could contain all the user authentication information for a Web server, FTP server, CMS, mail server, and so on. That means that only a single user account would have to be administered on the LDAP server, instead of individual records at all other servers.

Fortunately, through a plug-in that comes with the system, Joomla supports LDAP authentication. Although the group-level settings (such as registered, contributor, moderator, and so on) can't be stored on the LDAP server, username and password login can be.

Joomla LDAP Plug-In

To activate LDAP capabilities on Joomla, select the Plug-in Manager under the Extensions menu of the Joomla Administrator interface. You will find the LDAP extension under the name Authentication — LDAP. Click on the link to display the LDAP extension parameters, as shown in Figure 11-13. Set the Published parameter to Yes, because the plug-in is not activated with a default installation.

When setting the plug-in parameters, if available through the target LDAP server, select the Yes option for the Negotiate TLS parameter. Setting this parameter will make the system negotiate Transport Layer Security (TLS) that will encrypt traffic with the LDAP server so that passwords and authentication are not sent in plain text.

Set the Base DN parameter to the base *distinguished name* of the LDAP Server (which should be unique). Set the Search String to the query string with [search] substituted where the username or ID will be placed. For example, a search string of uid=[search] will send the entered username to be matched against values in the uid field. The Users DN is used only in direct binds and will send user-provided login strings, separated by a semicolon (;). For example, uid=[username], dc=mycompany, dc=com would log in to the LDAP server with those parameters.

Leave both the "Connect username" and "Connect password" fields blank for anonymous access. The final Map parameters are used to define the fields on the LDAP server that will contain the required information for a Joomla login.

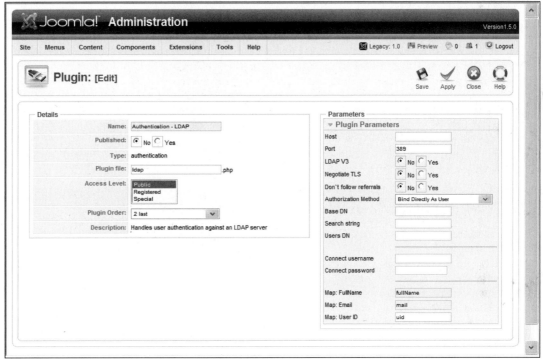

Figure 11-13: The LDAP plug-in parameters provide configuration details about the LDAP server to be addressed.

OpenLDAP

If you want to run an LDAP server, you can use OpenLDAP, an open source implementation of an LDAP server. It is available for the Linux, UNIX, MacOS, and BeOS operating systems at the main OpenLDAP site (www.openldap.org). For Windows, you can get LDAP at the ILEX Web site (www.ilex.fr/openldap .htm or http://download.bergmans.us/openldap). Note that most Windows-based networks will use Active Directory, which also supports LDAP.

For testing, you can address an LDAP server from modern Web browsers. Simply use the ldap prefix rather that the traditional http for the URL like this:

    ldap://ldap.itd.umich.edu

If you're doing a lot of LDAP work, consider downloading and installing Luma, which is an LDAP browser and testing tool. You can download it for free at the Luma home page (http://luma.sourceforge.net).

> *Configuring an LDAP server is no small task. Therefore, if you have no previous experience with LDAP, before you attempt an installation, I would suggest you purchase one of the many fine books available on the technology. You might try Implementing LDAP by Mark Wilcox (Wiley Publishing, Inc., 1999), which covers LDAP from the perspective of developers, as well as system administrators.*

Maintenance

As important as setup can be to the proper functioning of a Joomla site, maintenance can be just as important. A CMS is like a garden where weeds must be plucked, pests destroyed, and even the most desirable of flowers must be pruned.

By making sure your Joomla system continues to be properly tuned, you will maintain good performance. Letting unpublished content clog the system, or long-time inactive user accounts present a security threat, can make the time saved by avoiding routine maintenance seem like a bad choice.

Cleaning Joomla

The Joomla database can become cluttered over time with quantities of unpublished content, unused menus, inactive user accounts, and so on. You can begin the cleaning from the Joomla Administrator interface. However, there are many cleaning tasks that are too arduous and time-consuming to perform through the interface. These tasks can execute directly against the MySQL database.

> *Before you perform any cleaning manually, check the Joomla extensions site (`extensions.joomla.org`) for an extension that performs the task you need. An extension may take into account variables that affect the system functions. For example, you can't delete a category until all articles filed in that category are removed. Rather than going through the tedium of removing the articles and then the category, you may find an extension that will delete a category and all the articles in it.*

Using the Article Manager to Find Unpublished Articles and Menus

If possible, you should use the Joomla Administrator interface for any deletions or modification. Only the system itself understands the web of links a particular change might affect. The interface will also warn you of problems with executing the desired action, such as the performance penalties that may occur from activating search term logging.

The Article Manager can be used to instantly generate a list of all the unpublished articles. Examining this list is important at regular periodic intervals (once every six months, for example) to ensure that your database doesn't become bloated with unused content.

For unpublished articles, select the Unpublished option in the Article Manager, as shown in Figure 11-14. The list will now hold only the unpublished articles on the system.

Direct MySQL Access

Since all of the critical information for Joomla is stored within MySQL, you can directly search the database for errant information. It is also possible (but not recommended if you have another choice) to clean the database yourself. Some cleaning functions (especially those such as removing extensions, which require file deletion) should only be performed through the Administrator interface. However, the ability to make bulk changes and deletions to particular tables can sometimes only be handled directly through MySQL.

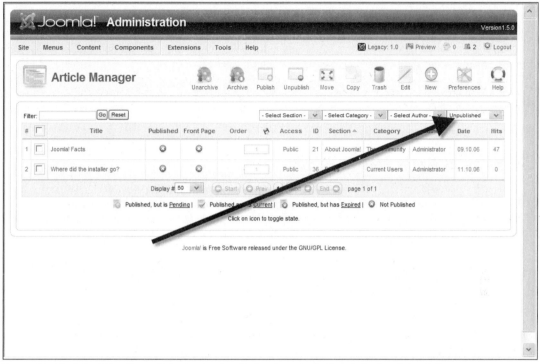

Figure 11-14: Select the Unpublished selection in the drop-down list at the far right of the screen.

> You are directly modifying the Joomla database that can be very hazardous if you don't understand exactly what you're doing. If you have any doubts about performing an action — don't do it. Also, before you make any changes, be sure that you have backed up the entire database, so in the case of a catastrophic fault, you can restore the database and, thereby, restore the Joomla site.

Finding Old Content

Content listed by modification date can show all articles that haven't been revisited in a substantial length of time. These articles can be updated to provide more current information or archived off the system.

You can find old content by executing the following SQL statement against the Joomla database, substituting the date specified as a desired value:

```
SELECT * FROM jos_content WHERE modified < '2007-01-01'
```

Finding Inactive Users

Joomla tracks the last visit date of all registered users. A query of these dates can provide a list of users who have not visited the site in some time. One of the best things you could do with such a list is to email these users to remind them of the site and invite them to return.

You can find inactive users by executing the following SQL statement against the Joomla database, substituting a desired value for the date specified:

```
SELECT * FROM jos_users WHERE lastvisitDate < '2007-01-01'
```

Finding Empty Data Fields

There are a number of fields that, if left empty, can be detrimental to your site ranking on search engines. Most important of these fields are the meta information (such as article description and article keywords) that provide the search engine with behind-the-scenes information about the content. A simple MySQL query can be used to find all of the articles that are missing this information, so the data can be created and the problem remedied.

You can find empty data fields by executing the following SQL statement against the Joomla database:

```
SELECT * FROM jos_content WHERE metakey = '' or metadesc = ''
```

Finding Unpublished Articles and Menus

Tracking unpublished items can be a big task with a popular, large, and mature Joomla site. Often, content is unpublished for convenience, since at a particular time, it is unknown whether the item will be needed again. After a certain age, however, the item (whether it's an article or menu) is unlikely to ever be used again. At that point, it is best to simply archive the item and then remove it from the database to increase performance.

You can find unpublished items by executing the following SQL statements against the Joomla database:

```
SELECT * FROM jos_content WHERE state = 0
SELECT * FROM jos_menu WHERE published = 0
SELECT * FROM jos_plugins WHERE published = 0
SELECT * FROM jos_components WHERE enabled = 0
SELECT * FROM jos_modules WHERE published = 0
```

Finding Most Recent Polls

There are many queries that you might want to perform on the Joomla system that show specific recent activity. For example, you may want to see all of the votes cast in polls in the last 10 days to determine if a recently posted poll has been popular. Performing such a query is simple through MySQL.

First, you need to look at the polls table to find the id the poll that interests you:

```
SELECT * FROM jos_polls
```

By executing the following SQL statement against the jos_poll_date table, a resultset will be returned with all of the votes within the last 10 days:

```
SELECT * FROM jos_poll_date  WHERE DATE_SUB(CURDATE(),INTERVAL 10 DAY) <= date;
```

Finding Empty Sections and Categories

When examining site organization, it can be useful to determine which sections or categories are unused. These unused filing groups can then be eliminated or merged with other designators for better organization.

You can find unused sections by executing the following SQL statement against the Joomla database:

```
SELECT * FROM jos_sections
    LEFT JOIN jos_content ON jos_content.sectionid = jos_sections.id
    WHERE jos_content.sectionid IS NULL and jos_sections.published=1
```

To find unused categories, execute this query:

```
SELECT * FROM jos_categories
    LEFT JOIN jos_content ON jos_content.sectionid = jos_categories.id
    WHERE jos_content.sectionid IS NULL and jos_categories.published=1
```

Summary

When you manage a professional Joomla deployment, you must ensure that your development and deployment process matches the needs of the undertaking. This chapter has provided an overview of how to configure and deploy Joomla by doing the following:

- ❏ Using the PHP CLI to test small code segments.
- ❏ Explaining the basics of backing up and restoring data on the Joomla system.
- ❏ Creating a virtual host configuration on the Apache server.
- ❏ Refining the MySQL server configuration to allow for best performance, depending on the Joomla deployment type.
- ❏ Adopting LDAP authentication for shared infrastructure services with other servers (such as the Web server and mail server).
- ❏ Querying with direct MySQL statements to find unpublished articles, inactive users, old content, empty data fields, and so on.

This chapter focused on the management of the resources on the Joomla site, but Joomla also includes capabilities that allow it to interact with remote information resources. Chapter 12 shows you how to set up Joomla to obtain outside content through everything from RSS feeds to performing manual screen scraping.

12

Interfacing with Outside Content

No Web site should be an island. Joomla makes it easy for a site to interface with outside content for everything from downloading Web feed articles to using Electronic Data Interchange (EDI) for commerce transactions to querying a database for XML data. There are literally dozens of extensions that support numerous types of system interaction. When you can't locate an extension that has the necessary communication capabilities, or you need a custom protocol, Joomla's developer-friendly framework makes it easy to develop your own extensions.

In this chapter, you'll learn how to configure your Joomla site to subscribe to external content and to publish your own on a Web feed. You'll also have a chance to see some of the affiliate programs that can be used effectively with Joomla through extensions created specifically to add the affiliate features to a Joomla site. Finally, you will use the development skills you have already gained to build custom extensions to wrap a Web API (to implement Google Maps), interface with a query server that returns a result set in XML (the U.S. Postal Service ZIP code finder), and develop a simple screen scraper to obtain data from another HTML site.

Pulling in External Content

By connecting to outside content from Web sites and newsfeeds, your Joomla site can supplement native articles. A Joomla site can supplement the existing content using Web feeds that deliver articles automatically for feed publishers.

Web Feeds

One technology that has done more for automated exchange of information than any other consumer protocol is *Web feed technology* (also called *newsfeed technology*). In a normal consumer situation, users can visit a Web site (such as www.CNN.com) and look at the current site content, as long as they are online. If the visitor desires more of the same type of content in the future (breaking stories, for example) and the site offers a Web feed, then that user can subscribe to a feed of the site.

By clicking on the Web feed link (typically labeled "RSS Feed," "RSS XML," or "Atom Feed"), a desktop application on the user's computer called an *aggregator* is notified of the subscription. The feed link URL points to the feed file (in XML format), which acts as an electronic table of contents pointing to (or containing) articles on the feed site. Depending on the preferences set for the aggregator, the program will automatically download new articles in the future by checking for additional entries in the newsfeed file. The new stories are saved on the user's local drive for later browsing.

As shown in Figure 12-1, the Mozilla Thunderbird email application includes an aggregator that will display feed content in email format. Simply select File ⇨ New ⇨ Account and, when the Account Wizard is displayed, click on the RSS News & Blogs option. Thunderbird will add a new folder titled `News & Blogs` where you can add any number of subscriptions. You can set parameters determining how the Web feed will be handled (frequency of updates, content presentation, and so on).

The Mozilla Firefox browser even includes a simple aggregator program. When the browser accesses a site that features a Web feed, the address bar displays a feed icon, as shown in Figure 12-2. The user only needs to click on the icon and select an option to add a Live Bookmark to access the feed content.

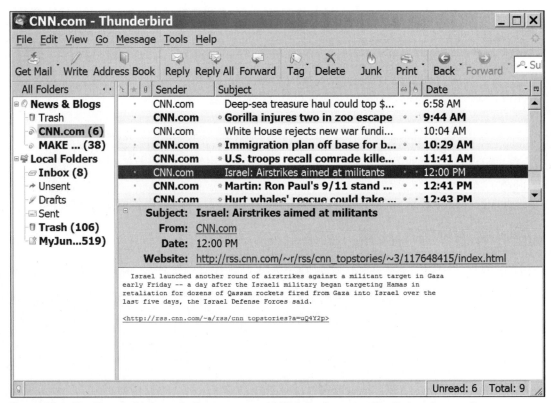

Figure 12-1: The Thunderbird email client can present Web feed content like it does for email.

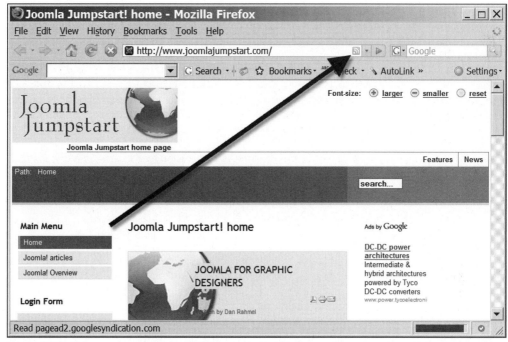

Figure 12-2: When a site provides a Web feed, Firefox displays a feed icon that can be selected for subscription.

Web Feed Format

There are two standard formats for Web feeds: RSS (Really Simple Syndication) and Atom. Both formats are stored in an XML-formatted file and, although an Atom feed uses the `.xml` extension (`atom.xml`, for example), an RSS feed may have either an `.xml` extension or an `.rss` extension.

For a long time, the two formats seemed neck and neck in the adoption race. But lately it seems as if RSS has become dominant, with many sites that used to offer both feed types dropping the Atom feed format.

For example, following is the URL to the CNBC feed:

```
http://rss.msnbc.msn.com/id/3098080/device/rss/rss.xml
```

The header and a few entries in a RSS feed file for filmmaking Web site looks like this:

```
<?xml version="1.0"?> <rss version="2.0">

<channel>
<title>Nuts and Bolts Filmmaking and Graphic Design</title>
<link>http://www.cvisual.com</link>
<description>Focused on Nuts and Bolts Filmmaking.</description>
<category>Arts/Movies/Filmmaking</category>
<language>en-us</language>
<copyright>Copyright 2007, Dan Rahmel</copyright>
```

```
<pubDate>Thu, 13 Jul 2007 11:10:00 PST</pubDate>
<lastBuildDate>Thu, 13 Jul 2007 11:10:00 PST</lastBuildDate>
<managingEditor>dan@example.com</managingEditor>
<webMaster>dan@example.com</webMaster>

<image>
<title>Nuts and Bolts Filmmaking Banner</title>
<url>http://www.cvisual.com/cover_test.jpg</url>
<link>http://www.cvisual.com</link>
<description>Nuts and Bolts Filmmaking banner image</description>
</image>

<item>
<title>Free 3D Modeling Checklist</title>
<link>http://www.cvisual.com/graphics-techniques/cgi-3d-modeling-checklist.asp</link>
<guid>http://www.cvisual.com/graphics-techniques/cgi-3d-modeling-checklist.asp</guid>
<description>Revised checklist for planning the creation of 3D models in Maya,
Lightwave, Blender, 3D Studio Max, Cinema 4D, Poser, or any other 3D
application.</description>
<pubDate>Mon, 17 Jul 2007 10:30:21 PST</pubDate>
<category>Arts/Movies/Filmmaking</category>
</item>
```

The file opens with the header information about the feed itself. The HTML header is followed by a header display section that holds the banner image to display for the feed. Finally, an `<item>` entry defines a story that can be downloaded or linked to by the aggregator.

> *Web feeds are becoming even more advanced. Podcasts (audio feeds) and vodcasts (video feeds) use nearly the same feed files as newsfeeds. The popular media aggregators (such as Apple's iTunes) perform exactly the same operations (for example, checking the feed file and automatically downloading the newest content) that a traditional news aggregator performs.*

Joomla Feed Subscription Module

The Feed module in Joomla allows you to integrate feed content directly into your Web site. Figure 12-3 shows the module titled Top Stories, presenting stories from the CNN newsfeed on a Joomla home page. Each time a Web visitor requests a page that includes the Feed module, the module accesses the remote feed file, retrieves the article information, and displays the most current feed entries.

To activate the Feed module, open the Joomla Administrator and display the Module Manager screen. Find the module named Feed Display and click on the entry. The module editor will display the current settings, as shown in Figure 12-4.

Begin configuration of the Web feed by setting the title of the module that will appear above the feed stories. In this example, I modified the Title from Feed Display to Top Stories. Change the Position of the module so that it won't appear at the bottom of the other modules in the left column. You can use the Right setting to have the feed stories appear in the right column. I set the position to User1 so the headlines would appear at the top of the page.

Figure 12-3: Including a Web feed on a Joomla page automatically displays new stories as they are added to the feed.

The Parameters pane on the right side of the screen has the settings that relate to the feed itself. The optional Suffix parameter allows you to set a suffix for a custom style (the suffix would be added to the `table.moduletable` style) in the CSS that would be used by this module. Enter the URL of the feed that you copied from a Web site. The `Feed URL` parameter will accept any standard URL pointing to an XML file formatted in either RSS or Atom format. You can also find links to various feeds in an RSS directory. For a list of the most popular directories, check out the RSS Specifications Web site (`www.rss-specifications.com/rss-directory.htm`). Since the feed in this example is supplied in English, there is no need to turn on the `RTL feed` (right-to-left) option that is useful if the feed language is provided in a language such as Mandarin.

Turn off the Feed Title and Feed Description parameters. The title and description are included in the feed file by the publisher, so you have no control over them. On a feed from a large company like CNN, you could be pretty confident nothing offensive would appear in these fields. However, a small, non-commercial Web feed (despite having great content) might put up something your visitors might find objectionable. Note that turning off the Feed Title does not turn off the display of the module Title (a text item you control).

Decide whether you want the feed image displayed. In most cases, you'll want to turn this off. It usually displays the logo of the feed originator, and that can cause some confusion for Web visitors. Additionally, I've seen some feeds that have really slow servers, which delays the time your server can return a requested page. Also, if you want a more compact display for the Feed module, turn off this setting.

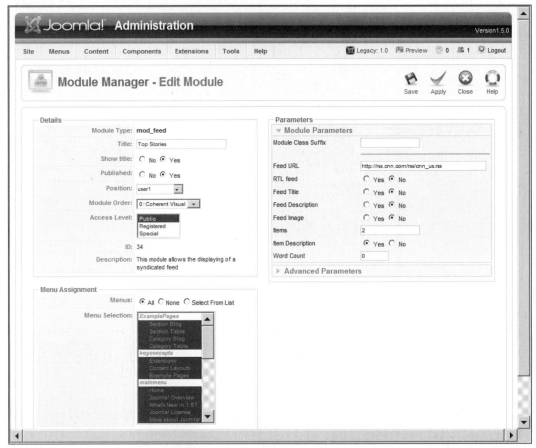

Figure 12-4: The Feed module settings will determine which feed is displayed and how the content is presented.

The Items parameter determines how many of the feed stories will be display. Since this will appear at the top of my page, I set the value to 2. The Items Description lets you determine whether you want to display just the headline links, or the headlines with the article summaries. The Word Count parameter allows you to control the number of words of the description that will be visible. The default setting of zero allows the entire description to be displayed.

> *To allow the Top Stories feed to be alone at the top of my page, I also unpublished the Latest News module in the Module Manager. The Latest News module was occupying the user1 module position and crowding my page display.*

That's it! Every time your page is accessed now, the page will read the newest stories from the configured Web feed and include links to these stories (and summary descriptions, if so set).

Joomla's Web feed capabilities don't end with subscribing to feeds. A Joomla site can also publish a feed of its own.

Joomla Syndication Publishing Module

Joomla also includes the capability to publish your own Web feed so that others can subscribe to your site.

In the Module Manager, click on the Syndication module to display the current settings. Ensure that the module is published and set the Position setting so the feed display appears in the left column. In the Parameters pane, set the Text parameter to the phrase you want to accompany the feed icon on the display page, as shown in Figure 12-5. You can choose the Format of the feed, although I recommend leaving the RSS 2.0 default. Save the settings to the module and your site now has its own Web feed!

When you view the Joomla page, it shows the feed icon and link. As shown in Figure 12-6, in the Firefox browser, the address bar indicates that this site is Web feed-enabled. When a user subscribes to the feed, the content items from the Frontpage Manager are included in the article list in order of their publication (with the newest content listed first).

If you publish a feed for your site, be sure to register it with one or more of the feed directories (`http://www.rss-specifications.com/rss-directory.htm`). Unlike Web search engines like Google that search out new content, feed search sites only include feeds that have applied for addition to the site. Before you get listed, though, be sure you have a decent amount of content that is updated regularly. Users on most engines can rate the feeds and, if your feed makes a poor showing, others will hear about it.

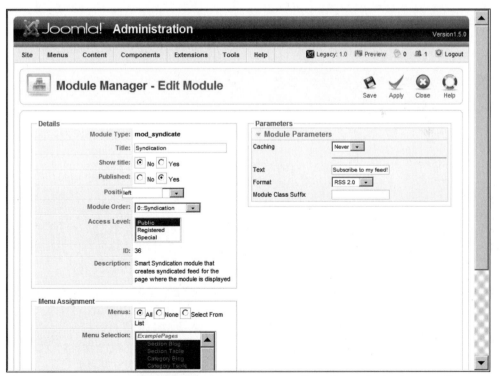

Figure 12-5: Setting the Syndication module parameters will configure the feed output file.

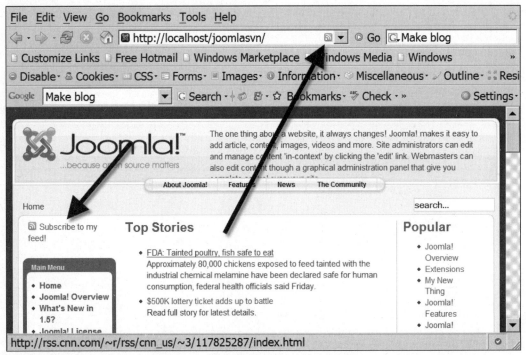

Figure 12-6: The Web feed icon and link are displayed by the Syndication module, and the address bar indicates the page is feed-enabled.

Auto Articles 3000 Extension

For search engine placement, it is questionable if a site gains any rank placement advantage from content supplied by Web feeds. Many search engine optimization (SEO) experts say that the search engines recognize content that is drawn from a feed and ignore it. If that is true, then feed content is not considered part of your site and, therefore, not indexed by the search engine.

One way to get supplemental content that becomes part of your site (and gains you search advantages) is to use an extension called Auto Articles 3000, which is shown in Figure 12-7. This extension downloads articles on specified topics from an ezine (electronic magazine) article archive and stores the article in your Joomla site database. Unlike a feed that retrieves off-site content dynamically, the Auto Article 3000 content creates an article store on your server that is updated as new articles become available.

Offered as a free service by Elerion, Ltd., Auto Articles 3000 is a package of components (one front-end component and one Administrator component) that can be installed on a Joomla site. The initial component installation includes 230 articles that are written into the Joomla database. New articles are downloaded automatically from the Web site at regular intervals (30 minutes is the default setting). You can download Auto Articles 3000 here:

    www.articles3000.com

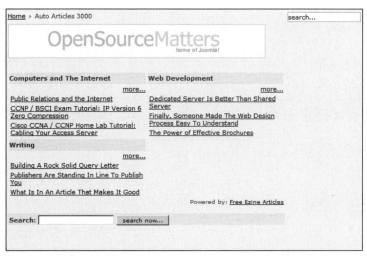

Figure 12-7: Auto Articles 3000 displays articles held in a table in the Joomla database.

You can determine which topics are downloaded for your site in the Administrator interface, as shown in Figure 12-8.

Unfortunately, the articles provided by the extension are not stored like standard Joomla articles in the Joomla content tables. That means the new material is invisible to Joomla interface features (such as site search) and also to other site extensions (such as sitemap utilities). The extension stores downloaded articles in the `jos_a3000_articles` table of the Joomla database.

However, one of the wonderful things about the world of open source is that it's open! You have full access to the source code and data for most extensions. In this case, it means that you could manually copy the Auto Articles 3000 content into the normal Joomla `jos_content` table. You would only need to coordinate the new records to Joomla-specific fields such as the section and category ID fields (`sectionid` and `catid`, respectively) so that the articles were properly filed. Copying the article data could be accomplished using the MySQL `INSERT INTO` statement, as shown here:

```
http://dev.mysql.com/doc/refman/5.0/en/insert-select.html
```

Another way you may want to get your hands dirty with this component is to modify the frequency that new articles are requested from the host site. You can set the site query to more or less than the 30-minute default. But to accomplish it, you can't simply modify a parameter in the Administrator interface. Rather, you must alter the component source code. Open the component file in your text editor with a path similar to this:

```
\components\com_a3000\a3000.php
```

In the file, look for the line that reads as follows:

```
if(time() - $last_checked > 1800) {
```

The parameter for `time` is coded in seconds, so the current value of 1800 is equal to 30 minutes. Set this value to any number of seconds you desire.

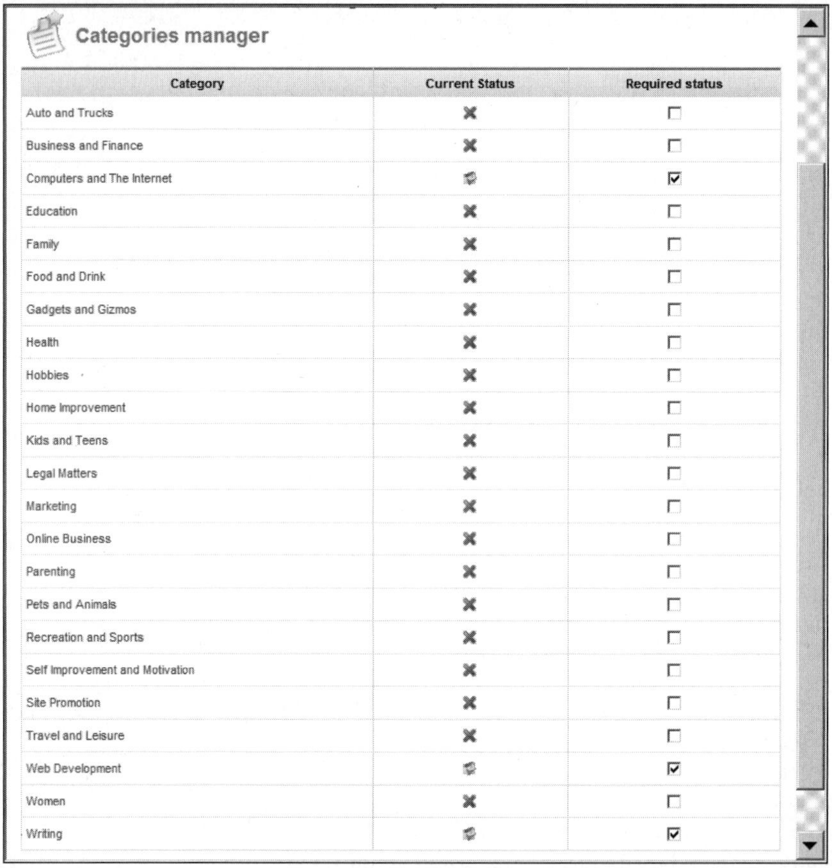

Category	Current Status	Required status
Auto and Trucks	✖	☐
Business and Finance	✖	☐
Computers and The Internet	🖉	☑
Education	✖	☐
Family	✖	☐
Food and Drink	✖	☐
Gadgets and Gizmos	✖	☐
Health	✖	☐
Hobbies	✖	☐
Home Improvement	✖	☐
Kids and Teens	✖	☐
Legal Matters	✖	☐
Marketing	✖	☐
Online Business	✖	☐
Parenting	✖	☐
Pets and Animals	✖	☐
Recreation and Sports	✖	☐
Self Improvement and Motivation	✖	☐
Site Promotion	✖	☐
Travel and Leisure	✖	☐
Web Development	🖉	☑
Women	✖	☐
Writing	🖉	☑

Figure 12-8: The Administrator interface shows all of the available article categories.

Managing Affiliate Programs

Affiliate programs are likely the most popular way to make money from a Web site. The Web master of a site signs up with a company such as Google or Amazon to allow advertisements to appear on the host site. Each time the user clicks on an ad or purchases something by following a link to the vendor's site, the Web master earns a fee. These programs can be so lucrative that large sites can earn literally thousands of dollars a month strictly from affiliate income.

Joomla can host most of the popular affiliate programs through extensions that encapsulate the code (HTML and often JavaScript) necessary to display the advertisements on the site. To activate most affiliate technology, you need only install the associated extension, set the parameters to match your service, and specify the location where the affiliate content will appear on your site.

Google AdSense Affiliate Program

One of the most popular affiliate programs on the Web is Google's AdSense. AdSense provides code that displays Google ads on a Web site that are relevant to the site visitors. Each time a user clicks on an ad, the owner of the Web site is paid a fee. These fees can results in large sums if the site is very popular, or if the content of the site targets a market where the advertisements for that sector are very expensive.

To host AdSense advertisements, you must first sign up for the program here:

```
www.google.com/adsense
```

When you first set up your Google account, only public service announcements are displayed (see Figure 12-9) until a Google representative examines your site. Once the site content is confirmed to comply with the user agreement (no pornography, illegal content, and so on), advertisements with links are provided by the Google servers.

The AdSense program has numerous options, including the capability to categorize content in separate "channels" so that placement of the ads on various parts of the site can be tracked. A Web master manages the account through a Web interface such as the one shown in Figure 12-10.

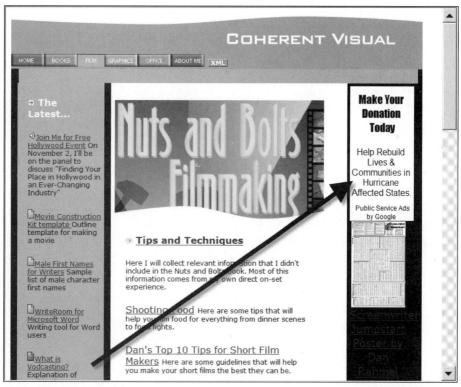

Figure 12-9: Google ads first appear as public service announcements until the Google team verifies your site.

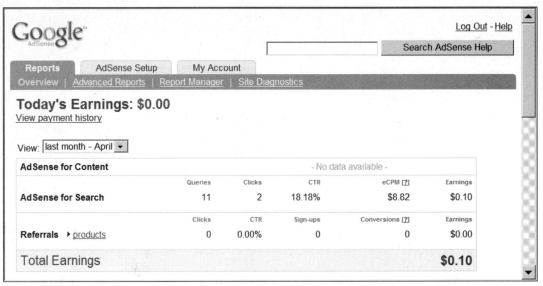

Figure 12-10: The Google AdSense administration screen reports queries, earnings, and other data.

Through the AdSense administrator, you can generate the link code you will need to add to your site. The code is simple JavaScript and appears like this:

```
<script type="text/javascript"><!--
google_ad_client = "pub-2440224655555555";
google_ad_width = 728;
google_ad_height = 90;
google_ad_format = "728x90_as";
google_ad_type = "text_image";
google_ad_channel ="1035475555";
//--></script>
<script type="text/javascript"
  src="http://pagead2.googlesyndication.com/pagead/show_ads.js">
</script>
```

To add the code to display AdSense to your Joomla site, download the extension called Mod HTML (http://fijiwebdesign.com). It is a very simple and straightforward module that allows you to insert any type of HTML and/or JavaScript for display on a Joomla site. By default, when the module is installed, one instance is automatically created called Html Module. You can edit this instance by clicking on the name in the Module Manager and the editor will be displayed, as shown in Figure 12-11.

Set the Title to something relevant (I chose Google01 because this is my first Google ad). Turn off the Show Title parameter, turn on the Published parameter, and choose a Position for the module display. Enter the code into the HTML box. After you click the Save button (in the upper-right corner of the screen), the Google AdSense advertisement should appear in the location you specified.

To create another module instance to display another Google ad, click on the New button at the Module Manager screen. Select HTML Module as the module type (see Figure 12-12), and click the Next button. From there, you can configure the module to contain other ad link code.

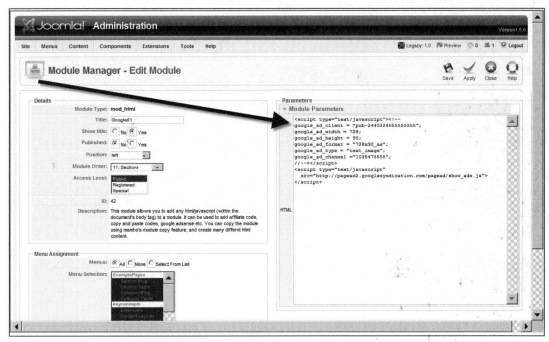

Figure 12-11: The Mod HTML administration screen provides the HTML parameter where any code can be entered.

Figure 12-12: Create a new module, and select the HTML Module as the module type.

Amazon Affiliate Program

Like Google, Amazon.com has an affiliate program (http://affiliate-program.amazon.com/gp/associates/join). While Google's program pays for clicks on the ads, Amazon's only pays if the click directly results in a sale. However, if the visitor to your Web site clicks on an item, you will earn a payment for that user if he or she buys anything on the site during that session — not just the item that was linked.

Amazon has a large variety of advertisement styles from specific products to context links. Figure 12-13 shows some of the advertisement links you can build in the affiliate program interface. Click on the "Build links" button next to any one of these items to generate a small segment of JavaScript code that the Web master needs to insert into the page of the Web site.

As people purchase goods through links on the site, Amazon includes reporting (see Figure 12-14) that breaks down the purchases and even the effectiveness of the click-through response. You'll want to track this information closely so that you know what products interest your site visitors and which items they never select.

A number of extensions can help you manage the Amazon ads that will appear on your Web site. You can use the Mod HTML that was demonstrated for the Google AdSense code, or select from a variety of Amazon-specific extensions.

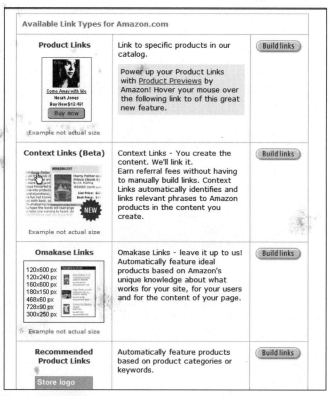

Figure 12-13: The Amazon program has a variety of ad types to choose from.

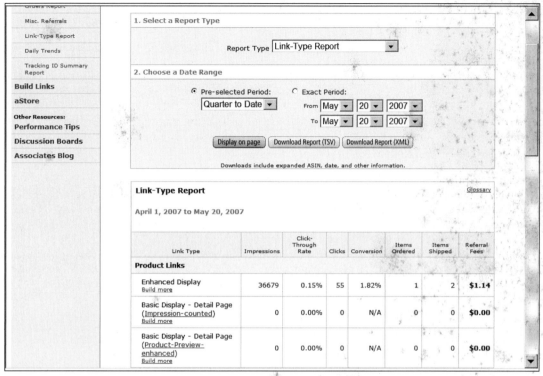

Figure 12-14: The Amazon program features a number of reports that break down link activity.

Amazon Associates Extension

The Amazon Associates extension is a plug-in that allows you to embed the affiliate advertisement directly in article text. It works with most international Amazon programs, including Amazon.com, Amazon.co.uk, Amazon.ca, Amazon.de, and Amazon.fr. You can download the plug-in from here:

    www.q-square.com/component/option,com_docman/Itemid,37/task,cat_view/gid,23

After you install the extension, you will need to set your affiliate ID by modifying the plug-in parameters through the Plugin Manager (see Figure 12-15). The Amazon ID parameter for the extension is the most important setting since it will tell Amazon when a click was generated through your Web site. The other settings regulate the presentation of the product link.

You will need to know the product ID of any items you want to list on your site. The IDs may be determined by finding the item on the Amazon site and looking at the URL for the currently displayed page. The URL will look something like the following (with the product ID number appearing here in bold):

    http://www.amazon.com/o/ASIN/0399154213/ref=s9_asin_title_1/103-8035767-9056638?pf_
    rd_m=ATVPDKIKX0DER&pf_rd_s=center-2&pf_rd_r=0DZV92ZKNE9Z5XJWBJ8J&pf_rd_t=101&pf_rd_
    p=279438201&pf_rd_i=507846

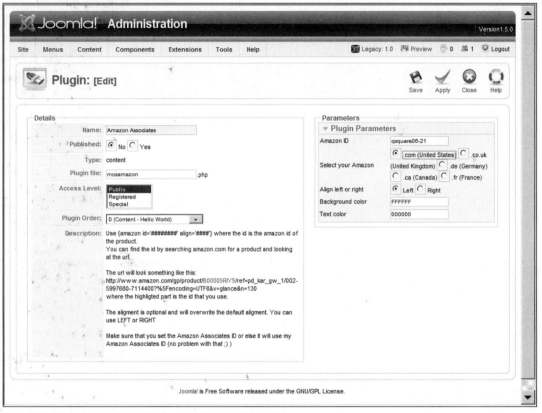

Figure 12-15: Amazon Associates extension configuration

Then, you need only add the following text to your article content with the ID of the desired item and (optionally) setting the justification to either LEFT or RIGHT:

```
{amazon id='0399154213' align='LEFT'}
```

You can add as many of these references to your content code as desired, although each ad must be retrieved from the Amazon servers. That means the rendering of your page may slow down if your server has a slow Internet connection, or the Amazon server is experiencing heavy traffic.

If your product isn't properly displayed on the page, try selecting No Editor and then reinput the code into the article. Some WYSIWYG editors corrupt the entry when trying to interpret it before the article saves.

Amazon Products Feed Bridge

Much more powerful is a package called Amazon Products Feed (APF). It is an Open Source, PERL-based application that accesses Amazon's Web services API. It provides a real-time listing of Amazon products on your Web site.

There is an APF Bridge extension that lets you use APF with Joomla. The extension features modules, components, and a plug-in that allows you to create a virtual Amazon store on your site. In Figure 12-16, you can see an example of a Joomla site providing Amazon search capabilities, while displaying a book with picture, pricing information, availability, and more.

APF is available for download here:

```
www.mrrat.com/aws
```

The APF Joomla bridge is available here:

```
www.deanmarshall.co.uk/demo/apf_bridge
```

Figure 12-16: The Amazon Products Feed Bridge bridges real-time Amazon features into a Joomla site.

The APF Bridge package is made up of a number of different extensions that provide various parts of the Amazon functionality to your Joomla site. The individual extensions include the following:

❑ *APF Bridge component* — Bridges the APF Perl library into Joomla.

❑ *mosAPF_0.5b3 Amazon plug-in* — Works in conjunction with the bridge component by scanning article text and replacing defined APF tags with the proper code for displaying Amazon information.

❑ *mosAPF_button WYSIWYG Editor Button plug-in* — Adds a button to the Joomla editor interface that will insert the various tags for the APF Bridge. Entering the tags through this extension saves typing time and minimizes typo errors.

❑ *mod_apf_search* — Displays a search box that will search an Amazon store for the selected country.

The APF Perl implementation uses the cURL library for transferring files. If your Web host doesn't have the cURL libraries installed, you won't be able to use APF.

Business Interaction with EDI

The surge in eCommerce on the Internet over the last decade has been astounding. Billions of dollars of transactions now occur through the Web and its related technologies. Chapter 4 mentions Joomla extensions that provide front-end e-commerce applications such as a shopping cart. However, the lion's share of money changing hands on the Internet occurs through business-to-business (B2B) transactions. Joomla is capable of handling B2B interactions through available extensions.

Electronic Data Interchange (EDI) is a set of standards that are used for transmitting information electronically between organizations. Despite the lack of publicity about this format, it remains the primary data interchange standard used in a vast majority of the electronic commerce transactions worldwide. The business-to-business nature of most implementations of EDI makes it more of a behind-the-scenes player than popularized formats such as XML.

Through an extension, Joomla is able to act as an EDI server.

EDI Documents

EDI is often used to automate purchase order commerce transactions. EDI documents can be transmitted by any means, including FTP, HTTP, MIME, direct modem, AS1, AS2, MQ, and value-added networks. *Value-added networks* (VANs) are private secure networks supplied by companies such as INOVIS, GXS, and BT*EDINET. Increasingly, however, technology is being put in place to allow secure transmission over the Internet to take advantage of free transmission and to minimize costs.

Wal-Mart, in particular, is advancing the *Applicability Statement 2* (AS2) standard that sets up a client-server model for EDI communication. This standard specifies a number of requirements (such as a static IP for the base server) that minimize the possibility of system compromise. The AS2 protocol is described in the RFC 4130 document available here:

```
www.ietf.org/rfc/rfc4130.txt
```

Most EDI documents mirror the content of the original paper versions they replace. The standards for the document format exist for many industries, including engineering (construction plans, work orders, and so on), medical (patient records, laboratory results, and so on), and transportation (bill of goods, purchase orders, container information, and so on). You can find descriptions of some of the EDI document standards here:

```
www.rapidnet.org/Standards_Tools/EDIStandards.asp
```

EDI Standards

There are two primary standards for EDI. The *ANSI ASC X12* standard (commonly referred to simply as *X12*) is the dominant implementation in the United States. Europe uses the *United Nations/Electronic Data Interchange For Administration, Commerce, and Transport* (UN/EDIFACT) standard, which is endorsed by the United Nations.

The X12 has document standards for a number of industries and are categorized in the set areas shown in Table 12-1 with the associated abbreviation.

Table 12-1: X12 Document Standards Categories

Category	What It Contains
Order Series (ORD)	Standards for items, including cooperative advertising agreements, coupon notification, grocery products invoice/purchase order/purchase order change, invoice, item maintenance, manufacturer coupon and coupon redemption, sales catalog, purchase order and PO acknowledgment, retail account characteristics, return merchandise authorization and notification, ship notice and manifest, and shipment and billing notice
Materials Handling Series (MAT)	Standards for asset schedule, item information request, material claim, material obligation validation, price authorization acknowledgment and status, price information, product authorization/deauthorization, request for quotation, requisition, and response to request for quotation
Tax Services Series (TAX)	Includes definitions for business credit report, electronic filing of tax return data, electronic filing of tax return data acknowledgment, income or asset offset, notice of employment status, notice of power of attorney, notice of tax adjustment or assessment, revenue receipts statement, statistical government information, and tax information exchange
Warehousing Series (WAR)	Standards for customer call reporting, deduction research report, market development fund allocation, market development fund settlement, response to a load tender, warehouse inventory adjustment advice, warehouse shipping advice, warehouse shipping order, warehouse stock transfer receipt advice, and warehouse stock transfer shipment advice

Continued

Table 12-1: X12 Document Standards Categories *(continued)*

Category	What it Contains
Financial Series (FIN)	Includes definitions for account analysis, account assignment/inquiry and service/status, application advice, application control totals, commission sales report, consolidated service invoice/statement, credit/debit adjustment, debit authorization, financial information reporting, financial return notice, freight invoice, functional group totals, invoice, lockbox, operating expense statement, payment cancellation request, and payment order/remittance advice
Government Series (GOV)	Standards for business entity filings, court and law enforcement notice, court submission, electronic filing of tax return data acknowledgment, Federal Communications Commission (FCC) license application, periodic compensation, royalty regulatory report, statistical government information, tax rate notification, unemployment insurance tax claim or charge information, uniform commercial code filing, and voter registration information
Manufacturing Series (MAN)	Standards for contractor cost data reporting, delivery/return acknowledgment or adjustment, delivery/return base record, inventory inquiry/advice, order status inquiry, order status report, planning schedule with release capability, product activity data, product transfer account adjustment, product transfer and resale report, production sequence, receiving advice/acceptance certificate, and response to product transfer account adjustment
Delivery Series (DEL)	Standards for cartage work assignment, consolidators freight bill and invoice, direct store delivery summary information, logistics service request, logistics service response, motor carrier summary freight bill manifest, purchase order shipment management document, response to a cartage work assignment, routing and carrier instruction, ship notice/manifest, shipment and billing notice, shipment delivery discrepancy information, shipment information, and shipping schedule
Engineering Management & Contract Series (ENG)	Standards for clauses and provisions, component parts content, contract abstract, contract completion status, contract payment management report, contract pricing proposal, contractor cost data reporting, excavation communication, logistics reassignment, maintenance service order, pricing history, procurement notices, product dimension maintenance, project cost reporting, project schedule reporting, specifications/technical information, trading partner profile, vendor performance review, and well information

Table 12-1: X12 Document Standards Categories *(continued)*

Category	What it Contains
Insurance/Health Series (INS)	Standards for annuity activity, automotive inspection detail, benefit enrollment and maintenance, cargo insurance advice of shipment, claim status report and tracer reply, claim tracer, eligibility, coverage or benefit information, eligibility, coverage or benefit inquiry, health care claim, health care claim payment/advice, health care claim status notification, health care claim status request, health care provider information, health care services review information, individual life, annuity and disability application, insurance plan description, insurance producer administration, insurance underwriting requirements reporting, insurance/annuity application status, loss or damage claim—motor vehicle, medical event reporting, patient information, property and casualty loss notification, property damage report, report of injury, illness or incident, underwriting information services, and wage determination
Miscellaneous ANSI X12 Transactions Series (MIS)	Includes definitions for cryptographic service message, data status tracking, electronic form structure, file transfer, functional acknowledgment, general request, response or confirmation, motion picture booking confirmation, name and address lists, set cancellation, and text message
Mortgage Series (MOR)	Standards for application for mortgage insurance benefits, loan verification information, mortgage credit report, mortgage credit report order, mortgage loan default status, mortgage note, mortgage or property record change notification, real estate information report, real estate information request, real estate inspection, real estate settlement information, real estate title evidence, real estate title insurance services order, residential loan application, residential mortgage insurance application, residential mortgage insurance application response, secondary mortgage market investor report, and secondary mortgage market loan delivery
Product Services Series (PSS)	Includes definitions for product registration, product service claim, product service claim response, product service notification, product source information, promotion announcement, and return merchandise authorization and notification
Quality and Safety Series (QSS)	Standards for animal toxicological data, commercial vehicle credentials, commercial vehicle safety and credentials information exchange, material safety data sheet, nonconformance report, report of test results, and testing results request and report

Continued

Table 12-1: X12 Document Standards Categories *(continued)*

Category	What it Contains
Student Information Series (STU)	Includes definitions for student application for admission to educational institutions, educational course inventory, grant or assistance application, request for student educational record (transcript), response to request for student educational record (transcript), student educational record (transcript) and acknowledgement, student enrollment verification, student loan application, student loan guarantee result, student loan pre-claims and claims, and student loan transfer and status verification

The European standard, UN/EDIFACT, has been adopted by the ISO as standard #9735. The standard doesn't have explicit set categories like X12. Instead, the various document standards are defined as messages with the individual abbreviations shown in Table 12-2.

Table 12-2: UN/EDIFACT Abbreviations

Abbreviation	Meaning
APERAK	Application error and acknowledgment
AUTACK	Secure authentication and acknowledgment
AUTHOR	Authorization
BANSTA	Banking status
BAPLIE	Bayplan/stowage plan occupied and empty locations
BAPLTE	Bayplan/stowage plan total numbers
BOPBNK	Bank transactions and portfolio transactions report
BOPCUS	Balance of payment customer transaction report
BOPDIR	Direct balance of payment declaration
BOPINF	Balance of payment information from customer
CALINF	Vessel call information
CASINT	Request for legal administration action in civil proceedings
CASRES	Legal administration response in civil proceedings
CHAMAP	Chart of mappings
COARRI	Container discharge/loading report

Table 12-2: UN/EDIFACT Abbreviations *(continued)*

Abbreviation	Meaning
CODECO	Container gate-in/gate-out report
CODENO	Permit expiration/clearance ready notice
COEDOR	Container stock report
COHAOR	Container special handling order
COLADV	Advice of a documentary collection
COMDIS	Commercial dispute
CONAPW	Advice on pending works
CONDPV	Direct payment valuation
CONDRA	Drawing administration
CONDRO	Drawing organization
CONEST	Establishment of contract
CONITT	Invitation to tender
CONPVA	Payment valuation
CONQVA	Quantity valuation
CONRPW	Response of pending works
CONTEN	Tender
CONTRL	Syntax and service report
CONWQD	Work item quantity determination
COPARN	Container announcement
COPINO	Container prenotification
COPRAR	Container discharge/loading order
COREOR	Container release order
COSTCO	Container stuffing/stripping confirmation
COSTOR	Container stuffing/stripping order

Continued

Table 12-2: UN/EDIFACT Abbreviations *(continued)*

Abbreviation	Meaning
CREADV	Credit advice
CREEXT	Extended credit advice
CREMUL	Multiple credit advice
CURRAC	Current account
CUSCAR	Customs cargo report
CUSDEC	Customs declaration
CUSEXP	Customs express consignment declaration
CUSREP	Customs conveyance report
CUSRES	Customs response
DATRAK	Data tracking
DEBADV	Debit advice
DEBMUL	Multiple debit advice
DELFOR	Delivery schedule
DELJIT	Delivery just-in-time
DESADV	Dispatch advice
DESTIM	Equipment damage and repair estimate
DIRDEB	Direct debit
DIRDEF	Directory definition
DOCADV	Documentary credit advice
DOCAMA	Advice of an amendment of a documentary credit
DOCAMI	Documentary credit amendment information
DOCAMR	Request for an amendment of a documentary credit
DOCAPP	Documentary credit application
DOCARE	Response to an amendment of a documentary credit

Table 12-2: UN/EDIFACT Abbreviations *(continued)*

Abbreviation	Meaning
DOCINF	Documentary credit issuance information
FINCAN	Financial cancellation
FINSTA	Financial statement of an account
GENRAL	General purpose
GESMES	Generic statistical
HANMOV	Cargo/goods handling and movement
IFCSUM	Forwarding and consolidation summary
IFTCCA	Forwarding and transport shipment charge calculation
IFTDGN	Dangerous goods notification
IFTFCC	International transport freight costs and other charges
IFTIAG	Dangerous cargo list
IFTMAN	Arrival notice
IFTMBC	Booking confirmation
IFTMBF	Firm booking
IFTMBP	Provisional booking
IFTMCS	Instruction contract status
IFTMIN	Instruction
IFTMSC	Single consignment forwarding and transport
IFTRIN	Forwarding and transport rate information
IFTSAI	Forwarding and transport schedule and availability information
IFTSTA	International multimodal status report
IFTSTQ	International multimodal status request
IHCEBI	Interactive health insurance eligibility and benefits inquiry and response
INSPRE	Insurance premium

Continued

Table 12-2: UN/EDIFACT Abbreviations *(continued)*

Abbreviation	Meaning
INVOIC	Invoice
INVRPT	Inventory report
ITRGRP	In-transit groupage
ITRRPT	In-transit report detail
JAPRES	Job application result
JIBILL	Joint interest billing report
JINFDE	Job information demand
JOBAPP	Job application proposal
JOBCON	Job order confirmation
JOBMOD	Job order modification
JOBOFF	Job order
MEDADR	Medical adverse drug reaction
MEDAUT	Medical preauthorization
MEDPID	Person identification
MEDREQ	Medical service request
MEDRPT	Medical service report
MESGEV	Social event
MIGRPT	Message implementation guide (MIG) report
MOVINS	Stowage instruction
ORDCHG	Purchase order change request
ORDERS	Purchase order
ORDRSP	Purchase order response
PARTIN	Party information
PAXLST	Passenger list

Table 12-2: UN/EDIFACT Abbreviations *(continued)*

Abbreviation	Meaning
PAYDUC	Payroll deductions advice
PAYEXT	Extended payment order
PAYMUL	Multiple payment order
PAYORD	Payment order
PCPRDR	Property and casualty property damage report
PRICAT	Price/sales catalogue
PRODAT	Product data
PRODEX	Product exchange reconciliation
PROLST	Promotional list
PRPAID	Insurance premium payment
QALITY	Quality data
QUOTES	Quote
RDRMES	Raw data reporting
REBORD	Reinsurance bordereau
RECADV	Receiving advice
RECALC	Reinsurance calculation
RECECO	Credit risk cover
RECLAM	Reinsurance claims
REMADV	Remittance advice
REPREM	Reinsurance premium
REQDOC	Request for document
REQOTE	Request for quote
RESETT	Reinsurance settlement
RESMSG	Reservation

Continued

Table 12-2: UN/EDIFACT Abbreviations *(continued)*

Abbreviation	Meaning
RESREQ	Reservation request — interactive
RESRSP	Reservation response — interactive
RETACC	Reinsurance technical account
SAFHAZ	Safety and hazard data
SANCRT	International movement of goods governmental regulatory
SCRIPT	Prescriptions and refill request and response — interactive message
SKDACK	Schedule acknowledgement — interactive
SLSFCT	Sales forecast
SLSRPT	Sales data report
SSCLDE	Social Security claim decision
SSDREQ	Social Security data request
SSIMOD	Modification of identity details
SSRECH	Worker's insurance history
SSREGW	Notification of registration of a worker
STATAC	Statement of account
SUPCOT	Superannuation contributions advice
SUPMAN	Superannuation maintenance
SUPRES	Supplier response
TANSTA	Tank status report
TESTEX	Test message explicit mode
TESTIM	Test message implicit mode
TINREQ	Tourism information request
TINRSP	Tourism information response
TRADES	Traffic or travel description definition

Table 12-2: UN/EDIFACT Abbreviations *(continued)*

Abbreviation	Meaning
TRADIN	Traffic or travel details of individual traveler
TRAILS	Traffic or travel route guidance and planning
TRALOC	Traffic or travel location definition
TRAREQ	Traffic or travel information request
TRAVAK	Traffic or travel information acknowledgment
TRAVIN	Traffic or travel situation information
VATDEC	Value added tax
VESDEP	Vessel departure
WKGRDC	Work grant decision
WKGRRE	Work grant request

Skylark Extension

The Skylark extension turns Joomla into an EDI Server. It allows management of trading partners, business processes, communication protocols, and document format translators. It has no restrictions on the particular document type that is handled, and can process both inbound and outbound documents.

The Skylark extension is actually made up of a number of components and modules. It supports the following transports (or communication protocols):

❑ Generic (including FTP, SMTP and POP3)

❑ ARI (uses HTTP)

❑ Honda (using IBM MQ)

❑ Stihl (uses HTTP)

It also supports the following translators:

❑ ARI

❑ Briggs

❑ GMI

❑ Honda

❑ Stihl

When you complete installation, you will be presented with a screen that has a link to an introduction (see Figure 12-17). Read this introduction because it contains a good explanation of the basic functioning of the component.

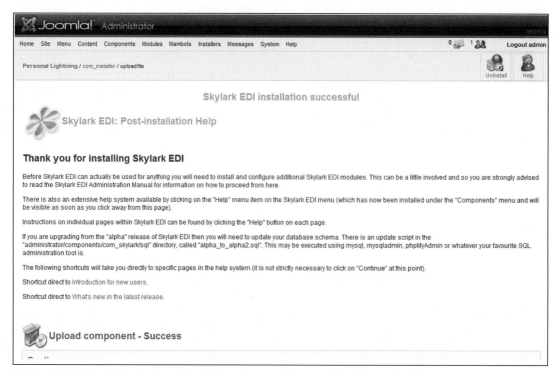

Figure 12-17: Select the Skylark introduction for a useful summary of the extension.

Custom Extranet Interaction

As you've seen in previous chapters, creating a simple custom component for the Joomla system doesn't require a great deal of work. Through the Joomla framework, most of the user interface is already in place, so you can focus on the implementation details of the capability that you want to add. That makes extranet interaction through Joomla not only practical, but also inexpensive when compared with creating stand-alone Web applications.

In this section, you'll implement three extensions that interface with external sites. The first small application will use HTML retrieval capabilities of PHP to retrieve data from a separate Web page, filter data from the page, and format it for display on the Joomla page. The second extension will wrap a remote system's Web interface (the Google Map API) and deliver the content to the Joomla site. The final extension will provide an example of having a component query a remote database and process the returned XML data.

All of these extensions will demonstrate extranet capabilities that can be customized to other real-world tasks. The number of Web APIs is growing constantly, and these examples should allow a developer to easily create an extension that can take advantage of any of these Web services.

Screen Scraper Component

The World Wide Web has made text data available like never before. Almost all sites accessible through the Internet can be addressed by either a browser or a program that retrieves the plain-text version of the page containing HTML tags. This availability of raw data has caused a renaissance of programs called *screen scrapers*. Screen scrapers access data normally targeted at a screen (or browser window) and scrape the desired data from the screen for storage, or repackaging and display.

Brief History of Screen Scrapers

Between the 1970s era of widespread deployment of text-based mainframe/terminal applications and the twenty-first century browser era came the age of the graphical user interface (GUI). Ushered in by the success of the Macintosh, computer applications began to feature windows, drop-down menus, checkboxes, and other user-interface elements that made using programs much more flexible than their text-based predecessors.

The revolution in GUI adoption caused a problem for organizations that had invested tremendous amounts of time and money in mainframe-based text applications. In less than a decade, these text-based applications went from being cutting edge to antiquated. For productivity reasons, organizations had to rewrite these applications to take advantage of the new GUI paradigm. Even more daunting than the mountain of reprogramming was the conversion of data stored in these mostly custom systems. Few standard data formats existed when they were initially designed, so retrieving and converting the data posed tremendous difficulties.

Enter the screen scraper. A screen scraper was a program that sat between the text-based application and either a user or a more advanced data retrieval program. For GUI applications, the screen scraper acted as a middle layer between the graphical interface in the foreground and the real text-based application in the background. Data would be scraped from the text-based screen and loaded into the front-end graphical interface. A user would work with a modern interface with all of the advantages provided by a GUI, including Undo, Cut, Copy, and Paste (among other functions). When the user clicked the Save button, the screen scraper would interface with the text-based application and act as if the user was punching in the keyboard codes and data by hand.

More commonly, a screen scraper would be used to access a system and "scrape" the screen for data held in the text-based system. The scraper might send a query into the text-based system and then scrape the results displayed by the mainframe and place it in a new data store such as a database management system (DBMS).

As time passed and text-based applications were retired, screen scrapers became less and less common. Organizations upgraded antiquated text-based systems and traded custom data storage for standardized database servers with flexible data stores. Scrapers were no longer needed when data retrieval through many different types of retrieval middleware was available.

The explosive growth of HTML changed all that. Almost overnight, oceans of data were being widely published in an unencrypted, public, and quickly accessible data format. Anything Web sites published for viewing by individual browsers could easily be harvested by a program, stripped of its formatting, and either reformatted for display or stored for later access.

Since PHP comes with built-in HTTP capabilities, it is a fairly easy task to write code to go to a Web site, grab the HTML code from the site, and strip the desired data from the page. Implementing such code as a Joomla component is only a short development step from there.

Pitfalls of Using a Screen Scraper

Whenever you are retrieving content from a remote site and publishing it for the use of your Web site visitors, a number of problems arise — technical, legal, and ethical. These problems should be taken into account before you undertake a screen scraping application.

On the technical side, using a scraper means that you have no access to a standard API for the data you need. That means any changes to the host Web page can instantly cause your scraper to stop functioning properly. Your program will rely on the data to be presented in a particular format. Unlike a human viewer who understands the information whether it is displayed in three columns or changed to four columns, a program must have consistency in order to process the page and retrieve the information. Therefore, a scraping application can go from working flawlessly one day to not working at all the next. Scrapers require constant monitoring.

Further technical problems arise when the site tries to discourage scraper applications. Some organizations hate scraping applications because the programs retrieve the information while expending site bandwidth and other resources. Further, the scrapers eliminate the possibility of obtaining visitor data from the user's browser, and avoid the display of Internet ads that generate revenue for the site.

On the legal side, even though the data may be publicly available, it may be illegal for you to redisplay it on your own Web site in the same way that you can't plagiarize a written article and claim it as your own. For Web-based content, these issues are very cloudy. Some Web data is compiled from numerous sources before being processed and published to the world, making determining the information's provenance difficult. Republishing it through scraping and reformatting further complicates the issue.

Additional legal problems arise when the terms of agreement for use of the site prohibits scraping processes. Google, for example, includes such a clause in their Terms and Conditions site document. That means that, although Google is very easy to scrape, it is illegal to do so.

On the ethical side, even though you may be able to retrieve the information and republish without any legal ramifications, it might not be ethical to do so. There is no question that an automated solution that queries a Web data store uses resources on the target Web server. It is also very likely that the site owner never intended the information published on the site to be accessed by a machine for unknown repurposing.

However, despite these significant pitfalls to screen scraping, there are numerous applications where scraping is not only possible, but extremely useful. Many government Web sites publish information to the Web that is free and in the public domain. The information is provided because the taxpayers have paid for it to be widely disseminated (for example, Center for Disease Control safety alerts). Often, this government data is located in difficult-to-find places, or in such cryptic form that a site republishing the information is performing a public service by making it accessible and usable.

However, even some public databases warn against using them for automated database retrieval. The California Department of Real Estate, for example, has the following on its search page:

> *The online status inquiry feature is a service for consumers. It is not intended for, nor capable of, automated database searches or sorts. If you desire such database files, contact the Department for information on availability and costs.*

While the technology of the scraper presented in this chapter can be used to obtain data from a site whether permission has been granted or not, you should respect the wishes of a site and not apply your scraper there.

Basic Component Source File

To effectively deploy a screen scraper that acts as middleware, the component must be designed to handle four tasks:

❑ *Take the request or query from the user* — Typically, the user query will be entered into an HTML form displayed by the component. Once the query data has been entered into the form, the user clicks a Submit button and the request is sent to the component.

❑ *Retrieve the data from the source Web site* — This is the scraping function that forms the heart of the program. The file sockets PHP library will be used to retrieve the entire HTML page from the site.

❑ *Process the retrieved information* — The power of regular expressions really comes in handy for scraping applications because a simple expression can process a huge amount of text data.

❑ *Reformat the data and return to the user* — In Joomla, there are a number of different methods of accomplishing this task. Often, the best method when dealing with data is to store the data in XML format and use an XSLT document to provide the formatting services. In the interest of simplicity, this component will simply output the data in an HTML table.

With this general component task outline, you can begin component construction, as shown in Figure 12-18.

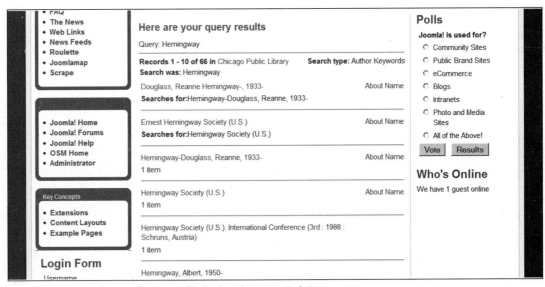

Figure 12-18: The Screen Scraper will display the current data.

Component Descriptor File

The component descriptor file is primitive and simply adds the component to the system. Enter the following file in your text editor, and save it under the name com_scrape.xml:

```xml
<?xml version="1.0" encoding="utf-8"?>
<install version="1.5.0" type="component">
    <name>scrape</name>
    <author>Dan Rahmel</author>
    <creationDate>July 2007</creationDate>
    <copyright>(C) 2007 Dan Rahmel. All rights reserved.</copyright>
    <authorEmail>admin@joomlajumpstart.org</authorEmail>
    <authorUrl>www.joomlajumpstart.org</authorUrl>
    <version>1.0.0</version>
    <description>Accepts a field input and then queries a remote site for the
information and scrapes the returned output.</description>
    <files>
        <filename component="com_scrape">scrape.php</filename>
    </files>
    <administration>
        <menu>Scrape</menu>
        <files>
            <filename component="com_scrape">scrape.php</filename>
        </files>
    </administration>
    <params>
        <param name="url" type="text" default=".gov" label="Target site"
description="URL of the server that will be scraped for information." />
    </params>
</install>
```

Scraper Component

The component will accept query values for book titles and send the request to the target Web site. When the page returns with the necessary data, a function will remove the data from the HTML code, reformat it, and return it to the user's browser.

Enter the following code in your editor and the file as scrape.php:

```php
<?php
/**
* @version $Id: scrape.php 5203 2007-06-15 02:45:14Z DanR $
* @copyright Copyright (C) 2007 Dan Rahmel. All rights reserved.
* @package ScreenScrape
* Accepts a field input and then queries a remote site for the information
* and scrapes the returned output.
*/

// no direct access
defined( '_JEXEC' ) or die( 'Restricted access' );
```

```
// Check the task parameter and execute appropriate function
switch( JRequest::getVar( 'task' )) {
    case 'query':
        doExecuteQuery();
        break;
    default:
        displayQueryEntry();
        break;
}

// Process data received from form.
function doExecuteQuery()  {
    // Get query from form posting values
    $fldQuery = JRequest::getVar('query') ;
    // Strip away anything that could be code, carriage returns, and so on
    $fldQuery = preg_replace("/[^a-zA-Z0-9 .?!$()\'\"]/", "", $fldQuery);
    // "
    $myData = doScrape($fldQuery);
    echo "<h1>Here are your query results</h1>";
    echo "<p>Query: " . $fldQuery . "<p>";
    echo "<hr />";
    echo $myData;
    echo "<a href=index.php?option=com_scrape>" .
        "Return to Scrape</a>";
}

function doScrape($queryStr) {
    $myUrl = "www.chipubweb.org";
    $myPath = "/cgi-bin/cw_cgi?alphaBrowse+8469d+2+-1+" . $queryStr;

    $myGet = "";
    $myAgent = "User-Agent: Mozilla/5.0 (Windows; U; Windows NT 5.1;" .
    " en-US; rv:1.8.1) Gecko/20061010 Firefox/2.0\r\n";
    $myApp = "Content-Type: application/x-www-form-urlencoded";

    $fp = fsockopen($myUrl, 80, $errNum, $errstr, 30);
    if (!$fp) {
        return "Error #": $errNum . "retrieving page.<br />\n";
    } else {
      $out = "GET " . $myPath . " HTTP/1.0\r\n";
       $out .= "Host: ". $myUrl . "\r\n";
       $out .= $myAgent . $myApp . "\r\n";
       $out .= "Connection: Close\r\n\r\n";

       fwrite($fp, $out);
       while (!feof($fp)) { $myGet .= fgets($fp, 128); }
       fclose($fp);

       $pattern = "/<table\sid=.m(.*)>([.|\s]*)<\/table>/i";
       preg_match($pattern, $myGet, $matches);
       return $matches[0];
    }
```

```
}

// Display form for query entry
function displayQueryEntry() {
?>
<h1 class="contentheading">Query form</h1>

<form id="form1" name="form1" method="post"
      action="index.php?option=com_scrape&task=query">
  <p>Enter your book query here:<br />
    <textarea name="query" cols="60" rows="1" id="query"></textarea>
  </p>
    <p>
    <input type="submit" name="Submit" value="Display Results" />
  </p>
</form>

<?php } ?>
```

Place both files in a ZIP archive named `scrape.zip`, and the component can be installed into the Joomla system. You can set the URL of the query site in the component parameters section. This code simply grabs a table with the results generated and places it in the Web page. For your target Web site, you will need to change the regular expression used by `preg_match()` to excise the portion of HTML code that you need to retrieve.

Google Map Component

Google provides a free mapping service where a Web site can display a custom Google street or satellite (or both) map within the Web page. Since the map is retrieved from the Google server, it contains the Google moniker and provides Google with additional demographic and other data. That is the return Google gets for providing this free service.

Although there is already a component that wraps the Google Map API for use on Joomla sites, it can be very instructive to create a component so that you can see how it is possible to interface with a remote API for display of information within your Joomla site. The component interface will allow the user to enter a standard address into a text field, as shown in Figure 12-19.

When the user clicks on the Display Location button, the component is called again, although this time with a task parameter of `goto` and the address information posted from the form. The component reads the form values, uses a geocoding routine to translate the address into latitude and longitude coordinates, and calls the Google Maps API to present the relevant map, as shown in Figure 12-20.

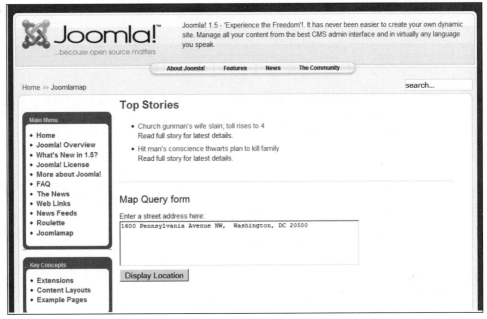

Figure 12-19: Enter a standard address into the Joomlamap address field.

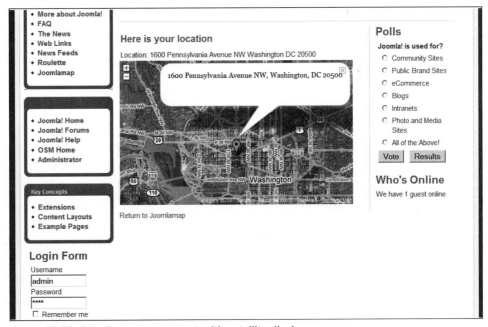

Figure 12-20: Joomlamap component with satellite display

Google Maps API Primer

Google has provided an excellent and simple API with which your program can request maps from its site. You can find a complete list of the API functions (as well as example code) here:

```
www.google.com/apis/maps
```

The Google Map Web application creates a map object that can be addressed by JavaScript code to govern such display parameters as location, zoom, type of display (street map, satellite, or hybrid), and others. All of these parameters are available for access from JavaScript code.

Registering for a Key

Each URL where a map will appear must have a unique Google key. In fact, when the map request is made, if the registered URL for the specified key does not match, the Google site will not return a map. That means you will need separate keys for your staging server and deployment server. Additionally, the URL that is registered with the key is case-sensitive, so www.example.com/map is not recognized as being the same as the registered www.example.com/Map.

You can register for a Google Maps API key here:

```
www.google.com/apis/maps/signup.html
```

Component Descriptor File

The component descriptor file is primitive and simply adds the component to the system. Enter the following file in your text editor and save it under the name com_joomlamap.xml:

```xml
<?xml version="1.0" encoding="utf-8"?>
<install version="1.5.0" type="component">
     <name>Joomlamap</name>
     <author>Dan Rahmel</author>
     <creationDate>July 2007</creationDate>
     <copyright>(C) 2007 Dan Rahmel. All rights reserved.</copyright>
     <authorEmail>admin@joomlajumpstart.org</authorEmail>
     <authorUrl>www.joomlajumpstart.org</authorUrl>
     <version>1.0.0</version>
     <description>Accepts a field input and then queries a remote site for the
information and scrapes the returned output.</description>
     <files>
          <filename component="com_joomlamap">joomlamap.php</filename>
     </files>
     <administration>
          <menu>Joomlamap</menu>
        <files>
             <filename component="com_joomlamap">joomlamap.php</filename>
        </files>
     </administration>
     <params>
          <param name="key" type="text" default="" label="Google Map Key"
          description="Enter the  Map key configured for this site." />
     </params>
</install>
```

Creating the Component Index File

The component must insert two pieces of information into the rendered Joomla page: the Google display script and the map object display tags.

Enter the following code into your text editor and save the file as `joomlamap.php`:

```php
<?php
/**
* @version $Id: joomlamap.php 5203 2007-06-15 02:45:14Z DanR $
* @copyright Copyright (C) 2007 Dan Rahmel. All rights reserved.
* @package Joomlamap
* This component accesses the Google Map API and displays the
* requested address.
*/

// no direct access
defined( '_JEXEC' ) or die( 'Restricted access' );

// Check the task parameter and execute appropriate function
switch( JRequest::getVar( 'task' )) {
    case 'goto':
        gotoLocation();
        break;
    default:
        displayAddressEntry();
        break;
}

// Process data received from form.
function gotoLocation()  {
    $userKey = $params->get('key', 0);
    // Get location from form posting values
    $fldLocation = JRequest::getVar('location') ;
    // Strip away anything that could be code, carriage returns, and so on
    $fldLocation = preg_replace("/[^a-zA-Z0-9 .?!$()\'\"]/", "", $fldLocation);
    // "
    echo "<h1>Here is your location</h1>";
    echo "<p>Location: " . $fldLocation . "<p>";
?>
        <script src="http://maps.google.com/maps?file=api&amp;v=2&amp;key=" .
        $userKey . " type="text/javascript"></script>

    <script type="text/javascript">

//<![CDATA[

    var map = null;
    var geocoder = null;

    function load() {
      if (GBrowserIsCompatible()) {
        map = new GMap2(document.getElementById("map"));
        map.setCenter(new GLatLng(37.4419, -122.1419), 13);
```

```
                geocoder = new GClientGeocoder();
            }
        }

        function showAddress(address) {
          if (geocoder) {
            geocoder.getLatLng(address, function(point) {
                if (!point) { alert(address + " not found"); } else {
                    map.setMapType( G_HYBRID_TYPE ); // default is G_MAP_TYPE
                    map.setCenter(point, 13);
                    var marker = new GMarker(point);
                    map.addOverlay(marker);
                    map.addControl(new GSmallZoomControl ());
                    marker.openInfoWindowHtml(address); } } );
          }
        }
        //]]>
        load();
        showAddress(<?php echo $fldLocation;   ?>);
        </script>

<?php
        echo "<a href=index.php?option=com_joomlamap>" .
            "Return to Joomlamap</a>";
} ?>

// Display form for address entry
function displayAddressEntry() {
?>
<h1 class="contentheading">Map Query form</h1>

<form id="form1" name="form1" method="post"
     action="index.php?option=com_joomlamap&task=goto">
  <p>Enter a street address here:<br />
    <textarea name="location" cols="60" rows="1" id="location"></textarea>
  </p>
  <p>
    <input type="submit" name="Submit" value="Display Location" />
  </p>
</form>

<?php } ?>
```

Archive the two files in a ZIP called joomlamap.zip and use the Extension Manager to install it into the system. You can set the Google map key in the parameters of the component.

Postal Address Finder with XML

The U.S. Postal Service (USPS) has a free Web tool where automated solutions can query the database for ZIP code and address information. The data is returned as a packet of XML data. Creating an extension that queries this Web tool provides a perfect example of the type of extranet application that you will most commonly need to construct.

Before you begin, you will need to sign up for a free account at the USPS.com Web site to obtain a user ID. You can sign up for the Web tools here:

```
www.usps.com/webtools/?from=zclsearch&page=webtools
```

The registration form asks for basic information about you, as shown in Figure 12-21. When you have filled out the form and submitted it, the system will send you an email with your Web Tools User ID. You will need to include this code in all queries to the system.

Also included in the registration email is the URL of your test server. This URL will be something like (but will not match) http://testing.shipping.com/ShippingAPITest.dll or https://secure.shipping.com/ShippingAPITest.dll for secure testing. The USPS wants you to have your application completely tested before you can start querying against the actual database. This saves the USPS resources for all of the queries your system will need to send when getting your extension debugged.

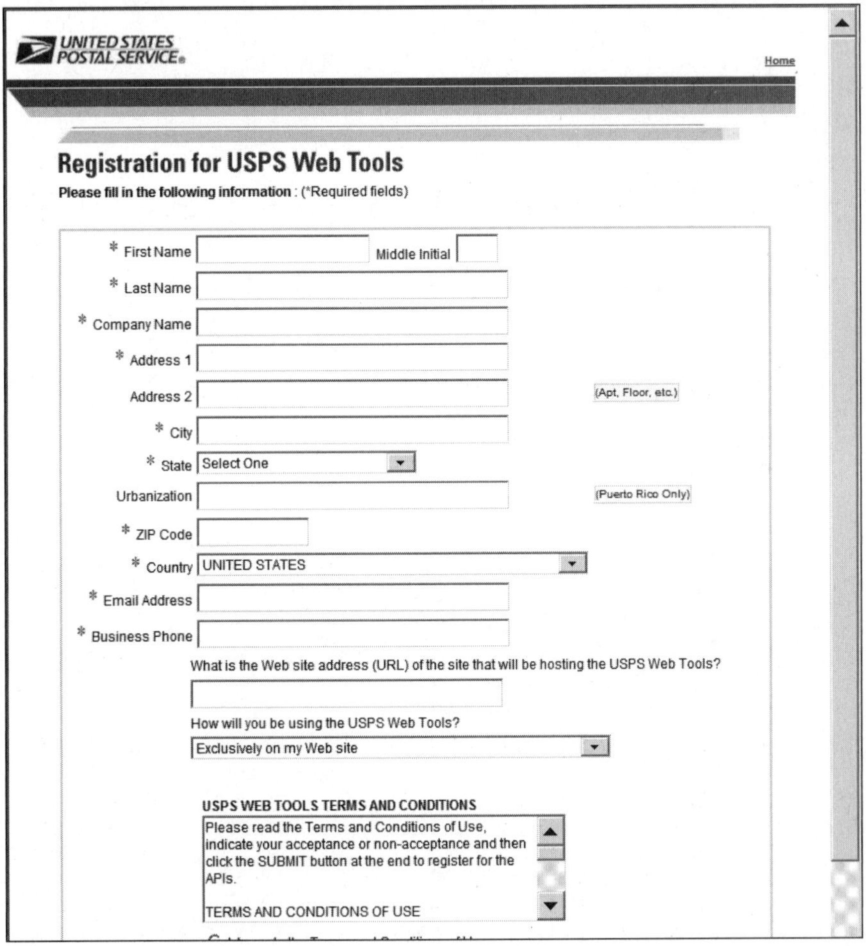

Figure 12-21: The USPS Web tools registration screen asks for basic information.

Manual Testing

With your user ID, you should do a manual test against the server to see if your browser can display the queried data. From the manual (available on the Web services section of the Web site), I entered the test request #1 that looks like this:

```
http://SERVERNAME/ShippingAPITest.dll?API=ZipCodeLookup&XML=
<ZipCodeLookupRequest%20USERID="MYID">
<Address ID="0"><Address1></Address1>
<Address2>6406 Ivy Lane</Address2>
<City>Greenbelt</City><State>MD</State>
</Address></ZipCodeLookupRequest>
```

Here, I have broken it up into multiple lines so that it is easier to read, but all the text should be entered into the single line of address bar of your browser. You also need to replace the SERVERNAME and MYID with the values you received in the registration email. When you press the Enter key to have your browser retrieve the information, it should be displayed in the window as XML-formatted text (see Figure 12-22).

If the system doesn't return the information you requested, make sure the user ID and server name are correct as entered. Then, if you entered the code provided here, check the USPS manual in case the query notation has changed.

Note that in the figure I have blacked out the returned ZIP code information because the postal service asks for this information to give you full access to the system — to verify that your application actually works.

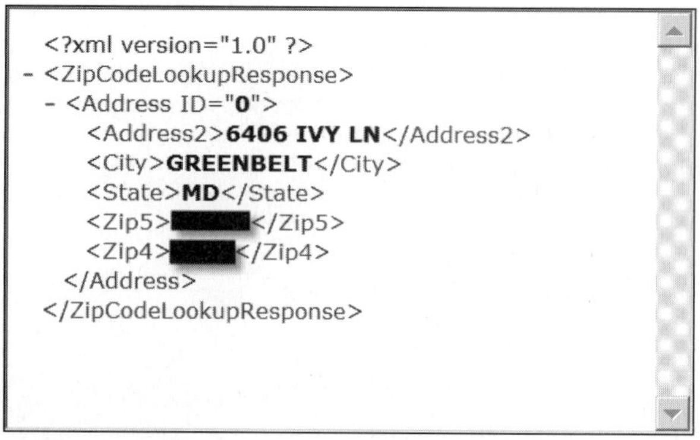

```
<?xml version="1.0" ?>
- <ZipCodeLookupResponse>
  - <Address ID="0">
      <Address2>6406 IVY LN</Address2>
      <City>GREENBELT</City>
      <State>MD</State>
      <Zip5>█████</Zip5>
      <Zip4>████</Zip4>
    </Address>
  </ZipCodeLookupResponse>
```

Figure 12-22: The retrieved information will be displayed as XML in your browser window.

Implementing a PHP Test Page

Having confirmed that your user ID is working correctly, it's time to implement a test using basic PHP code before attempting to embed the program logic into a complete extension. For extranet interfaces, I always recommend this intermediate step for extension development. Joomla is a complex system, and it is far easier to confirm baseline communication protocols outside a complete system to ensure that they work properly.

This example requires PHP version 5 running on the server. In PHP 5, standardized XML capabilities were added to load and parse an XML DOM. These functions are needed to process the postal data. You can add an XML extension to PHP 4 and adapt the example code to it if your Joomla site is hosted on a PHP 4 installation.

Enter the following code and save the file as `ziptest.php` at the Web root of your staging server:

```php
<html><body>
<h1>Zip Code Test</h1>
<?php

 $myWTID= "MYID";
 $myAddress = "6406 Ivy Lane";
 $myCity = "Greenbelt";
 $myState = "MD";

 $myUrl = "http://testing.shippingapis.com/ShippingAPITest.dll?" .
     "API=ZipCodeLookup&XML=<ZipCodeLookupRequest USERID='" . $myWTID ."'>" .
     "<Address ID='0'><Address1></Address1>" .
     "<Address2>" . $myAddress . "</Address2>" .
     "<City>" . $myCity . "</City><State>" . $myState . "</State>" .
     "</Address></ZipCodeLookupRequest>";

echo $myUrl;
echo "<hr />";
try {
     @$doc = DOMDocument::load($myUrl);
} catch(DOMException $e) {
     echo '<p>';
     print_r($e);
     echo '</p>';
}
// Echo all of the returned data in HTML
echo htmlspecialchars($doc->saveXML());
echo "<hr />";

$params = $doc->getElementsByTagName('Address');

foreach ($params as $param) {
      echo "ID=" . $param ->getAttribute('ID').'<br>';
}
echo "<hr />";

$params = $doc->getElementsByTagName('Zip5');
foreach ($params as $param) {
      echo "Zip 5=". $param ->textContent .'<br>'; // getAttribute('ID')
}
```

```
$params = $doc->getElementsByTagName('Zip4');
foreach ($params as $param) {
        echo "Zip 4=". $param ->textContent .'<br>'; // getAttribute('ID')
}
?>
<h2>Done.</h2>
</body>
</html>
```

Be sure to set the $myWTID variable to your USPS ID number. When you access this file through your Web browser, it should display a page similar to the one in Figure 12-23. If the test went properly, the Zip 5 and Zip 4 values should appear at the bottom of the page.

If the test failed, you should have enough data provided by the test to begin looking for the problem. The test file outputs the values that it uses as execution progresses. The output first displays the query being sent to the USPS system, then the full resultant XML is displayed, and finally three of the output values are displayed. When a test fails, you'll be able to compare it against the successful one on Figure 12-23 to look for differences.

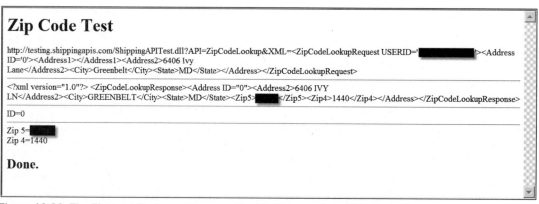

Figure 12-23: The Ziptest will attempt to query the USPS server for a ZIP code value.

Component Descriptor File

The component descriptor file is primitive and simply adds the component to the system. Enter the following file in your text editor and save it under the name com_zipfinder.xml:

```
<?xml version="1.0" encoding="utf-8"?>
<install version="1.5.0" type="component">
      <name>zipfinder</name>
      <author>Dan Rahmel</author>
      <creationDate>July 2007</creationDate>
      <copyright>(C) 2007 Dan Rahmel. All rights reserved.</copyright>
      <authorEmail>admin@joomlajumpstart.org</authorEmail>
      <authorUrl>www.joomlajumpstart.org</authorUrl>
      <version>1.0.0</version>
      <description>Accepts a field input and then queries a remote site for the
information and formats the XML output.</description>
```

```
    <files>
        <filename component="com_zipfinder">zipfinder.php</filename>
    </files>
    <administration>
        <menu>Zip Finder</menu>
        <files>
            <filename component="com_zipfinder">zipfinder.php</filename>
        </files>
    </administration>
    <params>
        <param name="accessid" type="text" default="" label="USPS Access ID"
        description="Enter the Access ID for the USPS web services." />
    </params>
</install>
```

Creating the Component Index File

The Zipfinder component will accept the address, city, and state values entered into a form. These values are sent in a query to the USPS server, which will return results in XML.

Enter the following in your text editor and save the file as zipfinder.php:

```php
<?php
/**
* @version $Id: zipfinder.php 5203 2007-06-15 02:45:14Z DanR $
* @copyright Copyright (C) 2007 Dan Rahmel. All rights reserved.
* @package ZipFinder
* Accepts a field input and then queries a remote site for the information
* and scrapes the returned output.
*/

// no direct access
defined( '_JEXEC' ) or die( 'Restricted access' );

// Check the task parameter and execute appropriate function
switch( JRequest::getVar( 'task' )) {
    case 'query':
        doExecuteQuery();
        break;
    default:
        displayQueryEntry();
        break;
}

// Process data received from form.
function doExecuteQuery()  {
    // Get query from form posting values
    $fldAddress = JRequest::getVar('address') ;
    $fldCity = JRequest::getVar('city') ;
    $fldState = JRequest::getVar('state') ;
    // Eliminate these 3 lines when you move off the test server
    $fldAddress = "6406 Ivy Lane";
    $fldCity = "Greenbelt";
    $fldState = "MD";
```

```php
        // Strip away anything that could be code, carriage returns, and so on
        $fldAddress = preg_replace("/[^a-zA-Z0-9 .?!$()\'\"]/", "", $fldAddress);
        $fldCity = preg_replace("/[^a-zA-Z0-9 .?!$()\'\"]/", "", $fldCity);
        $fldState = preg_replace("/[^a-zA-Z0-9 .?!$()\'\"]/", "", $fldState);

        $myData = getZip($fldAddress, $fldCity, $fldState);
        echo "<h1>Zip code results</h1>";
        echo "<p>Address: " . $fldAddress . "," . $fldCity . "," . $fldState . "</p>";
        echo "<h2>Zip+4: " . $myData . "</h2>";
        echo "<a href=index.php?option=com_zipfinder>" .
                "Return to Zip Finder</a>";
}

function getZip($myAddress, $myCity, $myState) {
        $myWTID= "MYID";

        $myUrl = "http://testing.shippingapis.com/ShippingAPITest.dll?" .
                "API=ZipCodeLookup&XML=<ZipCodeLookupRequest USERID='" . $myWTID ."'>" .
                "<Address ID='0'><Address1></Address1>" .
                "<Address2>" . $myAddress . "</Address2>" .
                "<City>" . $myCity . "</City><State>" . $myState . "</State>" .
                "</Address></ZipCodeLookupRequest>";

        try { @$doc = DOMDocument::load($myUrl);
        } catch(DOMException $e) {
                echo '<p>' . print_r($e) . '</p>';
        }
        $zip5 = "";
        $zip4 = "";

        $params = $doc->getElementsByTagName('Zip5');
        foreach ($params as $param) {
                if (strlen($zip5) > 0) $zip5 .= ", ";
                  $zip5 .= $param ->textContent;
        }

        $params = $doc->getElementsByTagName('Zip4');
        foreach ($params as $param) {
                if (strlen($zip4) > 0) $zip4 .= ", ";
                  $zip4 .= $param ->textContent ;
        }

        return $zip5 . "-" . $zip4;
}

// Display form for query entry
function displayQueryEntry() {
?>
<h1 class="contentheading">Zip Code Query form</h1>

<form id="form1" name="form1" method="post"
     action="index.php?option=com_zipfinder&task=query">
  <p>Enter your address here:
```

```
<INPUT type="text" name="address" size="80" ><BR>
  <p>Enter your city here:
<INPUT type="text" name="city" size="30" ><BR>
  <p>Enter your state abbreviation here:
<INPUT type="text" name="state" size="2" ><BR>
  </p>
   <p>
    <input type="submit" name="Submit" value="Find Zipcode" />
  </p>
</form>

<?php } ?>
```

Archive the two files in a ZIP called `zipfinder.zip`, and use the Extension Manager to install it into the system. When the component is executed and the user submits an address, in the version presented here, the address is ignored and the single test address used for the test server is used. That address is queried and the resulting ZIP code is displayed, as shown in Figure 12-24.

When you obtain your authorization to access the main ZIP code system, you will need to modify the URL to address that server, and delete the three lines that override the user-entered address.

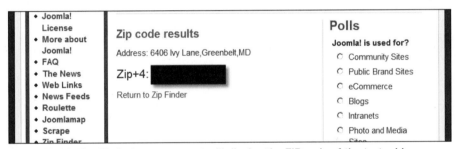

Figure 12-24: The Zipfinder component will display the ZIP code of the test address.

Summary

Accessing external resources from within a Joomla site can broaden the possible applications for the Joomla server. This chapter has provided an overview of the ways to connect Joomla to an extranet by doing the following:

❑ Pulling outside content through Web feeds and using the Auto Articles 3000 extension.

❑ Examining the Web feed format for proper deployment.

❑ Publishing the content on your Web site as an RSS or Atom feed that other users can subscribe to.

❑ Implementing affiliate programs with Google and Amazon to generate revenue for your Web site.

❑ Adopting the Skylark EDI extension to enable Joomla to process EDI interactions and act as an EDI server.

❑   Developing a custom screen scraper component to access text data on the Web.

❑   Encapsulating a Web API (such as the Google Map API) inside a component to add capabilities to the Joomla site.

❑   Creating a component that can query a remote site (in this case, the USPS), process returned XML result data, and format it for site display.

By interfacing with outside content, you can expand the depth of your site and, if your feed is successful, the popularity of your content will increase. Both factors are likely to increase your ranking on search engines where your site is registered. Chapter 13 provides a number of other options that can help you optimize your site for best placement on the search engines.

Search Engine Optimization (SEO) and Search Engine Marketing (SEM)

There is generally little point in having a Web site if interested users cannot find it. Making your site conspicuous in the search engines used on the Internet is one of the most important aspects of modern Web deployment. Search Engine Optimization (SEO) techniques will maximize your ranking in the search engines and minimize practices that keep your site with only an average placement.

This chapter examines SEO that relates most directly to a Joomla site. Joomla includes a number of features that make a site more Search Engine Friendly (SEF). The built-in settings help guide the search engines to more accurately represent the content of your site. There are also a number of general techniques that, if followed consistently, will aid in maximizing your site placement on every relevant search.

This chapter also takes a brief look at Search Engine Marketing (SEM), where paid advertising can help drive traffic to your Web site. SEM encapsulates SEO techniques, but large commercial organizations often hire an SEM firm (such as The Search Agency) to handle both sides of the search engine business. In contrast, small sites and noncommercial sites will emphasize SEO because of the low (or no) cost of implementation. Since a majority of Joomla sites are medium sized or small, this chapter will focus on SEO.

Keep in mind that the world of SEO is changing constantly. What may have a tremendous effect on search placement today may become much less important tomorrow. That said, none of the techniques described here should hurt your placement. If, in the future, the techniques described here lose some of their potency, they will likely always be useful for ranking improvement.

Joomla Settings

The developers of Joomla are aware of the importance of good Web site ranking. They have provided a number of options for a Joomla site to make itself as SEF as possible. By spending a little time with configuration settings and a little due diligence when posting new content, you can use the Joomla features to increase the opportunities of your site and to obtain high placement on the search sites.

With the adjustment of only a few global options, Joomla implements the changes for all the rendered content pages. As usual, implementing these features in Joomla requires only a few clicks in the Administrator interface.

Search Engine Friendly (SEF) URLs

By default, all Joomla URLs reference the same Web page (`index.php`) and use query string parameters to specify individual menus or articles to retrieve. For example, the URL to a standard Joomla article might look something like this:

```
http://www.example.com/index.php?Itemid=27&option=com_content
```

To a search engine, this URL is confusing. A *search engine spider* (the program that indexes a Web site) isn't very good at discerning that the query string holds the ID reference to the article. In general, a query string is just as likely to hold site visitor parameters as references to particular content. Here is the URL with query string for a common Web site that includes a query string ID:

```
http://www.example.com?userid=98239992107&viewsetting=ATVPDKIKX0DER
```

A search engine wouldn't want to record such user variables. It is difficult for a program such as a spider to know the difference between these user parameters and article reference information. For this reason, the spider will often ignore most of these parameters, so the default Joomla URL setting would generate very poor site ranking.

Fortunately, there is a solution to this problem in the Search Engine Friendly URLs settings in the Global Configuration. Figure 13-1 shows the SEO Setting frame in the Administrator interface. There are two options that related to SEF URLs: "Search Engine Friendly URLs" and "Use mod_rewrite."

If only the SEF URLs setting is activated, a Joomla article URL will appear like this:

```
http://www.example.com/index.php/joomla-overview
```

This type of URL is exactly what a search engine needs to properly index a Web site. New to Joomla 1.5, this setting uses a technique whereby the reference to the `index.php` file in the URL is executed by the Web server. When executing, it interprets the path that follows it and returns the requested page. This technique can work on both Apache server and IIS.

To work on Apache server, the `AcceptPathInfo` directive must be set to `On`. You can find complete information about this directive on the Apache site at `http://httpd.apache.org/docs/2.0/mod/core.html`.

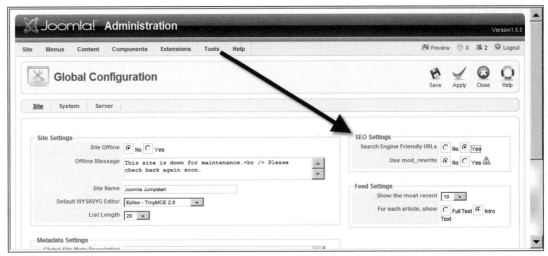

Figure 13-1: There are two SEF settings available on the Global Configuration screen of the Administrator interface.

If this directive is not active on your Web server (as sometimes is the case with ISPs), you must activate the "Use mod_rewrite" option to get SEF URLs. With this option active, the URL will look something like this:

```
http://www.example.com/home/44-godaddy-joomla-hosting-tips
```

In contrast to the first technique (which references the index file that interprets the path following it in the URL), mod_rewrite is an Apache module that detects if a URL that is being accessed does not really exist. If the URL is not found, the command settings in the .htaccess file are accessed, and the module will redirect the Web server in the background to the desired content.

For the mod_rewrite option to work, you must rename the htaccess.txt file at the Joomla root directory to .htaccess. On the Windows platform, Windows Explorer will reject this filename as illegal. You will need to use the ren (rename) statement at the command prompt, which will perform the operation.

Be sure to activate your SEF options before you register your Joomla site with the search engines. If they are activated after the site is already indexed (or potentially other sites have linked to the old URLs), your site could lose traffic or ranking, as the originally spidered URLs are no longer valid.

If you already have a site deployed on an older version of Joomla and are currently using an SEF extension, when you upgrade to Joomla 1.5, be sure to use this same extension. Since the Joomla 1.5 SEF URLs are likely different from your old URLs, old links will get a" page-not-found" error and potentially destroy your site ranking.

If you are converting a static Web site to a Joomla deployment, and you already have pages ranked on the search engine, use one of the available extensions (such as OpenSEF) instead of the built-in SEF functionality. Other extensions allow you to manually define the SEF URLs specifically for particular articles or categories. You can create URLs that match your original URLs, so the changeover will be transparent and you will not lose your ranking.

Metadata

One of the most important unseen aspects of SEO is the use of proper metadata information. *Metadata* is information about information. In the case of Web sites, metadata is article descriptions, keywords, and site information that is invisible to site visitors but is picked up by the search engine spiders. If you've looked at the source code for the header portion of a common Web page, you may have seen tags like these:

```
<meta http-equiv="Content-Type" content="text/html; charset=iso-8859-1">

<meta name="description" content="Filmmaking is a site focused on Nuts and Bolts
Filmmaking including storytelling, shooting tips, motion graphics, film technology,
3D rendering, and all aspects of movie creation.">

<meta name="GENERATOR" content="Microsoft FrontPage 4.0">

<meta name="keywords" content="filmmaking, movies, DV, MiniDV, Hollywood,
low-budget, guerilla, shooting, production design, cinematography, art direction,
cameraman, HD, VX2000, VX2100, Sony, GL1, GL2, XL1, XL2, Maya, 3D, design, film
critique, discussion, film links, free, articles">

<meta name="ProgId" content="FrontPage.Editor.Document">
```

This HTML code is metadata information about the Web site. You can see that the `description` metadata provides a summary of the page. The `keywords` metadata details search terms that are most relevant to the contents of the page. The `ProgID` and `Generator` are the page construction information (which is seldom used for site ranking). All of this data is recorded by the search engine spider and used in various degrees to understand and rank the Web site.

Site Metadata

The metadata for the Web site itself can be set in the Global Configuration screen. In the Metadata Settings frame shown in Figure 13-2, the metadata properties for the `description` and `keywords` may be set. This metadata is included on every page that is *not* an article. Descriptively setting this metadata is important, since it will provide information about the home page.

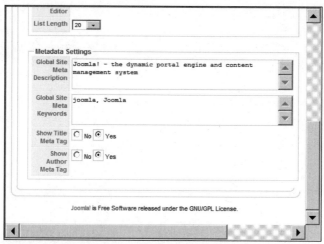

Figure 13-2: The Global Configuration screen holds the site metadata information.

Article Metadata

In Joomla, each article holds the metadata properties in the Metadata Information pane of the Article Editor (see Figure 13-3). The metadata properties allow you to set the `description`, `keywords`, `robot` settings, and `author` acknowledgment. These items will be included in the `<head>` section of the HTML rendered uniquely for each displayed article.

In the past, the text contained in the `keywords` section was very important because the keywords were used by the search engines to properly categorize the page. No more. Spammers have abused keywords so often and so extensively that many of the search engines almost entirely ignore this metadata today. Nonetheless, most search sites still record this information, so it is useful to spend a small amount of time including keywords relevant to the page.

The most critical metadata for each article is the page description. While the `keywords` metadata has diminished in importance, most search engines still mine the description for keywords that relate to the site. Almost equally as important, search engines often use the `description` metadata to provide a brief summary of the page in the results section of a search. For example, for the metadata presented in the earlier section "Metadata," you can see in Figure 13-4 that the site's listing on Google uses that `description` metadata to describe the site. Therefore, the `description` field is an opportunity for you to sell your site to potential visitors.

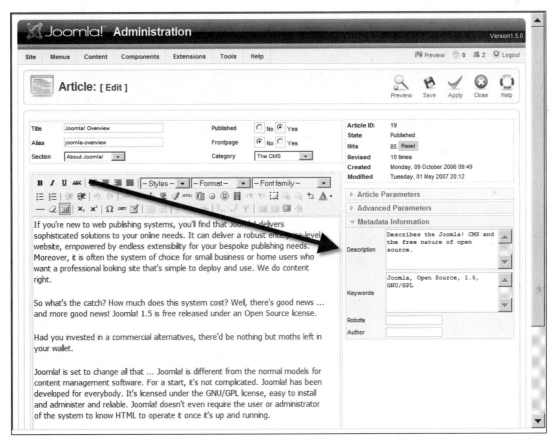

Figure 13-3: In the Metadata Information pane of the Article Editor, parameters including page description, keywords, robot settings, and author notation can be set.

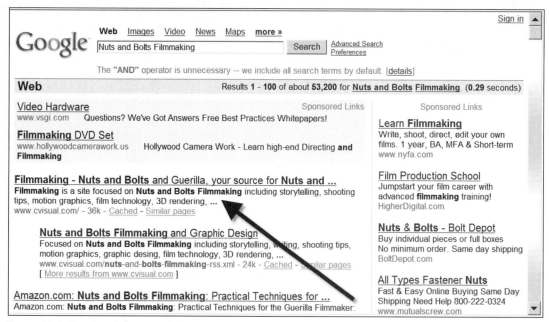

Figure 13-4: The description metatag is used by search engines to provide the page summary in the results list.

Activating Breadcrumbs

Breadcrumbs are the links that allow the user to understand and navigate the Web site hierarchically. If the visitor has jumped into the middle of your Web site (did not enter through the home page), the breadcrumbs will allow the user to ascend to any organizational level above the current page. Since breadcrumbs provide internal site referential links, they aid the search engine spiders in understanding the order of your Joomla site.

As shown in Figure 13-5, Joomla includes the Breadcrumbs module that will automatically create breadcrumbs for displaying on each Web page. Any template that includes this module will properly display the article's location in the hierarchy.

Figure 13-5: Joomla includes breadcrumb functionality that can aid your site in search engine ranking.

You'll find the breadcrumbs module in the Module Manager. As shown in Figure 13-6, it includes a number of parameters that will determine how it functions, including the Text Separator. If the Text Separator field is left empty, the default double arrow (>>) is used.

Figure 13-6: Through the Module Manager, you can change the settings of the Breadcrumbs module.

Sitemap

The more navigation aids that you can provide to the search engine spider, the more likely your content will be found and listed prominently on the search site. A *sitemap* is a tool that can help both your users and the spiders find everything on your site. Like a master index, the link to the sitemap is usually one of the lower items listed on the main navigation menu. Fortunately, there are a number of Joomla extensions that provide automatic sitemap generation.

Joomla Sitemap Extensions

There are a number of extensions on the Joomla site (extensions.joomla.org) that will create a sitemap of the Joomla system. Probably the most widely used and the most popular is an extension called Joomap. The Joomap extension uses the stylesheets from the currently selected default template to display the sitemap in the site style, as shown in Figure 13-7.

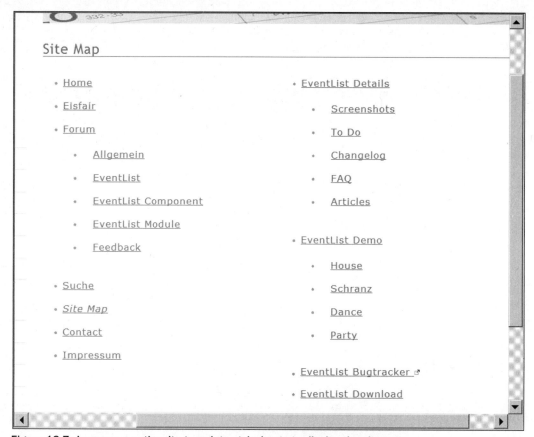

Figure 13-7: Joomap uses the site template stylesheets to display the sitemap.

Joomap will create a sitemap that includes the normal menu structure, categories, sections, and even Virtuemart categories (if you have that extension installed). Joomap will also output a sitemap in the XML format that Google Sitemaps requires. There are also a number of plug-ins for Joomap that will allow it to index content from other Web applications such as Gallery2.

Google Sitemaps

Google offers an online sitemap service that will automatically create and maintain the sitemap for you. Most Joomla sitemap components (including Joomap) use the Google API to integrate the Google Sitemap into the Joomla system. The Google Sitemap will help optimize the page spider to understand your site.

You can access more information on the Google Sitemap here:

```
www.google.com/webmasters/tools/sitemaps
```

General Techniques

Simply activating some of the Joomla site technology will help the search engines to understand your site but won't have a dramatic effect on search engine placement. However, there are a number of techniques that can be applied to any Web site (not just Joomla deployments) that will increase your search engine ranking.

Many of these techniques involve modifying the HTML of the site to make it more likely that your page will be located in a search. However, you will find that the best ranking increases come from getting links from other popular pages. Be sure to devote the most time to obtaining reciprocal links.

> *Any SEO technique can become obsolete the day after it is reported. Think of SEO like this: you're trying to divert the search engine from its main goal of supplying impartial information. Search engines are trying to provide information that is most germane to the user's search terms and the content that has proven itself to be useful to those searching. Aside from some of the basic techniques such as setting accurate page titles, with SEO techniques, you are trying to make your unproven site appear to the engine like a desirable, reliable, pedigreed site. Therefore, the programmers of search engines are constantly trying to see past SEO methods, because they don't want individual sites to choose if they are relevant to the search.*

Dominant Search Engines

The dominant search engine as of this writing is Google. Five years ago, it would have been Yahoo!. Five years before that, it would have been difficult to decide which was the frontrunner. Search engines are about finding the information you need. If a search engine called XYZ Search were to enter the Web arena tomorrow with unique technology, it's possible that in five years it would be the dominant search engine. Right now, it seems that Google has effective search technology that is difficult to duplicate, despite the best efforts of companies like Yahoo!.

That makes it possible for a newer, better search technology to take the mantle from Google. Unlike desktop applications where switching brands causes major hardships (years of archived files are generally invested in a particular file format), users can switch search engines by simply typing in a different URL.

By the time you read this, the horses may have changed positions. Nonetheless, the currently dominant search engines include (in order of importance) Google, Yahoo!, MSN, and Ask Jeeves. In the interest of maximizing your SEO time, it is a good idea to spend time on each in proportion to its popularity. For this reason, the examples in this chapter use Google for demonstration purposes.

Performing Keyword Research

One of the best investments in your SEO time is targeting the proper keywords for the type of people you want visiting your site. By explicitly choosing and targeting keywords on your site, you can maximize your site placement (and even page placement) on the search results list.

While it is most important to target the proper keywords for your main page, it is also very useful to perform the same targeting functions on your most important articles. Each page that ranks highly on the search engine will increase the amount of traffic on your site, as well as the likelihood the visitor will look at other content on your site. It is essential that you get the visitors "in the door."

Creating a Keyword Starter List

To obtain good ranking on the search engines, you need to know what popular keywords relate to the topic area of your Web site. For example, if your Web site focuses on personal improvement, do people enter "personal improvement" into the search engines when they are looking for your type of site? Or, do they instead look for "self help," "self improvement," or "life coaching"? Until you know this information, your site placement will depend more on luck than anything else.

Before you begin your research, spend 10 minutes creating a list of the terms that you think are most likely to relate to your site content. To find effective keywords, you need somewhere to start. Staying on the personal improvement topic, the list would begin like this:

- Personal improvement
- Self help
- Self improvement
- Life coaching
- Personal productivity
- Self reliance
- Support group
- Motivation

If you don't know where to begin, try looking up your central topic in an encyclopedia such as Wikipedia (`http://en.wikipedia.org/wiki/Main_Page`). The encyclopedia entry will likely have many of the terms that relate to the field that your page addresses.

Using a Keyword Finder Tool

Once you have your starter list of keywords, you'll need a keyword finder tool. You can use an online version such as Google Adwords Tools (`https://adwords.google.com/select/KeywordToolExternal`) or a desktop application such as the excellent freeware Good Keywords (`www.goodkeywords.com`).

If you put the previous starter list into Google Adwords Tools, it provides a list of all the most used search keywords that are related to the ones that were entered (see Figure 13-8). By default, the keywords are listed alphabetically. You can easily sort by any of the columns simply be clicking on the column header.

The top 10 keywords by search volume were the following:

- group support
- inspirational quotes
- motivation
- motivational
- self help
- support group
- support groups
- achievement motivation
- adhd support groups
- aids support groups

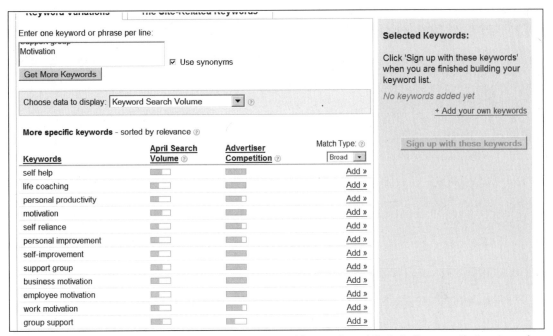

Figure 13-8: Google Adwords Tools can search on entered keywords and find similar ones that are popular.

As you can plainly see, the starter keyword list did not match the most used search phrases that the largest target audience would use. For the number one match, "group support," the starter list had these same two words, but in the opposite order! That would mean significant loss of page placement because other pages with the words in the correct order would look to the search engine as more relevant than your page. Knowing the popular variations of your main keywords is critical to pursuing an effective SEO strategy.

Take the top 30 terms you found in your keywords search and add them to your starter list — do not replace your starter list. The number one search term may mean it is the most popular entry that people use to find a particular sort of site, but it also likely means that there is the most competition in that area. By targeting keywords that are less popular, you will be able to be a large fish in a small pond (but that "small pond" will still be immense).

Finding the Sweet-Spot Keywords

Take your list of keywords, and start by entering the first term into a search engine. For simplicity, this discussion uses Google for these examples.

First, put the keywords into the engine using quotation marks so that only sites that have these exact words are returned. When you enter "group support," Google tells you that it found 1,190,000, and that's a lot of competitive Web sites. Just as important, by examining the list of returned sites, it becomes apparent that a number of them relate to electronic collaboration and groupware — not exactly the target audience.

Record the number of sites returned by Web search. Even though the keywords "group support" seem to have a large number of pages returned, some of the other terms may have even more. For example, on the fifth keyword phrase, "self help," Google returns 20,300,000 pages. The mere million pages for "group support" now looks more attractive.

Search for all of the terms on your keyword list, and record the number of pages returned. You will surely find a few of the pages hit the "sweet spot" where many people are searching using those terms, but there are relatively fewer sites that are returned by that search phrase. These sweet-spot keywords are the ones that you want to target for highest placement.

Look at the Top Pages

Imitation is said to be the sincerest form of flattery, but it is often also the best method of site promotion. To determine how your page can achieve the highest ranking on the sweet-spot keywords, you will need to look at the HTML source code of the pages to see what the others are doing.

Search on one of your keywords, and click on the top site for that search. Select the View Source command in your Web browser, and a window should be displayed showing the HTML of the page. One of my sweet-spot keywords was "motivational speech topics," and the top page as of this writing was `http://www.speech-topics-help.com`. When I executed the View Source command against this page, the source code appeared as shown in Figure 13-9.

> *The native View Source command in Internet Explorer launches the HTML code in Notepad. You can find instructions for changing this selection on the Web (you have to edit the registry). Alternately, if you haven't looked at the Mozilla Firefox browser already, it has an excellent HTML source parser built in. In Firefox, the View Source command opens a window that shows the HTML color formatted for easy reading. It makes examining HTML code painless.*

```
view-source: - Source of: http://www.speech-topics-help.com...

File  Edit  View  Help

<!DOCTYPE HTML PUBLIC "-//W3C//DTD HTML 4.01 Transitional//EN">
<html>
<head>
<title>2,500+ Speech Topics</title>
<link rel="alternate" type="application/rss+xml" title="RSS" href="http://www.speech-topics-help.com/speech-to
<META Name="Description" Content="Speech topics lists with persuasive and informative speech ideas and speechw
<META Name="Keywords" Content="speech topics,persuasive speech topic,informative speech topic,public speaking,
<link rel="shortcut icon" type="image/vnd.microsoft.icon" href="http://www.speech-topics-help.com/favicon.ico"
<script language="JavaScript" type="text/javascript">
<!--

function MM_swapImgRestore()
{
    var i,x,a=document.MM_sr; for(i=0;a&&i<a.length&&(x=a[i])&&x.oSrc;i++) x.src=x.oSrc;
}

function MM_preloadImages()
{
    var d=document;
    if(d.images)
    {
        if(!d.MM_p) d.MM_p=new Array();
        var i,j=d.MM_p.length,a=MM_preloadImages.arguments;
```

Figure 13-9: The View Source command in a Web browser displays the HTML code of the page.

You must now determine how the site placed so highly. The following factors generally lead to high placement:

❑ *Large number of links to site* — If the site has a large number of Web sites in the related topic area that link to it, a search engine will take this as a sign not only of popularity but also usefulness. Search engines judge a page by the company it keeps. When a large number of related Web sites think a page is valuable enough to link to it, a search engine recognizes it. Use the Google Toolbar to check the Page Rank to get an estimate of the link backs.

❑ *Keywords in the title text* — Keywords found in the `<title>` tags typically rank much higher than the keywords located at other places on the site.

❑ *Keywords in `<H1>` headings* — If the keywords are located in heading 1 (`<H1>` tags) text, the search engine determines that they are important to the site. If the heading keywords match the keywords in the page title, it considers them even more important.

❑ *Keywords bolded, italicized, or underlined* — Keywords that have special font styling are seen as important to the page.

❑ *Number of times keywords are included* — When the page contains repetitions of the keywords, that signals the search engine spider. Keep in mind, however, that search engine programs have become much more adept at determining when the keyword has been "spammed" on the page or repeated many times without relevance. This will hurt your ranking, rather then help it.

❑ *Keywords at the beginning and end of article* — Keywords appearing at both the beginning and end of the content will increase the page's ranking.

Examine the source of the top pages for these items. How many of them are present on the page? Execute the Find command (Ctrl+F in most View Source windows) and see how many times the keywords appear in the page. Where do they appear? After examining a few of the top-ranked pages for the search term, you should begin to see a pattern that explains how the search engine program chose those pages.

Repeat this process with your other sweet-spot keywords. By the time you are finished, you should have a good idea of how to make sure that your Joomla page imitates all of the strategies these sites used to achieve effective keyword placement.

Page Titles

For search engines, the page title is one of the most important items used in determining what content is included on the page. A short, descriptive title is an excellent way to increase the possibility that your page will be found. Before CMS systems, many Web sites had pages that included no title or titles undescriptive enough to make much of the Web site difficult for the search engine spiders to classify. Like other CMS applications, Joomla requires each article to be given a title, which is used for the page title.

Given that each article has a title, here are some guidelines to make your titles more effective for search engine placement:

❑ *Minimize the words used in each title* — Search engines cannot effectively weigh which words in a title are important and which are simply descriptive. Therefore, the shorter the title of the article, the more important the remaining words will seem.

❑ *Eliminate extraneous words* — You should eliminate short, simple words that have no relevance to your topic (such as "the," "and," "or," "but," "for," "nor," and so on). Instead of "this and that," use a simple character as a spacer such as a dash (–) to make your title read "this - that."

❑ *Combine words to avoid repetition* — Try to avoid repetitious words in the title. A title such as "Self improvement and self motivation" would serve you better as "self improvement motivation" because the search engine will still pick up all the keywords.

Of the page titles, the most important title is that of the home page. While the page title of articles is rendered from the article title itself, the title of the front page comes from the Home menu. Open the menu items of the Main Menu and click on the Home menu (or the first menu shown in the list).

In the System Parameters panel on the right side of the screen, you will find the `Page Title` parameter. By default, this parameter is set to "Welcome to the Frontpage", which is not very helpful to your site ranking. Be sure to change this to text that reflects the subject area of your site.

alt Attribute for Images and Other Media

Always use the `alt` attribute for any media that is included on your site. The `alt` attribute is a text representation of an image or other media displayed on the site that you can see when you mouse over an image, as shown in Figure 13-10. `alt` attributes are used primarily to allow text browsers to effectively represent a Web page or allow accessibility software such as text-to-speech page readers to present the page to those with disabilities. However, think of a search engine spider as a text browser — it can't see any graphic on the page. By setting the `alt` field to text that explains the graphic, the search engine will be able to use that text in determining page content.

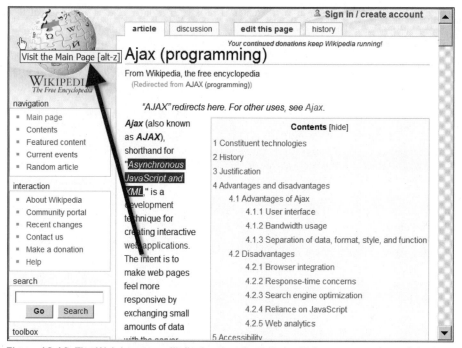

Figure 13-10: The Web browser will display the alt attribute during a mouse-over of the image.

In Joomla, when you insert a graphic into an article, you can enter text for the alt attribute in the Image Description field, as shown in Figure 13-11. If the image is the diagram of a business process, label it as such. However, if the image is a generic image used to add flavor and is not directly relevant to the content, use the alt attribute as another opportunity to use your keywords. If this technique is used with restraint, it can help your site ranking.

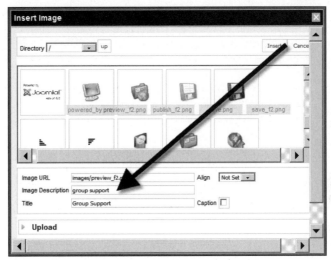

Figure 13-11: Enter alt attribute text into the Image Description field in the Insert Image window.

Google Page Rank

If you have the Google Toolbar installed, you may have noticed a small graphical bar labeled Page Ranking. For each site you visit, the page ranking of the site (on a scale from 1 to 10) is listed for this site, as shown in Figure 13-12. Note that the page-ranking bar will only appear if you allow the Google Toolbar to record your searches and site visits.

Examining the general ranking provides baseline useful information. However, this page rank is a general figure and not as important to site optimization as it might first appear. It is more important for a site to be found by a user during a search for the area you are targeting, rather than general popularity.

One of the tools you can use to determine how to increase your site's ranking is the Google Analytics visitor tracking tool. This free, Web-based service requires you to put a small amount of JavaScript code on your site page, and any visits to your page will be tracked in a variety of ways. For more information, see the section, "Google Analytics," later in this chapter.

Figure 13-12: The Google Page Rank provides a 1 to 10 index of the site's link popularity.

Reciprocal Links

The single most influential method of obtaining site ranking is through links that reference your site. Most search engines use the number of links to a site as an indicator of peer recommendations and are, therefore, a very important factor in generating a page ranking.

All links are not created equal, however. A single small link on a popular, high-ranked site (AOL.com, for example) is worth more to your site ranking than a hundred links on unpopular sites.

Reciprocal links are essentially a link exchange where you offer to include a link on your site in exchange for a link on someone else's site. These types of agreements can be very useful in generating a better ranking position as well as more site traffic.

Ajax and SEO

Ajax (also known as Asynchronous JavaScript and XML) is the incredible conjunction of Web technologies allowing a site to provide interactivity that compares with many desktop applications (see Chapter 7). Ajax allows a Web application to provide updates and interactivity on a Web page without refreshing the entire Web page. That can make a site far more dynamic and responsive.

The problem with Ajax is that the Ajax system is literally invisible to search engines. Ajax technology relies on a browser to execute JavaScript code to retrieve additional information from the Web server and display it in the browser window — most often in a pop-up window. Search engine spiders will not execute any client-side code. That means that the content displayed by the Ajax technology is not seen by search engines.

Presently, there is no ideal way to adopt Ajax and yet continue to obtain good search engine placement. Web designers that adopt Ajax have the following options to ensure continued good placement:

❑ *Duplicate content on general pages* — Even though a user will primarily view Ajax content through pop-up windows or interactive retrieval, be sure to keep all content that is provided through the Ajax interface also available as standard HTML content elsewhere on your site. You may have to develop a custom component to accomplish this task on Joomla, but ultimately for SEO it would be worth it.

❑ *Avoid using Ajax and JavaScript for navigation* — When a search engine spider indexes a Web site, it uses the internal links to find the content of the site pages. Since JavaScript is not executed by the spiders, nearly all of the navigation links displayed via JavaScript menus or Ajax live content retrieval will be invisible to the spider. Therefore, be sure to avoid using these technologies for your site navigation.

❑ *Have Ajax content be a summary of a traditional page* — Instead of making Ajax-specific content, have your Ajax extension provide a summary of traditional content. PHP can easily parse an HTML file, so your Ajax component could simply retrieve the content and reformat it for Ajax display. This would eliminate the need for any content duplication.

Ajax is so quickly gaining dominance as a method of providing site interactivity that the search engine will soon find a method by which site designers can signal to spiders the location of the content. Until that occurs, following these guidelines is the best way to adopt the new technology and keep a proper site ranking.

> *For the same reasons of invisibility to the spiders, you should be judicious in your use of Flash. While Flash can create an excellent impression on your visitor, Flash content is all but invisible to search engine indexing programs. Therefore, try to have a traditional HTML representation of all content, so the page is properly indexed by a search engine.*

Google Analytics

Google offers a free site statistics that you can activate on your Web site that allows complete traffic analysis. Google Analytics (`www.google.com/analytics`) provides a number of ways to examine the statistical data, including usage graphs, as shown in Figure 13-13. These graphs are only the tip of the iceberg in terms of available site statistics.

Figure 13-13: The Google Analytics usage graphs provide an overview of site activity.

For SEO, the Traffic Sources is the most important panel to examine, since it provides figures on not only the sources of referral traffic to your site but also the top keyword searches that resulted in visits to your site. This information can be critical to targeting the optimal keywords to use for your site.

Google Analytics can also be linked with any Adsense or Adwords advertising campaign. In fact, the system allows you to set up traffic goals and monitor the progress to those goals. You can determine the sources of Web traffic that offer the most return for the cost.

Note that when you add the Analytics code to your Web site, you are providing Google with all of your Web traffic information. Since many organizations consider this data private, be sure to recognize that this user data is being harvested outside the association.

What Not to Do

While this chapter has recommended many opportunities to optimize your site placement, there are also a number of bad practices that will hurt your placement. Some of these include the following:

❑ *Spamming keywords inside a page* — If your page has a high ratio of keywords-to-content (meaning most of the text on your page is keywords), the search engine spider will likely flag your page as spam, and the ranking for that page will suffer greatly. Try to ensure that each page on your site is human-readable and provides some useful information to prevent such categorization.

❑ *Avoid link farms* — There are sites called *link farms* that are simply lists of links. These will do your site no good and may harm your ranking.

❑ *No hidden text* — An early way to "game" the search engines was to set the background color, make text the same color as the background (so the spam text wouldn't confuse the user), and then load the page up with keywords. Search engines now look for this technique, and your site will be hurt if you attempt it.

❑ *A deal that is too good to be true probably is* — Scam companies regularly promise stupendous search engine ranking where you invest little time and effort — only money. Some of these schemes actually work for a brief time, but once discovered, are targeted by the search engines. There is no such thing as a free lunch in the real world or the Web world.

Search Engine Marketing (SEM)

The field of SEO attempts to influence site placement in search results. Search Engine Marketing (SEM) is the broader general field of increasing traffic through SEO technical refinements, as well as paid advertising. In fact, SEM encapsulates search engine advertising — both buying and selling. You can purchase advertisements to promote your business or allow your site to host ads supplied by a third party.

Writing an Effective Ad

Entire books have been written on creating good advertising copy, and many of them are excellent tools if you are going to be constructing ads. If you purchase some books on advertising copy, you should take a look at *Words that Sell* by Richard Bayan (McGraw-Hill, 2006) and *Tested Advertising Methods* by John Caples and Fred E. Hahn (Prentice-Hall, 1998). These books provide substantial help in creating an effective ad.

Nonetheless, here are a few guidelines that should help you craft better advertising copy:

❑ *Test, test, test!* — Successful copy is often like lightning striking. You can write the most wonderful copy that doesn't work, and yet the ad you tossed off in 10 minutes generates most of your hits. The only way to figure out what works and what doesn't is not to ask the experts but to test it in the real world.

❑ *Use short action words* — Motivate users to click with such phrases as, "NOW! Sale ends today. Download free software now. Buy today and save 50%."

❑ *Sell the benefits, not the features* — Whatever you are promoting with the ad, you should focus on the benefits to the user. One salesman famously (and accurately) stated that you should sell the sizzle, not the steak.

❑ *Make sure the ad uses hot-button words* — Use words that induce emotion and enthusiasm, such as "New," "Sale," "Free," and others.

❑ *Be succinct* — Remove all words that don't highlight the point of the site.

❑ *Target your audience* — Don't try to get everyone interested in your ad, just the target audience that you want.

❑ *Create landing pages for each ad* — For proper testing, you must be able to track the traffic generated by an ad. Use Joomla uncategorized content (so alternates of the same page don't show up in the section and category lists) to create a unique landing page for each ad placed.

Pay-per-Click and Impression Advertising

The most common form of ad marketing is the *pay-per-click* program. The advertisements are displayed on a site, but no revenue is generated until the visitor clicks on the ad link. Most search engines offer pay-per-click programs. Check the search engine for details.

No longer nearly as popular as during the dot-com boom, with *impression advertising,* the site hosting the ad earns revenue by the number of times an advertisement is displayed, regardless of whether the user clicks on the banner.

Impression advertising still has its place, particularly when an organization is trying to promote brand awareness. For example, many motion pictures use impression advertising as part of their marketing arsenal, since they want to raise awareness of an upcoming release — not just drive traffic to the movie's Web site.

Google Adsense

One method of generating income from your Joomla site is through the Google Adsense program (available at `www.google.com/adsense`). With this program, Google advertisements appear on your Web site. If a visitor clicks on one of the ads, you are paid for the click-through.

You can simply place the ads on your Web site and earn money for the clicks. However, the method of targeting ads benefits greatly from the SEO techniques that you have implemented. The Google Adsense application uses automated examination of your site to determine ad placement in much the same way that the SEO routines make your site more desirable to searchers. Therefore, ensure that you have all the SEO techniques implemented before you begin your Adsense subscription.

Summary

Search Engine Optimization (SEO) can be performed very effectively on a Joomla site, since it includes all of the necessary features to implement the technology. Most of the techniques don't require great genius or hidden secrets, but rather the application of simple elbow grease. This chapter has examined ways to implement SEO on a Joomla site by doing the following:

❑ Implementing the SEF URLs for the Joomla site organization.

❑ Improving the metadata included with every article.

❑ Adding a sitemap and creating a Google Sitemap XML descriptor file.

❑ Activating breadcrumbs so search engine spiders can better navigate the site.

❑ Performing keyword research to ensure that your site is found by the maximum number of people who *want* to find your site.

❑ Refining page titles for best ranking possibilities.

❑ Creating `alt` attributes for images to ensure that the images of your page help your ranking.

❑ Examining Google page ranks to determine the number of links referencing a site.

❑ Adopting an implementation strategy for Ajax that doesn't hurt your site popularity.

❑ Using Search Engine Marketing (SEM) to increase the visibility of your site.

If your SEO is successful, your site will gain a great deal more traffic — not all of it good. A Web site with greater visibility also becomes a much more attractive target for hackers. Chapter 14 examines aspects of security vulnerability and how the dangers of an attack can be minimized.

14

Joomla! Security

Because Joomla is easy to install and configure, many Web masters are lax when it comes to implementing proper security. Although the Joomla system does everything it can to prevent hacker breaches, it is important for any Web administrator to understand the basics of security and for you to understand the particulars of ensuring that your Joomla system can withstand an attack.

Because Joomla uses four interlocking server technologies (Apache, PHP, MySQL, and Joomla), you must maintain security protection at each link of the chain. For example, poorly handled PHP security can leave Joomla wide open to penetration even if Joomla, MySQL, and Apache are secure. This chapter examines each of the servers and how maximum security can be put into place to minimize the danger from the "Wild Wild West" environment of the Internet.

To minimize security problems you should perform a regular update of all your server software, including Joomla. New security problems are found all the time, and the developers of each software package patch the applications to close loopholes. By keeping your versions updated, you will be less vulnerable to attacks.

Types of Attack

Entire books have been written on aspects of hacking attacks, so a complete list is beyond the scope of this book. Nonetheless, there are a number of common attack methods (password, SQL Injection, cross-site scripting, and so on) that are extremely widespread. Any Web master should have at least a passing understanding of how they work.

The following sections provide a brief overview of the ordinary strategies used by hackers to gain access or fault a system. In later sections of this chapter, you'll learn how to configure your Web server, PHP system, and Joomla installation to minimize the likelihood of penetration by these or other methods.

If you want to obtain more detail in this topic area, a great deal of information on Internet security is available through the Unites States Computer Emergency Readiness Team (US-CERT). There are many freely available publications for technical and nontechnical users that are accessible on the US-CERT Web site (www.us-cert.gov).

Password Attacks

There are programs that will attempt to breach the security of a site through "brute-force" automated attacks on the password system. Most commonly, these attacks are performed using a dictionary of common terms and common passwords. It is always amazing to discover how many users use the word "password" or "1234" as their system password.

One method of promoting good user-selection of secure passwords is to encourage following these guidelines:

❑   Make a password at least seven characters long.

❑   Use uppercase and lowercase characters.

❑   Include numeric characters.

Users should incorporate two words and a number in their passwords. If one of those words is non-English (perhaps even "Joomla"), the chances of a dictionary or brute-force attack succeeding are almost nil.

> *In Hollywood movies, "hackers" use techniques like the brute-force method to break into a single user's account, but real hackers are much less choosy. The majority of successful brute-force attacks don't vary the password as much as the username. Since the word "password" is so common, a hacker will run this password against a user list to see if anyone has an account with that key. Therefore, it is advisable to shield your user list from general access.*

SQL Injection

One of the most common and effective forms of Internet attack is the *SQL injection attack*. In an injection attack, a hacker attempts to send unauthorized SQL code through an unfiltered SQL query. The hacker's SQL code may do anything from return secure information to execute a destructive procedure.

With basic precautions, you can protect against this type of security breach. The basic rule of thumb for protection against injection is to ensure that your program code never trusts raw data passed from an outside process (even if that process is a form you've created). All raw data accepted from outside the system should be processed and validated before it is used by the application.

Unfiltered Text Fields

For example, an HTML form may accept a field for a name. While a normal user would enter a simple name into the field, the hacker injects SQL code into the statement that alters the execution of the query. If the PHP code for the query placed the entered name into the variable $name and queried with it, the code for the query string might look something like this:

```
$sql = "Select * From jos_users Where name = '" . $name . "';";
```

The hacker would simply enter a last name that read as follows:

```
dummytext' or 'a' = 'a
```

The SQL code generated from this value would read as follows:

```
Select * From jos_users Where name = 'dummytext' or 'a' = 'a';
```

When the query is executed, the `'a' = 'a'` test would return a `True` value for every row, and the query would return the entire user list! Even scarier is that any valid SQL code can be injected, as shown here:

```
dummytext'; Drop Table jos_users; Select * From jos_polls Where title = '
```

That code would destroy the Joomla user table entirely. Sending the form input text through a simple processing routine would eliminate any danger from such an attack.

Handling Text Fields in Joomla and PHP

Joomla includes routines to generate escape characters for any characters that can't be properly stored inside a database string. For example, the single quotation mark (') cannot be stored without modification in a standard SQL `Insert` statement. Therefore, an escape sequence provided by the backslash (\) character on MySQL systems allows special characters to be included. Thus, a backslash followed by the quote (\') would store the single quote in a database field.

Creating an escaped string from the user-supplied string invalidates the injection attack because the single quote is no longer taken as a literal character for SQL execution. Instead, the quote (and any code that was intended for injection) is simply stored as part of the string. The likely result of such a query string would be the return of an error, since no records matching that value would be found.

For straight PHP code, you can instead use a database-specific method of generating a string that creates escape codes for special characters. For MySQL, PHP includes the `mysql_real_escape_string()` function. It can be used to format a string like this:

```
$name = mysql_real_escape_string($name);
```

Joomla provides an abstracted method called `getEscaped()` that will return the escaped string regardless of the target database. Although Joomla presently only supports MySQL, in the future when further data sources are added, code using the Joomla method instead of direct PHP will still work properly. You can get the escaped string from the JDatabase object like this:

```
$db =& JFactory::getDBO();
$name = $db->getEscaped($name);
```

If the first example of SQL Insertion attack were escaped, it would generate the following harmless string:

```
dummytext\' or \'a\' = \'a
```

The second example would look like this:

```
dummytext\'; Drop Table jos_users; Select * From jos_polls Where title = \'
```

There is a feature in PHP known as "magic quotes" that will automatically add backslashes to all input fields received from an outside source (such as a Web browser). In version 6 of PHP, the magic quotes option has been eliminated. Therefore, it is better to code manual escape processing as shown so that your code will securely run on PHP servers in the future without modification.

Untyped Fields

Another form of injection attack can occur when values that are not typed (set to be an `integer`, `float`, and so on) are passed directly to the SQL engine. For example, an `id` value retrieved from a query string might be passed directly into a SQL query with a line like this:

```
$sql = "Select * From jos_users Where id = " . $id . ";";
```

The same type of injection code could be used as the unescaped string:

```
1; Drop Table jos_users;
```

Therefore, whenever you accept values from a query string or form posting, be sure to type them through PHP. For example, to type the `$id` into an `Integer`, you could use the following PHP code:

```
$id = intval($id);
```

Typing code will automatically either outright eliminate any Injection code included in the field, or will generate an error when the code makes the typing nonsense.

If you use the `JRequest::getVar()` or `JRequest::get()` methods to obtain form and query string data, you are already protected because these functions provide a secure filter of all incoming data. Any outside data not obtained through these functions, however, should be escaped and typed wherever possible.

Custom Requests — Especially Through Ajax

SQL Injection attacks don't only come through form entry pages. Increasingly, Web sites are implementing Ajax technology that makes data requests of the system that skirt most common data-validation routines. That means that the explosion of Ajax use opens up a wide variety of potential security violation points.

Therefore, special attention should be paid to the portions of a system that provide responses to Ajax queries. When designing an Ajax responder, ask yourself the following questions:

❑ *Have I typed all of the request data?* — Every piece of information that comes from the outside should be processed and typed. That will prevent nearly every basic kind of injection attack. Limits should also be placed on strings to prevent any sort of overflow bug from rendering your system vulnerable. No last name should be more than 50 characters, so why not trim the string to that length to prevent false entry?

❑ *Should I limit the scope of the data accessible?* — For example, an Ajax component may provide a Who-Is display that shows the user's home country. However, the query is made off the entire contact table where a SQL Injection attack could possibly reveal personal information such as a home address. MySQL supports a table *view* that provides a filter for table data. By including only the data used by the Ajax component in the view, even a penetration would reveal no more than publicly available information.

❑ *Is this information you want to provide through Ajax?* — Many companies make available through Ajax requests whole databases or catalogs. However, a simple program can be constructed to make sequential requests to the Ajax responder and harvest all of the information in the database. Ensure that you understand the data you will be exposing or a competitor may use your own database for his or her competitive advantage.

These are just a few of the considerations you should examine in this infancy of Ajax implementation. The new technology will likely cause a tremendous number of security breaches before the weaknesses of the system are understood and protected. When implementing an Ajax solution, be sure to read the most current security literature so that you can understand the newest hacker threats.

Cross-Site Scripting (XSS)

Cross-site scripting (XSS) is a method of inserting some executing JavaScript code or object references into HTML code when an HTML editor is made available to the user. This code may open a hidden window on the user's system and record items such as usernames and passwords entered into other browser windows. Since this vulnerability occurs when a site allows user-posted content (a cornerstone of Web 2.0 dynamic interaction), it is very dangerous and must be guarded against.

These types of attacks can be controlled when they are attempted through the Joomla user interface (see the section "Joomla Security" later in this chapter). However, the prevalence of available extensions that allow HTML code entry (from guestbooks to forums) means that you should be on the alert to prevent these types of attack. Ensure that any new extensions filter the tags used by this method of attack (chiefly `<object>` and `<script>`) before you deploy the extension on your site.

PHP has a few built-in functions that can help you. The `strip_tags()` function will strip all HTML, XML, and PHP tags from a passed string and return the raw text. This can be used very effectively if your application is not expecting rich text formatting as input. For formatting, you could use BBCode, which is left unaffected by this function.

The `htmlentities()` function in PHP will convert all non-alphanumeric characters (such as quotation marks, greater than signs, and so on) to HTML formatting. You can also use regular expressions to strip everything from input fields except alphanumeric characters. For a last name field, you might use a statement like this:

```
$myString = preg_replace("/[^a-z 0-9]/i", "", $myString);
```

Directory Scanning

Many Web servers have the option set to allow directory browsing. Over an HTTP connection, a visitor can browse to a directory and see all of the files contained there, provided that there is no `default.htm`, `default.asp`, `index.html`, or `index.php` file found in the directory. Directory browsing is an open invitation for hackers to discover a great deal of information about your system. Everything from configuration filenames to general system information can be learned if that hacker has knowledge of the host applications and operating system.

By default, most Web servers now have this option disabled. If your site will be hosted on an older server, be sure to check that this directive is not set. This form of hacking is more likely to be performed manually by a hacker, since full knowledge must be used to recognize the weakness of a system.

As a preventative measure, Joomla includes a dummy `index.html` file in every site directory and sub-directory of the site to prevent this possible intrusion. Most extensions and templates, however, don't take this preventative step, as you should do with all add-ons that you create for the Joomla system.

Denial of Service (DoS) Attack

The *denial of service* (DoS) attack is an attempt to deny use of a server or other resource to authorized users. The most common form of this attack simply floods a router or server with so many requests that the machine is overwhelmed and cannot respond to authentic requests. In another common DoS attack, an attempt is made to force a reset of the server or router, which makes the resources unavailable during the restarting process. Of course, once the reset is complete, the attacker requests another reset and continues to repeat this process.

To prevent tracking of the hackers and also to reach a critical mass of false requests, the DoS attack is often launched with a virus or worm that spreads the attacking code to innocent computers. This is known as a *distributed denial of service attack*. At a particular time and date, the code activates and previously friendly computers simultaneously attack the target.

Most DoS attacks must be deflected at the hardware level, so if you are running the host server, be sure to have a good firewall in place. Special firewalls known as *stateful firewalls* will automatically recognize the difference between good traffic and DoS traffic, and will prevent the invalid traffic from being passed onto the network.

The OpenBSD packet filter program called `pf` supports a feature called *synproxy* that sits between a server and Internet traffic. It performs the same role as a stateful firewall in blocking faked traffic. You can find more information about `pf` at `www.openbsd.org/faq/pf`.

HTTP Sniffing

The nature of Web communication means the information sent and received is broken down into small chunks of data called *packets* and broadcast over the Internet. The packets eventually find their way from the broadcast computer to the target computer, passing through a variety of computers and routers before they reach their destinations. This makes it possible for a computer sitting somewhere between the broadcaster and the target to copy or "sniff" the packets that pass by.

Web data is sent and received in HTTP format encapsulated within packets. An HTTP Sniffer (EffeTech HTTP Sniffer, for example) gathers and decodes packets containing information in the HTTP protocol. The sniffer then rebuilds the HTTP session and can open files and data that it intercepts.

For a Joomla site (or any other site that has an unencrypted login), an HTTP sniffer can potentially intercept entered username and password information. For an Internet deployment of Joomla, it is fairly unlikely (and very difficult) to place a sniffer inline to make such interception possible. On a Joomla intranet run on a local area network, however, the opportunities and penetration points are greatly increased.

In those circumstances, you might consider purchasing an SSL security certificate to allow encryption of traffic between a browser and the Web server. Check out the Verisign Web site (`www.verisign.com`) for a complete explanation of how the certificates work and the way they provide encryption of data. Once you have an SSL certificate installed on your Web server, you should be able to access it with a URL like `https://www.example.com`. The `https://` address stands for "HTTP secure." The default port used by `https://` is `443` instead of port `80` for the normal Web interaction.

If you want all site interaction encrypted, you merely need to point the Web server at the Joomla root for the server location default. However, you can use Joomla's switchover technology, which lets you switch between secure and insecure versions of a Joomla site. That way pages for login, registration, personal information entry, e-commerce, and perhaps even Administrator interface access can use an encrypted communication while the rest of the interaction with the site is unencrypted.

To enable a secure login on a Joomla site, first you must have the SSL active on your Web server. Then, you must unpublish the Login module so that there is no insecure login available. Create a new menu item that will provide the link to display the login screen under the SSL encryption. It needs to address the User ➪ Login component as shown in Figure 14-1.

When the menu item screen is displayed, set the Title to `Login`. Expand the System Parameters frame, and set the SSL Enabled option to `On`, as shown in Figure 14-2. This option will make the link from the menu begin with an `https://`.

That's it! When the user clicks on the link from the front page, the login screen will be displayed as shown in Figure 14-3, and the small padlock in the bottom of the browser window will be locked, showing that the site is secure.

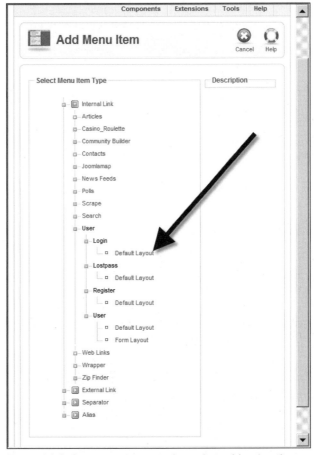

Figure 14-1: Create a new menu item that addresses the User ➪ Login component.

Figure 14-2: Set the SSL Enabled option to On.

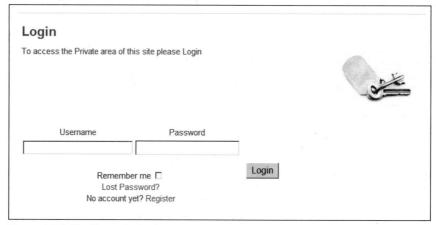

Figure 14-3: The User ⇨ Login component will be displayed on a secure page.

Web Server Security

The lowest level of attack and least likely place for penetration is the Web server. Both Apache Web server and Microsoft IIS are hosting literally millions of Web sites with few publicized breaches. Although such widespread adoption doesn't prevent the possibility of a security problem, the servers are very well debugged and protected.

Apache is even less likely to be the vector of an attack, since the execution of Web scripts (such as PHP or Perl) is not handled by the Web server itself, but rather a plug-in or component. Since script execution engines are perhaps the most directly vulnerable to attack, the Apache Web server itself does not have this point of jeopardy.

Securing Apache Server

Apache Server, out of the box, is extremely secure. Since Apache runs a large chunk of the Web servers of the world, it has been tested and probed from every which way. Therefore, without any changes to the configuration settings, a vanilla Apache install will handle most security needs.

Nonetheless, there are a few places where you can add a little extra safety. Although Apache is very secure by default, it can easily be made insecure by a poor setting choice. Therefore, be sure to give careful consideration before you edit any of the default settings.

.htaccess Configuration

With Apache server, the file and folder permissions can be stored in a file called .htaccess. Access permission, password protection, PHP blocking, and other security settings may be specified in the file. Because of the power available through the file, Apache includes (by default) a configuration to make the file inaccessible from outside the system through a browser.

Joomla users generally use the .htaccess file to set the permissions to allow the use of mod_rewrite to create Search Engine Friendly (SEF) URLs (see Chapter 13 for more information). The Joomla installation includes a usable htaccess file named htaccess.txt that you can activate for mod_rewrite enabling if your system is not currently set up to use it. To activate it, simply rename the htaccess.txt file to .htaccess instead.

> On Windows, the Explorer file interface will not allow you to rename a file to an empty filename with an extension (which is how .htaccess appears to the system). You can either add a directive to the httpd.conf file to look for the access file under a different name or you can open the command prompt window and use the ren command.

ServerSignature Directive

The more information a hacker obtains about your system, the more exact the methods that he or she can use against your site. While it will be fairly obvious to the beginning hacker what type of Web server you are running, providing extra information such as the version number, operating system, and so on, is not in your best interests. Unfortunately, much of this information is provided by the ServerSignature whenever the server generates a page (such as a server error message).

Adding the following directive to your httpd.conf file will turn off the signature output:

```
ServerSignature Off
```

ServerTokens Directive

Much of the information supplied by the signature is also returned with every page request. The `ServerTokens` directive lets you set the amount of information about the server to provide with the page request. There are six settings available for this directive. In descending order, these include `Full`, `OS`, `Minimal`, `Minor`, `Major`, and `Prod`.

You should add a directive to provide the least information, like this:

```
ServerTokens Prod
```

Denying Access to File Extensions

A helpful security feature included in Apache is the capability to deny access to particular types of files from a Web browser. By using this capability, you can deny outside access to any file types that have no reason to be addressed by a browser (such as `.log` files).

Your default `httpd.conf` file should contain an entry to deny a browser access to the `.htaccess` file. Examining the configuration file, you should see code like this:

```
<FilesMatch "^\.ht">
    Order allow,deny
    Deny from all
</FilesMatch>
```

This code tells Apache to deny browser access to all `.htaccess` files (and `.htpasswd` files, too). To deny access to log files, you can copy the previous section and then modify the `FilesMatch` statement like this:

```
<FilesMatch ~ "\.log$">
```

To deny browser access to a particular directory, you need to use the `Directory` element like this:

```
<Directory ~ "C:/Program Files/Apache Software
Foundation/Apache2.2/htdocs/libraries">
    Order allow,deny
    Deny from all
</Directory >
```

When a browser attempts to access files in the `\libraries` directory or any directory inside it (existing or not), a `403 Forbidden Page` error will be returned.

PHP Security

PHP security will likely be the most important server technology to secure because it is the most vulnerable to attack and also has a number of administrative configurations that can open security holes. If an attacker can successfully execute script code outside narrow limitations, there is great potential that the villain can take complete control of the system.

The first step in minimizing potential jeopardy to your system is ensuring that there are no files on your server that call the phpinfo() function. While this function is superb for examining your system and determining configuration settings, it can provide a hacker with a complete window into your PHP system. That information can give clues on exactly how a breach might be accomplished.

After you have made sure that your server doesn't expose itself, there are a number of PHP directives that can seal up the server to ensure that it isn't a promising target for the visiting hacker. Although a Joomla server can function correctly without these security precautions in place, you will potentially save yourself a lot of grief if you ensure that your Joomla server is securely configured.

> *In PHP version 6, three common features (register globals, magic quotes, and safe mode) have been eliminated. In the case of magic quotes (see the section "SQL Injection" earlier in this chapter), the removal of the feature will require novices to pay closer attention to their coding.*

PHP Safe Mode

When *safe mode* is activated on a Web server, execution scripts can only access files within their own Web site directory. This prevents hackers on a shared system from executing a script in one directory that can read files and information from a directory that doesn't belong to them. Safe mode also limits script execution time, memory utilization, and access to certain system functions (such as exec(), unlink(), and copy()). It is good to have safe mode turned on in many situations, although some programs and components won't function completely if this mode is enabled.

Safe mode is activated on most shared remote PHP hosts. You can check if the mode is set to On by executing the phpinfo() function and looking in the Configuration ⇨ PHP Core for the safe_mode directive. You can change the setting by searching for the safe_mode directive in your php.ini file.

If you are running PHP on Microsoft IIS, you do not need to use safe mode, since each virtual host can be configured to run from a separate user account. As long as the privileges of the user accounts are properly set, there is no need to prohibit cross-account access because it will not be possible.

> *Safe Mode is removed in PHP version 6 and above. The restrictions it provided are thought to give a false sense of security. From its initial implementation, it was a stopgap measure until Web servers (where the problem should be handled) had reached a level of sophistication where it would no longer be needed. Servers have been at that level for some time.*

PHP doc_root

The doc_root directive accepts a string that specifies the execution root directory for PHP scripts. If safe_mode is enabled, then no scripts will be allowed to execute outside of the cited directory. The directory should be set in the php.ini file like this:

```
doc_root = "C:\Program Files\Apache Software Foundation\Apache2.2"
```

PHP disable_functions

With PHP safe mode deprecated, there are a number of other functions that can be used to secure individual items in PHP. For example, the disable_functions directive can be set to deactivate particular functions that might be exploited by a hacker. In your `php.ini` file, inserting the following directive will deactivate the functions listed without affecting Joomla's operation:

```
disable_functions = file,fopen,popen,unlink,system,passthru,exec,popen,
    proc_close,proc_get_status,proc_nice,proc_open,proc_terminate,shell_exec
```

On a deployment server, you may consider including the `phpinfo` function in the `disable` list. That way, if any errant files exist that call the function, even if a hacker locates that file, it can't be exploited for the information it would supply.

Before you make this sort of configuration change, ensure that you understand PHP fairly thoroughly. Otherwise, you are likely to disable a function that is used by an extension, and thereby limit the functionality of your Web site.

PHP disable_classes

Like `disable_functions`, the `disable_classes` directory accepts a comma-delimited list of items to be disabled. This function will deactivate the specified object-oriented class from executing under PHP. While this directive has only limited usefulness as of this writing, in the future, when class frameworks (including the Joomla framework) become more extensive and present security risks, this setting will prove very useful.

To disable the `Directory` class, include this directive in your `php.ini` file:

```
disable_classes=Directory
```

PHP display_errors

One setting that you will almost certainly want turned on when using a staging server and definitely want off on a deployment server is the `display_errors` setting. When this is enabled, any errors or warnings that occur during PHP execution are echoed to the browser, along with the file and line number where the error occurred. You can enable this option in the `php.ini` file with this directive:

```
display_errors = On
```

During development, you will want all errors displayed to allow fast resolution, and all warnings displayed because they will tend to be overlooked if they are only entered into the error logs. With this setting disabled, the messages from the system will not be lost. Whether activated or deactivated, errors and warnings are written into the `error.log` file of the `\logs` directory on an Apache server as long as `log_errors` is left enabled (which is the default).

Be sure to set this parameter to `Off` on a deployment server. If left on, any error can provide a hacker with a variety of information about your Web server, including filenames, directory paths, variables, and permission settings. These may be exploited to provide unauthorized access or damage to your site.

PHP expose_php

The Apache `ServerTokens` mentioned earlier sends server information with each page request. The `expose_php` directive will append information about the PHP server to the information returned during a page request. By default, this option is enabled, but for best security, you should disable it on your deployment server.

To deactivate the supply of the PHP server information, set this directive in your `php.ini` file:

```
expose_php = Off
```

MySQL Security

The MySQL database server can hold a great deal of important private information. If the Joomla platform is used for contact management or eCommerce, the potential access to user's private identity information can be substantial. Therefore, you should read the brief (but significant) MySQL "General Security Issues" guide that you'll find at the following URL:

```
http://dev.mysql.com/doc/refman/5.0/en/security.html
```

Joomla Security

The Joomla system is created to provide a great deal of turnkey security, so even a default installation will be fairly secure. However, there are a number of fine adjustments that you can make to tighten up a few Joomla weak points. New security problems arise all the time as hackers devise new methods of breaching security. You should always keep your Joomla installation updated to the most recent available version.

The best method of staying informed about possible Joomla security issues is to subscribe to the Joomla "Security Related Announcements." You will receive emails relating security information and any alerts that require special attention. To subscribe, search on the Web (in case the location has changed) or go to this forum topic:

```
http://forum.joomla.org/index.php/topic,125221.0.html
```

Delete Installation Files

Be sure that, once you have completed installation, you delete the `\installation` folder and all of the files in it. If a hacker were able to reactivate the installation process on an existing server, it would be possible to wipe the site clean. To make sure this doesn't happen under any circumstances, be sure the installation execution files are removed from your Web server.

Joomla HTML Editor

If you allow contributors on your Web site, there is the potential of someone using an account to attack the system through an XSS attack, as described earlier in this chapter in the section, "Cross-Site Scripting (XSS)." Be sure to limit the capabilities of the editors that are available to contributors.

Through the Plugin Manager, you can access the parameters for the rich text editors used by Joomla. These editors nearly always contain functionality that allows automatic stripping of potentially hazardous content from user-entered content.

TinyMCE can strip security risks found in articles through the "Code Cleanup" and "Code Cleanup on startup" options (see Figure 14-4). By default, Code Cleanup is set, while the startup option is not. You only need the startup option if you believe there is already unclean code in you article database.

There are certain conditions where the Code Cleanup function will prevent you from doing something you want to do (such as inserting a YouTube video into an article) because it thinks the code is dangerous. Rather than disabling the option, select the No Editor option and edit directly in HTML when making changes to articles that have such content.

A more powerful setting on the TinyMCE parameters screen is the Prohibited Elements setting that allows you to specify HTML elements that can be stripped from the entered text. By default, only `applet` is entered in this field. For greater security, you might consider setting the list to `object,applet,iframe`, which will prohibit almost all element types that might be used for XSS attacks, among other things. Of course, it will also stop users from adding Flash animation and other dynamic content.

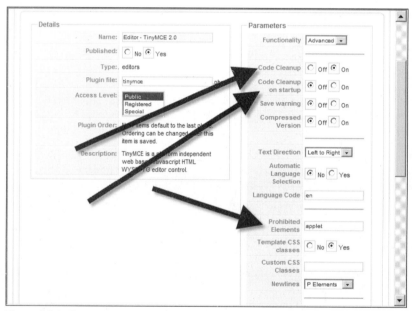

Figure 14-4: The Code Cleanup option will strip the code of certain HTML elements and script tags for security.

Execution within the System

When a hacker can directly execute a PHP file from outside the system, all sorts of mischief is possible. If you are developing new extensions (modules, components, or plug-ins), always add the code that ensures that the extension is being run by Joomla itself. At the top of your code file, add the following line:

```
defined( '_JEXEC' ) or die( 'Restricted access' );
```

If the _JEXEC parameter is not defined (meaning Joomla isn't executing the process), the execution of the code terminates. Even a primitive test extension should include the line just in case it is left installed on the server and forgotten, only to be found later by a hacker and exploited.

Testing and Development

If you are going to deploy a protected Joomla system, you must be able to test configurations and extensions on a safe system. This testing should all be done on a staging server. The staging server can be fairly insecure and include all types of rough extensions and code.

A staging server is even more important for security if you are performing development. Test scripts and example extensions are only two of the items that you will need to execute when performing development that can create large gateways of opportunity for a hacker to enter. Attacks generally occur at a system's weakest point, and a development system will have many.

Once development is complete, you should move the configured system to a deployment server. You should *not* move the configuration files such as php.ini and httpd.conf because the deployment server should have vastly different settings. When certain portions of the system break under the new stricter deployment (and they will), track down the problem instead of disabling the problem setting. This will lead to a stronger Joomla deployment and more solid code.

Summary

Joomla is intrinsically a very secure system. And yet, its coordination of multiple Web technologies makes it vulnerable unless security threats are understood and proper countermeasures put into place. This chapter has provided an overview of the ways Joomla security concerns can be addressed by doing the following:

❑   Understanding the types of attacks that can be attempted against a Web server.

❑   Improving the security configuration settings of the Apache server.

❑   Refining the php.ini file to limit execution and access.

❑   Creating a MySQL security policy to prevent unauthorized information access.

❑   Configuring Joomla parameters to best prevent potential attacks.

Security from outside attacks is very essential, but having effective control of user access within a system is very important as well. Unfortunately, this area is one that is somewhat lacking in Joomla. Chapter 15 examines all of the areas where Joomla lacks capability that is included in higher-end CMS systems.

15

What Joomla! Can't Do

As you know by now, Joomla is a phenomenal Content Management System (CMS). On the CMS Matrix Web site (www.cmsmatrix.org), which tracks features of all of the major CMS applications, Joomla has 124 out of 140 features listed for comparison. The tremendous feature list makes Joomla comparable to systems that sell for hundreds of thousands of dollars. However, there are areas where Joomla lacks the sophistication or advanced implementation that would make another CMS application a better choice for certain types of deployment.

This chapter provides a snapshot of some of Joomla's shortcomings as of this writing. Joomla development continues, and many of these features are slated for addition to Joomla in the coming years. However, other CMS vendors will not be idle either, so this chapter will portray Joomla accurately as it can be compared with other products in the near future. When Joomla adds a first version of a given feature, the products that already include the feature will likely be releasing version 2.0 capabilities. Therefore, this chapter should continue to provide an effective way of judging Joomla's deficiencies in relation to other products of the CMS category.

> *Some Joomla proponents would argue that many of Joomla's shortcomings can be overcome by adding available extensions. In the cases where a widely adopted extension integrates a particular feature in a seamless way (the way Virtuemart adds e-commerce capabilities), I have not included the non-native item as a Joomla limitation. When available extensions add only the most primitive or poorly supported implementation of the functionality (such as version control), I have cited Joomla's weakness in that area.*

Document Version Control

One of the most significant features Joomla lacks is *document version control*. Nearly every commercial CMS (and all the high-end CMS products that are comparable to Joomla) provide complete version control functionality. Version control is critical to content management when the number of contributors and editors grows beyond a handful. It is also a key feature that allows article content to be processed through an administrative workflow.

To understand the importance of document version control to a content-based organization, imagine the workflow of an online newspaper. A reporter writes an article and initially submits it to the system. One or more editors look through the article and make suggestions, add notes, or execute changes to the content. Next, fact checkers vet the article for accuracy, and note recommendations for modifications. The legal department then adds its input for any controversial issues.

Finally, the original author works through the article — accepting changes, responding to criticisms, making modifications, and performing rewrites. Only after many revisions occur does the article actually appear for public viewing. If new information is discovered or inaccuracies are uncovered, the article may be changed again after publication.

In the workflow outlined for the online newspaper, each stage requires changes to the initial content. These changes may be destructive (deleting a paragraph, for example), constructive (draft of an additional explanatory sentence by the editor), or corrective (change a mistaken punctuation mark). For a CMS with revision control, each save creates an historical copy or version of the article before the changes were made.

If it is necessary to step back into earlier versions or to examine a particular revision, the CMS allows the archive for the earlier version to be retrieved. A majority of systems allow a side-by-side comparison of two different versions of the document with the changes highlighted in a different color for easy recognition. Many editors (including jEdit and Microsoft Word) offer side-by-side comparative versioning, as shown in Figure 15-1.

Joomla is lacking any form of version control. When modifications are made to an article and saved, the old version is written over and there is no way to restore it. That means that there is no real possibility of implementing a workflow system for document management. There is an extension called Versioning that makes a backup copy of the last version of a document when a new save is made, allowing a one-revision "undo." This elementary implementation, however, does not provide true version control.

Import, File Conversion, and Export

While Joomla shines in the area of new content creation, import capabilities are virtually nonexistent. There is no automated method of importing articles from external files. Joomla also lacks a conversion feature that would allow the creation of articles from one or more files in a rich text format (such as Microsoft Word, PDF, RTF, and so on).

Since existing article libraries and author file submissions are two common content sources, this oversight is significant. Commercial CMS systems allow direct or bulk import for numerous document types, including Microsoft Word, Microsoft Excel, Microsoft Outlook, Web capture, Extensible Stylesheet Language Transformations (XSLT) formatting of XML data, TeX, and BBCode. CMS applications such as the Vignette Web Content Management system even allow bulk import of images for full document-management capabilities.

Until substantial conversion capabilities are added, Joomla will not be able to meet the needs of organizations with a large archive of existing content. Content conversion can be easily added as extensions, but as of this writing, the only Joomla converter I could locate supplied DocBooks conversion capabilities.

Figure 15-1: A side-by-side comparison of historical changes to an article can be incredibly useful.

Export functionality is equally lacking. While MySQL can be used to directly access and export content data, there is no built-in capability to export content or other data from the Joomla system. That makes it difficult to move data out of the Joomla system for use elsewhere, as well as making the archiving of older content for removal from the database problematic.

Limited Security and Authentication Features

The Joomla security model is primitive when compared with other systems. Joomla has only eight groups (Registered, Author, Editor, Publisher, Public Backend, Manager, Administrator, and Super Administrator) under which a user may be categorized. In comparison, many database systems include user groups as well as role designations, so security settings can have a high level of specificity (or granularity).

For example, if you wanted to grant an assistant administrator the capability to approve or edit articles in only one category in Joomla, it is impossible to grant privileges that specific. Likewise, if you wanted to grant a registered user viewing access to only two sections, that type of restriction is not currently possible.

There are extensions that broaden the security settings for Joomla. The JACLPlus extension, for example, allows the administrator to create additional groups that can have restricted viewing privileges. However, the type of control and level of security that many commercial CMS systems tout must be integrated on the framework level for security reasons, and can't realistically be added as a plug-in.

Additionally, there are no advanced modes of authentication such as Kerberos, network information system (NIS), Windows NT LAN Manager (NTLM), or Server Message Block (SMB) authorization. That limits the level of security offered by Joomla, since, by default, username and password logins are sent in plain text to the server, making interception possible.

Fortunately, for password login pages and e-commerce solutions, Joomla version 1.5 added native Secure Sockets Layer (SSL) compatibility. SSL allows a client browser to establish a secure session with a Web server, so all traffic between them is encrypted. That allows for secure site login, protection when submitting personal information (on an online dating site, for example) or hosting an e-commerce site.

Load Balancing and Replication

Because the deployments are meant for extremely heavy traffic loads, most of the commercial CMS systems have load-balancing capabilities that integrate with the underlying application server. Unfortunately, Joomla does not provide this type of combined approach.

Further, Joomla includes no native capability that allows for replication. Joomla lacks the features and tested architecture that would allow a distributed cluster of servers that hold (and allow editing of) the same content. Although MySQL does provide replication services, it is never a good idea to implement replication when the application whose data is being replicated is unaware of the data merge that is taking place in the background.

There are several methods of creating distributed, multi-server, load-balanced Joomla deployments as detailed in Chapter 11. However, these solutions are not native to Joomla and are, therefore, not supported like those created by the developers of CMS systems that incorporate load balancing and replication into the system infrastructure.

User Interface Levels and Skinning

Joomla has two main user interfaces: front-end and Administrator. On other CMS systems, multiple levels of user interface complexity may be created that are customized to user, role, or group privileges. That means that different WYSIWYG editors, forms editors, and general interface attributes are presented, depending on the user who is logged in to the system. The small changes to menu systems based on the user's group are not comparable to user-interface levels.

Additionally, many CMS systems let the user customize the user interface experience with a selection among multiple skins. Joomla presents the same template to all users. Some personalization (particularly relating to a user profile) is offered through the Community Builder extension. However, this extension requires substantial customization to allow for the type of individual page personalization offered out of the box by other systems.

Standard Groupware Capabilities

Groupware is a software category that includes applications that allow online collaboration among a set of users. Lotus Notes is perhaps the most famous example of this type of network-based application. Common features available through groupware applications include the following:

❑ *Web publishing* — One of the most important aspects of groupware is the capability for members of a group or project to publish documents and information. Often, this type of publishing does not mean publishing for general public access, but instead for use by a focused task group. Typically, the publishing portion of a groupware application includes complete versioning and markup of documents, so collaborative (and nondestructive) modification of documents is possible.

❑ *Forums/message boards/discussion boards* — Communication, essential in group collaboration, is made possible by forums and message boards. Board topics are available for all current shared projects, and postings can direct the user directly to a project resource (such as a spreadsheet, online conference, or current document).

❑ *Synchronous conferencing* — Conferencing may include video, audio, chat, application sharing, or shared "whiteboard" tools. Users can interact in real time, and generally have the capability to modify a shared document or whiteboard together.

❑ *E-mail and Instant Messaging* — Email systems for groupware are integrated with other applications so that notifications can be sent by the system to inform users of new publications, uploaded documents, events, and so on.

❑ *Event calendars/time management* — Event calendars can be used to coordinate resources, both physical and virtual. For example, an actual conference room or virtual chat room can be reserved for a weekly meeting. Time management is also possible, since under some groupware solutions, users will spend most of their work time within the application.

❑ *Project management systems* — Some applications include complete project management capabilities that allow online tracking of a project, management of resources and people, construction of milestone and critical path charts, and other management features.

❑ *Workflow systems* — These allow for the guiding of a project through a knowledge-based business process. With a workflow system, when a user signals to the system that a stage is complete, the documents or information for the project are automatically routed to the people responsible for the next stage.

❑ *Knowledge management systems* — The systems collect, organize, manage, and share various forms of information.

❑ *Extranet systems coordination* — A project, once complete, may be published or shared through an extranet with an outside organization or system. For example, architectural groupware may automatically share a project's construction plans with the outside contractor as various aspects of the plans are complete.

Some CMS systems are chosen for their groupware functionality. Groupware allows users to share documents (such as budget spreadsheets or presentation files), to communicate through the system (using forums, system email, and so on), and to track changes to these documents on the system. Organizations (especially those with geographically disparate employees) have seen incredible productivity increases when they employ a groupware solution.

Joomla offers many of the groupware features through individual extensions, but the lack of integration of these tools makes it very difficult to use Joomla for collaborative tasks. In fact, attempting to use Joomla for groupware would be inadvisable in most cases, because groupware requires very robust security arrangements, which Joomla lacks.

Portal Capabilities

CMS sites are most often a powerful way to present a version of an online newspaper or periodical. However, many CMS systems are used as a Web portal that provides single-point access for instantaneous information (stock prices, breaking headlines, weather, and so on), Internet-based applications (Web-based email, online mapping, photo galleries, and so on), personal Web page configuration, and commerce (auctions, classifieds, yellow pages, and so on).

Generally, when users access a portal, they will stay within the portal site for the duration of their activities. Visitors to the Yahoo! portal such as the one shown in Figure 15-2 might monitor stock prices, check their email, listen to an online radio show, read the latest news, browse the personal ads, and download music in one site stopover. Once logged in to the system, the user's information (personal and financial) can be used for any of the online applications of the portal without a separate login or configuration.

Figure 15-2: Yahoo provides a full range of portal services that can be used without leaving the site.

Here are some of the most common integrated features offered through a portal, and suggestions on how Joomla may be configured to provide the functionality:

❑ *Web search capabilities* — The most popular portals are the ones hosted by search engines such as Google and Yahoo! However, most portals provide some form of Web searches, even if the search technology is provided by another company. You can add this technology for free to your Joomla site through the Google Custom Search Engine (`http://bizsolutions.google.com/services`) program. It allows you to create both a site search and a Web search form that can be integrated into the look and feel of your site.

❑ *Email accounts* — Most portals offer Web-based email and provide an amount of online storage for mail or remote files. While Joomla has many Private Message System (PMS) extensions and ships a primitive PMS with the default installation, hosting an actual email server is beyond the capabilities of Joomla.

❑ *Maps* — A popular portal service is the ability to access maps and directions to a particular destination. You can develop a custom Joomla solution to access the Google Maps API (`www.google.com/apis/maps`), or you can look in the Joomla Extensions directory for one of several Google Map wrapper extensions (such as Plug-in Googlemaps, Geo Visitors, and Google Maps API).

❑ *Personal Web page* — Very popular on sites, such as MySpace and Friendster, having the capability for users to create their own Web page within your portal can help create homesteaders out of your visitors. The commercial component Ravenswood User Home Pages allows user Web page creation or "mini-sites" that are managed within the Joomla environment.

❑ *Classified and personal ads* — On the Joomla Extensions directory, you will find a number of classified ad extensions, including the well-reviewed AdsManager.

❑ *Job search* — On the Joomla Extensions directory, you will find a number of job search extensions, including the well-reviewed Jobline.

❑ *Travel information* — Although there are many specialized sites for travel such as `Expedia.com`, portals are gaining a growing slice of the online travel pie. Featuring travel guides, flight bookings, cruise specials, vacation packages, and car rental discounts, portals are becoming a trusted source for setting up travel plans, as well as performing what-if exploration into travel options. The Joomledia extension allows a Joomla site to access the Expedia affiliate program.

❑ *Directories (white pages/yellow pages)* — Often, portals will provide phone reference information from white and yellow page directories. You can provide white pages listings on your site through the `WhitePages.com` Affiliate Program (`https://affiliates.whitepages.com`). There are also a number of Joomla components for constructing your own yellow pagelike directories (such as Sigsiu Online Business Index and JAddresses).

❑ *Financial information* — Stock market and other financial information are staples of portals that generally provide near real-time information, often with a time lag of only 15 minutes. Joomla has extensions such as the Mortgage Rates Module that displays current rates such as the Freddie Mac National Averages for the 30-Year Fixed-Rate Mortgage (FRM), 15-Year FRM, and 1-Year Adjustable-Rate Mortgage (ARM).

❑ *Games* — Portals generally offer some method of playing online multiplayer games. Web-based games generally consume very few server resources, and yet have visitors online for hours, during which time banners can be displayed regularly. Nonviolent multiplayer games are also incredibly popular with the 18–39 female demographic, if that is the target market of your Web site. The Playgames extension is a Joomla component that wraps the German Play.de for free access to multiuser and casino-type games.

❑ *Music and media downloads* — With the explosive growth of YouTube.com, many portals are beginning to allow the uploading of music, video, and other media. This type of service is extremely bandwidth and server resource intensive, and not recommended for Joomla-based sites. However, the AllVideos plug-in for Joomla does allow streaming of audio and video content for an all-in-one media solution if that fits your needs.

❑ *Sports information* — The displaying of sports scores and current match-ups is a very popular feature of many portals. Joomla has a number of modules that can host a basic score display.

❑ *Weather* — Portals generally have the geographic location of registered users and provide simple weather forecasts for the user. There are excellent Joomla extensions to present this information including JVTempo Easy Weather, Weathermaster, and Z Weather.

While the Joomla extensions can add most of the portal features to Joomla, effective management of a portal requires a unified, consistent, and integrated administration system. The presentation of each part should be consistent and easy to modify. Joomla lacks the integration that would make it a valid choice for portal construction and deployment.

Summary

Although Joomla is a phenomenal application, it is not the perfect solution for all CMS needs. This chapter has provided an overview of the shortcomings of Joomla that include the following:

❑ Lack of document version control and workflow tools to allow medium to large document collaboration.

❑ Nonexistent import, export, and bulk document handling.

❑ Limited security and authentication features that, although they can be augmented by third-party extensions, need to be incorporated into the Joomla core for true security protection.

❑ Load balancing and replication only offered at the Web server level (not through Joomla), making custom load management difficult. A lack of integrated replication (MySQL could perform dumb replication without Joomla's knowledge) means that running a large multi-server cluster of Joomla servers is not recommended.

❑ Substantial limitations in terms of user interface levels and no capability to allow user selection of a custom site skin.

❑ Little integration of groupware features means hosting online collaboration is not easy, attractive, user-friendly, or administrator-friendly.

❑ Few portal capabilities such as personal Web pages, social markers, and other hallmarks of portal hosting that are available from other CMS products.

Up to this point in the book, you've learned about almost every aspect of the Joomla system. Chapter 16 provides a survey of popular Web sites that are powered by the Joomla CMS. Visiting these pages can be instructive because you can see the deployment choices and extensions that have been chosen by popular sites.

16

Spotlight on Successful Joomla! Sites

The Joomla CMS has been successful in supporting topic areas as diverse as property management to children's television. Because the Joomla community is so varied, it is sometimes difficult to know where to begin when studying peer sites to better your own. This chapter provides a window into many successful Joomla sites. Visiting these sites will help generate new ideas for layout and functionality.

Each site spotlighted in this chapter is evaluated in terms of its use of Joomla technology, including the extensions used on the site, the Internet service provider (ISP) that is hosting the site, the template used by the site, the virtual community and e-commerce features, and more. I have also tried to ensure that each site has been around for at least two years because that makes it more likely the site will continue to exist.

Web sites included in the survey had the following characteristics:

❑ *Significant presence among the community to which the site caters* — The site must feature a decent amount of content that has been updated at least semi-recently, so "ghost sites" were avoided. As a rough guide, I tried to pick sites with a Google page ranking of 5 or above.

❑ *Clean use of the Joomla interface and professional design* — With the widespread availability of both free and commercial templates, a Joomla site has little reason to look shabby.

❑ *Adoption of one or more Joomla extensions to supplement site functionality* — Visiting these sites allows a developer to see some of the Joomla add-on technology in action.

Selecting sites by these criteria stopped me from including those that, while popular, were poorly designed, and other sites that had amazing presentations, but had little or no content. As the constellation of Joomla sites has grown on the Internet, selecting a few sites among the masses is difficult. However, the sites spotlighted in this chapter show the versatility of the Joomla CMS and the pervasive adoption of Joomla by every type of Web master.

I have only included English sites in this list. Unfortunately, I only speak two languages (and the second poorly), so I felt that I couldn't effectively evaluate and summarize non-English Web sites. However, there are obviously many, many excellent international Web sites (such as www.iearn.cat*), and I urge you to check out the Joomla Powered Sites section (*www.joomla.org/content/blogcategory/35/69*) of the main Joomla site for excellent sites in every language.*

Academic Sites

There are numerous academic sites that have embraced Joomla. Beyond the exceptional CMS capabilities of Joomla, universities around the world have embraced and promoted the use of open source software. Students are some of the most prolific developers of extensions and add-ons for a variety of open source systems.

Princeton Molecular Biology Department

The Princeton University Molecular Biology Department computer support site (see Figure 16-1) features not only traditional information in the form of FAQs, it also maintains general interest stories on design and genetic breakthroughs.

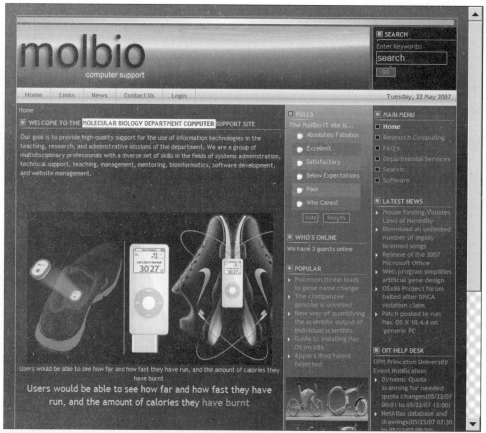

Figure 16-1: The Princeton Molecular Biology Department site provides computer support.

❑ *URL* — `http://mol-lamp.princeton.edu/joomla`

❑ *Started* — 2004

❑ *Owned by* — Princeton

❑ *Google Page Ranking* — 3/10

❑ *Affiliate programs* — None

❑ *Extensions used* — `com_expose`, Poll, google-analytics

❑ *Web feed* — None

❑ *Template* — `rhuk_planetfall`

❑ *Search-engine-friendly URLs* — No

❑ *Breadcrumbs* — Yes

❑ *Top sections* — Research Computing, FAQs, Departmental Services, Search, and Software

❑ *Default width* — 800

❑ *E-commerce* — No

❑ *Community features* — No

Shakespeare Birthplace Trust .

The Shakespeare Birthplace Trust site (see Figure 16-2) represents the charity that owns and cares for the five Shakespeare Houses and the Harvard House. The site also promotes the works of Shakespeare around the world. If you're going to visit Stratford-upon-Avon, this site is a must-visit.

Figure 16-2: Shakespeare Birthplace Trust

- ❏ *URL* — www.shakespeare.org.uk/index.php
- ❏ *Started* — 2004
- ❏ *Owned by* — Shakespeare Birthplace Trust educational charity
- ❏ *Google page ranking* — 6/10
- ❏ *Affiliate programs* — None
- ❏ *Extensions used* — com_virtuemart, Mambomap
- ❏ *Web feed* — None
- ❏ *Template* — Custom

❏ *Search-engine-friendly URLs* — Yes

❏ *Breadcrumbs* — No

❏ *Top sections* — William Shakespeare, Online Shopping, Activities and Events, Outdoor Plays, Lunchtime and Evening Lectures, Family Events, Children's Activities, The Stratford-upon-Avon Poetry Festival, Library & Archives, Education, Museums, Supporting Us

❏ *Default width* — 800

❏ *E-commerce* — Yes

❏ *Community features* — No

Journal of Intercultural and Interdisciplinary Archaeology

This is the host site (see Figure 16-3) of the periodical archaeological publication *Journal of Intercultural and Interdisciplinary Archaeology* (JIIA). Each issue of the *Journal* has the privilege of being placed in the National Library online catalogues of several countries.

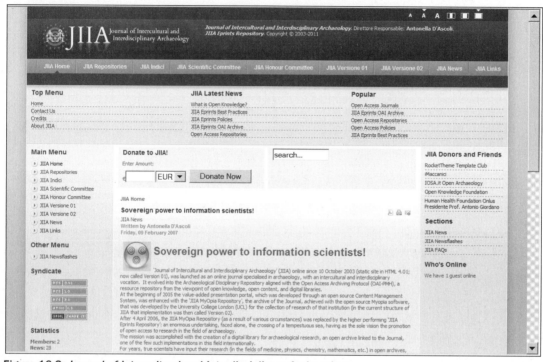

Figure 16-3: *Journal of Intercultural and Interdisciplinary Archaeology*

- □   *URL* — www.jiia.it
- □   *Started* — 2003
- □   *Owned by* — *Journal of Intercultural and Interdisciplinary Archaeology*
- □   *Google page ranking* — 5/10
- □   *Affiliate programs* — Google AdSense
- □   *Extensions used* — Contact, RSS, PayPal
- □   *Web feed* — RSS
- □   *Template* — Rockettheme.com Versatility II template
- □   *Search-engine-friendly URLs* — No
- □   *Breadcrumbs* — Yes

❑   *Top sections* — JIIA Repositories, JIIA Indici, JIIA Scientific Committee, JIIA Honour Committee, JIIA Versione 01, JIIA Versione 02, JIIA News, JIIA Links

❑   *Default width* — Full

❑   *E-commerce* — Yes

❑   *Community features* — No

Graphic User Interactive Learning and Development (GUILD)

The Graphic User Interactive Learning and Development (GUILD) site (see Figure 16-4) aids in multimedia training for the career development of students and industry professionals.

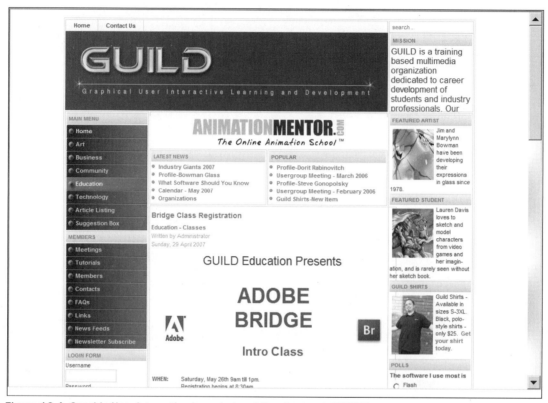

Figure 16-4: Graphic User Interactive Learning and Development (GUILD)

- ❏ *URL* — `http://mguildonline.com`
- ❏ *Owned by* — Graphic User Interactive Learning and Development
- ❏ *Google page ranking* — 5/10
- ❏ *Extensions used* — Ajax Shoutbox, RSS, Contact, `com_extcalendar`, Banners, Poll,
- ❏ *Web feed* — RSS & Atom
- ❏ *Template* — ddj005
- ❏ *Search-engine-friendly URLs* — Yes
- ❏ *Breadcrumbs* — No

- ❏ *Top sections* — Student Profiles, Artist Profiles, Jobs, Interviews, Organizations, Community News, Classes, Teachers Group, Gaming News, In My Opinion, Technology News
- ❏ *Default width* — 800
- ❏ *E-commerce* — No
- ❏ *Community features* — No

Virgin Islands Department of Education

This site includes resources from the Virgin Islands Department of Education (VIDE), which include parent-teacher forums, event calendars, surveys, and articles about all aspects of education (see Figure 16-5).

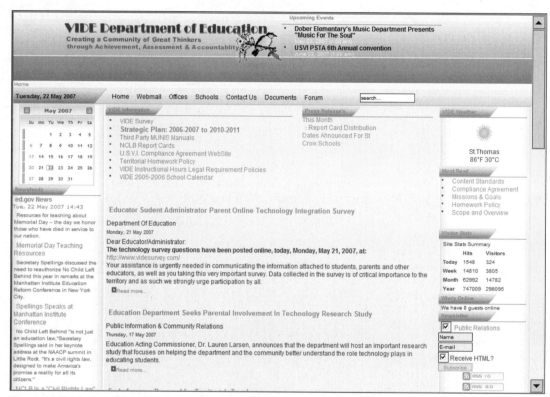

Figure 16-5: Virgin Islands Department of Education

❏ *URL* — www.doe.vi

❏ *Started* — 2004

❏ *Owned by* — United States Virgin Islands Department of Education

❏ *Google page ranking* — 5/10

❏ *Affiliate programs* — None

❏ *Extensions used* — RSS, JCalPro, com_acajoom, bsq_sss_ssscom_table, Fireboard

❏ *Web feed* — RSS & Atom

❏ *Template* — vide-blue

❏ *Search-engine-friendly URLs* — Yes

❏ *Breadcrumbs* — No

❑   *Top sections* — Parent Teacher Student Association , VIDE Report Cards, Federal Grants, ERP Munis Training, Parent/Teacher Corner, Debates in Education, Special Educational Needs, Learning Outside School, E-Learning, Health and Social Care,

❑   *Default width* — Full

❑   *E-commerce* — No

❑   *Community features* — Yes

Family/Health Sites

The ease of installation and setup of Joomla makes it perfect for people who are very technically savvy, as well as those who only have a basic grasp of how Web sites work. The low barrier to entry has resulted in a large number of family- and health-oriented Web sites springing up around the world.

SeniorNet

Celebrating its 20th year online, SeniorNet of Puget Sound (see Figure 16-6) is an all-volunteer organization with a mission to establish and operate a Learning Center for basic computer education for seniors age 50 or older.

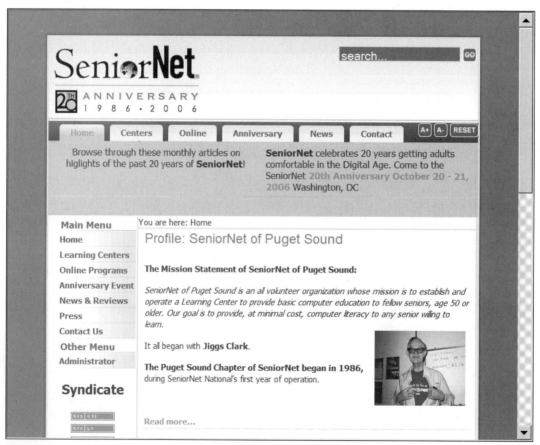

Figure 16-6: SeniorNet — seniors teaching technology to seniors

- ❑ *URL* — http://seniornet2007.org
- ❑ *Started* — 1986
- ❑ *Owned by* — SeniorNet Puget Sound

- *Google page ranking* — 4/10
- *Affiliate programs* — n/a
- *Extensions used* — RSS, Contact
- *Host*: eNom, Inc. (www.enom.com)
- *Web feed* — RSS & Atom
- *Template* — Custom
- *Search-engine-friendly URLs* — No
- *Breadcrumbs* — Yes
- *Top sections* — Learning Centers, Online Programs, Anniversary Event, News & Reviews, Press, Contact Us
- *Default width* — 800
- *E-commerce* — No
- *Community features* — No

KidsCHANNEL

KidsCHANNEL (see Figure 16-7) is Canadian portal that offers games, activities, lessons, articles, and the most comprehensive Yellow Page style directory of children's resources by province, region, and city.

Figure 16-7: KidsCHANNEL

❑ *URL* — http://kidschannel.ca

❑ *Started* — 2005

❑ *Owned by* — Kids Channel

❑ *Google page ranking* — 4/10

❑ *Affiliate programs* — Google AdSense, Futura Rewards, Feedpark, Link Exchange

❑ *Extensions used* — fisheye_menu module, com_mtree, RSS

❑ *Host* — My Real EBiz

❑ *Web feed* — RSS & Atom

❑ *Template* — Custom

❑ *Search-engine-friendly URLs* — Yes

❑ *Breadcrumbs* — No

❑ *Top sections* — Just for Kids, More Just for Kids

❑ *Default width* — 800

❑ *E-commerce* — No

❑ *Community features* — Resource Guide

A Story for Bedtime

This is a community sharing site for parents and children that hosts MP3 audio files of bedtime stories to play to the kids (see Figure 16-8). Registration provides access to the children's-story-focused forums and message boards.

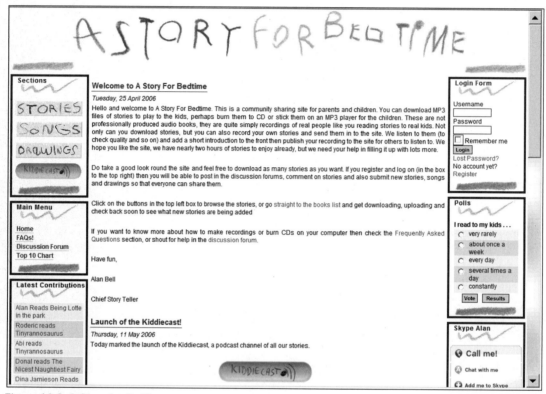

Figure 16-8: A Story for Bedtime

❑   *URL* — www.astoryforbedtime.com

❑   *Started* — 2005

❑   *Google page ranking* — 5/10

❑   *Affiliate programs* — Google AdSense

❑   *Extensions used* — Remository, Pony Gallery, Simple Board, Graphitory, Poll, Chat, Skype

❑   *Web feed* — RSS Podcast

❑   *Template* — Custom

❑   *Search-engine-friendly URLs* — No

❑   *Breadcrumbs* — No

❏   *Top sections* — FAQs!, Discussion Forum, Top 10 Chart

❏   *Default width* — Full

❏   *E-commerce* — No

❏   *Community features* — Yes

Second Wives Club

This site focuses on the "sisterhood for stepmoms" and includes forums, a weekly newsletter, legal information, and more in relation to stepfamilies, remarriage, and ex-wives (see Figure 16-9).

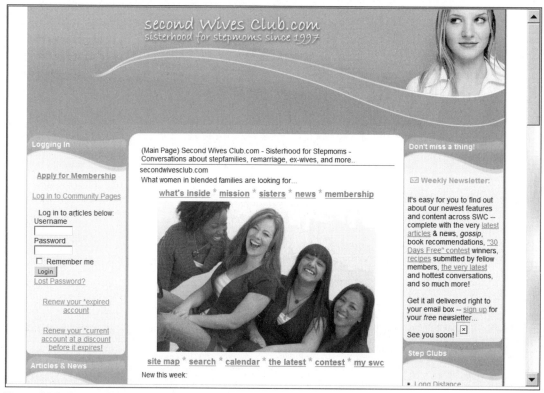

Figure 16-9: Second Wives Club.com

- ❏ *URL* — www.secondwivesclub.com/portal
- ❏ *Started* — 1997
- ❏ *Owned by* — Secondwivesclub.com
- ❏ *Google page ranking* — 4/10
- ❏ *Affiliate programs* — Google AdSense
- ❏ *Extensions used* — pcajaxcomment, jomcomment, com_magazine, Contact, com_recommend, com_weblinks, Joomap, mod_smo_ajax_shoutbox_css.php,
- ❏ *Web feed* — RSS & Atom
- ❏ *Template* — Custom
- ❏ *Search-engine-friendly URLs* — Yes

❑ *Breadcrumbs* — No

❑ *Top sections* — And Baby Makes..., Alimony, Book Reviews, Child Support, Christian Stepfamilies, Collaborative Law, Co-parenting, Custody, Divorce, Divorced Dads, eCourses, Ex-Files, Family Law, Infidelity, Money, Parental Alienation, Relationships, Remarriage, Starting Over, Again, Stepfamilies, Stepparenting, Stress Management, Visitation, Weddings, Wives Of Widowers, Wonderful — Not Wicked

❑ *Default width* — 800

❑ *E-commerce* — Yes

❑ *Community features* — Yes

Better Health Here

This is a diabetes site that provides a wellness program, including on-site specialists, a self-management program, insurance advice, diabetes test kits, and home delivery of a variety of diabetes supplies (see Figure 16-10).

Figure 16-10: Better Health Here

- ❑ *URL* — www.betterhealthhere.com
- ❑ *Started* — 2005
- ❑ *Owned by* — BetterHealthHere
- ❑ *Google page ranking* — 4/10
- ❑ *Affiliate programs* — n/a
- ❑ *Extensions used* — Virtuemart, AkoForms, com_magazine, com_registration, poll, tabnews, Contact, Joomap

- ❏ *Web feed* — No
- ❏ *Template* — `md_digitalether`, Transmenu powered by JoomlArt.com
- ❏ *Search-engine-friendly URLs* — No
- ❏ *Breadcrumbs* — Yes
- ❏ *Top sections* — All About Diabetes, Manage Diabetes, Buy Diabetes Sample, Ask an Expert
- ❏ *Default width* — 800
- ❏ *E-commerce* — Yes
- ❏ *Community features* — Yes

Professional Sites

Professional Web sites are focused on commercial ventures or career topics. There are a great number of professional Web sites in the technology field, but only Joomla has numerous sites that cross over a wide variety of nontechnical pursuits.

World Cup 2010 South Africa

This site provides information and news relating to the World Cup 2010 from South Africa (see Figure 16-11). Data updated frequently includes articles relating to travel and World Cup ticket availability.

Figure 16-11: World Cup 2010 South Africa

- ❑ *URL* — www.worldcup2010southafrica.com
- ❑ *Started* — 2006
- ❑ *Owned by* — World Cup 2010 South Africa
- ❑ *Google page ranking* — 5/10
- ❑ *Affiliate programs* — Google AdSense, Shopzilla.co.uk, Cybercapetown.com, 888 Casino

- ❑ *Extensions used* — RSS, Joomap, Sobi2, Contact, Poll

- ❑ *Web feed* — RSS

- ❑ *Template* — jw_inetgazette

- ❑ *Search-engine-friendly URLs* — Yes

- ❑ *Breadcrumbs* — No

- ❑ *Top sections* — World Cup Tickets, World Cup 2006, Stadiums (Cape Town, Durban, Johannesburg, Nelspruit, Rustenburg, Pretoria, Polokwane, Port Elizabeth, Bloemfontein), Directory

- ❑ *Default width* — 1024

- ❑ *E-commerce* — No

- ❑ *Community features* — No

Best Association Resources and Tools

These are community Web sites that feature resources for association membership development, member benefits, event marketing, event registration, meeting planning, non-dues revenue, member retention, government affairs, and association jobs (see Figure 16-12).

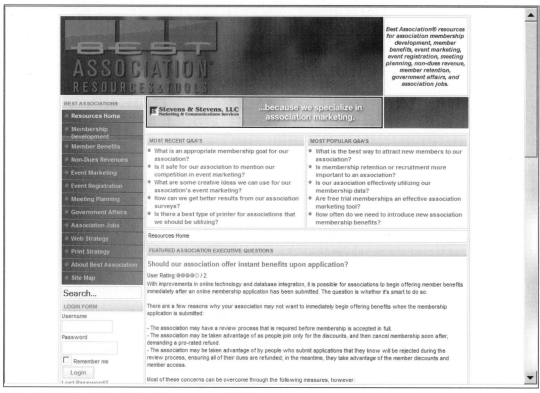

Figure 16-12: Best Association Resources and Tools

❏ *URL* — www.bestassociation.com

❏ *Started* — 2006

❏ *Owned by* — Best Association Resources

❏ *Google page ranking* — 6/10

❏ *Extensions used* — Banners, Joomap, AkoComment, Security Image

❏ *Web feed* — RSS, Atom, and OPML

❏ *Template* — rhuk_solarflare_ii

❏ *Search-engine-friendly URLs* — Yes

❏ *Breadcrumbs* — Yes

- ❑ *Top sections* — Resources Home, Membership Development, Member Benefits, Non-Dues Revenues, Event Marketing, Event Registration, Meeting Planning, Government Affairs, Association Jobs, Web Strategy, Print Strategy, About Best Association, Site Map

- ❑ *Default width* — 800

- ❑ *E-commerce* — No

- ❑ *Community features* — Yes

Randall Wood Travel Writing Site

This site (see Figure 16-13) focuses on the travel writings of Randall Wood, who is currently working with National Geographic Society on its World Heritage Survey (which attempts to analyze the world's most valuable cultural and environmental sites).

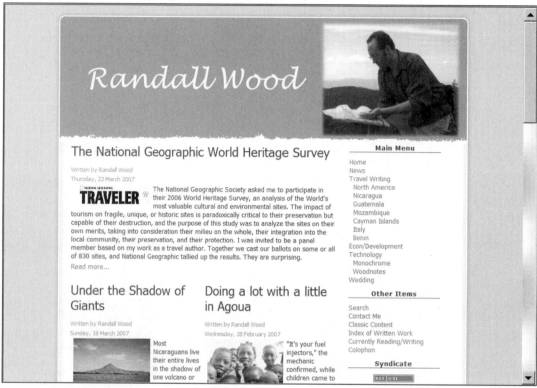

Figure 16-13: Randall Wood travel writing site

❑ *URL* — www.therandymon.com

❑ *Started* — 2003

❑ *Owned by* — Randall Wood

❑ *Google page ranking* — 5/10

❑ *Affiliate programs* — None

❑ *Extensions used* — ds-syndicate

❑ *Web feed* — RSS, Atom, and OPML

❑ *Template* — ms_thinking_green

❑ *Search-engine-friendly URLs* — Yes

- ❑ *Breadcrumbs* — No
- ❑ *Top sections* — Home, News, Travel Writing, North America, Nicaragua, Guatemala, Mozambique, Cayman Islands, Italy, Benin, Econ/Development, Technology, Monochrome, Woodnotes, Wedding
- ❑ *Default width* — 800
- ❑ *E-commerce* — No
- ❑ *Community features* — No

Turbo Trade

This site features an online trading company that offers extremely low per-trade fees (see Figure 16-14). It offers a variety of financial services, including equities, options, currency, and global futures.

Figure 16-14: Turbo Trade

- ❑ *URL* — www.turbotrade.com
- ❑ *Started* — 2005
- ❑ *Owned by* — MMVI TurboTrade Financial, Ltd
- ❑ *Google page ranking* — 5/10
- ❑ *Affiliate programs* — Google AdSense
- ❑ *Extensions used* — com_facileforms, com_contact
- ❑ *Web feed* — No
- ❑ *Template* — Custom
- ❑ *Search-engine-friendly URLs* — Yes

- *Breadcrumbs* — Yes
- *Top sections* — Equities/Options, Forex/Currency, Global Futures, Services, Open an Account, Why TurboTrade, FAQs
- *Default width* — 800
- *E-commerce* — Yes
- *Community features* — No

Sonnetto

This is a real estate site that focuses on property in North Cyprus (see Figure 16-15).

Figure 16-15: Sonnetto

- ❏ *URL* — www.sonnetto.com
- ❏ *Started* — 2006
- ❏ *Owned by* — North Cyprus Property
- ❏ *Google page ranking* — 5/10
- ❏ *Affiliate programs* — Google AdSense
- ❏ *Extensions used* — com_hotproperty, poll, contact, joomap
- ❏ *Web feed* — No
- ❏ *Template* — Custom
- ❏ *Search-engine-friendly URLs* — Yes

❑   *Breadcrumbs* — Yes

❑   *Top sections* — North Cyprus, Travel guide, Bogaz, Kyrenia, Famagusta, Cyprus holidays, Property Title, Expats Living in Cyprus

❑   *Default width* — 800

❑   *E-commerce* — No

❑   *Community features* — No

John Avon Illustration

This is a Web site of a professional illustrator who has created images that have graced the covers of books by authors including Steven King, Terry Pratchett, and Arthur C. Clark (see Figure 16-16). He has produced more than 200 paintings for the collectable trading card game Magic the Gathering in cooperation with Wizards of the Coast.

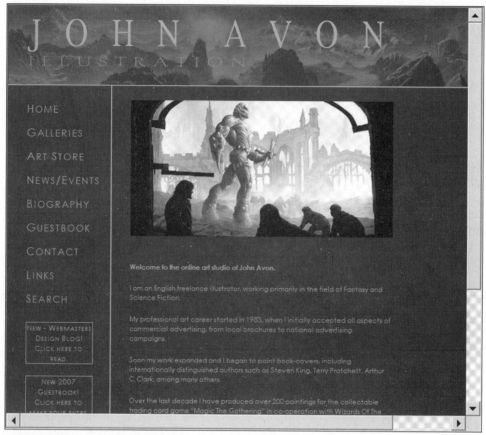

Figure 16-16: John Avon Illustration

- ❏   *URL* — www.johnavon.com/index.php
- ❏   *Started* — 2006
- ❏   *Owned by* — John Avon
- ❏   *Google page ranking* — /10
- ❏   *Affiliate programs* — No
- ❏   *Extensions used* — Pony Gallery, EZ Store, Easy Guestbook, Contact,
- ❏   *Web feed* — RSS & Atom

- ❑ *Template* — Custom
- ❑ *Search-engine-friendly URLs* — No
- ❑ *Breadcrumbs* — No
- ❑ *Top sections* — Galleries, Art Store, News/Events, Biography, Guestbook, Contact, and Links
- ❑ *Default width* — 1024
- ❑ *E-commerce* — Yes
- ❑ *Community features* — Yes

Media (News, Magazines, and so on) Sites

As a content management system, Joomla is custom-made to host all sorts of media. In fact, the number of musical sites that Joomla hosts is legion, although they haven't been included here because of their generally low Google page ranking (those sites are more of a cottage phenomenon). Here you will find online magazines, information resources, and even a very popular satirical newspaper.

MainSPOT.NET

This site is devoted to automobiles and motorcycles, and includes a great amount of diagnostic information for poorly operating motor vehicles (see Figure 16-17). It also gathers a number of auto-related news-feeds for the latest car information.

Figure 16-17: MainSPOT.NET

❑   *URL* — www.mainspot.net

❑   *Started* — 2005

❑   *Owned by* — MainSpot.NET. Automotive Resource and Car Care

❏   *Google page ranking* — 5/10

❏   *Affiliate programs* — Google AdSense

❏   *Extensions used* — Joomap, Simple Machines Forum, Newsfeeds, Contact, Poll, RSS

❏   *Web feed* — RSS

❏   *Template* — Custom

❏   *Search-engine-friendly URLs* — Yes

❏   *Breadcrumbs* — No

❏   *Top sections* — Car Technical Data, Automotive Tips, Headlines

❏   *Default width* — Full

❏   *E-commerce* — No

❏   *Community features* — Yes

PanNatural Environmental News Source

This is a central portal site similar to a Drudge Report, but it focuses on the environment instead of politics (see Figure 16-18). It also hosts the blogs of more than a dozen environmental activists.

Figure 16-18: PanNatural Environmental news source

- ❏   *URL* — www.pannatural.org
- ❏   *Google page ranking* — 4/10
- ❏   *Affiliate programs* — Google AdSense
- ❏   *Extensions used* — Feedgator
- ❏   *Web feed* — RSS, Atom, OPML
- ❏   *Template* — News_rh+
- ❏   *Search-engine-friendly URLs* — Yes
- ❏   *Breadcrumbs* — No

❏ *Top sections* — Eco Lifestyle Treehugger, Lime, Sustainable Style, Hippyshopper, Eco Worrier, Ecorazzi, Hugg, Inhabitat, New Consumer, Greener Magazine, Green Options, Personal Blogs The Conscious Earth, Strat. for Sustainability, Greenthinkers, Green Trust, Clean Break, Pract. Environmentalist, Triple Pundit, Eco-Enterpreneur, Sustainablog, Joel Makower, EcoSherpa, Eco Street, The Future Is Green, Enviroblog, The Green Guy, Green LA Girl, The Green Side, People Tree, Recycle Chat, It's Getting Hot in Here, Ivan Enviroman, Earth Architecture, Minding the Planet, The Green Geek, The Hip and Zen Pen, GreatGreenGoods, Urban Eco, The Ecologist Blog, SusHI, Celsias

❏ *Default width* — 1024

❏ *E-commerce* — No

❏ *Community features* — No

United Nations Regional Information Centre for Western Europe

The United Nations Regional Information Centre for Western Europe (UNRIC) hosts a magazine (see Figure 16-19) that is devoted to providing information on educational and environmental issues. The UNU recently participated in the World Summit on the Information Society.

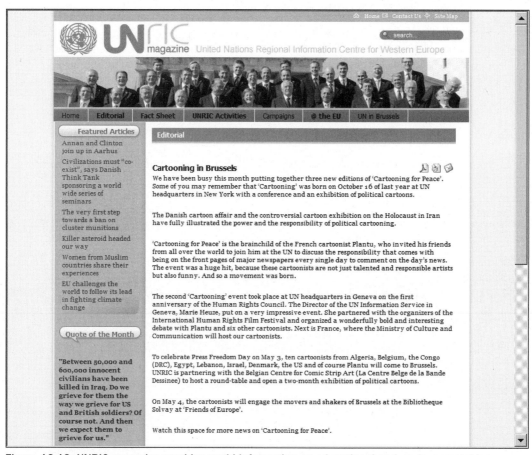

Figure 16-19: UNRIC magazine provides world information on educational and environmental issues.

- ❑ *URL* — www.unric.org
- ❑ *Started* — 2006
- ❑ *Owned by* — United Nations
- ❑ *Google Page Ranking* — 6/10
- ❑ *Affiliate programs* — None

❑ *Extensions used* — Joom!Fish, Joomap, Contacts, iJoomla Magazine, Flash, `com_extcalendar`, `com_artbanners`

❑ *Web feed* — RSS

❑ *Template* — `RocketTheme!`

❑ *Search-engine-friendly URLs* — Yes

❑ *Breadcrumbs* — No

❑ *Top sections* — UN in Brussels, UN and the EU, UNRIC Magazine, UK & Ireland and the UN, UNRIC Library Newsletter, UN Associations, Multimedia Resources, Guest Columnist, Observances, 10 Stories: Somalia, Book Review, UN-Appointments, Goodwill Ambassadors, Back in Time, Friends of the UN, What our interns say, Who we are at UNRIC, UNRIC Library, Cartooning for Peace, Join the discussion, and Previous issues

❑ *Default width* — 800

❑ *E-commerce* — No

❑ *Community features* — No

HCJB Global

This is an evangelist site (see Figure 16-20) that focuses on "empowering dynamic media and health-care ministries." It includes a monthly newsletter *Truth in Motion* and hosts the blogs of several industry professionals.

Figure 16-20: HCJB Global

- ❑ *URL* — www.hcjb.org
- ❑ *Started* — 2001
- ❑ *Owned by* — World Radio Missionary Fellows
- ❑ *Google page ranking* — 5/10
- ❑ *Affiliate programs* — None
- ❑ *Extensions used* — com_jomcomment, com_linktrack, *iJoomla Magazine*
- ❑ *Web feed* — RSS

- ❏ *Template* — Custom
- ❏ *Search-engine-friendly URLs* — Yes
- ❏ *Breadcrumbs* — Yes
- ❏ *Top sections* — Mass Media, Healthcare, Education, Getting Involved, Download Now, Worldwide, Downloads
- ❏ *Default width* — 800
- ❏ *E-commerce* — Yes
- ❏ *Community features* — No

Asiaing.com

This is a portal that focuses on books, magazines, newspapers, and other documents that relate to technology's use in the commerce sector (see Figure 16-21).

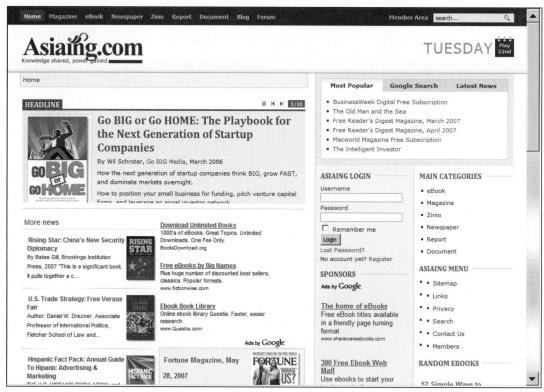

Figure 16-21: Asiaing.com

❑   *URL* — www.asiaing.com

❑   *Started* — 2005

❑   *Owned by* — Asiaing.com

❑   *Google page ranking* — 5/10

❑   *Affiliate programs* — Google AdSense

❑   *Extensions used* — Newsportal, Fireboard, Community Builder, RSS

❑   *Web feed* — RSS

❑   *Template* — ja_teline

❑   *Search-engine-friendly URLs* — Yes

❑   *Breadcrumbs* — Yes

❑ *Top sections* — Magazine, eBook, Newspaper, Zinio, Report, Document, Blog, Forum, Member, Area

❑ *Default width* — 1024

❑ *E-commerce* — No

❑ *Community features* — Yes

The Chaser

The Chaser is a satirical news site that features a comedic look at most of the day's current events (see Figure 16-22). It includes a number of feature columns.

Figure 16-22: The Chaser

- ❏ *URL* — www.chaser.com.au
- ❏ *Started* — 2006
- ❏ *Owned by* — Chaser Publishing
- ❏ *Google page ranking* — 5/10
- ❏ *Extensions used* — com_artbanners, Simple Machines Forum, RSS, Virturemart, com_performs, com_jombok, com_blastchatc, com_acajoom, Poll, GigCal,
- ❏ *Web feed* — RSS, Atom, and OPML
- ❏ *Template* — Rocket Theme versatility_ii_sienna
- ❏ *Search-engine-friendly URLs* — Yes
- ❏ *Breadcrumbs* — No

❑ *Top sections* — Hansen Online, NewsJunkie, Cubisia, Gregor, Tim Brunero, Charles Firth's Postcards, Dominic Knight

❑ *Default width* — 800

❑ *E-commerce* — Yes

❑ *Community features* — Yes

Creative Guy Publishing

This is the site of a cottage publisher of alternative forms of literature (see Figure 16-23). This is primarily a publisher of the novella form, in ebook, chapbook, and audiobook formats. It also publishes in trade paperback format, including an annual anthology of humorous speculative fiction called the *Amityville House of Pancakes*.

Figure 16-23: Creative Guy Publishing

- ❑ *URL* — www.creativeguypublishing.com
- ❑ *Started* — 2003
- ❑ *Owned by* — Creative Guy Publishing
- ❑ *Google page ranking* — 4/10
- ❑ *Affiliate programs* — Amazon, Books-a-million
- ❑ *Extensions used* — Newsfeeds, RSS, Banners, Poll

- ❑ *Web feed* — RSS, Atom, and OPML

- ❑ *Template* — `mcportal`

- ❑ *Search-engine-friendly URLs* — No

- ❑ *Breadcrumbs* — No

- ❑ *Top sections* — About the Books, Books - Catalogue, CGP Blog, Reviews, Author News, Authors, Liaison Press, Press Releases, Contact Us, Submissions

- ❑ *Default width* — Full

- ❑ *E-commerce* — No

- ❑ *Community features* — No

Hobbyist Sites

Hobbyist Web sites that were popular on the Web were the most difficult to find. Joomla seems to be *the* Web software for niche interest sites, but few of them gain more than their core audiences. The following sites (even some that are geographically specific) have generated a substantial amount of interest in the Web community.

Success and Sport (S.A.S.)

This is a Community Interest Company that support sports projects across Sussex, England (see Figure 16-24). It includes an online magazine, forum, local sports directory, and local business directory.

Figure 16-24: Success and Sport (S.A.S.)

- ❑ *URL* — http://sassussex.com
- ❑ *Started* — 2005
- ❑ *Owned by* — Sussex Academy of Sport & IVARX

❑ *Google page ranking* — 5/10

❑ *Affiliate programs* — Google AdSense

❑ *Extensions used* — Digg, RSS, Sobi2, `com_linx`, Virtuemart, Joomap, `com_fpslideshow`, `com_facileforms`, PHPBB

❑ *Web feed* — RSS & Atom

❑ *Template* — `jj_absolute`

❑ *Search-engine-friendly URLs* — No

❑ *Breadcrumbs* — Yes

❑ *Top sections* — About SASSussex, Who's Who, What We Do, Membership, SAS Testimonials, The UK Entertainer Mag, The UK Entertainer - Download, Media Pack , Rates , Sussex Business Directory, Sussex Sports Directory, SASSussex Web Links, Forum , Store, Magazine Advertising, Website Advertising, SAS Membership, Donations, Savers Hand Book

❑ *Default width* — 800

❑ *E-commerce* — Yes

Safari Ventures

This is a company site that offers safari adventures around the globe (see Figure 16-25). The site aids in trip planning, geographic selection, value tours, corporate tours, and group tours.

Figure 16-25: Safari Ventures

- ❑ *URL* — www.safariventures.com
- ❑ *Started* — 2006
- ❑ *Owned by* — Safari Ventures
- ❑ *Google page ranking* — 4/10
- ❑ *Affiliate programs* — Varied
- ❑ *Extensions used* — Google Translation, Contact, com_facileforms, com_xegallery, com_events, com_eweather
- ❑ *Web feed* — No
- ❑ *Template* — Custom
- ❑ *Search-engine-friendly URLs* — No

❑   *Breadcrumbs* — No

❑   *Top sections* — Select a Journey, Plan Your Journey, Expectations, Value Tours, Corporate Tours, Group Tours, Request Information

❑   *Default width* — 1024

❑   *E-commerce* — No

❑   *Community features* — No

Sky Systems

Sky Systems offers information relating to recreational aviation, including paragliding, paramotors, light aircraft, and microlighting (see Figure 16-26). The site features news and information relating to these aerial sports.

Figure 16-26: Sky systems

❑ *URL* — www.skysystems.co.uk

❑ *Started* — 2005

❑ *Owned by* — Sky Systems

❑ *Google page ranking* — 4/10

❑ *Affiliate programs* — Google AdSense

❑ *Extensions used* — com_directory, Weblinks, Contact, com_marketplace

❑ *Web feed* — RSS

❑ *Template* — jw_geosync

❑ *Search-engine-friendly URLs* — Yes

❑ *Breadcrumbs* — Yes

❑ *Top sections* — Air Sports Directory, Kites, Paragliding, Paramotor, Hanggliders, Gliders, Microlights, Light Aircraft

❑ *Default width* — 800

❑ *E-commerce* — Yes

❑ *Community features* — Bo

KISSin' UK

This is a fan site of the rock group KISS, including tour information, articles about the members, fan stories, and band merchandise (see Figure 16-27).

Figure 16-27: KISSin' UK

- ❏ *URL* — www.kissinuk.com/cms
- ❏ *Started* — 2005
- ❏ *Owned by* — KISSin' UK
- ❏ *Google page ranking* — 3/10
- ❏ *Affiliate programs* — Google AdSense
- ❏ *Extensions used* — RSS, Contact, Newsfeeds, Banners, phpBB
- ❏ *Web feed* — RSS

- ❏ *Template* — Custom
- ❏ *Search-engine-friendly URLs* — Yes
- ❏ *Breadcrumbs* — No
- ❏ *Top sections* — News Archive, News Feeds, Reviews, Links, Tribute Bands, Television, Downloads, Air-Brush & Gear, Trade Board, KISStories, Search, , KISSin' UK Forums, Guestbook, Mailing List, Lyrics, Contact Us, Syndicate
- ❏ *Default width* — 800
- ❏ *E-commerce* — No
- ❏ *Community features* — Yes

Calialive.com

This is a California site that focuses on metal news, upcoming California hardcore shows, downloads, links, hardcore album reviews, and just about everything relating to the California hardcore scene (see Figure 16-28). The site also features a hardcore and metal webzine.

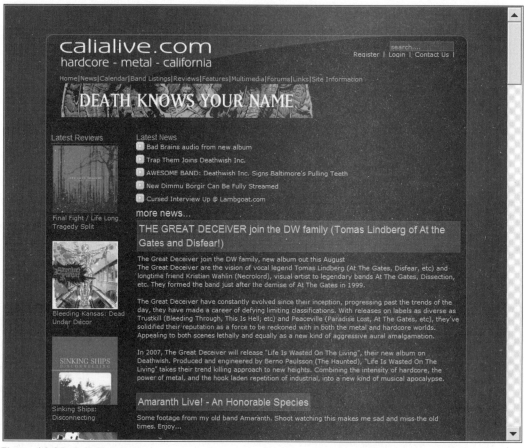

Figure 16-28: Calialive.com

❏ *URL* — http://calialive.com

❏ *Started* — 2005

❏ *Owned by* — Calialive.com

❏ *Google page ranking* — 3/10

❏ *Affiliate programs* — Varied

❏ *Extensions used* — Contact, Community Builder, ExtCalendar, Pony Gallery, BSQ Stats, Joomlaboard, Staff, Banners, com_comments

❏   *Web feed* — RSS & Atom

❏   *Template* — `js_empire` by Joomla Shack

❏   *Search-engine-friendly URLs* — Yes

❏   *Breadcrumbs* — No

❏   *Top sections* — News, Calendar, Band Listings, Reviews, Features, Multimedia, Forums, Links, Site Information

❏   *Default width* — 800

❏   *E-commerce* — No

❏   *Community features* — Yes

Technology Sites

The Internet acts like a magnet to those who are interested in technology. This topic area was the one where it was not a matter of choosing a Joomla site popular enough to break the guideline threshold, but rather to choose the sites either were mainstream, or those that contribute directly to the Joomla community.

I also included the OScar site because I thought the idea of applying open source techniques to creating a car was particularly novel. Also, the site is leveraging several of the Joomla technologies in its attempt to achieve an interesting result.

Joomla Main Site

This is a central Joomla site where more than 2.5 million people have downloaded Joomla (see Figure 16-29). This site is proof positive that Joomla can take the pounding of volumes of traffic and function effectively.

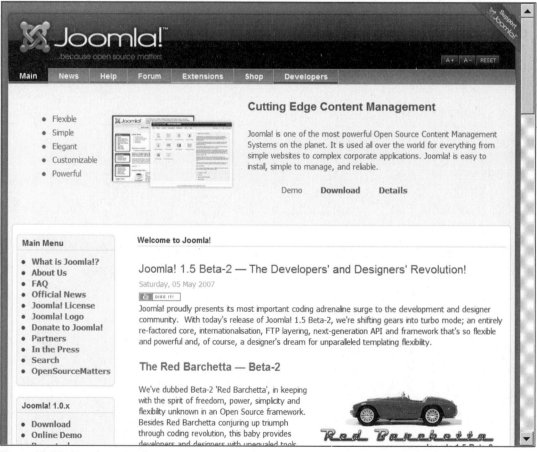

Figure 16-29: Joomla main site

- ❏ *URL* — www.joomla.org
- ❏ *Started* — 2005
- ❏ *Owned by* — Open Source Matters
- ❏ *Google page ranking* — 9/10
- ❏ *Affiliate programs* — No
- ❏ *Extensions used* — com_faq, Banners, RSS, com_submissions, com_jd-wiki, Simple Machines Forum
- ❏ *Host* — www.rochenhost.com
- ❏ *Web feed* — RSS, Atom, and OPML
- ❏ *Template* — jw_joomla
- ❏ *Search-engine-friendly URLs* — Yes
- ❏ *Breadcrumbs* — Yes
- ❏ *Top sections* — What is Joomla!?, About Us, FAQ, Official News, Joomla! Team Blog, Joomla! License, Joomla! Logo, Donate to Joomla!, Partners, In the Press, Search, OpenSourceMatters, Download Joomla
- ❏ *Default width* — 1000
- ❏ *E-commerce* — Yes
- ❏ *Community features* — Yes

VOIPSpeak.net

The focus of this site is voice-over-IP (VOIP), including tutorials and articles that describe the technology and how it can be implemented (see Figure 16-30).

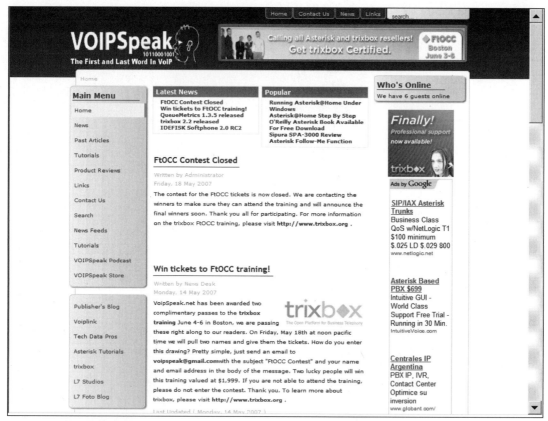

Figure 16-30: VOIPSpeak.net

❑ *URL* — www.voipspeak.net

❑ *Started* — 2005

❑ *Owned by* — VoipSpeak.net

❑ *Google page ranking* — 5/10

❑ *Affiliate programs* — Amazon, Buy.com

❑ *Extensions used* — RSS, Contact, Newsfeeds,

❑ *Web feed* — RSS, Atom, and RSS Podcast

❑ *Template* — madeyourweb

❑ *Search-engine-friendly URLs* — No

- ❑ *Breadcrumbs* — Yes

- ❑ *Top sections* — News, Past Articles, Tutorials, Product Reviews, Links, Contact Us, Search, News Feeds, Tutorials, VOIPSpeak Podcast, VOIPSpeak Store, Publisher's Blog, Voiplink, Tech Data Pros, Asterisk Tutorials, trixbox, L7 Studios, L7 Foto Blog

- ❑ *Default width* — 800

- ❑ *E-commerce* — Yes

- ❑ *Community features* — No

Open Workbench

This site focuses on the Open Workbench application that is an open source, Windows-based project featuring a scheduling and management program (see Figure 16-31). The program is free to distribute, and the site features development information, source code, and a forum for project discussion.

Figure 16-31: Open Workbench

- ❑ *URL* — www.openworkbench.org
- ❑ *Started* — 1998
- ❑ *Owned by* — Computer Associates
- ❑ *Google page ranking* — 5/10
- ❑ *Affiliate programs* — No
- ❑ *Extensions used* — google-analytics, RSS, phpBB, com_docman,

- ❑ *Web feed* — No
- ❑ *Template* — Custom
- ❑ *Search-engine-friendly URLs* — No
- ❑ *Breadcrumbs* — Yes
- ❑ *Top sections* — Downloads, Forums, News, Support & Training, Get Involved, Developers, Partners, Contact Information
- ❑ *Default width* — 1024
- ❑ *E-commerce* — No
- ❑ *Community features* — Yes

Joomlahut

This is a popular Joomla/Mambo site that features free templates and tutorials that can aid in the production of a professional Web site (see Figure 16-32).

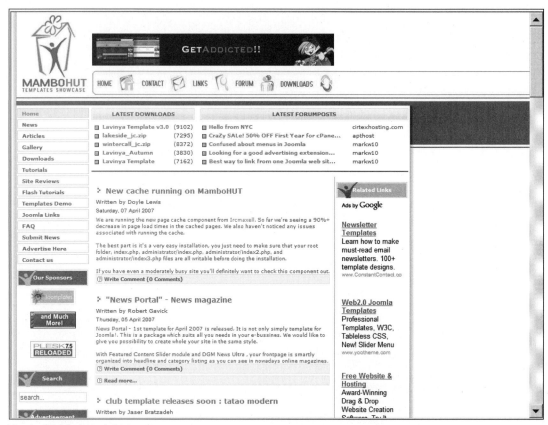

Figure 16-32: Joomlahut

- ❏ *URL* — www.joomlahut.com
- ❏ *Started* — 2003
- ❏ *Owned by* — BuyHTTP, LLC
- ❏ *Google page ranking* — 5/10
- ❏ *Affiliate programs* — Google AdSense, Joomplates, BuyHTTP.com, vBulletin
- ❏ *Extensions used* — RSS, Contact, com_mtree, com_remository, com_submissions, com_virtuemart
- ❏ *Web feed* — RSS, Atom, and OPML
- ❏ *Template* — mambohut_red

❑ *Search-engine-friendly URLs* — Yes

❑ *Breadcrumbs* — No

❑ *Top sections* — News, Articles, Gallery, Downloads, Tutorials, Site Reviews, Flash Tutorials, Templates Demo, Joomla Links, FAQ, Submit News, Advertise Here, Contact us

❑ *Default width* — 800

❑ *E-commerce* — Yes

❑ *Community features* — No

OScar Project (Open Source Car)

This site hosts the OScar Project that attempts to develop a car according to open source principles (see Figure 16-33). The target is an automobile of simple and functional concept to spread mobility. OScar is about new ways of mobility and the spreading of the open source idea in the real (physical) world. The site features community features for open source collaboration.

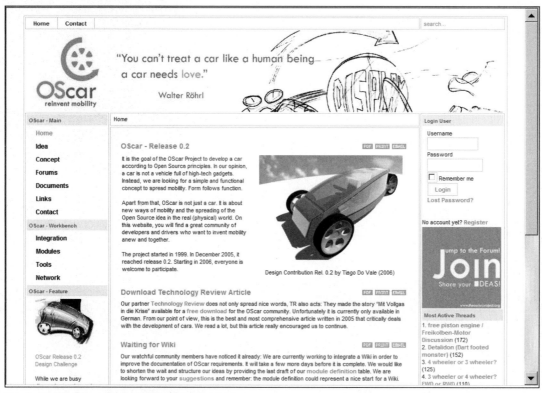

Figure 16-33: OScar Project (Open Source Car)

❑ *URL* — www.theoscarproject.org

❑ *Started* — 2005

❑ *Owned by* — OScar - Reinvent Mobility

❑ *Google page ranking* — 5/10

❑ *Affiliate programs* — No

❑ *Extensions used* — com_icms, Contact, Joomlaboard, com_docman, com_user_extended

❑ *Web feed* — RSS & Atom

❑ *Template* — rhuk_solarflare_ii

❑ *Search-engine-friendly URLs* — No

❑ *Breadcrumbs* — Yes

❑ *Top sections* — Idea, Concept, Forums, Documents, Links, Contact, OScar - Workbench Integration, Modules, Tools, Network

❑ *Default width* — 1000

❑ *E-commerce* — No

❑ *Community features* — Yes

Summary

Joomla sites seem to represent pages that focus on almost any human endeavor. The amount of power Joomla puts in everyone's hands is quite amazing. This chapter has provided a survey of some of the Web world served by Joomla to show the following:

- ❑ Academic Web sites that provide distance learning, support, history, literature, archeology, and parent-teacher interaction.

- ❑ Family and health Joomla sites that feature health information, children's television programming, bedtime stories (both written and audio), healthcare, and stepfamily relations.

- ❑ Professional Web sites that focus on networking, paid travel, stock and equities trading, expert illustration, and real estate.

- ❑ Online media sites that include pharmaceutical clearinghouses, automotive magazines, environmental news, Asian markets, humor, and small publishing houses.

- ❑ Hobbyist sites for sports, safari, recreational aviation, fan clubs, and music interests.

- ❑ Technology Web sites for open source development, commercial product support, and add-on repositories.

Thank you for taking this journey through the world of Professional Joomla deployment. You have learned a tremendous amount of material, and I hope you can put much of it to practical use. I hope to see you on the Joomla forums (http://forum.joomla.org), or you can visit the Joomla Jumpstart site (www.joomlajumpstart.com) that I created to publish free tutorials and other information relating to Joomla.

Index

SYMBOLS

$this statement, 48–49
& (AND), 28
_ (underscore) method, 120
| (OR), 28
~ (NOT), 28
\ (backslash) in plug-in code, 205
/ (forward slash) in plug-in
    code, 205

A

abbreviation replacement plug-in,
    200–205
abstract factory patterns, 181
academic sites
    Graphic User Interactive Learning
        and Development, 384–385
    Journal of Intercultural and
        Interdisciplinary
        Archaeology, 382–383
    overview, 378
    Princeton University Molecular
        Biology Department,
        378–379
    Shakespeare Birthplace Trust,
        380–381
    Virgin Islands Department of
        Education, 386–387
access, framework. See
    framework access, Joombla
Account Expiration Control &
    Subscription Manager (AEC)
    extension, 97–98
ACL (Access Control List), 235
action words in ads, 349
adapter patterns, 183
address finder with XML, 322–329
administration
    MySQL, 34–36
    professional deployment,
        276–277
    resetting passwords, 39–41
administrator events, 197–198

administrator guestbook editor,
    150–152
Administrator user interface,
    210, 372–373
Adobe Photoshop, 65–68
AdSense, 293–295, 348, 350
advanced extensions.
        See components
advertisements
    Amazon program, 296–300
    community planning, 221
    implementing classified,
        113–115
    Joomla limitations, 375
    SEM, 349–350
AEC (Open Source Account
        Expiration Control &
        Subscription Manager)
        extension, 97–98
affiliate programs
    Amazon, 296–300
    Google's AdSense, 293–295
    managing, 292
aggregators, 103, 284
Ajax (Asynchronous JavaScript
        and XML), 163–178
    BlastChat, 229–231
    custom requests, 356–357
    disadvantages, 177–178
    SEO and, 347
    server-query component,
        169–177
    simple component, 165–169
    structure, 163–164
    summary, 178
    utChat, 231–233
AkoComment, 107, 239–241
alert setting, 19
alt attribute for media, 344–345
Amazon affiliate program,
    296–300
Amazon Products Feed (APF),
    298–300
Analytics, Google, 347–348
AND (&), 28

ANSI ASC X12 standard,
    301–304
Apache Web server
    command line control, 263–265
    configuration overview, 18–21
    deployment checklist, 261
    directives, 21–23
    htdocs folder, 25
    vs. IIS, 13–14
    Joomla server constellation,
        9–10
    log files, 23–24
    modules and extensions folders,
        24–25
    securing, 361–362
    SEF URLs, 332–333
    virtual hosts configuration,
        262–263
APF (Amazon Products Feed),
    298–300
Applicability Statement 2 (AS2)
    standard, 300
Application Package, 206
architectural design patterns,
    184–186
archiving guestbook component,
    154–155
Article Manager, 278
articles
    document version control,
        369–370
    finding in Joomla database,
        176–177
    metadata, 334
    page titles, 343–344
AS2 (Applicability Statement 2)
    standard, 300
Asiaing.com, 418–419
Associates extension,
    297–298
Asynchronous JavaScript and
    XML (Ajax). See Ajax
    (Asynchronous JavaScript
    and XML)
Atom, 285

K

keywords
metadata, 335
SEO, 339–343
spamming, 349
KidsCHANNEL, 390–391
KISSin' UK, 430–431

L

languages
Easybook support, 225
Jambook support, 227
setting in utChat, 232
LDAP (Lightweight Directory
Access Protocol)
authentication, 276–277
legal liabilities
copyrighted images, 95
screen scrapers, 314
virtual communities, 251–252
licensing information, 72–73
Lightweight Directory Access
Protocol (LDAP)
authentication, 276–277
limitations of Joomla. See
Joomla limitations
link farms, 349
links
reciprocal, 346
SEO, 343
Linux, 12
live chat rooms, 108
load balancing
Joomla limitations, 372
site deployment, 265–266
load profile, 265
local installation vs. remote
deployment, 11–12
log files, 23–24
logic, template, 47–51
login module, 61
login system, 90–91
LogLevel directive, 19–20
logs, error
LogLevel directive, 19–20
staging server setup, 42

M

MacOS, 12
magic quotes, 356

MainSPOT.NET, 410–411
maintenance
Joomla! communities, 252–253
professional deployment,
278–281
Mambo, 7–8, 79
management extensions
adding, 87–88
CB. See CB (community builder)
defined, 83
manager, instance, 264
managing professional
deployment. See professional
deployment
manual testing, 324
maps
Google, 318–322
Joomla limitations, 375
marketing, 222–223. See also
advertisements
MD5 (Message-Digest algorithm 5),
39–41
media. See also images
alt attribute for, 344–345
Joomla download limitations, 376
media attribute tag, 77
media sites
Asiaing.com, 418–419
The Chaser, 420–421
Creative Guy Publishing,
422–423
HCJB Global, 416–417
MainSPOT.NET, 410–411
overview, 410
PanNatural Environmental news
source, 412–413
United Nations Regional
Information Centre for
Western Europe (UNRIC),
414–415
message boards, 233–236, 373
Message-Digest algorithm 5
(MD5), 39–41
metadata
SEO, 334–336
templates, 55–56
MicroShop PayPal shopping
cart, 98
Microsoft Internet Information
Server (IIS), 13–14
Missus extension, 113
mobile browser templates, 76–77
mod_articleajax, 172–175

Model
creating Hello World
component, 188
in MVC patterns, 186–187
Model-View-Controller (MVC)
pattern, 186–191
moderators, 252
modules, 119–135
changing, 68–70
contact us, 130–135
creating Ajax, 172–177
defined, 65–68
hello world, 120–123
holiday greetings, 124–129
Joomla feed subscription,
286–288
Joomla syndication publishing,
289–290
overview, 119
summary, 135
template layout, 60–62
modules folder, 24–25
money through affiliate programs.
See affiliate programs
mouse-over pop-up information
Ajax, 164
in server-query component. See
server-query components
simple Ajax component, 165–169
music download limitations, 376
MVC (Model-View-Controller)
pattern, 186–191
mvc.php, 188
My EBay Store extension,
101–102
MySQL
creating database table,
127–128
index optimization, 270–274
installation/configuration,
31–36
instance manager, 264
Joomla server constellation,
9–10
maintenance with direct access,
278–281
performance tuning, 267
problems source, 269
profiling, 274–275
querying database, 171
security, 365
setting server type, 267–269